A HISTORY OF CHRISTIANITY IN WALES

T0351390

A History of Christianity in Wales

Barry J. Lewis, Madeleine Gray,
David Ceri Jones and D. Densil Morgan

UNIVERSITY OF WALES PRESS
2022

www.uwp.co.uk

British Library CIP Data
A catalogue record for this book is available from the British Library.

ISBN   978-1-78683-821-6
eISBN   978-1-78683-822-3

The rights of Barry J. Lewis, Madeleine Gray, David Ceri Jones and D. Densil Morgan to be identified as authors of this work have been asserted in accordance with sections 77 and 79 of the Copyright, Designs and Patents Act 1988.

Typeset by Gary Evans
Printed by CPI Antony Rowe, Meklsham, United Kingdom

The publisher acknowledges the financial support of the Books Council of Wales.

CONTENTS

Contents

THE AUTHORS

Barry J. Lewis is a native of Welshpool, Montgomeryshire. He worked in the University of Wales Centre for Advanced Welsh and Celtic Studies in Aberystwyth (2001–14), and now holds a professorship in the Dublin Institute for Advanced Studies. His research focuses on medieval Welsh language and literature, especially poetry. In addition, he is interested in hagiography. He has edited the works of several medieval Welsh poets and is the author of *Medieval Welsh Poems to Saints and Shrines* (2015). He is currently working on an edition of the genealogies of the Welsh saints.

Madeleine Gray is Professor Emerita of Ecclesiastical History at the University of South Wales. She has close links with a number of heritage and community organizations, and is an honorary research fellow of the National Museum of Wales. She has published extensively on late medieval and early modern history with a particular focus on visual and material evidence for the history of religious belief and practice. She is currently working on a survey of medieval tomb carvings in Wales.

David Ceri Jones is Reader in Early Modern History at Aberystwyth University. His most recent publications include: *The Fire Divine: Introducing the Evangelical Revival* (2015); as co-author, *The Elect Methodists: Calvinistic Methodism in England and Wales, 1735–1811* (2012); and as co-editor, *George Whitefield: Life, Context and Legacy* (2016); *Making Evangelical History: Faith, Scholarship and the Evangelical Past* (2019); and *Evangelicalism and Dissent in Modern England and* Wales (2020).

D. Densil Morgan is Emeritus Professor of Theology at the University of Wales, Trinity Saint David, Lampeter. Previously he was Professor of Theology at Bangor University and Warden of Coleg Gwyn, the North Wales Baptist College. An ordained Baptist minister, he has written extensively on Christianity in Wales, aspects of modern Church History and the theology of Karl Barth. Among his publications are the two-volume *Theologia Cambrensis: A History of Protestant Religion and Theology in Wales, 1588–1900* (2018 and 2021), *The Span of the Cross: Christian Religion and Society in Wales, 1914–2000*, 2nd edition (2011), *Barth Reception in Britain* (2012) and *The SPCK Introduction to Karl Barth* (2010). He is a Member of The Center of Theological Inquiry at Princeton, and a Fellow of the Learned Society of Wales.

The history of Welsh Christianity and the history of the Welsh language in any recognizable form begin at very much the same point, and it is not surprising that they continue to be deeply interwoven. Until the last quarter of the last century, most of the population of Wales – churchgoing or not, Welsh-speaking or not – would have taken for granted a cultural hinterland deeply imbued with the Christian imagination, especially as crystallized in the tradition of hymnody. 'Hymns and arias': it's a folk memory that lingers even in the very secularized environment that is contemporary Wales. But how many under sixty now know (let alone sing) the words of those hymns? In a very postmodern twist, more people at rugby internationals probably know the words of Max Boyce's nostalgic evocation of communal singing at sports events than know the hymns themselves. That most formidable of twentieth-century Welsh Anglophone poets, R. S. Thomas, famously wrote of living under 'The last quarter of the moon / of Jesus' ('The Moon in Lleyn').

The waxing and waning of public faith in Wales, though, is not a new thing. In post-Roman Britain, Christian teachers and ascetics salvaged from the wreckage of imperial rule a remarkably vigorous Christian culture which consolidated the identity of highland Britain, especially Cornwall, Wales and Cumbria, as a bastion of Christian truth against barbarian incursions. A rich and intellectually lively cultural commonwealth united Wales with Ireland and indeed with continental Europe, before the trauma of the Viking age, and the destruction of the greatest centres of learning by raids from outside and local wars within regions. A brief period of recovery was interrupted by the Norman conquest and the total reorganization of church administration; a native tradition of learning and spirituality was edged aside by the importation of foreign clergy at the most senior level. Yet some of these imported leaders and their successors were drawn into projects and dreams that affirmed Welsh identity (think of Gerald of Wales). 'Foreign' religious orders like the Cistercians became in many areas indispensable allies of the indigenous rulers and even patrons of the bardic tradition.

The brutalities of the thirteenth-century suppression of independence and the universally shared devastation of plague in the fourteenth century left church and society alike deeply damaged; yet the fifteenth century saw a further flowering of writing and the visual and monumental arts. The Welsh church on the eve of the Reformation is not exactly a beacon of discipline, learning and ascetical piety, but it is very far from being (as some historians were once wont to suggest) a morass of superstition and illiteracy. The Reformation, when it arrived, started badly, with Welsh language and tradition being readily identified by some zealots with religious reaction; but the extraordinary generation of Protestant humanist scholars who promoted the translation of Bible and Prayer Book into Welsh saved the country for Reformed Christianity and began to lay the groundwork for popular literacy and a popular religious literature aimed at a new and wider public.

Poverty, the dissolution of traditional social patterns, and an often demoralized, undereducated and inadequately supported clergy had led, by the early eighteenth century to a widespread pessimism about the spiritual condition of the people at large, despite all the effort of the preceding century (including initiatives from some of the much-maligned bishops of the era, not all of whom were indifferent English placemen). The fields were ripe for a harvest of new educational and evangelistic labour; and – ironically – projects designed to reinforce the hold of the Anglican church helped to prepare the ground for the unexpected and unparalleled outpouring of energy and devotion from the mid-eighteenth century onwards which led to the majority of the Welsh population abandoning the Established Church. Nonconformity came to be seen as the religion of the people, as against the *hen estrones*, 'the old foreigner', a Church of England that seemed distant from the bulk of the population, especially the Welsh-speaking population. By the middle of the nineteenth century, Nonconformity and national identity were deeply intertwined, and the language was a vehicle for this alliance, with enormous quantities of Welsh-language theology and devotional material appearing from Welsh presses. The disestablishment campaign reflected this confident and expansive spirit; yet its eventual triumph on the eve of the First World War left a legacy of sour hostility and a degree of exhaustion. Nonconformity began its twentieth-century decline, increasingly precipitous after the Second War. Anglicanism, briefly and often tactlessly triumphant in the mid-twentieth century, followed suit, as the country became both more politically self-conscious and more culturally diverse.

R. S. Thomas's poem stops and turns on itself about half-way through, with the challenge, 'Why so fast, / mortal?' We are constantly tempted to premature closures in any human story. The history is already one of advance and retreat, of the decay and the rediscovery of Christian identities; only the crudest determinism can consign Wales's Christian past to the museum. These chapters do an impressive job not only of chronicling the diverse and dramatic history of Christian practice in Wales but of helping us spot the continuities, the unexpected points of growth and change, the fluidity and resilience of faith in its multifarious relations to wider society. At point after point, they gently challenge myths and sentimental fictions; throughout, they remind us of the cultural depth and sophistication that Christian practice and imagery have brought to Wales and its language. This book will be a sound reference point for scholars. But it will also be a work to which the reader can turn to understand both Welsh society and the resources of the Christian tradition across the centuries.

Rowan Williams
Archbishop of Wales, 1999–2002
Archbishop of Canterbury, 2002–12
Cardiff, Lent 2021

PREFACE

In the late medieval tale 'Ystoria Taliesin', the story is told of the supernaturally gifted poet Taliesin defeating the poets of Maelgwn Gwynedd in song. Towards the end of the tale he sings a long prophetic poem 'Ef a wnaeth Panton' ('The Lord of all made'), which starts with God's creation of the world and moves systematically throughout sacred history until it reaches the Anglo-Saxon invasions of Britain in the fifth and sixth centuries. As the culmination of the poem, he prophesies about the future of the Britons after Maelgwn's time. 'Eu Nêr a folant'/'Their Lord they shall praise', he writes, and their language they will keep, though they will lose most of Britain, except for Wales.[1]

This book charts the many and varied ways in which the Welsh have lived out Taliesin's prophecy, maintaining a witness to the life-giving power of the death and resurrection of the Lord Jesus Christ over the course of almost two thousand years. It begins with the origins of Christian witness in Wales in Roman times and follows the story with increasing detail right down to 2020. It builds on the best and most recent scholarship on the history of Christianity in Wales in each period but attempts to present this in an accessible and attractive way, maintaining a focus throughout on the chronological and narrative development of Welsh Christianity. The scholarly apparatus has, therefore, been kept to a minimum, and a bibliographical essay included at the end to guide interested readers to the more specialist literature on each theme and period.

There have been a couple of other attempts to retell the Welsh Christian story in recent years. Gwyn Davies's *The Light in the Land: Christianity in Wales, 200–2000* (2002) is a lavishly illustrated brief account with an evangelical flavour, while John I. Morgans and

Peter C. Noble's *Our Holy Ground: The Welsh Christian Experience* (2016) is a more personal set of reflections on the uniqueness of the Welsh experience of the Christian faith. *The Religious History of Wales: Religious Life and Practice in Wales from the Seventeenth Century to the Present Day*, edited by Richard C. Allen and David Ceri Jones with Trystan O. Hughes (2010) contains chapters on all of the main Christian denominations in Wales as well as introductions to other faiths too, but concentrates exclusively on the early modern and more recent past. This book does not seek to replace any of these, but attempts something slightly different, not least in terms of its detail, and ambition to cover the distant past in as much detail as the better-known post-Reformation past.

The inspiration for this book stemmed from the enthusiasm of successive cohorts of students who joined my classes on church history as part of the Aberystwyth Academy of Christian Discipleship and latterly the Momentwm course at St Michael's, Aberystwyth, between 2002 and 2016. Their passion for the study of the history of Christianity in Wales in particular, and my increasing frustration that there was not a single-volume study in English that I could recommend, spurred me into action. The idea for much of what follows can be directly traced back to those memorable Saturday afternoon sessions in which Christians from all corners of Wales and sometimes beyond, made their pilgrimage to Aberystwyth and joined me on excursions into Wales's Christian past.

A book of this nature, that seeks to tell a long story and distil so much scholarship into an accessible form, calls for a team of expert authors. I am deeply indebted to my three co-authors both for their initial interest in the project, and their commitment to producing chapters that have more than exceeded my initial expectations for the volume. I am grateful to Inter-Varsity Press for permission to reuse some material from Chapter 3 of my *The Fire Divine: An Introduction to the Evangelical Revival* (2015) in Chapter 8 of the present study. I am also indebted to the University of Wales Press for their enthusiasm and commitment to the project, and to Llion Wigley in particular for his periodic and always impeccably timed encouragements to see it through to completion. The anonymous reader appointed by University of Wales Press provided early enthusiasm for the project, and then invaluable advice on the final shape of the book. And, finally, to Rowan Williams for kindly agreeing to write such a warm commendatory 'Foreword'.

The place and role of Christianity in the history of Wales is slipping from contemporary public consciousness. It is my hope that this book will provide readers in Wales and further afield with a fresh appreciation of the ways in which Christianity has shaped the history of Wales, and also inspire Christians today to persevere, thereby ensuring the continued fulfilment of Taliesin's prophecy.

David Ceri Jones
February 2021

Notes

[1] *Ystoria Taliesin*, edited by Patrick K. Ford (Cardiff: University of Wales Press, 1992), p. 86.

Chapter 1

Roman Beginnings, *c.AD 1–c.AD 400*

BARRY J. LEWIS

The origins of Christianity lie many hundreds of miles away from Wales, in Palestine, where Jesus was born around the year now designated AD 1. At that time, Jesus' homeland lay at the eastern fringe of the territories ruled by Rome. Westwards from the Holy Land the Roman empire stretched in an unbroken expanse all around the Mediterranean Sea and up through Gaul (modern France) as far as the Atlantic Ocean. Beyond this western shore, the island of Britain was largely still unconquered in Jesus' time; indeed, to most Romans and other Mediterranean people, Britain was so remote as to be little more than a rumour. And yet, within a few centuries, Christianity managed to span this great distance to reach Wales in the far west of the island. How that happened will be the subject of this first chapter.

One difficulty we must confront at once is that Wales, as a country or even as a concept, did not yet exist. Neither, for that matter, did England or Scotland. The familiar division of Britain into three parts lay in the future. Instead, our historical sources refer either to the whole island or to individual peoples who inhabited it, such as the Atrebates, the Catuvellauni or the Silures. Wales, being divided between several of these peoples, was not a unit, nor was it distinct from the rest of Britain. It is hard to write the history of a country that was not recognized and did not have a name, and we run the risk of distorting the past if we do so. For this reason, the story of these early centuries cannot be told without overstepping the familiar boundaries of Wales. A second difficulty is the thinness of the historical record for the Roman era. An acute shortage of documents makes it far from easy to trace the course of events. Richer material is offered by archaeology, and unlike historical sources, it keeps on growing as new finds are made. Unfortunately, archaeological evidence poses great problems of interpretation. Bluntly put, we know precious little about the spread of Christianity into what we now call Wales, and we can form only an incomplete idea of its progress and character until records begin to become more abundant; that is, at the end of the eleventh century. Unavoidably, therefore, the first few chapters of this book will contain many gaps, uncertainties and hesitant suppositions.

Wales in Roman Britain

Greek and Roman authors grouped together everybody who lived in Britain as one ethnicity, the Britons; for Romans, the island was *Britannia* and its people were *Britanni*. Of course, classical commentators lived far away and were liable to make generalizations about a region that most of them had never visited. Yet the Greek and Latin names for the island and its inhabitants were borrowed from the Britons themselves, who do, therefore, seem to have shared some sense of common identity. One thing that held the Britons together was their language. British, also called Brittonic, was spoken through much if not all of Britain. It is the ancestor of Welsh, Cornish and Breton, and a close relative of the Gaulish language spoken by the Britons' neighbours across the Channel. Both British and Gaulish belonged to the Celtic language group, and there were very close cultural and political ties between the Britons and the Gauls, maintained by much travel and trade across the Channel. To the west, in Ireland, yet another Celtic language was spoken. Neither Britons nor Irish, however, seem to have thought of themselves as Celts, even though they certainly shared a cultural inheritance with continental Celtic peoples like the Gauls.

As the Romans became better acquainted with Britain, they came into contact with the many diverse peoples of the island. Before the conquest no single people or ruler was dominant, and political and economic development varied hugely from region to region. In the south and east were major kingdoms with close ties to the Continent and long experience of living alongside the Roman empire. For the peoples of the west and north, though, relations with Rome were more distant or did not exist at all. The area which we know as Wales was shared by several such peoples. In the south-east, roughly modern Glamorgan and Gwent, lived the Silures. West of them were the Demetae. North and mid-Wales seem to have been the domain of the Ordovices. We cannot draw the boundaries of these territories on a map, because we do not know where they ran. There were more peoples along what is now the border, namely the Cornovii in Cheshire and Shropshire, and the Dobunni in Gloucestershire. It is quite likely that the territories of these groups extended into Wales: the Severn valley, for example, may have belonged to the Cornovii. Finally, the Deceangli of north-east Wales may have been a subgroup of the Ordovices or the Cornovii.

The inhabitants of late Iron Age Wales were not hunter-gatherers or nomadic herders. They were settled farmers who grew cereals as well as raising animals. They lived in permanent homesteads in a landscape that had long been cleared and parcelled out into fields; the land was well populated and thoroughly exploited. There was trade in iron and other valuable materials, often over long distances, and craftsmen such as metalworkers were often itinerant too. A social hierarchy operated, as is revealed by the larger settlements – hill-forts and defended enclosures – dotted among the more humble farms. These belonged to an armed elite who lived off the labour of the rest of the population and doubtless fought amongst themselves for the privilege. Nevertheless, these were societies that had no concept of city life, and for Roman observers that marked them out as inferior. Roman terms for such peoples – *gens* or *natio* – often had dismissive connotations, like the English word 'tribe'. But Romans also used a third term, *civitas*, whose basic meaning was 'political community', and it could be applied to any polity from the Ordovices of western Britain right up to their own mighty city.[1] They recognized, in short, that even the Ordovices and the Silures were organized communities with their own social structures, laws, identities and sense of belonging.

The *civitates* of south-eastern Britain had been under loose Roman domination since the 50s BC, when Julius Caesar twice took his army to Britain.[2] Just under a century later, in AD 43, the emperor Claudius (r. AD 41–54) decided to finish what Caesar had started. Much of lowland Britain was quickly incorporated into a new province of *Britannia*. But as the Roman forces pressed further west and north, they encountered tougher resistance. The *civitates* of western Britain seem, from the Roman accounts, to have violently opposed the conquest, the Silures and Ordovices being particularly stubborn. It was not until AD 77 or 78 that the last resistance in Wales was crushed, when the Roman governor Agricola occupied Anglesey.[3] For some decades after that, the western *civitates* were heavily garrisoned through a network of forts. Some of these can still be seen today, as at Segontium, now Caernarfon, or the Gaer a little to the west of Brecon. They were typically placed at intervals of a day's march and linked by newly built permanent roads. At Chester in the north-east, and Caerleon in the south-east, larger fortresses were founded to house the elite troops, the legions. This heavy military occupation seems to have been needed for about half a century. Gradually, though, the garrisons were wound down and the *civitates* were allowed to govern their own internal affairs, like hundreds of similar communities elsewhere in the empire. We know this for certain in the case of the Silures, whose administrative centre was Caerwent. Here we have the solid evidence of an inscription set up by decree of the *ordo* or 'council' that governed the *res publica civitatis Silurum*, the 'republic of the *civitas* of the Silures'.[4] For the Demetae the evidence is indirect: a city was founded at Moridunum (Carmarthen) which, along with the closing of the forts in their territory, indicates that they too had a civilian government of their own from around the time of the emperor Hadrian (r. AD 117–38). More signs of peaceful conditions are Romanized farms and estate centres, the so-called villas. They are most common in lowland Gwent and Glamorgan, where the agricultural and trading economy was strongest, but there is a scatter through southern

Carmarthenshire and Pembrokeshire too. In 2003 a modest villa was discovered at Abermagwr near Aberystwyth, much further north than any previously known in Wales. It is a sign that central Wales too was capable of supporting an aspirational, if modest, Roman lifestyle for its elite.[5]

The rest of Wales lacked cities and has revealed few villa-like or Romanized buildings away from army bases. As a result, it was long thought that northern and central Wales remained within an underdeveloped 'military zone' throughout the Roman period. This term, however, is misleading. Most of the forts were closed by the middle of the second century, while at the rest the garrisons were much smaller or only present now and again. Such a modest contingent of troops could not have kept the population down by force. It did not need to: archaeological evidence supports the view that Roman rule was now accepted. Roman goods were in circulation, even if not so commonly as in richer areas. Dozens of hoards of Roman coins have been found across Wales. For everyday buying and selling, people may have continued to use barter, but coins were required for paying taxes, so the coin hoards are indirect but clear testimony that taxes were being levied, and paid. Evidence is gradually accumulating for the spread of Roman building techniques and urbanization. Besides the Abermagwr villa, a substantial settlement has been uncovered at Tai Cochion on the south coast of Anglesey. It is large enough to count as a 'small town' and must have served a ferry crossing towards Segontium on the mainland.[6] Further evidence for intense contact between the population of Wales and Roman culture emerges a little later, in the early Middle Ages, when we have better written records. At once we discover that many people bore names adopted from Latin, like Einion, Meirion, Edern or Padarn. Likewise, the British language absorbed great numbers of Latin words. Some, like *mur* 'wall' and *melin* 'mill', were borrowed along with new technologies, but others cover basic concepts like 'go up' (*esgyn*) and 'go down' (*disgyn*), and even 'arm' (*braich*).

Roman rule worked through co-opting local elites. The native landowners were turned into intermediaries between the population and the Roman administration. It was they who raised taxes and found recruits for the army and labour for duties like building roads. This will have been true among the Ordovices, as elsewhere. Upland Wales, with its thin soils and harsher climate, was different from the more urbanized south, but in an empire that extended from Scotland to the fringes of the Sahara desert, there were bound to be innumerable varieties of landscapes and local economies, and just as many different ways of being Roman. In the countryside as in the towns, everyone had some contact with the wider Roman world. This was true also in the sphere of religion, to which we turn next.

Religion in Roman Wales

We know very little about religious beliefs in Britain before the Roman conquest. Iron Age Britons did not use writing, so there are no texts from Britain itself. Julius Caesar described British society in the 50s BC, but he saw only the south-east, on two brief visits, and he tells us little about religion beyond the isolated fact that Britons would not eat hare, chicken or goose.[7] Other authors who describe Celtic religion refer only to regions far away from here, like southern Gaul. Often the accounts draw on earlier authors rather than first-hand experience. It is also a problem that Greek- and Latin-speaking observers were intelligent, highly educated men who interpreted foreign religions in the light of their own beliefs. They do not, in other words, give us a plain picture of what they themselves saw. Again, Caesar provides a partial exception in that he spent much time in Gaul, but what he says about Gaulish religion need not be true of Britain.

If we do not want to rely on outsiders' views, then we are forced back on sources produced within British society. That means the physical remains left behind by Iron-Age Britons, and the medieval literature written by their descendants many centuries later. Both raise troubling difficulties. Without written accounts to guide us, sites and objects have to be interpreted using models that may not be appropriate. Exploiting later literature is an even more fraught alternative. Medieval Welsh writings, as it happens, do mention a few figures who look as though they were supernatural beings in the distant past. In the *Mabinogi* stories, Rhiannon may derive from an ancient horse-goddess, and Manawydan from some kind of sea-god; his Irish counterpart, Manannán, appears in the early tale *Voyage of Bran* driving his chariot across the sea, which for him is a flowery plain while the leaping salmon are calves and lambs.[8] The difficulty with this kind of interpretation is that it cannot be confirmed by texts from the actual pagan period, because we have none, and so it remains frustratingly speculative. The *Mabinogi* tales were composed around the twelfth century, after Wales had been Christian for hundreds of years; the *Voyage of Bran* is earlier but still from a medieval Christian milieu. What they give us is a medieval and Christian perspective, even if, as is plausible, some of the characters and motifs did have ancient and pagan origins.

Native religion was focused on individual sacred places and a multitude of divine spirits. Votive offerings to deities, with the sacrifice of animals and even human beings, seem to have been important. There was a tradition of depositing valuable objects in water, apparently as offerings to whatever spirits dwelt there. A famous example is the ironwork from Llyn Cerrig Bach on Anglesey, placed in a lake along with signs of animal and human sacrifice.[9] We also know that there was a class of religious experts, the druids. Caesar gives us a detailed account of these men, although he was describing Gaul, not Britain.[10] Druids presided at sacrifices, interpreted religious laws, and judged legal cases and political questions. They wielded the sanction of banning people from sacrifices, which Caesar describes as the worst punishment conceivable to Gaulish society. They were exempt from tax and from warfare. They studied astronomy and other aspects of the natural world, taught that the soul was immortal and took apprentices, whose training might last twenty years. To judge from this description, the Gaulish druids must have dominated the religious sphere and wielded great political power besides. Was this true in Britain too? According to Caesar, the druid order originated in Britain, and Gauls would travel to the island for advanced training in druidism. The later Roman historian Tacitus mentions druids here as well, so it may be legitimate to extend Caesar's account to Britain.

About Roman religion we are much better informed. Romans worshipped numerous gods. By the first century AD their city abounded in cults, some ancient, others more recently introduced. It was essential for the whole of society to maintain a good relationship with these gods, for only in that way could peace, prosperity and social harmony be preserved. Rome's extraordinary success in conquering most of the known world was taken as evidence that the gods remained favourable, but it was a tense equilibrium, riven by fear that the vast, fragile edifice of empire might collapse. To keep the gods happy, Romans performed traditional rituals, at the heart of which was the sacrificing of animals. Sacrifices were performed at every level of life, from the highest offices of the state down to individual households. But within this framework there was some freedom. Individuals could choose particular deities for devotion, without denying the claims of others, and their choice could vary greatly depending on their gender or social class, or what part of the empire they came from. In general, the worship of Roman gods was not demanded from non-Romans. Anyone who received Roman citizenship, though, was expected to adopt some cults of the city of Rome, and there would be strong incentives for many provincials to do so too as they adapted to the new order. Furthermore, all inhabitants of the empire were expected to acknowledge the emperor somehow in their religious devotions, through praying to his divine spirit, or honouring dead emperors as gods. This is the set of behaviours that historians loosely call the 'imperial cult'; it became an important symbol of loyalty to the state.

With conquest, Roman religion was abruptly thrust into space where only native beliefs had been known. In Wales, the soldiers and officials based in the forts must have been the main protagonists in this encounter. The army had a very marked religious identity of its own. It followed a common calendar of festivals and worshipped a range of strongly Roman deities in classically Roman ways, as we see from the altars preserved at Caerleon: for instance, a dedication made in AD 244 to the divine spirits of the emperors and the *genius* of the Second Legion.[11] It is safe to assume that most of the dedicators came from outside Britain. At the other extreme of the religious spectrum, native farmers may have continued to worship nameless spirits in traditional numinous places, just as their ancestors had done. But over time, the brutal colonial division of the conquest period gave way to more complex and sympathetic interactions. Religious influence did not all travel in one direction. As polytheists – believers in many divine beings – Romans did not find it insuperably difficult to accept other people's gods. They knew that there were many gods besides those of their own city, and they might be powerful and dangerous. Conversely, if the good will of these alien gods could be obtained, then they became supporters of Rome's power. The adoption of local deities by incoming colonists was, arguably, as much an act of conquest as the building of forts and roads.

It is certain that local gods were transformed by this process, which we see repeated all over the Celtic regions. Sanctuaries were endowed with stone buildings, gods were represented by images following Greco-Roman artistic traditions, and inscriptions recorded the names of gods, many for the first time. Moreover, native and Roman gods were paired or identified with one another. Two inscriptions from Caerwent honour Mars Ocelus, combining a well-known Roman god with a Celtic one.[12] At Bath, the native spirit Sulis was equated with the Roman Minerva. A Latin term for this process, *interpretatio Romana*,[13] has been found in a passage in Tacitus. We cannot be certain that the term was in fact used more widely, nor about the implications for belief: did worshippers completely identify the two? If Roman incomers saw Sulis as a local manifestation of the goddess whom they knew as Minerva, they still called her Sulis, since that was the name that she had chosen for herself at this sacred site, marked out by its marvellous hot springs.

Roman soldiers, campaigning in and subsequently garrisoning a frontier region like Wales, would have encountered native religion almost immediately, not least through the civilian settlements that grew up around their forts. As most of our information comes from forts or their environs, it is very hard to know what wider society made of *interpretatio*, or of the imperial cult, or of all the other religious changes. But it is implausible that the amalgam was created solely by the incomers. *Interpretatio* required, at the least, dialogue between Roman and native. Some shrines were developed by local communities in response to Roman culture. Both Caerwent and Carmarthen had stone-built temples. Another is known from a rural site at Gwehelog, near Usk. Gwehelog is a strong candidate for a pre-existing, native religious site which was provided with a stone temple building under Roman rule.[14] Most other sites were not developed in this way, so far as we can tell. But rural Wales has much less high-status archaeology of all kinds than other areas of the empire, so this does not have to mean that the religious ideas and practice of the population did not alter. They probably did, though not in ways that archaeology can show us. Indeed, amidst this welter of change we have to wonder how much of the religion of Roman Wales was inherited from the Iron Age past at all. The question itself is open to objections. Certainly, by the later empire it makes no sense to divide belief crudely into 'native' and 'Roman' parts. Religion was a functioning system that reflected generations of integration. So-called 'Roman' religious practice was always a negotiation between different groups of people in different places. The new stone temples like Gwehelog, so far from being purely 'Roman', actually follow a design that was regionally distinctive to Gaul and its Celtic neighbours.

Polytheism fostered religious acculturation, because it was flexible and adaptable. One thing it did not endorse, however, was anything like the modern ideal of religious tolerance. 'Tolerance' implies acceptance of things that we ourselves do not believe in or even dislike, and it is a modern virtue. Romans, like other ancient peoples, were not tolerant of beliefs that they did not share; rather, they were anxious to control and absorb the power of alien gods who seemed as real to them as their own. Nor was openness unconditional. Roman society set boundaries in religion. Devotion that seemed pious, proportional and appropriate was termed *religio*, while everything beyond that was regarded as fanatical, extreme or wicked *superstitio*. As we might expect, opinions varied as to what kinds of belief and, more importantly, behaviour, fell on the wrong side of the dividing line. From an early date, however, the druids were victims of the distinction. Roman authors emphasize that they carried out human sacrifice, which was the epitome of *superstitio*. This accusation was probably justified, but there can be little doubt that it suited the Roman authorities, who saw a compelling political need to suppress the druids. Both in Gaul and in Britain, the druids seem to have been strong supporters of resistance to Rome. Tacitus records how a Roman army, invading Anglesey in AD 60 or 61, faced a British force across the Menai; among them were druids 'raising their hands to the sky and pouring out dreadful prayers'. After the Romans won, they cut down the druids' sacred trees.[15] Druids did not disappear after the conquest, but they lost most of their status and dwindled into mere magicians. Their name perhaps survived in medieval Welsh as *dryw*, but frustratingly we really do not know whether they were still a force when Christianity began to spread here.[16] A few early medieval texts mention wizards or magicians. The female witches who attacked St Samson of Dol, according to his *Life*, may be a lingering echo of these once powerful figures, and the same *Life* records that the important early Welsh saint Illtud was a *magicus* by descent.[17]

Roman religion was not just a matter of rules. Individuals could develop powerful emotional bonds to particular deities and sacred places. There were also opportunities for deep commitment within the so-called mystery cults. These typically had a closed membership, so that newcomers had to be initiated, usually in stages, and they promised some kind of transformation in the lives of their adherents. Some may have prepared people for an afterlife, a subject on which traditional Roman religion had nothing definite to say. The best-known is the worship of Mithras, which belonged originally to Persia (modern Iran), though the Mithraism of the Roman empire was so transformed that we must regard it as a Roman religion. Only men were admitted to this cult, and it was especially popular among soldiers. There was a temple of Mithras somewhere at Caerleon, as we know from an altar, and a complete *mithraeum* was excavated just outside the fort of Segontium (Caernarfon).[18] Like other *mithraea* all over the empire, it was a small, dark chamber, evoking the Persian cave in which Mithras slew the mighty sacred bull. It is a vivid reminder of the religious possibilities available in Roman Wales. But we do not know if anyone other than army officers, probably natives of far-off parts of the empire, ever worshipped in it.

The *mithraeum* at Caernarfon shows the power of Rome's empire to transmit ideas across vast distances. Between Iran and Wales there stretched roads, rivers and sea routes used by uncountable numbers of people – soldiers, officials, ambassadors, merchants, grain suppliers, tax collectors, spies, physicians, entertainers, pilgrims, slaves, beggars and prostitutes. New religious beliefs travelled along with these people and, not to forget, with the families who often accompanied them. The worship of Mithras was one such belief. Another, and the one that most concerns us, was the cult of the Christians. Mithraism, although it made great play of its exotic origins, remained on the approved side of *religio* and could be accommodated into the polytheistic worldview. Christianity, however, could not. It proved altogether more challenging to the Roman religious order, which it ultimately overthrew.

Written evidence for the earliest Christianity in Britain

Christianity had some things in common with the mystery cults: a lengthy initiation, and rituals that were open only to members (the eucharist). But in other regards it was radically different, for it rejected the whole concept of polytheistic religion and its offer was of personal salvation in the afterlife, not fulfilment in this world. After Christ was crucified in about AD 33, the new religion spread around the eastern Mediterranean, following the roads and sailing routes. It soon arrived in Rome, traditionally brought by the apostles Peter and Paul. Britain, much further away, may not have seen any Christians for many decades, but that is not a certainty; it is easy to imagine some Christian merchant or official or soldier happening to have business in Britain, even within a few years of the crucifixion. A precise answer will never be found, but there are two avenues for research: written records and archaeology. I shall look at written evidence in this section and archaeological evidence in the next.

No literature survives from Roman Britain, and authors who lived elsewhere paid little attention to this remote land. Where they do mention Christians in Britain, it is to praise the marvellous providence of God that succeeded in carrying the faith to the very margins of the inhabited earth. The African theologian Tertullian, writing around AD 200, listed peoples all around the Roman world to whom the name of Christ had become known, including 'regions of the Britons, inaccessible even to the Romans'. A few decades later, Origen of Caesarea in Palestine boasted that the power of Christ had reached 'those in Britain who are sundered from our world'. Classical writers were inclined to think of Britain as impossibly remote and cut off from civilization by the encircling sea that they called Ocean.[19] For Christians, the carrying of the gospel beyond even Ocean triumphantly fulfilled the commandment of Christ, 'Go therefore and make disciples of all nations' (Matt. 28:19). This was an enduring topos: the great eastern theologian John Chrysostom (*c.*AD 349–407) made repeated use of it, while Jerome, writing in the Holy Land in AD 385, marvelled at pilgrims coming from the distant island: 'the Briton, cut off from our world, once he has progressed in the faith, abandons his western horizon and comes to seek the place known to him only by repute and from what Scripture tells.'[20] We cannot prove that these authors knew anything concrete about British Christians, though they may have done, but their general claims are plausible enough. Christianity must have reached Britain before the third century AD, but whether there were extensive Christian communities, as opposed to individual believers, is doubtful.

Elsewhere in the empire Christians were found mainly in cities. Only in some eastern provinces was the countryside much affected. Conversion was not an easy choice. Quite apart from the emotional ties that bound believers to their traditional gods, there were severe social obstacles, so severe in fact that Christianity soon became an illegal and persecuted religion. Christians denied the existence of all gods except their own, and since rituals in honour of the gods suffused all public, social and even family occasions, committed Christians might feel obliged to refuse any part in these. Likewise, Christians could find it difficult to perform civic duties or hold any public office, because these too entailed sacrificing to the gods. And Christians proselytized, thus increasing the number of people who held these subversive views. Not only did this lead to conflict between citizens, and even within families, but it threatened to break the precious contract with the gods that kept humanity safe and secure. Many thought that Christians ignored their civic and moral duties to their fellow citizens in pursuit of a goal – individual redemption and eternal life after death – that seemed selfish, if not downright bizarre. In short: Christianity came to look like a peculiarly nihilistic form of *superstitio*. Once the Roman authorities had decided that it was illicit, anyone who professed it had always to reckon with the possibility of personal disaster. It was not that Christians were threatened everywhere all of the time – indeed there were long periods of calm with tacit toleration – but local and sporadic outbreaks of trouble were common enough, and there were several waves of general persecution led by emperors, notably Decius, Valerian and above all Diocletian. We do not know if, or how, persecution was carried out in Wales, but the sixth-century author Gildas mentions two martyrs, Julius and Aaron, who suffered at Caerleon.[21] How – if – their cult had persisted down to Gildas's day is not known. Gildas himself knew no details. He simply guessed that they were killed during the Great Persecution that marked Diocletian's last years in power (AD 303–5), but we have some evidence to suggest that Diocletian's orders were not enforced as strongly in the western provinces as in the east, and if so, the deaths of Julius and Aaron must be placed earlier, probably in the third century. As to their place of martyrdom, a church bearing their name (*merthir iun et aaron*) is mentioned in a charter in the Book of Llandaf, which probably preserves ninth-century evidence.[22] There is no guarantee that it really stood on the site of a late Roman martyr shrine, but the possibility exists. Hopefully the site will be investigated by archaeologists in the future.[23]

The last of the persecutions was brought to a close when the emperor Constantine came to power in the west (312). After his 'Edict of Milan' of the following year, Christianity was both legal and officially encouraged. Almost immediately we find evidence for an organized church in Britain. In 314 three British bishops attended a council at Arles, in southern Gaul. They were Eborius of York, Restitutus of London and Adelfius, probably from Lincoln, though the name of his see is damaged in the record. A priest named Sacerdos and a deacon, Arminius, also attended, representing unnamed churches.[24] As elsewhere in the empire, the hierarchy of the church copied the structure of local government. By this time there were four provinces in Britain, and each of the bishops in this list represented the capital of a British province. Frustratingly for us, the capital of *Britannia Prima*, in which Wales lay, is missing. We cannot read too much into this: Cirencester may have had a bishop who could not attend for some reason, but it is equally possible that western Britain did not yet possess an organized hierarchy. Nor does the evidence tell us whether there were further bishops in the *civitas* capitals such as Silchester or Caerwent. However, the existence of bishops of London, York and Lincoln as early as 314 argues that Britain had shared in the general growth of Christianity during the third century, for it is hardly likely that they had all been appointed since the peace of the church in the previous year.

By 359 there were certainly more than three bishops. In that year a council was held at Rimini in Italy, at which the bishops of Aquitaine, Gaul and Britain refused the emperor's offer to maintain them from public funds during their stay. Three of the British bishops alone accepted the offer, on the grounds that they were too poor to bear the costs themselves.[25] By implication, therefore, there were more than three British bishops present. In 358 or 359 Hilary of Poitiers, exiled to Phrygia for his theological views, wrote a letter addressed, among others, to the 'bishops of the provinces of Britain'. Around 396, Bishop Victricius of Rouen in northern Gaul visited Britain, as he tells us in his work, *In Praise of the Saints*. His mission was to settle a dispute, but he does not say what was at stake, beyond indicating that it was the British bishops who asked for him.[26] Though slender, the written record indicates that Britain had a hierarchy which was in contact with other parts of the empire, and more especially with its near neighbours in Gaul.

At the very end of our period, Christian culture in Britain was strong enough to produce two outstanding intellectuals and writers: Pelagius and Faustus of Riez. This is an indication that a solid Christian training was now available in the island. Yet both men left for the Continent at an early age. Britain remained on the margins of the public life of the empire, so it was natural for ambitious men to pursue their careers in more central places. Pelagius was in Rome by the 390s, while Faustus, who was born in the first decade of the fifth century, appears at the famous monastery of Lérins in the south of Gaul as early as the 420s.[27] There will be more to say about Pelagius in the next chapter.

Archaeological evidence for Christianity in Roman Britain and Wales

The written sources tell us only a small amount about Christianity in fourth-century Britain and nothing that can be linked to Wales apart from the martyr cult that probably existed at Caerleon. Archaeology is a little more helpful, though only a little. It is hard to identify Christian objects, and there was no reason for Christianity to leave much obvious archaeology behind. Early Christians worshipped in their own houses or in those of fellow believers. Such 'house-churches' are all but impossible to distinguish from ordinary dwellings, unless some decoration survives that shows Christian motifs. One definite house-church is known from a villa at Lullingstone in Kent. There are also Christian mosaics at the villas of Hinton St Mary and Frampton in Dorset.[28] It cannot be shown that these rooms were used for communal worship but they must indicate that the rich and influential owners of these grand houses were Christians.[29] Purpose-built churches are no easier to find since they too just look much the same as other public buildings. Other than that, we have to deal with portable objects decorated with Christian inscriptions or symbols such as the Chi-Rho (the first two letters of Christ's name in the Greek alphabet). Hoards of late fourth-century silverware decorated in this way have been found at Mildenhall in Suffolk and Water Newton in Huntingdonshire, and elsewhere.[30] They may be the plate from Roman churches, hidden in the face of some emergency and never recovered. Equally they could have belonged to wealthy Christian households. The survival of this material is obviously very haphazard, and so are our chances of finding it. It is not surprising that nearly all of it belongs to the wealthier lowland areas of Britain, far away from Wales, because that is where the archaeology is richest. By contrast, late fourth-century Wales is very poor in archaeology of every kind. Welsh villas seem to lose access to easily datable things like coins and pottery around the middle of the century. This does not have to mean that they were abandoned, but it does leave us puzzled as to what was happening in them. We fall back on the towns, and it is only Caerwent that offers us any hint of the new religion. A pewter bowl was found hidden with other utensils in a house in the Roman town, and on its base a Chi-Rho was scratched. The set may have been used for the *agape* or love-feast after the eucharist, though this is speculative. A silver spoon, with a Chi-Rho, Alpha and Omega, was discovered near Roman remains in Monmouthshire in the nineteenth century, but the find was not properly recorded. Apart from that there is only a very speculative idea that one of the buildings in Caerwent was used as a house-church. The theory is, again, very dubious.[31] Outside the south-east, we have only a belt fixture inscribed with a peacock, fish and tree of life, found in the hill-fort at Pen-y-corddyn in Denbighshire. It is likely to be from an official, military belt, and as the design incorporates no less than three motifs with Christian significance, it is probably Christian and a sign that Christian symbolism was now promoted by the authorities.[32]

Our direct evidence for Christianity from Wales itself is tiny. Moreover, paganism was very much alive. At Llys Awel near Abergele, bronze figurines and votive plaques were deposited not earlier than the 390s. They point to a functioning pagan shrine.[33] The temple at Caerwent was founded in the early fourth century, a sign that Constantine's embrace of Christianity was not followed by everyone, even among local elites. It remained in use to the end of the city's life. The Gwehelog shrine was also active until late in the fourth century. In this it compares with the great pagan sanctuary of Lydney in nearby Gloucestershire, which may have ceased to function at a similar date.[34] In the fourth century, religious life was in flux. Constantine's conversion was, arguably, a rupture rather than a natural development, for Christians were certainly still a small minority, especially in the west. As a Christian ruler Constantine faced an aristocracy that, for the most part, remained attached to their older religious heritage. And Christianity itself was far from set in stone. With no leader and no geographical centre, it subsisted in myriad small communities scattered across the empire and overseen by bishops who had to act largely for themselves. Questions such as to what degree Christians could compromise with traditional religion were very much open, and social pressure to convert was slow to build up. Only late in the fourth century, in the 380s and 390s, do we find the weight of the Roman state beginning to be turned against pagan worship, as the emperors placed restrictions on public sacrifice. By that time the issues were becoming much sharper. The church had grown enormously in wealth and influence and an ideology of Christian rulership was emerging. Slowly Christianity was becoming a marker of Romanness in contrast to 'barbarian' religions. But we have no idea how all that impacted on Wales, if at all.

There are two ways of interpreting the very small body of evidence for Christianity in Roman Wales. The poverty of material might suggest that the faith had made only very modest progress by around AD 400. Alternatively, since all other aspects of the Welsh archaeological record are inadequate as well, archaeology may simply be incapable of telling us how Christian the country was. We do at least have evidence for Christians living in urban south-east Wales. Christianity had made progress among the rural landowners of Gloucestershire, Somerset and Dorset, so it is likely, though not demonstrable, that there were Christian families among the landowners of the Silures, whose region was also the part of Wales most tightly integrated with the rest of the empire. Nothing can be said of the upper ranks of society elsewhere in Wales. As to the poorer people, if we compare Wales with other rural parts of the western empire, we can assume that conversion in the countryside had not yet got very far.

The poor evidence for the faith in the fourth-century led some scholars to argue that later Welsh Christianity owed little or nothing to the Roman period. In their view, either Christianity never made much headway against Celtic paganism, or if it did, it was abandoned in the chaos after Roman rule ended. Instead, they thought that the faith had to be reintroduced from the Continent, and especially from Gaul, during the fifth and sixth centuries. This idea was one of the building blocks in the theory that there was a separate and distinct 'Celtic church' in western Britain and Ireland that was decisively different from the Roman church. We will see in the next chapter that this is quite unlikely. Welsh Christianity has its roots firmly in the Christian church of Roman Britain, but by 400 that church, though well established in lowland southern Britain, had not yet made decisive progress in the remote west. It is a paradox that the Romano-British church would continue to expand after Roman secular rule failed, encompassing Wales and extending further into Ireland. That is why the next chapter will be called 'The Age of Conversion'. The title does a certain amount of injustice to the Roman centuries, but perhaps not too much.

Notes

1   Compare Tacitus, *Agricola*, ch. 18, *Ordovicum civitas* with *Histories*, 1.19.
2   On the period after Caesar's intervention, see John Creighton, *Britannia: The Creation of a Roman Province* (Abingdon: Routledge, 2006).
3   Tacitus, *Agricola*, ch. 18. The arguments regarding the date are finely balanced and not vital here.
4   *www.romaninscriptionsofbritain.org*, no. 311. It is now kept in Caerwent parish church.
5   Jeffrey L. Davies and Toby Driver, 'The Romano-British Villa at Abermagwr, Ceredigion: Excavations 2010–15', *Archaeologia Cambrensis*, 167 (2018), 143–219.
6   David Hopewell, 'A Roman Settlement at Tai Cochion, Llanidan, Anglesey', *Archaeologia Cambrensis*, 165 (2016), 21–112.
7   Julius Caesar, *De bello Gallico*, v.12.
8   *The Voyage of Bran Son of Febal to the Land of the Living*, edited and translated by Kuno Meyer (London: David Nutt, 1895), vol. 1, pp. 18–19.
9   C. Fox, *A Find of the Early Iron Age from Llyn Cerrig Bach, Anglesey* (Cardiff: National Museum of Wales, 1946); H. N. Savory, 'Llyn Cerrig Bach Thirty Years Later', *Transactions of the Anglesey Antiquarian Society* (1973), 24–38.
10 Caesar, *De bello Gallico*, vi.13–16.
11 *www.romaninscriptionsofbritain.org*, no. 327.
12 *www.romaninscriptionsofbritain.org*, nos. 309, 310.
13 Tacitus, *Germania*, ch. 43, interpreting two German gods as Castor and Pollux.
14 The most recent account is in Oliver Davis and Toby Driver, 'Llancayo Farm Roman Marching Camp, Usk, Monmouthshire', *Archaeologia Cambrensis*, 163 (2014), 177–80.
15 Tacitus, *Annals*, xiv.30.
16 *Dryw* is found a few times in medieval Welsh poetry preserved in the Book of Taliesin. Its etymology is disputed, however. The word now used for druid, *derwydd*, is not related to the ancient term.

[17] See Chapter 2 for this important text.

[18] George C. Boon, 'A Temple of Mithras at Caernarvon-Segontium', *Archaeologia Cambrensis*, 109 (1960), 136–72.

[19] Diarmuid Scully, '"Proud Ocean has become a servant": a classical topos in the literature of Britain's conquest and conversion', in *Listen, O Isles, unto Me: Studies in Medieval Word and Image in Honour of Jennifer O'Reilly*, edited by Elizabeth Mullins and Diarmuid Scully (Cork: Cork University Press, 2011), pp. 3–15.

[20] The passages cited, and others, are gathered in *Councils and Ecclesiastical Documents relating to Great Britain and Ireland*, edited by A. W. Haddan and W. Stubbs (Oxford, 1869–78), vol. 1, pp. 4–16.

[21] Gildas, *De excidio Britanniae*, i.10. Gildas will be discussed more fully in chapter 2.

[22] For the date, Wendy Davies, *The Llandaff Charters* (Aberystwyth: National Library of Wales, 1979), p. 121 (no. 225). In the text the site is also referred to as *territorium sanctorum martirum iulij et aaron*.

[23] See Andy Seaman, 'Julius and Aaron "Martyrs of Caerleon": In Search of Wales' First Christians', *Archaeologia Cambrensis*, 164 (2015), 201–19; 'The Church of Julius, Aaron and Alban at Caerleon', *Monmouthshire Antiquary*, 34 (2018), 3–15; Jeremy K. Knight, 'Britain's Other Martyrs: Julius, Aaron and Alban at Caerleon', in *Alban and St Albans: Roman and Medieval Architecture, Art and Archaeology*, edited by M. Henig and P. Lindley (Leeds: British Archaeological Association, 2001), pp. 13–29.

[24] *Councils and Synods*, edited by Haddan and Stubbs, i, p. 7; more up to date references in Richard Sharpe, 'Martyrs and local saints in late antique Britain', in *Local Saints and Local Churches in the Early Medieval West*, edited by Alan Thacker and Richard Sharpe (Oxford: Oxford University Press, 2002), p. 77.

[25] *Councils and Synods*, edited by Haddan and Stubbs, i, pp. 9–10; Sharpe, 'Martyrs and local saints', p. 78.

[26] For Hilary, see *Councils and Synods*, edited by Haddan and Stubbs, i, p. 9; more recent references, and discussion of Victricius, in Sharpe, 'Martyrs and local saints', pp. 78–9.

[27] On these men, see Thomas Charles-Edwards, *Wales and the Britons, 350–1063* (Oxford: Oxford University Press, 2013), pp. 192–202.

[28] Lullingstone, Hinton St Mary, Frampton: David Petts, *Christianity in Roman Britain* (Stroud: Tempus, 2003), pp. 79–83, with illustrations.

[29] A nuanced analysis in Susan Pearce, 'The Hinton St Mary Mosaic Pavement: Christ or Emperor?', *Britannia*, 39 (2008), 193–218, argues that the image combines imperial and Christian themes.

[30] Petts, *Christianity in Roman Britain*, pp. 118–22; Charles Thomas, *Christianity in Roman Britain to AD 500* (London: Batsford, 1981), pp. 108–22.

[31] For the Caerwent evidence, see Christopher J. Arnold and Jeffrey L. Davies, *Roman and Early Medieval Wales* (Stroud: Tempus, 2000), p. 132; Thomas, *Christianity in Roman Britain*, pp. 123, 167–8.

[32] Petts, *Christianity in Roman Britain*, pp. 110–13; F. Mawer, *Evidence for Christianity in Roman Britain: The Small-Finds*, BAR, British Series, 243 (Oxford: BAR Publishing, 1995), p. 60.

[33] Arnold and Davies, *Roman and Early Medieval Wales*, pp. 130–1.

[34] P. J. Casey and B. Hoffmann, 'Excavations at the Roman Temple in Lydney Park, Gloucestershire in 1980 and 1981', *Antiquaries Journal*, 79 (1999), 115.

Chapter 2

The Age of Conversion,
c. 400–c. 600

BARRY J. LEWIS

Unlike their neighbours, the medieval Welsh lacked a good story of how they had become Christians. Ireland fostered the legend of St Patrick, apostle and saviour of the Irish people. For the English, the mission from Pope Gregory the Great that arrived in 597 took on the same significance. But nothing similar is found in Wales. The sixth-century British writer Gildas offers only the vaguest of outlines. 'Christ', so Gildas says, 'made a present of his rays' to Britain, 'an island numb with chill ice and far removed, as in a remote nook of the world, from the visible sun.' This happened, he alleges, in the last years of the emperor Tiberius.[1] The date, so soon after the crucifixion, is probably just a guess. Later a more satisfying narrative was devised, albeit one that rested on a misunderstanding. Far back in the second century a Syrian king called Lucius wrote a letter to the bishop of Rome. Because Lucius ruled from a citadel called *Britium*, a much later reader mistook him for a king of 'Britain' and thought he had asked the pope for a mission and converted to Christianity along with all his people.[2] This 'Lucius legend' proved popular and was retold many times, but in reality Gildas came nearer to the truth. Christ's 'rays' reached Britain, and Wales, through uncountable and untraceable channels of communication. We know nothing of the men and women through whom the Christian message travelled. Some of their names may be preserved among the early saints, but our sources for the fifth and sixth centuries are not good enough to tell us, so we will have to be content with tracing hints of cultural influences using insubstantial and ambivalent evidence.

The end of empire

From the late third century raiders from the north German and Danish coasts were threatening eastern Britain, while others from Ireland began to attack the west. In response, the authorities reopened coastal forts like Neath or founded new ones, as at Holyhead. Little is known of the late Roman garrison in Wales or the fleet that supported it, but they operated at least into the 390s. The last sign of Roman forces is items of military equipment in the town of Caerwent, dating to the years around 400. They may have been carried by soldiers billeted on the town or by civilians who had armed themselves to defend it. It was not Irish raids in the west that brought about the end of Roman Britain, however, but problems on the Continent. On the last day of 405, so it appears, a great force of Vandals, Alans and Sueves invaded Gaul.[3] Britain faced being cut off from the rest of the empire, and this seems to have set off a series of revolts in the island. The third, early in 407, brought a man called Constantine (III) to power. He took much of the army from Britain to Gaul. By 409, as Saxon raiders once again threatened the Channel coasts, there was a fourth revolt in Britain. We do not know what kind of regime now came to power, but neither Constantine III nor the legitimate emperor Honorius ever regained control over Britain. Whether by choice or compulsion, Roman Britain now set out by itself. It did not go well. Archaeology points to a rapid collapse of much of Romanized life: coins ceased to circulate, the glass and pottery industries failed, towns shrivelled, and the material culture of the island reverted to a level of poverty that was considerably below what it had been before the Romans. Some archaeologists think that these changes happened at a brutally rapid speed, within a decade or two, while others suggest that there was a much slower transition. It seems unlikely, however, that any centralized government or taxation survived for long.

Eastern Britain began to pass under the control of Germanic invaders. Many Britons moved to the Continent, and by the sixth century they were holding swathes of the Armorican peninsula, which became Brittany. In the west of Britain, new British kingdoms emerged. They were based, for the most part, on the old *civitates*. The kingdom of Dyfed, in south-west Wales, continued the name of the Demetae, while the south-eastern kingdom of Gwent bore the name of the chief town of the Silures, *Venta* (Caerwent). In the north, a new name appeared, *Gwynedd*, apparently replacing the Ordovices. At the same time many Irish settlers took land in Dyfed and Gwynedd, as well as Cornwall and the west of Scotland. New people were now in charge in Wales, and we see dramatic changes in the archaeology as well as in the historical sources. It was during these two centuries that Christianity became the sole religion of the ruling elite, as far as we can tell. Unfortunately the sources are much poorer for the bulk of the population, whose beliefs remain hard to establish.

Archaeology of the early Welsh kingdoms: the evidence for belief

Most Roman-style archaeology vanishes in the turmoil of the early fifth century, be it pottery, glass, brick, tile, coinage or masonry buildings. This makes fifth-century society very difficult to study and it suggests that there was massive economic and social upheaval that must have been traumatic to live through. But in some ways the people of Wales become more visible now than they had been in Roman times, or at least the most influential among them. We find new centres of political power in hill-forts and other defended places; a well-studied example is Dinas Powys near Cardiff. These must have been the seats of kings or other local strongmen. Some goods were still imported from the Mediterranean and Gaul, a trade that we can trace through types of pottery found in these strongholds. It was a small and select trade, under the thumb of the local rulers, who controlled access to the rare prestige goods that were transported in this pottery.[4]

The new elite also found another way to assert themselves: they began setting up inscriptions on stone to commemorate their dead.

In Roman times, stone epitaphs were confined essentially to the families of soldiers and officials living in a few major centres like Caerleon. In the fifth century this changes, as sub-Roman inscriptions appear widely through the British-held lands, from northern Britain down into Brittany. There is a special concentration in Gwynedd and Dyfed, with further groups in Glamorgan and Brycheiniog. Inscriptions were carved in Latin, using capitals, which were the traditional script for Roman epitaphs. All this looks very Roman and doubtless it was meant to. And yet the stones themselves are generally rough, undressed blocks or pillars, not the shaped tombstones that we know of from Roman times, so perhaps they owe something also to prehistoric standing stones. Only a few were set up in early churchyards. Most were erected away from churches, in older burial grounds out in the countryside, often along the roads, where Romans had put their tombs in previous centuries, and sometimes on or near older prehistoric monuments. If the people who erected these memorials wanted to look back to the Roman past – and they clearly did – they also chose to lay visible claim to their land and to assert some kind of connection with the monuments left behind by even earlier generations.

As an assertion of power and status, graves marked in this permanent way were a privilege of the few, not the many. Some belonged to secular rulers like the Voteporix, buried near Castell Dwyran, Carmarthenshire, who was probably a king of Dyfed, but others commemorated churchmen, such as the *Sanctinus sacerdos* ('priest' or 'bishop') remembered on a stone near Llandudno.[5] The stones are quite revealing about the nature of the new ruling class. The personal names are a mixture of Roman and British. The Latin is usually very faulty, but this does not mean that it was a foreign language to the carvers or the people who paid them. The 'mistakes' are actually normal features of the kind of Latin that people used every day, and they tell us that some people still spoke Latin as a native language in west Wales in the fifth and sixth centuries. Besides Romano-Britons, other people were present as well. Some of the inscriptions are in the Irish language, using a special script, ogam. The ogam alphabet was a unique Irish response to Latin writing. Its letters consisted of notches carved along a line, usually the edge of the stone. In Ireland ogam was used alone, but in Wales most ogam stones are bilingual, carrying an Irish message in ogam and a Latin one in Roman script. Voteporix, for instance, was commemorated in both languages, while at Nevern in Pembrokeshire, a man with the Latin name Vitalianus Emeretus was honoured in Latin and also in ogam Irish.[6] It is clear that the elite of post-Roman Wales included many Irish-speakers. Later sources suggest that the royal family of Dyfed were of Irish origin.

The great question for us is: were the inscriptions Christian? The answer is yes in many cases. Some use the words *hic iacit* 'here lies'. This was a formula favoured by Christians all over the Latin world, reflecting their hope for the resurrection of the body. In ogam inscriptions the word *xoi* 'here' seems to be an Irish adaptation of this formula. Unusually, the word is spelled in Latin letters, *hoi*, on the lead coffin of a certain Camuloris from Rhuddgaer, Anglesey, a burial that may even be late Roman in date.[7] Other stones have crosses or the Chi-Rho symbol. Christianity is most obvious in the memorials of churchmen. At Llansadwrn, Anglesey, there is the epitaph of Saturninus, the founder of the church that still bears his name. Still on Anglesey, a stone recently discovered at Llanfaelog honours an Irishman, *Máel Ísu*, 'devotee of Jesus'. This Irish Christian gave his name, in the Welsh form *Maelog*, to the church.[8] Yet many of the inscriptions are silent as to religion. Not all need have been Christian, and it does not seem very likely that they were at this early date. A stone from Trawsfynydd in Merionethshire declares that *Porius hic in tumulo iacit homo [x]pianus fuit*, 'Porius lies here in the tomb. He was a Christian man.'[9] Presumably not everyone in Porius' community was a Christian if it was worthwhile to single him out in this way.

The stones, then, bear witness to Christianity even if they were not used exclusively by Christians. They also leave little doubt that Christianity was in the ascendancy. As Wales came under new rulers – made up of local Britons, Irish settlers and, in all likelihood, refugees from the eastern regions of Britain that were falling to the Anglo-Saxons – so people sought to create a new identity for themselves, at once local and Roman. And by this time to be Roman was, increasingly, to be Christian. A stone from Ffestiniog, Merionethshire, commemorates one *Cantiori*, 'citizen of Gwynedd' and 'cousin of Maglus the magistrate'. Both men have British names but their kingdom of Gwynedd looked back to Rome for its political language, while the *hic iacit* formula confirms that the memorial is Christian.[10] Alongside this secular elite, the stones give us a remarkable picture of the emerging church. There are memorials of bishops and priests and 'brothers', presumably monks. Clerical marriage seems to have been common. Saturninus was married and his 'holy spouse' (*sancta coniux*) was buried with him at Llansadwrn. From Cynwyl Gaeo parish, Carmarthenshire, there is an elaborate memorial in Latin verse: 'Preserver of the faith and always lover of his homeland, here Paulinus lies the most devout supporter of righteousness.' At the other end of the country, in Llantrisant in Anglesey, the wife of a priest or bishop, himself apparently a disciple of this Paulinus, was laid to rest. Her own name is missing but her husband, Bivatisus, receives a long section of rhetorical praise.[11] It is remarkable to think that this kind of language was meaningful now in regions that had been on the outer margins of the Roman world, and of how closely Latin culture was coming to be associated with the church.

Inscriptions like those of western Britain are found all over the Latin-speaking world in the fifth and sixth centuries, even down into North Africa. They assert Romanness and a claim to membership of the wider western world. What is so very odd, though, is that they should appear in the far west of Britain, *after* Roman rule had ended, while there are few or none in places like the West Midlands, the Cotswolds or Somerset, areas which were richer, much more Romanized and still under the control of Romano-Britons. Even within Wales, areas like the north-east, Powys and Gwent never adopted the new memorials. The distribution of these inscriptions strongly hints that the idea of setting them up spread by sea. Accordingly, it was once thought that the habit was brought here by churchmen from Gaul; indeed it was taken as evidence that a wave of Christian missionaries sailed to western Britain and converted the Britons after the end of Roman rule.[12] In such a simplistic form, this theory is no longer credible. There is no evidence that the Gallic church undertook a mission to Britain. But there were certainly comings and goings between Gaul and the coastal lands around the Irish Sea, as imported pottery shows. It is quite likely that the habit of putting up stone epitaphs was introduced by people who knew them from Gaul, for example. But this is unlikely to be the whole story, as the inscriptions do seem to retain habits from older Romano-British epigraphy as well: either these were brought into fifth-century Wales from further east, or there was more continuity between these stones and earlier practice in Wales than we can currently see.[13]

Even if there was influence from Gaul, this cannot be taken as proof that Christianity itself came to Wales by the same routes. Those stones that have Christian markers help us to see the faith being adopted around the western coasts, but the *absence* of stones from other parts of Wales tells us nothing about its progress there. For whatever reason, most of the regions that were still British never took up the habit of erecting these inscriptions. Yet the bulk of the Christian influence spreading into Wales must have come from the Romano-British church, which by now was well-established further east. The difficulty lies in tracing it when we have so little other evidence to use. Unsurprisingly, therefore, archaeologists have looked to another innovation of this period – the appearance of burial grounds – for more information about conversion to Christianity. This is an even more complex matter than the memorial stones, however. Without words or symbols to guide us, graves are a risky basis for drawing conclusions about people's beliefs. There is a continuing, unresolved debate about whether, and when, we see Christianity reflected in Roman and early medieval burial customs. In the first and second centuries, the commonest custom in the Roman world was to cremate the dead. From the third century onwards there was a striking change, as people began to bury the dead uncremated. This great shift from cremation to inhumation occurred throughout the Roman west, though at varying speeds, and appears to have begun in Rome as early as the second century. It is tempting to think that it was inspired by Christianity, because of the Christian idea that the whole body would be resurrected in eternity. But the change started too early. Inhumation came to be the norm long before Christians can have been anywhere near a majority of the population, so the change to unburnt burial remains one of the perplexing mysteries of Roman history. It is no easier to interpret other customs. In late Roman

Britain bodies were laid out on their backs in fairly neat rows in regulated cemeteries. They were oriented roughly west–east, with the head to the west, facing east. Few or no goods like clothing, pots or tools were left in graves. This whole arrangement looks Christian to us because it came to be the norm for Christian burial in later centuries, but did it arise under the influence of the church or is it rather just the late Roman norm? None of it is essential to any dogma of Christianity. Indeed, the writers of the later Roman empire never mention any distinctively Christian way of disposing of the dead. That was an idea that took centuries to develop. Eventually these customs would become the Christian standard, but that may just be because they were in use at the same time as Christianity was becoming the accepted religion.

In Roman Wales, burials of any kind are hard to find. People seem to have disposed of the dead in ways that left few traces. The exception is around the forts and towns, where the inhabitants, many of them not natives, followed the common Roman customs that I have just outlined; that is, cremation in the early centuries, and inhumation later on. It is only in the fifth century, after the collapse of Roman authority, that burials begin to be visible throughout Wales, but when they do, they clearly follow the late Roman pattern. Burial grounds look regulated, if not completely regular. Many graves were lined with stones; archaeologists call these 'long cists'. Others were lined with wood, or wood and stone together, while the remaining graves were unlined, and hence are called 'dug graves'. In general, though, the bodies were laid out on their backs, oriented west–east, and have few or no grave-goods. The appearance of these customs in Wales, after a long period when different rites were in use, does suggest a change in mentalities, but – as elsewhere – archaeologists cannot agree on whether the new rites are specifically Christian or not. Charles Thomas, in his classic *The Early Christian Archaeology of North Britain*, not only argued that the burial grounds were Christian, but even declared that they should be seen as 'the primary field-monuments of insular Christianity'.[14] Indeed, he believed that many of our parish churches evolved out of them, a theory that will be discussed in more detail in chapter 3. Recent opinion has turned quite sceptical. In the fifth and sixth centuries churchyard burial was for clerics, their families and dependants, and monks, people who had taken vows of religion and so cut themselves off from the ties of family and community that bound the laity to their ancestral burial plots. Almost everyone else would have been laid to rest in their own cemeteries. There is no evidence until much later that church authorities expected or encouraged lay people to abandon these places for churchyards; we do not even know whether clerics attended the burial of lay people in this period. Most of the early medieval burial grounds discovered so far look unecclesiastical, were distant from church sites and were not controlled by any church, so far as we can tell. Instead they were near settlements, beside roads as was common in Roman times, and often in or near prehistoric monuments that provided a visible link with the past. Few if any of these cemeteries were enclosed, and it is unlikely, therefore, that they were consecrated.[15] It would be rash to assume that everyone buried there was a Christian. Porius, whose memorial was cited above, probably rested alongside non-Christians.

On the Continent, Roman cemeteries often developed into churches because they contained, or were thought to contain, the graves of martyrs killed during the persecutions. After persecution ended, churches were founded over the martyrs' tombs. There is, however, no certain example of this from Wales, and only one fairly trustworthy case in all of Britain, which is St Albans in south-east England. The lost church of Julius and Aaron at Caerleon, a possible Welsh site of this kind, has not been fully investigated.[16] One other candidate is Llanbeblig, Caernarfon, a church that stands in a Roman cemetery next to the fort of Segontium and whose saint may have a Roman name, if Peblig is from Publicius.[17] Perhaps it was a Roman burial place that became a church site, but it is not likely that a martyr grave inspired the change. Only provincial governors could pass the death penalty, and so we would expect martyr graves only at major towns where governors held their assizes, not small outposts like Segontium. The vast majority of the cemeteries that appear in the fifth and sixth centuries had no continuity with the much earlier time when Christians were persecuted. Some do, admittedly, contain what archaeologists call 'special graves', that is, graves marked out in some way, by a surrounding ditch or small building. It has been suggested that these were saints' graves, if not of martyrs, then of later, confessor saints. But in burial grounds away from churches it is more likely that they distinguished prominent laymen.

Both the inscriptions and the new burial practices owe something to late Roman Britain, but it is a paradox that they only really began to spread in Wales after the collapse of Roman power. For centuries Wales had been marginal to the empire. Heavy taxes and requisitions would have drained resources away to maintain the army and bureaucracy elsewhere, and local landowners could not accumulate great wealth. With the ending of Roman rule this drain would have stopped, for a while. For the first time in centuries kings ruled in Wales and were able to build up their resources. Naturally those kings and their supporters looked for ways to express their power, and the symbols they would choose would be those of the Roman world out of which they were emerging. Neither inscriptions nor oriented, unfurnished burials started out as exclusive markers of Christianity, but in this profoundly changed world, Christianity was coming to look more and more like the true Roman religion and a powerful way to set the Britons apart from the incoming Germanic peoples.

A new Christian language

The church worked through Latin, the medium of the Scriptures, theology, religious services, education and literacy. Latin was still spoken by some as a mother tongue in fifth- and sixth-century Britain, but the British language gradually ousted it from everyday use, so recruits to the church increasingly had to learn Latin as a foreign language. British – now on its way to becoming early Welsh – had its own class of professional language-users, including poets, lawyers and keepers of historical tradition, and naturally these men would have had many dealings with the new clergy. The two languages were thus in intimate contact, and since people needed to express their new faith in their British vernacular, so many dozens of words for Christian concepts were borrowed at this time. Words were needed for the church (*eglwys*), its personnel (*offeiriad* 'priest', *esgob* 'bishop'), vestments and furniture (*casul* 'chasuble', *mwys* 'paten', *allor* 'altar', *cloch* 'bell'), sacraments (*segrffyg*) such as baptism (*bedydd*) and the Mass (*offeren*), penance (*penyd*), parts of worship such as the sermon (*pregeth*) or lesson (*llith*), feasts and seasons (*gŵyl* 'vigil, feast', *Nadolig* 'Christmas', *Grawys* 'Lent'), and concepts like 'sin' (*pechod*), 'faith' (*ffydd*), and Christian names (*Iesu, Crist, Mair, Pedr*). We know that this influx of Latin words into Brittonic happened as early as this because the words show sound changes that are datable to the period. Linguistic archaeology can be as illuminating as that of stones and graves.

The British church after 409: St Germanus of Auxerre

In the fifth and sixth centuries, the western kingdoms remained just a part of the lands of the Britons. Further east, in the lowlands, the church was well entrenched. The political rupture of 409 did not cut the church in Britain off from the Continent. The next event recorded is the visit of a Gallic bishop, Germanus of Auxerre, in 429. Germanus' visit is recorded in an excellent contemporary source, the chronicle of Prosper of Aquitaine. The movers behind the mission were Germanus himself, a deacon called Palladius, and Pope Celestine. Germanus' task was to suppress the Pelagian heresy, which had taken hold in Britain. Pelagius himself, as we saw in the previous chapter, was a Briton, though his controversial career took him to Rome, Africa and Palestine. Pelagius acted as a spiritual adviser to wealthy aristocrats, but his emphasis on the role of the human will in salvation seemed to some critics to challenge the importance of God's grace. He was attacked by Jerome and Augustine, and in 418 his doctrine was declared heretical and he was exiled. His ideas, however, still had supporters. Prosper says that a Pelagian called Agricola, the son of a Pelagian bishop called Severianus, corrupted the British church. We know nothing more of either man. It is not stated that either was British, nor whether the problem in Britain was a long-standing one or had only recently arisen. One theory is that the Pelagian party fled to Britain after their condemnation in 418, because the island lay beyond the power of the emperor. Another is that the 'Pelagians' were local British Christians whose thinking on salvation was traditional but who, in the sharpened atmosphere of the Pelagian controversy, had found themselves on the wrong side of orthodoxy. It is in fact very difficult to know how influential Pelagianism was in fifth-century Britain, or whether it was even a movement at all, rather than a set of attitudes which would have been quite widely shared by Christians of the time.[18]

All that Prosper tells us about the mission is that Germanus succeeded. We do have a later, fuller account: a *Life of St Germanus* by Constantius of Lyon, a work that dates to the 460s or 470s. Unfortunately, though Constantius wrote elegantly and with theological sophistication, he had precious little evidence with which to work, and he resorted to set-piece stories that he took from Scripture or other saints' *Lives*. In one well-known passage, Germanus and his companion Lupus confront the Pelagians at an assembly. The 'heretics' arrive richly dressed, whereas the orthodox bishops are wearing modest clothes. This is symbolically loaded: the Pelagians' sumptuous clothing draws attention to the cardinal sin underlying their theology, as their detractors saw it, which was pride. In Constantius' words, 'on one side stood divine authority, on the other, human presumption.'[19] In this light, it would be rash to treat the Pelagians' rich clothes as a literal fact, still less as evidence for worldliness in the British church. Another highly symbolic episode is the famous 'Alleluia Victory'. An invading army of Saxons and Picts appears. Germanus and Lupus lead the Britons in raising a great cry of 'Alleluia', at which the enemy run away without spilling a drop of blood. It is, sadly, another piece of imaginative writing, illustrating 1 Samuel 17:47 with a hint of Joshua at the walls of Jericho, and not at all likely to have happened. Another problem with the *Life* is that it records a second visit by Germanus to Britain, and this is not mentioned in any other source. Historians continue to argue as to whether Germanus really did visit a second time, in the 430s or 440s, or not.[20]

One important detail remains which must have been factual, however. Germanus went to pray at the tomb of the martyr, St Alban. This is confirmed by another short text, the *Passion of St Alban*, a very early work, probably based on inscriptions put up in Auxerre while Germanus was bishop.[21] It tells the story of Alban's death, and also adds details about what Germanus did when he visited. The bishop opened the martyr's tomb, deposited some relics of the apostles, and took away some of Alban's relics for Auxerre. There is good evidence that the cult of Alban was established very early at Auxerre, from which it passed to other continental churches.

Difficult to handle as the sources for Germanus are, they show that the British church was still in touch with Rome and the Continent, and shared in theological and devotional developments with the rest of western Christendom, in spite of the political upheavals and the increasing pressure of barbarian attacks on the island.

Christianity spreads to Ireland

Germanus' mission was linked with a momentous event in the history of Christianity in these islands, the sending of the first bishop to Ireland. This is again recorded by Prosper of Aquitaine, who says that Palladius was sent in 431 'to those Irish who believe in Christ'.[22] It can hardly be a coincidence that this happened within two years of Germanus' visit to Britain. The deacon Palladius involved in sending Germanus to Britain in 429 must have been the same man as the bishop dispatched to Ireland in 431. It is very likely that the mission was planned between Germanus, the British bishops and representatives of the Irish Christians while Germanus was in Britain. But who were 'those Irish who believe in Christ'? There would have been many opportunities for Irish people to encounter Christianity. For centuries Ireland lay just beyond the boundaries of the Roman empire, and there would have been many links forged through trade and by individual Irishmen seeking a career in the empire. From the third century Irish raiders began to attack the western coasts of Britain and then settle around them, as we saw earlier. In these colonies Irish people encountered Christianity, as some of the inscribed stones attest, and through them the faith could have passed to Ireland. We must also reckon with intermarriage across the Irish Sea, and with the taking of British slaves to Ireland – St Patrick being a famous example. Thus it is no surprise that there were already Irish Christians by 431.

Though the routes by which Christianity could have reached Ireland are clear, the process of Christianization is not well documented because the fifth and sixth centuries lie before the time from which we have many reliable historical records. Palladius vanishes from sight after 431 and no trustworthy source tells us what he achieved in Ireland. He must have had some impact, however, for the Irish monk Columbanus, writing in 613, declares that the Irish church sprang from Rome, which must be a reference to this mission.[23] But quite soon afterwards memory of Palladius faded away, or else was obliterated by the growing cult of St Patrick. Everything about Patrick is frustratingly obscure, be it his dates, his career or his exact achievements. Within two centuries of his death he was being written of as the national apostle, but as we have just seen, the idea that he was the first to bring the faith to Ireland is a gross simplification. Patrick lived around the middle of the fifth century. He was born in a small British community called *Bannavem Tabernae*. The name has been damaged slightly in transmission and unfortunately we do not know where it was, except that it must have been near the west coast. Patrick's father, Calpurnius, was a deacon and local councillor (*decurio*), while his grandfather, Potitus, had been a priest. Here was a local landowning family, all bearing Roman names, that had embraced Christianity for at least three generations. As the son of local gentry, Patrick should have received some education, but it was cut short when he was abducted by raiders and taken as a slave to Ireland. There he worked as a shepherd for several years before escaping and returning to Britain. Later, however, he felt a vocation to return and convert the Irish people to Christianity.

For his Irish mission, Patrick was ordained as a bishop, but it seems that he, or his mission, had opponents within the British church, for he was forced to defend himself, his authority and his behaviour in Ireland. He has left us two works, the oldest literature that we possess from either Britain or Ireland. One, the *Confessio*, is his case for his own defence, aimed at those in Britain who might be influenced by his opponents: in it Patrick tells the story of his own life, defends his mission in Ireland and his own fitness to undertake it. The second, much shorter work, is a letter addressed to a British king called Coroticus, demanding that he release Irish

Christians seized in a slave raid. Neither text can be dated closely. They show us a church under construction and are full of hints as to the kinds of processes that must have operated in Wales, but regrettably the unnamed missionaries who worked here have left us nothing comparable. Thanks to his writings, it is Patrick who is the first Christian in these islands whose spiritual life we can approach in any detail.

For a couple of generations, Britons dominated the Irish church. Many words for religious matters, borrowed from Latin into the Irish language, show traces of a distinctive British pronunciation. Examples are *paidir* 'prayer', *altóir* 'altar', *Peadar* (the apostle Peter), *easpag* 'bishop', *sagart* 'priest', *eaglais* 'church', and the name of *Pádraig* himself.[24] Among later British missionaries, the most significant was probably a man called *Uinniau* (this would be *Gwynio* in today's Welsh). He settled in Ulster, founding the church of Moville in County Down, where he is known as Finnian. He taught St Columba, who left Ireland to found his famous church of Iona in 563.[25] With the establishment of great institutions like Iona and Clonmacnoise, the Irish church came into its own and British influence faded. Soon, as the Anglo-Saxon catastrophe overwhelmed most of Christian Britain, the balance of power shifted decisively to Ireland. But for a while, the two churches remained in the closest contact, as we will see in the next chapter.

Gildas

While the church was expanding westwards, in the east it was to suffer devastation. Raiders from Germanic Europe, the Angles and Saxons and others, began to colonize Britain's eastern and southern coasts. Around the 440s they wrested control of much of the island from whatever British authority had been in charge.[26] East Anglia and Kent were conquered early, and so probably was eastern Yorkshire, south-central England and the Thames valley. The colonists were pagans. There have been lively disputes as to how many there were: either so many that they annihilated or expelled the existing British population, or just a conquering elite who left most Romano-Britons in place and gradually assimilated them. Probably it varied from place to place. Either way, the conquest was by no means easy. Large areas remained under British control: the West Midlands, the West Country, Wales. From somewhere in this swathe of British territory, a lone voice survives who provides the richest testimony that we have concerning the early British church. This is the voice of Gildas.

Of Gildas himself we know next to nothing except that he lived during the short window of time between the establishment of the first Anglo-Saxon kingdoms in the east and the collapse of British rule in lowland Britain, and he was a deacon in the church. He wrote probably in the first half of the sixth century. We do not know where he lived, but it was most likely in what had been the heartland of late Roman Britain, Gloucestershire or Somerset or Dorset. It adds a note of poignancy to our reading to reflect that Gildas probably lived in a place that, a generation after him, became English for ever. He has left us one complete work, the *De excidio Britanniae* ('The Ruin of Britain'), and its title conveys its tone. It is a furious diatribe against the moral failings of the British people and a desperate call to repentance. Gildas begins by explaining how reluctant he was to speak out: he had hesitated for ten years, but duty now impelled him. Then he gives an account of the history of Britain and its church down to his own time. It is a dismal record of sin, wickedness and weakness. Britons were poor Christians, forever rebelling against proper authority but lacking the courage or strength to govern themselves. The coming of the dreadful Angles and Saxons was God's punishment upon them. Only if they repented and returned to the path of true religion would they survive. Next Gildas rounds on Britain's kings, of whom he names five. At least two ruled in Wales, Vortiporius in Dyfed and Maglocunus (Maelgwn) in Gwynedd.[27] Gildas accuses them of numberless crimes, ranging from hypocrisy and lust for praise through fornication to murder. A call for better kingship follows, with many references to ideals from Scripture. Finally, Gildas castigates Britain's priests in a similar thoroughgoing fashion, though no individuals are named.

Gildas wrote artistic, rhetorical and very difficult Latin.[28] In this western zone it was clearly still possible to receive a fine Roman-style education and to have access to an excellent library. More striking still is that he tells us that Maelgwn of Gwynedd received a rhetorical education too, at the hands of 'the refined master of almost all Britain'.[29] The phrase puts us in mind of the memorial stone at Llantrisant with its snippets of Latin panegyric, deep within Maelgwn's own kingdom. There were people around who were able to understand and appreciate the message of *De excidio Britanniae*.

As Gildas presents matters, the society of his own day was appallingly corrupt:

> Britain has kings, but they are tyrants; she has judges, but they are wicked. They often plunder and terrorize – the innocent; they defend and protect – the guilty and thieving; they have many wives – whores and adulteresses; they constantly swear – false oaths; they make vows – but almost at once tell lies; they wage wars – civil and unjust; they chase thieves energetically all over the country – but love and even reward the thieves that sit with them at table.[30]

In spite of all Gildas's fury, it is possible to see that the ideological basis of kingship was becoming closely intertwined with Christianity, even if practice lagged sadly behind Gildas's ideals. By now, this was a Christian society.[31] Famously, among all the sins of the Britons, Gildas does not mention paganism except as an error of the distant past. Within his lamentations, we find references to the right of church sanctuary, preaching, the swearing of oaths at altars, the cult of martyrs, church buildings, monasticism, chaste widowhood and much else that reveals a fully operational Christian church that maintained the standard hierarchy of bishops, priests and deacons, as well as monks and nuns. Relations between kings and churchmen were intimate. Kings were surrounded by clerics even if, in Gildas's account, the latter spent much of their time lamenting the dreadful behaviour of the former. Maelgwn himself became a monk for a while, though he later broke his vows. Gildas exclaims: 'your wicked return (like some sick hound) to your disgusting vomit has brought grief and weeping.' Behind Gildas's anger, a model of Christian kingship, strongly influenced by the

Old Testament, can be discerned. Kings should be continent and uphold sexual morality, and cherish their own kin rather than murdering them. Furthermore, they should fight only just wars, administer justice and protect the weak and the poor against oppression. It is an ideal that, needless to say, has proved unattainable in every age. Within the church, Gildas laments that holy orders were bought and sold, while wholly unfit candidates simply went abroad to be ordained. Some church offices were bought off the wicked kings, who exercised far too much control over matters spiritual. Another of Gildas's bugbears was incontinent clergy, but as we saw from the memorial stones, others regarded the taking of a wife by priests and even bishops as upright Christian behaviour. Indeed, it is fair to be sceptical about the true extent of all the abuses. What is hard to deny, though, is that the church was now established, powerful and well endowed with property.

Gildas put forward the ideal of a committed minority fighting for reform within the church. This suggests that he saw the ascetic ideal as the way forward. Uinniau consulted him on the rules of the monastic life, which must indicate that Gildas became a monk himself. Even in his own lifetime Gildas was an authority. Interestingly, the fragments of his correspondence with Uinniau reveal a more lenient side to the man, since he criticizes monks who go to extremes like ploughing the fields with their bare hands rather than using animals, or refusing to travel by horse, or eating only bread and water – and boasting constantly about it.[32] Gildas disparaged such antics as the fruit of pride rather than the spirit. After his death he was revered in Britain and Ireland: a short penitential, or set of rules for the behaviour of clerics and monks, survives that bears Gildas's name, though it is unlikely to be by him. His genuine work, *The Ruin of Britain*, is the most influential book ever written on the history of the Britons, and this was not altogether fortunate, as we shall see in the next chapter. But his motives were admirable and for all his anger, he advocated moderation in the religious life.

Monasticism, David and Samson

Both Patrick and Gildas bear witness to the growth of the monastic ideal. Christian asceticism seems to have begun in Egypt in the third century and spread from there to Palestine and beyond. In the west, a pioneer was Martin of Tours, who died in 397. The ascetic ideal was spread by word of mouth and by such important works as Sulpicius Severus' *Life of St Martin*. The son of the usurper Constantine III was a monk for a time, very possibly in Britain, which would push the origins of monasticism here back to the beginning of the fifth century. A generation or so later, Patrick's writings confirm that there were monks and nuns in Britain, and that they were beginning to attract Irish converts. A young Irishwoman whom Patrick baptized took a vow of chastity, much to the anger of her relations. He also mentions 'widows and the continent', and he worried particularly about female slaves who tried to follow ascetic vows while still in service, and who were threatened and beaten by their owners.[33] This, however, is almost all that we hear of lower-class recruits to monasticism. Overwhelmingly our sources give the impression that 'opting out' was a choice made by the wealthy and powerful. This is not surprising. Monasteries required land and the labour of peasants to maintain them, and these assets would come mainly as gifts from converts or from families who wished to devote their children as oblates. Gildas confirms that the monastic movement was widespread in the sixth century. It has been suggested that his own writings acted as a catalyst for a turn to the monastic life in the generations after him. Though this is strictly speculative, it is plausible that the chaos of the Germanic invasions and the dreadful plagues that hit in the middle of the century did create an atmosphere in which Gildas's call for repentance was listened to by many.[34] By now the ascetic movement was generating rival schools of thought. Gildas, it will be recalled, criticized extremist monks who ploughed their fields by hand, and if we choose to be a little daring, we can put a name to one of them: David. The evidence is, admittedly, not ideal. The *Life of St David* belongs to the end of the eleventh century, five hundred years later than his lifetime.[35] But it does seem as though Rhygyfarch, who composed the *Life*, used an old document from one of David's churches that reflected the saint's own rule for his monks. And one of its stipulations was that monks should not presume to use draught animals for ploughing. This looks like a view of the same sixth-century controversy, but from the opposing side.[36]

Of David himself little is securely known. It is safe to accept that he founded St Davids and some other churches, though certainly not all the ones that bear his name. The tradition that he settled first at Henfynyw in Ceredigion is also credible, and so is his death on 1 March, for the death of a founder saint would be preserved as a feast-day by his successors. But that is really all that we can say, for the rest of Rhygyfarch's *Life of St David* is built out of local place-lore, common miracle stories, anecdotes from Irish saints' *Lives* and episodes that relate to controversies between churches that arose long after David's own time. At least we can say more about David than many other saints. The sixth century was the 'age of the saints', and that idea is not just a modern myth, but one propagated already by medieval Welsh writers, who looked back on it as the time when the heroes of Welsh Christianity had lived and worked. The later *Lives* of the saints show them confronting and browbeating sixth-century kings, especially the Maelgwn made infamous by Gildas, and the legendary Arthur. Moreover, the genealogies of the saints attach them to royal and aristocratic families and imply that they all belonged to the same few generations around this time. How much of this is factual is impossible to tell. We cannot trace the founding of Welsh churches and monasteries in any detail. St Davids and Bangor were sixth-century foundations in all likelihood; Bangor was already important enough to be called 'the Great' in an Irish chronicle under the year 632.[37] Another very early foundation was St Illtud's house at Llanilltud Fawr in Glamorgan, about which more will be said below. Such men as David, Deiniol, Illtud, Cadog, Teilo, Padarn and others probably did live in the sixth century. But the much later *Lives* and genealogies are simply too untrustworthy and derivative to be used as historical documents for this early time.

However, a few individuals are illuminated by one fascinating early work. Around 700, or somewhat earlier, a *Life of St Samson* was written at Dol in Brittany.[38] St Samson, Dol's patron, lived around the mid- to late sixth century. His first home was south

Wales. Some eighty-odd years after Samson's death, a Breton author crossed the sea to retrace the steps of his hero. Much of his information he got at a church in Cornwall, very possibly Golant, but he also visited Llanilltud Fawr and Caldey Island in south Wales. The *Life* preserves precious information, transmitted in writing and through a chain of eye-witnesses. Samson's family were secular aristocrats, his father from Dyfed, his mother from Gwent. Early in his life he entered the monastery of St Illtud, who is described as 'the most learned of all the Britons', not only in Scripture but also in grammar, rhetoric, arithmetic and other school subjects. The hagiographer adds the interesting detail that Illtud came from a family of *magici* (prophets or wise men, perhaps distant descendants of Caesar's druids) – an indication of how the learned classes of pagan society might have transitioned into the Christian church on conversion. At this monastery, which we can safely identify with Llanilltud Fawr in Glamorgan, Samson is ordained by Bishop Dubricius (Dyfrig). Dubricius' see and sphere of jurisdiction are unclear; Llanilltud is in south-east Wales, but later in the *Life* we see Dubricius regularly spending Easter on Caldey Island in Dyfed. But at least the importance of the bishop is clear, as inspector of monasteries and ordainer of clergy. Presently, Samson withdraws to a more austere life on Caldey. The hagiographer relates, with obvious discomfort, an extraordinary story of the death of Caldey's abbot, Piro (Pyr): wandering through the monastery precinct one night, and the worse for drink, Piro fell down the well. The preservation of such a bizarre and inappropriate detail is one hint of many in the *Life* that the author went to pains to get authentic material and has passed it on conscientiously. Samson's parents, his five brothers and his uncle and aunt and their three children all convert to the monastic life and found various, unnamed houses. Since the author notes that the names of Samson's relatives were still commemorated during Mass at Dol, his account carries conviction. It is a unique portrait, in a British context, of a spectacular conversion to the ascetic life by an entire aristocratic family. Samson now founds another small community in an old fort beside the river Severn, near a cave into which he withdraws as a hermit. The author implies that he visited the spot and saw the saint's little church (*oratorium*), but frustratingly does not say where it was. Soon Samson is extracted, somewhat unwillingly, from his hermitage and made into the abbot of a nearby monastery, and then a bishop. That was the culmination of his career in south Wales, for he soon leaves for Cornwall and, eventually, the Continent. Samson is the great example of the wandering 'Celtic' saint; in fact he has been very influential in forming the popular image of the early Welsh saints as wanderers. Too influential, probably, for Samson must have been quite special. Most church-founders would have stayed much closer to home.

Since Gildas's time it is evident that the monastic movement had taken further hold. There were large and rich houses like Llanilltud Fawr, deeply intertwined with the life of its region, but also rougher island monasteries and hermitages. Disputes over laxity and austerity continued: Samson eventually left Llanilltud Fawr because it was *tumultuosum et expendiosum per patriam*, which may mean that it was rich and greedy and burdensome to the peasants whose hard work sustained it, perhaps also too involved in politics.[39] More light is cast on the early monks by four short penitential texts from Wales or some other British region, but preserved in Continental manuscripts. Alongside the penitential ascribed to Gildas, these are the *Synod of North Britain*, the *Synod of the Grove of Victory* and some 'excerpts from a book of David'.[40] Their rules are intended, above all, for monks, but clergy who had not taken monastic vows are addressed as well. Many and varied sins are catalogued: theft, drunkenness, in one case providing aid to the barbarians (presumably Saxons), but above all various types of sexual misbehaviour. The punishments – years of penance on starvation rations – are harsh, more so perhaps in the text attributed to David than in the one claimed to be by Gildas. The way of the monk was a narrow one, and the standards required of the rest of the clergy were almost as demanding.

By 600 'official' Wales was Christian. The tide of power and patronage had ebbed away from the older beliefs, and wealth and influence now flowed through the church. A small minority of believers reacted by embracing the monastic ideal, as in the rest of Christendom, but monasteries could not escape the need to own land and thus were bound to secular society with its family loyalties and powerful but capricious kings. Strictly speaking, we know little of the religion of the peasantry. It is unlikely yet that all were baptized or within easy reach of a church, but institutions like St Davids and Llanilltud Fawr were beginning to address the need for pastoral care. Spiritually and intellectually, the British church was vibrant, but it faced huge challenges: the growth of English power in the east, the loss of most of its own territory and flock, and the danger of being cut off from the rest of the Christian west. These problems will feature in the next chapter.

Notes

[1] Gildas, *De excidio Britanniae*, i.8.

[2] On Lucius see Barry J. Lewis, 'The saints in narratives of conversion from the Brittonic-speaking regions', in *The Introduction of Christianity into the Early Medieval Insular World: Converting the Isles I*, edited by Roy Flechner and Máire Ní Mhaonaigh (Turnhout: Brepols, 2016), pp. 440–4. The mistake was unravelled by A. Harnack, 'Der Brief des britischen Königs Lucius an den Papst Eleutherus', *Sitzungsberichte der königlich-preussischen Akademie der Wissenschaften* (1904), 909–16.

[3] The date is that suggested by Michael Kulikowski, 'Barbarians in Gaul, Usurpers in Britain', *Britannia*, 31 (2000), 325–45.

[4] Ewan Campbell, *Continental and Mediterranean Imports to Atlantic Britain and Ireland, AD 400–800* (York: Council for British Archaeology, 2007).

[5] Nancy Edwards, *A Corpus of Early Medieval Inscribed Stones and Stone Sculpture in Wales 2: South-West Wales* (Cardiff: University of Wales Press, 2007), no. CM3; Nancy Edwards, *A Corpus of Early Medieval Inscribed Stones and Stone Sculpture in Wales 3: North Wales* (Cardiff: University of Wales Press, 2013), no. CN21.

[6] Edwards, *Corpus 2*, no. P71.

[7] Nancy Edwards, 'Christianising the landscape in early medieval Wales: the island of Anglesey', in *Making Christian Landscapes in Atlantic Europe: Conversion and Consolidation in the Early Middle Ages*, edited by Tomás Ó Carragáin and Sam Turner (Cork: Cork University Press, 2016), pp. 183–5.

[8] Llansadwrn: Edwards, *Corpus 3*, no. AN45. Llanfaelog: Edwards, *Corpus 3*, no. AN13.

[9] Edwards, *Corpus 3*, no. MR23.

10   Edwards, *Corpus 3*, no. MR8.

11   Cynwyl Gaeo: Edwards, *Corpus 2*, no. CM5. Llantrisant: Edwards, *Corpus 3*, no. AN46.

12   V. E. Nash-Williams and E. G. Bowen were proponents. For discussion, see Sharpe, 'Martyrs and local saints in late antique Britain', pp. 95–102.

13   For various possibilities, see Mark Handley, 'The Origins of Christian Commemoration in Late Antique Britain', *Early Medieval Europe*, 10/2 (2001), 177–99; and Carlo Tedeschi, 'Some observations on the palaeography of early Christian inscriptions in Britain', in *Roman, Runes and Ogham: Medieval Inscriptions in the Insular World and on the Continent*, edited by John Higgitt, Katherine Forsyth and David N. Parsons (Donington: Shaun Tyas, 2001), pp. 16–25.

14   Charles Thomas, *The Early Christian Archaeology of North Britain* (London: Oxford University Press, 1971), p. 50.

15   David Petts, 'Cemeteries and boundaries in western Britain', in *Burial in Early Medieval England and Wales*, edited by Sam Lucy and Andrew Reynolds (London: The Society for Medieval Archaeology, 2002), pp. 24–46.

16   See Chapter 1 above.

17   Andrew Davidson, 'The early medieval church in north-west Wales', in *The Archaeology of the Early Medieval Celtic Churches*, edited by Nancy Edwards (Leeds: Maney Publishing, 2009), pp. 42–3.

18   For theories about the British Pelagians, see R. A. Markus, 'Pelagianism, Britain and the Continent', *Journal of Ecclesiastical History*, 37 (1986), 191–204. G. Márkus, 'Pelagianism and the "Common Celtic Church"', *Innes Review*, 56 (2005), 165–213, argues against a Pelagian influence on later British and Irish churches. Ali Bonner, *The Myth of Pelagianism* (Oxford: Oxford University Press, 2018), suggests that Pelagius' views were quite conventional at the time and that it was Augustine and his supporters who were the innovators.

19   Constantius, *Vita S. Germani*, 3.14.

20   See A. A. Barrett, 'Saint Germanus and the British Missions', *Britannia*, 40 (2009), 197–217.

21   Richard Sharpe, 'The late antique Passion of St Alban', in *Alban and St Albans: Roman and Medieval Architecture, Art and Archaeology*, edited by Martin Henig and Phillip Lindley (Leeds: Maney Publishing, 2001), pp. 30–7; Michael Winterbottom (ed.), 'The Earliest Passion of St Alban', *Invigilata Lucernis*, 37 (2015), 113–27.

22   *Ad Scottos in Christo credentes*; see T. M. Charles-Edwards, 'Palladius, Prosper and Leo the Great: mission and primatial authority', in *St*

Patrick, A.D. 493–1993, edited by David N. Dumville (Woodbridge: Boydell Press, 1993), pp. 1–12.

[23] Columbanus, *Epistle* 5.v.14, to Boniface IV.

[24] The most important study to date is Damian McManus, 'A Chronology of the Latin Loan-Words in Early Irish', *Ériu*, 34 (1983), 21–71.

[25] I present a view of Uinniau not shared by all historians. For the rather complex debate on his identity, see Richard Sharpe, 'Gildas as a father of the church', in *Gildas: New Approaches*, edited by M. Lapidge and D. Dumville (Woodbridge: Boydell, 1984), pp. 193–205, and Richard Sharpe, 'Martyrs and local saints', pp. 136ff. For those who want to pursue the contrary arguments, a chapter in the same volume (above n. 12), provides full references: Thomas Owen Clancy, 'Scottish saints and national identities in the Early Middle Ages', pp. 412ff.

[26] The *Gallic Chronicle of 452* notes, for the year 441, that 'Britain, having hitherto been overrun by various calamities and events, is subjected to Saxon authority'. See discussion in Ian Wood, 'The Fall of the Western Empire and the End of Roman Britain', *Britannia*, 18 (1987), 253.

[27] Vortiporius has been thought to be the man commemorated on the Castell Dwyran stone, but the names are slightly different, so that they may have belonged to two members of the same dynasty. See Patrick Sims-Williams, in Edwards, *Corpus 2*, p. 206.

[28] Michael Lapidge, 'Gildas's education and the Latin culture of sub-Roman Britain', in *Gildas: New Approaches*, edited by Lapidge and Dumville, pp. 27–50; and Neil Wright, 'Gildas's prose style and its origins', in the same volume, pp. 107–28.

[29] Gildas, *De excidio Britanniae*, ch. 36.

[30] *De excidio Britanniae*, ch. 27.

[31] David N. Dumville, 'The idea of government in Sub-Roman Britain', in *After Empire: Towards an Ethnology of Europe's Barbarians*, edited by G. Ausenda (Woodbridge: Boydell, 1995), pp. 177–216.

[32] The correspondence is available in Michael Winterbottom, *Gildas: The Ruin of Britain and Other Documents* (Chichester: Phillimore, 1978), pp. 80–2, 143–5.

[33] Patrick, *Confessio*, ch. 42.

[34] Sharpe, 'Gildas as a father of the Church', pp. 193–205. The idea is further developed by David N. Dumville, 'The Origins and Early History of Insular Monasticism: Aspects of Literature, Christianity, and Society in Britain and Ireland, A.D. 400–600', *Bulletin of the Institute of Oriental and Occidental Studies, Kansai University*, 30 (1997), 85–107.

[35] Its author Rhygyfarch died in 1099 according to *Brut y Tywysogion*.

For the text of the *Vita S. David* and a translation, see Richard Sharpe and John Reuben Davies (edited and translated), 'Rhygyfarch's *Life* of St David', in *St David of Wales: Cult, Church and Nation*, edited by J. Wyn Evans and Jonathan M. Wooding (Woodbridge: The Boydell Press, 2007), pp. 107–55.

[36] *Vita S. David*, ch. 22 (above n. 35). For the idea, see David Dumville, *St David of Wales*, Kathleen Hughes Memorial Lecture 1 (Cambridge: Hughes Hall and Department of Anglo-Saxon, Norse, and Celtic, 2001), pp. 11–26, pursuing a theory of John Morris.

[37] T. M. Charles-Edwards, *The Chronicle of Ireland*, 2 vols (Liverpool: Liverpool University Press, 2012), vol.1, p. 138.

[38] The date has been argued about for a long time, but a consensus now seems to be emerging. See *St Samson of Dol and the Earliest History of Brittany, Cornwall and Wales*, edited by Lynette Olson (Woodbridge: The Boydell Press, 2017).

[39] *Vita S. Samsonis*, i.20.

[40] Texts and translations in *The Irish Penitentials*, edited by Ludwig Bieler (Dublin: Dublin Institute for Advanced Studies, 1963), pp. 60–73.

Chapter 3

The Definition of Christian Wales, c. 600–c. 800

BARRY J. LEWIS

The church had expanded over the whole of Wales. Kings and nobles seem to have gone over wholesale to the new religion. But it is an almost inevitable conclusion that the church was still thinly spread. There had simply not been time to bring everyone, everywhere, inside a comprehensive system of pastoral care. An episode in the *Life of St Samson* is telling.[1] Landing on the north coast of Cornwall, Samson encounters a group of villagers enjoying a horse race. They insist that this is merely a traditional and harmless custom, but the saint can see that it is unambiguously the survival of a pagan festival, performed in front of an 'abominable image'. When a boy falls off his horse and is fatally wounded, Samson cures him, and the locals then agree to destroy the idol and give up their wicked customs. Thereupon, Samson confirms them – which tells us that these were not pagans, but baptized Christians. Nevertheless, it does not seem that there was a priest on hand to discipline them, and any pastoral care that they received was incomplete, at least in the view of a rigorist like the author of the *Life*. Neither land nor people had been fully cleansed of the influence of the demons that haunted all pagan landscapes. To early medieval Christians these demons were no mere symbols, but real beings with terrifying powers. They had to be exorcized, as Samson saw; half-measures would not do. Samson's Cornish adventure is a symbolic and tendentious episode that must not be taken as historical fact, but it shows what an author in the late seventh century thought about rural Christians: they were far from fully integrated into the new religion and were in dire need of pastoral care. The centuries 600–800 were an age of consolidation, as many more churches were founded to meet this need. Yet, at the same time, the Britons were under immense pressure from the resurgent Anglo-Saxons to their east, pressure that did not end when the latter too became Christians.

The collapse of Britain and the emergence of Wales

In the second half of the sixth century, the peace in which Gildas lived was shattered for ever. The Anglo-Saxon conquests began afresh, and this time the Britons found no respite from the expanding English polities to their east. By the early seventh century the independent British kingdoms were confined to Wales and what are now the border counties, the West Country and a shrinking territory in northern Britain. Furthermore, within the conquered zone the individual Anglo-Saxon kingdoms were consolidating, developing stronger kingships and links with neighbouring countries. Æthelberht of Kent married a Frankish princess and began to think of converting to Christianity. Many Britons must have been left behind within English-controlled areas. In some places it is likely that they formed the majority of the population, but they were reduced to a low political and social status. The pressure to assimilate would have been intense, be it by learning English, dressing and eating like Saxons, or abandoning the Roman religion, Christianity, for paganism.

The church is unlikely to have survived undisturbed in the English-controlled areas. In a few places, there are hints of continuity. St Albans, for example, preserved the cult of Alban and perhaps even a Roman church building. Another martyr, Sixtus, was still venerated somewhere in south-eastern Britain around 600.[2] On the other hand, there is no sign of any organized hierarchy that survived the conquest and settlement. Bereft of bishops and priests,

Christian communities could have struggled on, maintaining their faith and some of its rituals for a few generations, and that may be what we see at St Albans. But without anyone to administer the sacraments, they would be weak and vulnerable to assimilation. More could have survived further west, in the West Midlands and south-west of Britain. These lands were conquered later, which might mean that there were fewer settlers, and much less time passed between the conquest and the restoration of official Christianity. Indeed, some British areas were seized so late that their conquerors were themselves already Christian: west Devon, for instance, or much of northern and western Northumbria. In parts of Northumbria an organized British church survived under English rule until the later seventh century, when the British clergy were violently expelled and their churches handed over to English priests. Meanwhile, in the far west, beyond the limits of English conquest and settlement, independent British kingdoms endured. Here the world of Gildas was not overwhelmed, but rather transformed.

Local churches

The memorials that were so informative up till now decline rapidly in the seventh century. One of the latest was put up at Llangadwaladr, Anglesey, in the 620s, to honour King Cadfan of Gwynedd.[3] After that, they fell out of use except at a handful of the larger churches, where kings and senior clerics were still occasionally honoured with inscriptions down to the Norman era. Instead, we now find much simpler stones marked only with crosses. Like the small number of later inscriptions, these cross-marked stones cluster around church sites. An important shift was under way: people were abandoning their kin- and community-based burial grounds dotted around the wider countryside, and choosing instead to bury their dead at churches. This change was a slow process, beginning before the period covered in this chapter and not completed until well after 800. It was closely connected to the cult of saints. People looked to the saints to help them on Judgement Day, and this led to the literal idea that those buried near saints – *ad sanctos* – would have better access to their assistance. As early as the 390s St Ambrose arranged to be laid to rest between his patrons, the martyrs Gervase and Protase, in their church in Milan. From clerics the idea spread to the lay elite. In Wales, as church-founders came to be revered as saints, their graves too acquired a powerful holy attraction. Welsh rulers began to arrange for their bodies to be buried at churches, and once they did so, the rest of society was bound to follow. By the high Middle Ages burial had migrated so completely into churchyards that it was essential for all Christians to be buried in consecrated ground; anyone who was refused churchyard burial was, in effect, damned.

Logically, the same result could be achieved by building churches on older burial grounds and thus Christianizing them. This certainly happened on the Continent, especially where a cemetery contained a martyr's tomb. The archaeologist Charles Thomas put forward a famous model of how early cemeteries in Celtic Britain gradually developed into churches: first a cemetery would be enclosed with a wall, hedge or ditch, to mark it off as sacred space; then a cross might be erected, then a small chapel (sometimes over a special, saint's grave), and finally the whole site would become a parish church.[4] It is a possible model, but actual examples are not common. One is Capel Maelog in Radnorshire, which seems to have been a burial ground for centuries before the first church was built on it. Moreover, the church enclosed an older 'special grave' within its chancel. Another is the burial ground of Tywyn y Capel, Anglesey, to which a small chapel was added at some point.[5] Unfortunately, at most medieval churches it is impossible to test the hypothesis because they remain in use and cannot be excavated. What is more, archaeology has now revealed dozens of early medieval burial grounds across Wales that did not develop into churches. They were not deliberately enclosed (though they might be placed in older, prehistoric enclosures) and show no signs of ever being used as places of worship. The more of these that we find, the harder it is to maintain Thomas's model of 'development'.

We now suspect that, for the most part, churches were founded on new sites, away from older burial grounds. Unlike these, church sites would be enclosed from the outset to mark them off as sacred. Some were (or became) very substantial institutions, while others were served only by a priest or two. All had some land and a settlement attached to them so that the clergy could be supplied with food, clothing and other necessities. The lay inhabitants became church tenants. Such an arrangement arose because Wales lacked towns or villages to provide a framework for the new church. Most people lived in individual farmsteads scattered across the land. New churches were therefore inserted into underused spaces in the landscape, or perhaps more often attached to an existing farmstead. Nowadays, many of them stand in picturesque isolation among the fields. But churches such as Eglwys Gymyn in Carmarthenshire or Llanbabo in Anglesey, however lonely they look today, were not built as the remote retreats of monks or hermits. They served a local community that no longer exists; often, the last remnant of it is a single modern farm next to the church.

This pattern of small church settlements, within a landscape of scattered farmsteads, accounts for a striking feature of place-names in the Celtic-speaking regions: the number of places that are named after churches. Wales has more than six hundred places called '*llan* X'. One example will have to stand for many. In the north-west of Anglesey, *Llanfaethlu* is the name of a parish and a small hamlet. St Maethlu's church served the dispersed population of a secular district called *Carneddor*, but that name is now attached to a single farm in the parish.[6] Because the church settlement stayed where it was put while other habitations were affected by the vagaries of inheritance and changing land use, the ecclesiastical name flourishes while the secular one just about clings to life. The map of Cornwall looks much like that of Wales, with many place-names incorporating the Cornish *lann*, while Gaelic Ireland and Scotland have innumerable places named after their *cell* ('church'), such as Kildare and Kilbride. Most English churches, in contrast, were built at long-lived centres of manors, with the result that these places have kept their secular names and the parish name is simply that of the manor.

Place-names may give us precious evidence regarding the early church, but extracting it is no easy matter. Most names are only recorded centuries after they were coined, making it difficult or impossible to be chronologically precise. Nor are the nuances of place-name elements as clear as we might like. The most usual Latin word for a church is *ecclesia*, ultimately from Greek and meaning an 'assembly'. It was borrowed early into British, giving *eglwys* in Welsh. It is not very common in place-names: examples are *Eglwyswrw* in Pembrokeshire and *Eglwys Gymyn*, Carmarthenshire. Formerly there were more, but the word has often been replaced by *llan*, as in *Llangeinor*, Glamorgan, and *Llangain*, Carmarthenshire.[7] In late antique Latin *ecclesia* was used for the chief church of a community, while other major churches were called *basilicae*.[8] That word is found just once in Wales, in *Basaleg* near Newport. It is unknown as a common noun in Welsh. Basaleg must have been a very early foundation, and medieval records indicate that it was the mother church of a wide region. Another word that has provoked a lot of discussion is *merthyr*. It is quite widespread: examples are *Merthyr Caffo* (now *Llangaffo*), Anglesey, and of course *Merthyr Tydfil* in Glamorgan. Though *merthyr* is the ordinary Welsh word for a 'martyr', borrowed from Latin *martyr*, that does not make very good sense in the names of places. Perhaps, then, the *merthyr* of the place-names comes from Latin *martyrium* 'martyr-shrine'. But that raises another problem: as we saw above (chapter 2), martyr graves must have been vanishingly rare in Wales, so *martyrium*/*merthyr* would have to refer to a secondary shrine for relics that had been obtained from elsewhere, such as from Rome or Gaul. Recently, however, David Parsons has pointed to names in southern France in which *Les Martres* has the meaning 'graveyard'.[9] This French form has come either from a plural of *martyrium* or else from the plural *martyres* 'martyrs', which could have developed the sense 'martyrs' relics' and then simply 'place where Christian relics were kept, i.e. graveyard'. Either of these Latin forms would give *merthyr* in Welsh, and the French place-names do provide a good parallel to the Welsh ones. *Merthyr* names are early, though we do not know how early exactly. Already before the twelfth century they were being superseded by *llan*, as at *Merthyr Cynfall*, Herefordshire, now *Llangunville*.

By far the commonest word was *llan*, and its meanings have been much debated. The word is cognate with English *land* and refers to a spot enclosed for some purpose. In this basic sense it is found in *perllan* 'orchard' and *corlan* 'sheepfold'. Obviously it came to be used of church sites because they too were enclosed. Unfortunately the history of the word has become tangled up in the problem of whether medieval churches arose from older graveyards. Those who think they did have argued that *llan* applied first to graveyards and later to the churches that grew up on them. In truth we do not know whether a burial ground that had no church could be called a *llan*, but since most of them seem not to have been enclosed, this is looking increasingly doubtful. If most churches were founded on virgin sites, as recent views suggest, then *llan* may have been applied only to these new church enclosures, not to burial grounds in general. Medieval Latin writers translate *llan* both as *coemiterium* and *monasterium*, and sometimes also with *podum*, meaning a 'raised site' or a 'site with a raised boundary'.[10] It is clear that from the basic meaning 'enclosure' it came to refer to a church site as a whole. When, and why, did it become so popular in place-names? One school of thought argues that *llan*-names only became prevalent from about the eighth century, when the faithful were choosing to be buried in churchyards and abandoning their ancestral burial grounds. The rise of *llan* would thus accompany the rise of the churchyard.[11] The theory is appealing, and it is likely that churches called '*llan* X' were founded over centuries rather than all together in the conversion period. Llanfihangel-y-traethau in Merionethshire was founded as late as the reign of Owain Gwynedd (1137–70).[12] But the evidence for early *llannau* is also strong. Llantwit Major existed in the sixth century, as we saw in Chapter 2 (though, to be scrupulous, its actual name is not recorded before the tenth century). But the matter is put beyond doubt by the churches of St Tygái. The *Llandygái* beside Bangor is matched by no less than three others, in Cornwall (recorded as *Landighe* in Domesday Book), Devon (now *Landkey*) and Somerset (*Lantokay*). The Somerset name can hardly have been coined after the English conquests and so is almost certainly as old as the sixth century, and the same applies to *Lanprobi*, the British name for Sherborne in Dorset.[13]

Llan, then, belongs among the oldest British names for church sites. But its rise was gradual. No one was under an obligation to use it, or for that matter, any other 'church' word. Many important early churches have names unrelated to the concept of 'church'. *Mynyw*, for instance, the usual medieval name for St Davids, seems to mean 'bramble' or 'thicket', while *Clynnog Fawr* refers to holly (*celyn*). Where a 'church' word was chosen, *llan* competed with *merthyr* and *eglwys*. If Parsons is right in taking *merthyr* as '(Christian) graveyard', then its meaning was very close to that of *llan*, while *eglwys* focused on the building inside the *llan* or *merthyr*. There is no pressing reason to think that the choice of descriptive word reflected any particular difference between the churches themselves – it is often tempting to wring meaning out of such linguistic variation where perhaps none existed. Eventually *llan* became so prevalent as to invade other place-names, displacing many an *eglwys* and *merthyr*, and turning *Nant Carfan* into *Llancarfan* and *Nant Hoddni* into *Llanthony*.

Perhaps even more interesting than the various generic elements in place-names are the specific elements that follow them. A few of these are river names (*Llandaf, Llanelwy*) while others are descriptive (e.g. *Llanfor* 'the big church'). But the great majority are the names of people, hundreds of whom are remembered in this way all over Wales. But who were they? As an example of a unique name we can consider *Llangynhafal* in the Vale of Clwyd. The place is clearly named after a Cynhafal, and the church is regarded as dedicated to him as a saint. A Welsh poem was composed in his honour a few years before the Reformation.[14] All that, however, tells us nothing about the man himself. The name *Llangynhafal* first appears in writing in 1254.[15] We cannot possibly tell when Cynhafal lived nor what exactly he did. Perhaps he was a lay donor. Perhaps he was the first priest of Llangynhafal. These two possibilities are illustrated by another *llan* name, *Llandogo* in Monmouthshire. This *llan* is named after Bishop Euddogwy, who founded it, but a second name for it was *Llaneinion*, after the lay donor who gave the land on which it stands.[16] Only the survival of some early documents allows us to see the complexities at Llandogo, but for Llangynhafal we have no early source. All over Wales, places called *llan* and *merthyr* tenaciously preserve the names of individuals, but without, frustratingly, telling us when they lived or what they did to be remembered in this way.

Place-names are not dedications, but in Wales the distinction is easily lost sight of. It is assumed that churches like Llangynhafal are dedicated to the person after whom they are named. But this is historically something of a problem, since a living person can hardly dedicate a church in their own honour. Whether Cynhafal was a lay donor or an early cleric, the problem remains: either Llangynhafal had a different dedication back in his lifetime, or it had no dedication at all. If Cynhafal was regarded as a saint while he was alive, then the rededication could have happened as soon as he died. It is equally possible, however, that the idea of treating him as a saint only arose centuries later. Because his name was permanently preserved in the place-name, it was always available for reinterpretation. 'St Cynhafal' might have grown gradually over centuries, slowly acquiring a feast, a liturgical commemoration, a backstory, a grave, some relics and a place in the landscape, as in his holy well near the church. The problem is repeated all over Wales: we simply do not know anything firmly historical about the dozens of local 'saints'. It is a reasonable supposition, however, that the habit of naming churches after people has helped these saints' cults to survive, and – it must be suspected – given rise to some of them in later centuries.

The situation is quite different when we come to churches that bear the names of well-known saints, such as the numerous places called *Llanddewi*, *Llandeilo* or *Llangadog*. No one doubts that David, Teilo and Cadog were treated as saints from a very early date. The question is whether they were personally responsible for founding all these churches, as the traditional view holds. It is much more likely that they founded no more than a handful in their lifetimes; the rest were built by devotees at later dates. Of course, once we accept that many of these churches were founded long after the deaths of their saints, then the problems that we encountered at Llangynhafal do not arise in these cases. The churches could have been dedicated to, and named after, their saints from the moment that they were built, just as many a *Llanfair* or *Llanbedr* honours the Virgin Mary or St Peter. It should not, finally, be assumed that non-Celtic dedications are all late or arose under Norman influence, still less that they have replaced older ones. Under whose invocation did David, Cadog and the others dedicate their first churches if not that of a universal Christian saint?

Wales's local churches were founded over many centuries. In some cases, the initiative could have come from a wandering charismatic holy man, but other, more prosaic possibilities would be the local bishop, a nearby monastery, a lay donor or the local community acting in unison. Medieval writers, looking back on all this, preferred to tell a simple, clear story of heroic pilgrim-saints travelling tirelessly and founding churches wherever their names were commemorated. Historical truth was far messier and can rarely be recovered in full.

The British church and the English

The conversion of the Angles and Saxons to Christianity created pressing new difficulties for the older British church. Our major source for these events is the *Ecclesiastical History of the English People* by Bede, finished in 731. Bede was a monk of Wearmouth-Jarrow, in what is now County Durham. He was a gifted and influential writer in many branches of learning, including scriptural exegesis, grammar and *computus* (the study of the calendar). But the *Ecclesiastical History* is the best-remembered of his works today – with good reason, since it was the first great piece of historical writing in English culture. For our purposes, though, it has its problems. Bede was not well informed about the British-controlled regions and, what is worse, he had a very negative view of the Britons as a people.

In 597 a mission sent by Pope Gregory the Great arrived in Kent. It was led by Augustine, an Italian monk. The mission was a success and the king, Æthelberht, soon converted. Augustine returned to Gaul to be consecrated as bishop and metropolitan, so that he would have the authority to supervise the new church. The question now arose as to how he should deal with any other bishops that he encountered in Britain. Pope Gregory told him, flatly, that he was to take them all under his authority. Bede recounts a long story, in three parts, of how this mandate was rejected by the Britons.[17] Augustine first met with some British bishops at a place on the border, probably Aust on the Bristol Channel. He demanded that the Britons abandon their reckoning of the date of Easter, as well as 'many other customs contrary to church unity', and join with him in spreading the gospel among the pagans. According to

Bede, the British clerics obstinately refused until Augustine trumped them by miraculously curing a man of blindness. Even then, they agreed only to summon a larger synod, claiming that they needed to consult more widely. In the second part of the story, the Britons assemble seven bishops and many learned men, especially from their famous monastery of Bangor (*Bancornaburg*). Firstly, however, they consult a holy hermit. The hermit tells them to submit to Augustine, but only 'if he is a man of God': if Augustine rises in respect when they enter, he is to be accepted, but if he stays seated, he is 'ungentle and proud', and they should reject him. Augustine remains in his seat, and a bitter argument follows, as the Britons refuse all of his demands. Augustine foretells that, if the Britons will not live in peace with their English 'brothers', they will suffer death at their hands. In the third part of Bede's story, this prophecy is fulfilled. A battle is fought at Chester between the Britons and another English king, the pagan Æthelfrith of Northumbria. A great band of monks, mostly from Bangor, accompany the British army to pray for its victory. But Æthelfrith orders them to be attacked first of all, and they are slaughtered.

That such a devout author as Bede could rejoice in the slaughter of hundreds of monks is a reminder of the chasm that separates us from the eighth century. It is also a sign of how embittered relations between the two sides had become. For Bede, the Britons were inveterate disturbers of the Christian peace, schismatics who deserved to be punished by God through the weapons of their English enemies. Yet there is one oddity in his account: though the Britons are shown behaving badly in the first section of the story and being justly punished in the third, yet in the middle section they have right on their side, for Augustine is shown up as a vain and hard-minded autocrat.[18] The presence of British names, spelled in British orthography, supports the theory that the whole story has been put together from a mixture of English and British sources. It is a hint that the confrontation was not as black-and-white as Bede tells us, but that some contact was carried on between the churches; such contact is also apparent from the fact that Bede got hold of, and studied, a copy of Gildas.

Bede does not conceal the existence of the British church nor its strength. There were numerous bishops in Wales and the still

British West Country. We learn of one famous monastery, which Bede calls by an English name, *Bancornaburg*, but also by an Old Welsh form, *Bancor*. This great monastery, it has always been assumed, lay at Bangor-on-Dee, a few miles from Chester. In fact Bede does not say where it was, and we should not ignore the possibility that it was actually the much more famous Bangor in Gwynedd. Its size as reported in Bede – at least 2,100 monks – is quite incredible. We can accept, however, that it was large and complex. Besides monks, the British church also had hermits. Another important group were the *doctores*, or 'teachers', who attended synods alongside the bishops. These high-ranking scholars practised exegesis of Scripture and had their equivalents in the early Irish church, where the evidence is much fuller.

The arrival of a Christian mission among the English might have led to a new understanding between them and the already Christian Britons. Instead it produced a diplomatic disaster. What went wrong? From the pope's point of view, it was only natural that his representative would assume authority over the isolated British bishops as part of the task of re-establishing the traditional hierarchy of the church in Britain. But Gregory took no account of the political realities and probably did not understand them. Other provinces of the western Roman empire had passed under Germanic kings quickly and with much of their social structure and institutions intact, but Britain had been ripped apart by decades of destructive warfare and reduced to a mosaic of warring kingdoms, some of which defined themselves as conquest territories seized by Germanic newcomers while others, notably in Wales, looked back to a British identity. Gregory sent Augustine to an aggressive and expanding kingdom of Kent which was attempting to rule all of southern Britain, and it was inevitable that Augustine would be seen in Wales as just another threat from the Anglo-Saxon power. The Britons could not accept Æthelberht's bishop as their metropolitan, which meant that the church of Britain was never restored. Instead, a new church of the English was created, opening a rift between the Britons and Rome that would have fateful consequences.

Easter and other disputes

Augustine accused the Britons of following 'customs contrary to church unity'. Unity was not in fact a hallmark of the early medieval church. The liturgy differed between Spain, Gaul and Italy, and indeed from place to place within them. Some people worried about this while others were unfazed: Pope Gregory, for instance, argued that practices should be judged on their merits, not on the prestige of whatever church upheld them. Unfortunately, in Britain the question of different customs melded with that of Augustine's authority, which was anything but trivial, not to mention political and ethnic division. In this atmosphere, differences that could have been settled peaceably became quite intractable, and as people turned to the Scriptures to justify their positions, so the issues hardened into questions of fundamental belief. Their origin, however, lay simply in the political fragmentation and difficulties of communication of the early medieval world. The Britons kept an older form of ecclesiastical tonsure, and Bede also mentions some difference in the baptismal rite. But it was the Easter question that caused most trouble. It arose because the calculation of the date of Easter was complex and there were differing views not just on the details but also regarding the basic principles. Both the British and Irish churches followed an eighty-four-year Easter table known as the *Latercus*, probably made in Gaul *c.* AD 400. Subsequently Rome adopted a different, nineteen-year table devised by Victorius of Aquitaine around 457. Frankish Gaul went over to this system in 541, but this decision was not followed in Britain or Ireland, partly at least because the Victorine reckoning was open to serious criticism. A third reckoning, the Dionysiac from Alexandria in Egypt, would eventually triumph, but in the meantime there were substantive arguments both in favour of and against all the various Easter tables, which made the argument very hard to resolve.

The Easter dispute actually started before Augustine came to Britain. When the Irish monk Columbanus moved to Gaul in 591, he put the *Latercus* to use in his new foundations, to the dismay of the local bishops. In response, Columbanus appealed to Pope Gregory, and his letters provide our only account of the viewpoint

---

of adherents of the *Latercus* apart from the arguments of their enemies. Columbanus makes clear that the dispute had deep theological meaning for his side as much as for the Victorine party. In no way whatsoever did *Latercus* supporters see themselves as a 'Celtic' opposition to Rome. They revered the seat of St Peter as much as their opponents, and Columbanus was dismayed to find that the pope did not accept what he saw as the true Christian Easter. Nor is it correct to see the 'Celtic' side as more tolerant or pluralistic than their opponents. Columbanus denigrated the Victorine Easter as 'this error of Gaul',[19] and though he did argue, eventually, that more than one Easter dating should be tolerated, this was a counsel of desperation to which he was driven when he could not persuade the pope or the Gaulish bishops that the *Latercus* reckoning was correct.

The problem spread back to Britain, and Ireland, when Augustine arrived with the Victorine table in his baggage, and it continued to fester under his successor, Lawrence; unfortunately Bede did not preserve the letter that Lawrence sent to the British bishops, but he makes clear that they did not yield. It was only a matter of time before Canterbury fell out with the equally deviant Irish. An Irish bishop Dagán, visiting Canterbury, refused to eat with Lawrence or even in the same lodgings.[20] The dispute remained unresolved at Columbanus' death in 615, but his monasteries probably abandoned the *Latercus* in the 620s. However powerful the theological arguments for it, the weight of its opponents was greater. In Ireland, too, a party emerged that sympathized with Roman claims. The competing parties within the Irish church came to be known as *Romani* and *Hiberni* – Romans and Irish. By the 630s the southern half of Ireland had abandoned the older Easter reckoning. Meanwhile, the situation in the Anglo-Saxon kingdoms drifted towards a mishmash. The Gregorian mission, sustained by a tiny personnel, was vulnerable to events. By the 630s Northumbria had lost its Gregorian bishop and was ruled by a king, Oswald, who had lived among the Irish on Iona, spoke Irish and followed the Insular Easter. Oswald introduced an Irish bishop, Aidan, and so began what Bede calls the 'episcopate of the Irish', which lasted until the 660s, and out of which sprang further missions to East Anglia, Essex and the Midlands.

The English church was now dominated by leaders trained in the Irish tradition. We hear little of relations with the Britons at this time, but it is likely that they were easier and there was now an opportunity for cooperation rather than confrontation. The British role in the formation of English Christianity has been underestimated. Bede insists that the Britons played no part in converting the English, but this cannot be true. He himself reports that Bishop Chad of York was ordained in Wessex by one English bishop and two British ones, a sign that British Christians were cooperating with the fledgling English church in that region at least.[21] Archaeology too provides important hints of British churches that survived into the Anglo-Saxon era, especially in western England. In places like Gloucester it is likely that Christianity never wholly died and was transmitted from the British church.

Nevertheless, pressure to reopen the dispute built up, as it was bound to do. In Northumbria the instigator was Wilfrid, who trained in Rome and Lyon. By now Rome had abandoned the Victorine system for the Dionysiac, and the struggle would henceforth be between the Dionysiac system and the *Latercus*. In 664 the Northumbrians decided, at a synod held at Whitby, to accept the Roman, i.e. Dionysiac, Easter. Supporters of the *Latercus*, including the bishop, Colmán, were forced to leave. The pace of confrontation greatly increased in 669, when Theodore, from Tarsus in what is now Turkey, became archbishop of Canterbury and allied with Wilfrid to take a hard line on Easter deviancy throughout the English lands. Theodore deposed Bishop Chad and forced him to be reconsecrated, while Wilfrid had many British clergy violently driven from their churches in Northumbria.

Such harsh measures made the 670s a watershed in the relations between British and English Christians. Both Theodore and Wilfrid treated the *Latercus* Easter as outright heresy. Wilfrid's biographer, writing shortly after 709, brutally called the Britons and Irish 'Quartodecimans',[22] using the name of an old Easter heresy which was not strictly correct or fair when applied to adherents of the eighty-four-year Easter cycle, but was a powerful calumny nonetheless. Bede took a slightly more moderate position since he admired the Irish for their work in evangelizing his native

Northumbria and wished to spare them the accusation of heresy, but he had no time at all for the Britons. In Bede's view, the Britons had deliberately cut themselves off from communion with the rest of Christendom. They rejected the universal church and denied the claims of Rome and Roman order, and worst of all they refused to share their faith with the English, thus showing a lack of Christian charity, without which their rigorous monastic tradition was no more than a perverted expression of sinful pride. In contrast, English rulers, and especially those of Northumbria, were legitimate monarchs who had inherited Rome's tradition of *imperium* and law. Being English increasingly meant being an orthodox, Roman Christian, obedient to the hierarchy and a full member of the universal church, unlike the schismatic and quasi-barbarian Britons.

Bede's reading of the past encouraged his disregard for the Britons. In common with other early medieval authors, he believed that history was the working-out of God's will. The Britons had been defeated and lost most of their country: it followed, therefore, that they must have incurred the anger of God. Equally, the triumphant English must be God's chosen instrument to chastise them. Devastatingly, Bede did not need to think all of this through for himself, for a British author had already laid much of it out for him: Gildas. Of course, Gildas wrote not simply to condemn his people but to rescue them by leading them to redemption. Bede, though, lived two centuries later and knew of two vital developments that cast Gildas's story into a completely different light: firstly, the Britons had been crushingly defeated, so evidently they had not done what Gildas had warned them to do; and secondly, the English were now faithful Christians. Reading Gildas with this hindsight, Bede was bound to conclude that the English were not merely blind deliverers of divine justice: as faithful members of the universal church, they were rightly the new owners of Britain. It was God's plan that the Britons would be defeated like the biblical Canaanites and a new, better Christian people would take their place. In this way Gildas's message, which he had written to rouse his countrymen to repentance, was turned into a weapon to attack them.

Feelings on the British side could be equally bitter, but lack of sources compels us to study them through the words of their opponents. At some point towards the end of the seventh century the English abbot Aldhelm wrote to Gerent, king of Dumnonia.[23] This was a British kingdom in the south-west of Britain, roughly corresponding to modern Cornwall and Devon. Aldhelm urged Gerent and his clergy to cease their schismatic attacks on 'Catholic' Christians, to adopt the tonsure worn by St Peter, and to celebrate Easter on the Roman date. What is particularly interesting for us is that Aldhelm warns the Dumnonian clergy not to imitate the awful extremes in Dyfed, 'beyond the river Severn'. In Dyfed, so Aldhelm says, churchmen would refuse to take communion with any 'Catholics' who came to visit them. Indeed, they would not eat with them either. Any food that the visitors left would be thrown to dogs and pigs, and any cups and bowls used by them would be thoroughly scoured afterwards. Demetian clergy would not give such visitors the kiss of peace, nor offer them water or a towel to wash with in the traditional manner, or a bowl to cleanse their feet. Any 'Catholic' who went to live in a Christian community in Dyfed was required to do forty days of penance before being admitted. It is unlikely that such treatment was regularly given to English visitors during the more pluralistic period before 664, when so many churches in Anglo-Saxon regions followed Irish customs, which would have been the same as those followed in Wales. Rather, it was a response to the rupture at Whitby and the new demands for uncompromising Roman rectitude in the English church.

By the middle of the eighth century there must have been a danger that the Britons would be pushed out of Christendom altogether. Physically their culture had retreated to the outer margins of the known world. Their territories were small, fragmented and dispersed. Far more economically and militarily powerful kingdoms, both English and Frankish, now sat between the Britons and the rest of Christendom. They had long ceased to be seen by other western Europeans as fellow Romans, indeed commentators in these aggressive, expansionist kingdoms were busy redefining them as barbarians. And now, religious differences threatened to rob them of the name of 'Christians' as well.

A 'Celtic church'?

Readers may be puzzled, and even upset, at the way in which I have told the story of the Easter dispute without ever using the term 'Celtic church'. But the fact is that there was no Celtic church. Historians began abandoning the idea from the 1970s. It is important for anyone who wishes to study the origins of Welsh Christianity to understand why this has happened.

One quite simple, if superficial, problem is the term 'Celtic'. Medieval Irish and Welsh people never called themselves 'Celts', nor did they have any concept that they, or their languages, were closely related. That on its own should rule out using the term 'Celtic' to describe an institution that was founded and developed among them during the early medieval centuries. A more profound point, however, is that the churches of the separate Gaelic- and British-speaking regions never made up an identifiable single church, distinct in its organization and hierarchy from the rest of Christendom. Contemporaries certainly did not think in such terms. The nearest they came to it was to talk of the 'western church', meaning that of Ireland and (British) Britain, as Columbanus did, but only as a full member of the body of Christ, alongside others. British and Irish Christians revered the see of St Peter as much as anyone else in the West.

Various peculiarities of organization and ritual have been put forward as 'Celtic': the Easter date, the tonsure, and the other bones of contention in the seventh and eighth centuries. As explained above, these were formerly widespread customs that endured in Ireland and Britain after falling out of use elsewhere. Those who cherished them believed that they had been handed down in a chain of witness from the apostles to their own revered teachers, men like David in Wales and Columba in the Gaelic world. They were not treasured for being 'Celtic' or 'Irish' or any other ethnicity, but for being truly Christian. Confronted with evidence that the rest of Christendom disagreed, churchmen in Ireland and Wales ultimately proved willing to change their customs.

Another powerful idea is that the early church in Ireland and Wales downgraded its bishops and came to be controlled instead by the abbots of individual monasteries. This was not a frivolous theory: it arose from serious contemplation of the evidence, especially from Ireland. Nevertheless its supporters overgeneralized on the basis of certain cases – especially Iona – and misunderstood the way in which monastic terminology pervaded the early medieval church. In these centuries, words like 'monastery' and 'abbot' were used much more loosely than would later be the case, and the distinction between the active and contemplative life was not yet strongly institutionalized. Early medieval churchmen very often followed a monastic rule while also holding pastoral office. Large churches like St Davids or Bangor were multi-purpose institutions with bishops and priests who carried out pastoral and missionary work, but they also housed monks and hermits. As a result, *monasterium* came to be used as a catch-all term for a major church, while every *monasterium* reached its own accommodation between the active and the contemplative life. All of this is equally true whether we turn to early medieval Wales, or Ireland, or England, or Francia, or Spain.

As the idea of the Celtic church as an institution has faded, so the less concrete idea of a 'Celtic spirituality' has taken on its inheritance. Various beliefs form a part of this notion: that early Irish and Welsh churches were peculiarly interested in nature and the created world, or that they provide powerful models of individual Christian belief, or that they were unusually accommodating towards women. These beliefs are supported by readings of particular early Irish and Welsh texts. It must be said that these readings are highly selective and partial, and inevitably, as there is so little material surviving from Wales, it is early Irish literature that predominates, be it the many short lyrics on the hermit life in remote outdoor settings, or longer, theologically and spiritually profound works like Adomnán's *Life of St Columba*. There can be no objection at all to modern Christians going back to early medieval texts in search of whatever might be of benefit to their own personal spiritual needs, choosing what is helpful and laying aside what is disagreeable or unacceptable. Early Irish and Welsh religious literature is rich and often still speaks to today's Christians, who have the perfect right to approach this spiritual inheritance of the Christian past for guidance. But this is a different way of reading from that of the historian. It is a selective reading, concerned with usefulness, not representativeness. Considering the evidence as a whole, it is arguable that the early Welsh church was not vastly different from other European churches. It offers examples of profound spirituality, fine poetry and moving devotional writing, as we will explore in chapter 4. On the other hand, it belonged to its own, early medieval society, whose hierarchical structures it upheld. The church was sustained by land and, just as importantly, the peasants who worked it: it had no other way of existing. Churches, like everyone else, owned slaves and relied heavily on their labour. Bishops and higher clergy were drawn from royal and aristocratic families and did not forget this when they entered the church. For every austere anchorite there would have been plenty of the kind of comfortable clergy that Gildas objected to so strongly. The role of women was harshly limited, as in other medieval societies, by laws and social expectations. Nature was perceived as a strict hierarchy, with God at the top, man below him, woman below man and the rest of creation under man's hand. Most intellectual life was shared with the rest of western Christendom. The same books were read, the same school curriculum followed in Wales as elsewhere, with quite minor variations.

The idea of a Celtic church has its remote origins in the time after the Reformation, when Protestants sought to disassociate the ancient Christian tradition of these islands from Rome. In the nineteenth century this view morphed into a Romantic nationalist vision of the Celts as anarchic, nature-loving free spirits in contrast to the allegedly rigid, moralizing, hierarchical world of Rome. These are stereotypes that frankly serve modern agendas with no relevance to a proper understanding of the past. Early medieval Wales was one among many successor societies to the late Roman empire, one with some marked local characteristics such as its own distinct, non-Latin language, but its inhabitants saw themselves as members of western Christendom, whatever their neighbours thought. The labels 'Celtic church' and 'Celtic spirituality' do it a disservice.

The end of the Easter controversy

One thing on which all western Christians agreed was the prestige of Rome. If one group was able to insist that it represented the Roman way of doing things, then other points of view would be placed at a great, and ultimately fatal, disadvantage. This is indeed what happened. Bede tells us that Aldhelm's letter did its job, and Dumnonia accepted the demands of the Roman party, perhaps already in the 670s. In 716 the community of Iona yielded, which ended the divide in the Irish church. Pictland followed suit, and the Britons of the north seem to have conformed at this time as well. Thus, when Bede was writing in 731, it seems that Wales was the last to hold out. The period after Whitby is known as a time of isolation for the Welsh church. In reality we do not know how true this was. It seems implausible that the virulent hostility of the 670s endured for a whole century or that there was no communication of any kind between churchmen on either side of the border. It was noted above that some British material reached Bede. But this is still a very poorly documented period, and little is known of what happened. Not even the final end of the *Latercus* Easter in Wales is very well understood. Our sole source is a single, brief entry in a chronicle: 'Easter is altered by the Britons, Elfoddw, a man of God, correcting it.' The year was 768. Under 809 in the same chronicle we read that 'Elfoddw, archbishop of the Venedotian kingdom (Gwynedd), died.'[24] In later centuries Elfoddw was associated with Abergele, Denbighshire, and there are indications that Abergele was a significant church in this period and that the chronicle was maintained there for a time. But the internal workings of the Welsh church, and how the decision to accept the Roman Easter was made, are mysteries to us. It is not even possible to be certain that the decision of 768 affected all of Wales. Since we never hear of the Easter problem again, however, it is likely that Elfoddw was able to influence or persuade a synod that embraced the whole country. Nothing is preserved of the debates, arguments or political background of this event.

The settling of the Easter problem no doubt opened up new channels of communication between the Welsh and the English. A late eighth-century manuscript from Mercia, perhaps specifically from Worcester, contains Latin prayers attributed to *Moucan*. The name is that of an early saint whose churches are scattered across south Wales, though the prayers are likely to be later than his time. Since the form *Moucan* is Welsh, these intricate little texts, based on a complex intertwining of Old and New Testament passages, must have been composed in Wales before passing to the neighbouring English kingdom. They are almost unique as a spiritual document from eighth-century Wales:

> My soul [is the] one thing I have sought from the Lord; this I require, that in eternity I shall never thirst. Lord Jesus, receive my spirit, because my soul is greatly disturbed. Into your hands I commend my spirit in its own fashion, so that I may not sleep in death, so that I may not fear from the night-time fear nor from the mid-day demon.[25]

Meugan's prayers were not the only text that travelled this route: a commentary on the letters of St Paul went the same way. It was signed by a scribe, Meirion, apparently the disciple of a certain Peibio, and dated by the deaths of two Welsh kings whom we cannot now identify. The date of transmission is far from certain, as the manuscript itself perished and we have only later transcripts of it, but it fell some time in the eighth century.[26] The author of the commentary was none other than the notorious Pelagius, but this may well not have been known either to the Welsh scribes or to the English copyists who reproduced it.

By 800 Wales had emerged as a well-defined territory with a distinct culture and political life. Christianity was, as far as we can see, the only accepted religion. The Welsh church was distinct, though it regarded itself as part of the universal church under Rome. In spite of frequent warfare, some friendly contact was maintained with churchmen in Ireland and England. In the next period, from the ninth to the end of the eleventh centuries, we will see much more interaction between the Welsh and English churches, as Wales found itself caught between the power of Scandinavian raiders from the west, and the emerging kingdom of England to the east.

Notes

1 *Vita S. Samsonis*, chs 48–50.
2 Sharpe, 'Martyrs and local saints in late antique Britain', pp. 123–5.
3 Edwards, *Corpus 3*, no. AN26.
4 Thomas, *The Early Christian Archaeology of North Britain*, pp. 50–1.
5 Capel Maelog: W. Britnell, 'Capel Maelog, Llandrindod Wells, Powys: Excavations 1984–87', *Medieval Archaeology*, 34 (1990), 27–96; Tywyn y Capel: A. Davidson, 'Excavations at Tywyn y Capel, Trearddur Bay, Anglesey, 1997 and 2002–3', *Archaeologia Cambrensis*, 158 (2009), 167–223.
6 Now spelled *Cae Nethor*, Ordnance Survey Grid reference SH 309 866. The twelfth- or thirteenth-century collection of genealogies of Welsh saints, *Bonedd y Saint*, lists 'Maethlu in Carneddor'; see *Early Welsh Genealogical Tracts*, edited by P. C. Bartrum (Cardiff: University of Wales Press, 1966), p. 59 (§29).
7 See Gwynedd O. Pierce, 'The Welsh *Mystwyr*', *Nomina*, 23 (2000), 121–2.
8 T. M. Charles-Edwards, *Early Christian Ireland* (Cambridge: Cambridge University Press, 2000), pp. 249, 378.
9 David N. Parsons, *Martyrs and Memorials: Merthyr Place-Names and the Church in Early Wales* (Aberystwyth: University of Wales Centre for Advanced Welsh and Celtic Studies, 2013).
10 *Dictionary of Medieval Latin from British Sources*, fascicle 11 *Phi–Pos*, edited by D. R. Howlett (London: British Academy, 2007), p. 2329 s.v. *podium*, of which *podum* appears to be a variant form.
11 See John Reuben Davies, 'The saints of south Wales and the Welsh church', in *Local Saints and Local Churches in the Early Medieval West*, edited Thacker and Sharpe, pp. 393–4.
12 V. E. Nash-Williams, *The Early Christian Monuments of Wales* (Cardiff: University of Wales Press, 1950), no. 281.
13 O. J. Padel, 'Christianity in medieval Cornwall: Celtic aspects', in *A History of the County of Cornwall*, ii: *Religious History to 1560*, edited by Nicholas Orme (Woodbridge: Victoria County History, 2010), p. 113.
14 S. Baring-Gould and J. Fisher, *The Lives of the British Saints*, 4 vols (London: Honourable Society of Cymmrodorion, 1907–13), vol. 4, pp. 386–7.
15 See the online version of the Melville Richards place-name archive at Bangor University: *http://www.e-gymraeg.co.uk/enwaulleoedd/amr/cronfa. aspx,* under *Llangynhafal*.

[16] Davies, 'The saints of south Wales', pp. 390–1.

[17] Bede, *Historia Ecclesiastica*, book 2, chapter 2.

[18] See Clare Stancliffe, 'The British church and the mission of Augustine', in *St Augustine and the Conversion of England*, edited by Richard Gameson (Stroud: Sutton, 1999), p. 125.

[19] Columbanus, *Epistle* 1, ch. 4.

[20] Bede, *Historia Ecclesiastica*, book 2, ch. 4.

[21] Bede, *Historia Ecclesiastica*, book 3, ch. 28.

[22] *The Life of Bishop Wilfrid by Eddius Stephanus*, edited and translated by B. Colgrave (Cambridge: Cambridge University Press, 1927), pp. 24–5.

[23] *Aldhelm: The Prose Works*, translated by M. Lapidge and M. Herren (Cambridge: D. S. Brewer, 1979), pp. 155–60.

[24] *Annales Cambriae, A.D. 682–954: Texts A–C in Parallel*, edited by David N. Dumville (Cambridge: Department of Anglo-Saxon, Norse, and Celtic, 2002), pp. 6–7, 8–9.

[25] Edited and translated in David Howlett, '*Orationes Moucani*: Early Cambro-Latin Prayers', *Cambridge Medieval Celtic Studies*, 24 (Winter 1992), 71–2. The background is discussed in Patrick Sims-Williams, *Religion and Literature in Western England, 600–800* (Cambridge: Cambridge University Press, 1990), pp. 320–2. The saint is now called Meugan in Wales, and may be the same as Mawgan in Cornwall.

[26] David Dumville, 'Late-Seventh- or Eighth-Century Evidence for the British Transmission of Pelagius', *Cambridge Medieval Celtic Studies*, 10 (Winter 1985), 39–52.

Chapter 4

Vikings to Normans, c.800–c.1070

BARRY J. LEWIS

From about 800 our sources become much fuller. A chronicle was maintained at St Davids. The historical tract, *Historia Brittonum*, was made in 829 or 830. For the 880s and 890s Asser, probably bishop of St Davids, supplies us with some information about Wales. A Latin schoolbook, *De raris fabulis*, tells us about life in a Welsh or Cornish religious house. Not only do we have more texts from these three centuries, but we now have actual surviving books as well: the earliest is the Lichfield Gospels with their precious Welsh annotations. Just before 1100 we meet the first *Lives* of Welsh saints. Some twelfth-century works cast light backwards onto our period: the unique biography of the Gwynedd king, Gruffydd ap Cynan (died 1137); three poems addressed to saints that give us our first sustained picture of early churches through the Welsh language; the great Book of Llandaf, written about 1130, which preserves a wealth of early charters, albeit drastically rewritten; and finally the works of Gerald of Wales.

As a result, there is far more to say about these centuries than earlier ones. The record is still fragmentary, however, when compared with later times. The narrative of events is incomplete, making it hard to relate developments in the church to wider society. The organization of the Welsh church is not known in any detail. It remains almost impossible to gain access to the spiritual life of groups beyond the ruling elite, or to women's religious experience. Our sources are a series of spotlights. Each one illuminates a small area of knowledge for a time and then winks out.

Politics c.800–c.1070

From the 790s Scandinavian raiders – Vikings – attacked all parts of these islands. By the 830s they were settling in Ireland, especially at Dublin. In the 860s and 870s they attempted nothing less than to conquer all the English kingdoms. They failed to defeat Wessex, and over the next decades the Wessex kings expanded their rule to build the first, still fragile, kingdom of England. Welsh rulers found themselves sandwiched between dangerous rivals. The annals tell us of raids against the major churches of Wales: St Davids in 906, Holyhead in 961, Clynnog Fawr in 978, St Davids again in 982, Llanbadarn Fawr, St Davids, Llanilltud Fawr, Llancarfan and St Dogmaels in 988, St Davids yet again in 992, 999 and 1012, and so on. This record is certainly incomplete. The perpetrators might be Scandinavians, or English, or local Welsh rulers, often in shifting alliances. For the people who lived in and around these churches, raids would have been horrific. Some people were killed, others were driven off into slavery or saw their loved ones taken away for ever. Livestock and crops would have been lost and people would have gone hungry, precious objects would have been stolen, and perhaps treasured relics of the saints sullied or destroyed. But the churches themselves survived, because their true wealth lay in land, and they could recover within a few years.

War was endemic at all times in the early Middle Ages, and it is an open question whether these Viking centuries were really worse than before or whether the violence is just better recorded. Nor is it clear whether Welsh politics became more unstable. The historical record may just look worse because we now have more and better evidence for all the various wars, raids, usurpations, assassinations and violent changes of dynasty. Sometimes the balance of power allowed powerful kings to emerge, while at others the very existence of the Welsh kingdoms came into doubt. While Powys was threatened with absorption into English Mercia, Gwynedd expanded from 825 under a new dynasty. Rhodri Mawr and his sons were powerful rulers who pushed into south-west Wales by the early tenth century, but even they had to come to terms with the English kings next door. Presently Scandinavian pressure increased dramatically, which may have contributed to what looks like an ever greater instability in the eleventh century, when all regions of Wales seem to be fought over by a confused welter of competing rulers and families. In the 1050s Gruffydd ap Llywelyn, a member of one of the intrusive dynasties, built up a remarkable hegemony over all of Wales, but it was brittle and lasted barely a decade. After his fall in 1063, the country was left poorly prepared for the arrival of the Normans, who began to encroach from the late 1060s, firstly into lowland Gwent, and then more widely.

The organization of the church

The structure of the Welsh church is incompletely known before the twelfth century. Bangor and St Davids always had bishops, so far as the evidence lets us see. Llandeilo Fawr in Carmarthenshire had bishops in the ninth century, while in the eleventh Llanbadarn Fawr near Aberystwyth was claiming that it used to be a bishop's seat as well. At one time there were bishops also at St Cynidr's church, which was Glasbury in Brecknockshire. The situation in the south-east is puzzling. The charters in the Book of Llandaf were doctored to pretend that all south-eastern bishops were based at Llandaf. Such was not the case. There is no reliable evidence for bishops at Llandaf before Joseph, who died in 1045 and whose gravestone survived long enough to be seen by Edward Lhuyd in the late seventeenth century.[1] Before Joseph's time, the bishops of the south-east seem to have been based in Gwent, perhaps at Caerwent or Llandogo. Not only did the bishopric move westwards, but it also acquired a new patron saint, for Joseph is described in the Welsh chronicles as 'Teilo's bishop'. Through some mysterious process Llandaf had gained control of the patron saint of Llandeilo Fawr. This probably happened during the reign of Rhydderch ab Iestyn (1023–33), who ruled in both Glamorgan and Ystrad Tywi, but we do not know how. Given, however, that the beautifully decorated gospel book of St Teilo turned up at Lichfield cathedral at some point in the tenth or early eleventh century, it is a safe guess that Llandeilo Fawr had suffered a major disaster. With Teilo, Llandaf also inherited the claims of the bishops who had sat at Llandeilo, out of which arose the famous dispute with St Davids later on. If the south-east is complex, the north-east is a blank. No bishopric is known before a chronicler's chance remark that one 'lay empty' in that region in 1125. Control probably fluctuated between Bangor and the neighbouring English diocese, until St Asaph was founded – or reconstituted – in the 1140s.

Some historians think that there were, or once had been, many more bishops, maybe even one for each of the medieval administrative units known as cantrefs. The mainstay of this idea is a short tract in the Welsh laws on the 'seven bishop-houses of Dyfed': the number of churches matches the seven cantrefs in Dyfed.[2] There are other ways of accounting for the 'bishop-houses', however: as previous bishops' seats, or as bases between which a bishop circulated. If there really were seven bishops in Dyfed – that is, Pembrokeshire and the western half of Carmarthenshire – the number that implies for all of Wales would be difficult to credit. However, many bishops there were, it does not seem that they had an acknowledged leader, a metropolitan for all Wales. The idea was in the air, however, and by the end of the eleventh century St Davids had its eyes on the privilege. The oldest *Life of St David*, from the 1080s or 1090s, insisted that David was summoned to preach to the whole British church at a synod held at Llanddewi-brefi, where 'the whole episcopate gave power, sovereignty and princely authority to the holy David', including Deiniol (representing Bangor) and Dyfrig (for Glamorgan/Llandaf).[3] The claim was hotly disputed at Llandaf, which ran its own cottage industry in historical fabrication, and it never achieved full acceptance.

Below the bishops' sees were other important and influential churches. They are the ones that are mentioned in the annals, had famous patron saints, ran large estates, controlled other churches and supported communities of clergy. People saw that there was a difference between these institutions and smaller ones, though they had no single term for them. Gerald of Wales wrote about 'the bigger churches, to which the people of older times assigned a greater reverence'.[4] Welsh law distinguished a 'mother church', with an abbot, priests and community, from other churches, while the *Life of Gruffudd ap Cynan* mentions the 'major churches' to which Gruffydd bequeathed money in 1137.[5] A large church housed a community who were called in Welsh the *clas*, from Latin *classis*, a 'group, band', or 'class' in a school. Modern writers, seeking a convenient term for these churches, have chosen to call them *clas* churches, which is a reasonable solution inasmuch as it highlights the presence of a community of clerics as their most significant feature. Identifying all *clas* churches is no easy task. Only a few have proper written evidence from the early Middle Ages, while a handful more are revealed by later documents in which the abbot (*abad*) or *clas* are mentioned. Archaeologists have looked for other criteria, such as the size of the church, or how elaborate it was, or subsidiary chapels, or the size of the churchyard. The problem with these criteria is that they are not necessarily confined to churches of the highest status. Even quite minor sites could have elaborate structures. What is more, a simple distinction between *clas* churches and others may not be enough: churches came in many shapes and sizes.

Another problem is whether *clas* churches were founded in a planned manner or haphazardly. In many cases we can identify one *clas* church in each cantref or in each of the smaller subdivisions, the commotes: Tywyn, for instance, in Meirionnydd, or Llanymawddwy in Mawddwy. This might suggest that a *clas* church supervised the smaller churches in its assigned area. But reality was more complex. Churches had dependencies that crossed these borders: for example, the prominent *clas* church of Clynnog Fawr, on the Llŷn peninsula, had estates and dependent churches in Anglesey, claimed some kind of supremacy over the pilgrimage site of Holywell in Flintshire, and even had a wider network southwards as far as Gwent. The pattern of one *clas* church per district is also overdrawn. In Talybolion (north-west Anglesey), the *clas* of Holyhead did not have a monopoly, for there are signs that Llanfechell was another, if smaller, *clas* institution. The pre-Norman Welsh church was a tangled skein of networks: some of these quite naturally formed within local units, but others extended more widely. In the south, it seems that churches dedicated to David, Illtud, Cadog and Teilo were claimed by those saints' chief foundations, or at least that seems to be what twelfth-century writers thought when they looked back at earlier arrangements: they assumed that all 'David' churches had been founded by him and so belonged rightly to his successor at St Davids, and similarly in the case of the other saints.[6] Subordinate churches would have paid renders, and their personnel may have been appointed by the mother-house. Yet some of these dependencies were major *clas* churches in their own right, like Llanddewi-brefi (David) or Penally (Teilo).

Below the *clas* churches were smaller ones. We are even more poorly informed about these. Charters give us clues as to how local churches came to be founded. We have a big collection in the Book of Llandaf, and a smaller one attached to the *Life of St Cadog* from Llancarfan. Unfortunately the Llandaf charters have been rewritten, and Llancarfan's are not above suspicion either, but they can be trusted to give a fair impression of the kinds of processes that operated, even if the individual details are not secure. In one charter, St Cadog founds a church in Gwent, intending to reside there whenever he is visiting his Gwent estates, and entrusts it to his disciple Macmoil. In another, a disciple called Elli founds his own church (the modern Llanelli), subject to Llancarfan. In a third, an existing church called Llangadwaladr (probably Bishton, Gwent) is transferred to Llancarfan's ownership.[7]

Some local churches were thus founded from the *clas* churches. Others were estate churches, endowed by the initiative of the local landowner. A pious donor might give land freely – 'for the sake of his soul and that his name be written in the book of Cadog' – while a less pious one might be compelled to hand it over in compensation for a crime. We do not know how smaller churches were staffed and run, but the sources – which overwhelmingly focus on the *clas* institutions – give the impression that the larger churches exercised control over them. Over time it is likely that many broke free, acquired rights of their own – especially the rights to receive burials and tithes – and so became the parish churches of the high Middle Ages. We cannot follow this process in any detail. Nor do we know for certain how many churches there were in tenth- or eleventh-century Wales. What evidence we do have suggests that they were abundant. The Llandaf charters name over seventy. The number is biased towards lowland Gwent, but then so are the charters. Gwent was a rich area, but evidence from less favoured regions supports the same picture. A tenth-century list of saints from central Cornwall gives a strong hint that many local churches were established by then, while archaeological remains in Kerry in the west of Ireland reveal an abundance of small early medieval churches in that not particularly wealthy or central region.[8] The later parish system rested on foundations laid in the early Middle Ages.

A little is known about the layout of major churches. At the centre lay the cemetery (*mynwent*) containing the church (*eglwys*). Beyond that was a larger enclosure called the *corflan*, whose name probably contains *corf* 'defence' rather than *corff* 'body'. Both were marked by banks and ditches, or perhaps fences, and standing crosses. Members of the *clas* lived beyond the outer *clawdd* or ditch. A fascinating document attached to the *Life of St Cadog* describes the property assigned to each member of the *clas* of Llancarfan. Each had a house and a garden, worked by gardeners who looked after the orchards and guest rooms as well, and in addition a farmstead 'from which they had the essentials of clothing and food'. One of these parcels was the abbot's, another the priest's, one belonged to the *doctor* (i.e. the head of the church school), one to the cook, one to the bakery.[9] As the charters make clear, churches, like everyone else, needed access to food and other essentials: cereals for making bread and beer, meat, milk and butter, honey, fish, wool for clothing, wood and timber for building. A major church was the centre of a great estate worked by free tenants, unfree tenants, domestic servants and slaves, and would acquire outlying lands as well. Often the donors of lands stayed behind on the estates that they had given, becoming 'tenants of the saint', to be followed by their descendants in perpetuity. Probably in the eighth century, a certain Tewdwr ap Meurig gave Llancarfan a sword and a garment with which to buy itself a piece of land. Abbot Cynyng of Llancarfan sold these for an estate. The previous owners were to remain on the land and pay renders of beer, bread, meat and honey yearly. They also bought out the royal rights, sending three cows as a payment to the lord. Then the abbot and the lay donors walked the bounds with St Cadog's cross and threw soil from Cadog's land onto the estate to signify the saint's taking possession.[10] Cadog himself was of course long-dead by then, but nevertheless the land was 'his' because it had passed to the church of which he was the heavenly protector.

Big churches claimed extensive rights of sanctuary (Latin *refugium*, Welsh *nawdd/noddfa*). This institution was based on the traditional right of high-status people to protect fugitives who appealed to them, combined with the biblical idea of 'cities of refuge'. Around the church would be an area in which wanted people could shelter from their enemies, including angry kings. Both the Welsh Laws and Gerald of Wales indicate that the largest churches had sanctuaries extending as far as their pastures stretched up the hillsides, which could be for miles. The right was lucrative, since frightened people would pay handsomely to be kept safe, and it was jealously guarded against kings and lords who tried to snatch people out of *nawdd*. Churches claimed other privileges too. Their land was not supposed to pay renders to the king. Early charters have plenty to say about this perk. Llandogo was (allegedly) granted to Llandaf

> with all its dignity and all its liberty and all its commons, in woods and fields, in waterways and pastures, with its four pools, and with its fishweirs and woods and without any dues to any wordly man except to God and the church of Llandaf in perpetuity, and with its sanctuary, like an island free on all sides and set in the sea.[11]

To be like an island in the sea, free from the demands of territorial lords, was the ideal to which churches aspired. Kings, naturally, had other ideas, and resisted making churches exempt from providing men for royal armies or coastguard duty or other public needs.

We should not imagine places like St Davids or Llancarfan as they are today, dominated by a single, architecturally complex church. Early medieval church buildings were small and simple, but in recompense more than one would be built on many sites. At Clonmacnoise in Ireland, there are the remains of eight churches, while at Maughold, the most important early foundation on the Isle of Man, the large churchyard contains the foundations of four early keeills (small churches) besides the medieval parish church. Welsh sites do not appear so complex, but then they are nearly all still in use and cannot be dug up to investigate them. But a glance at the huge churchyard at Meifod, Montgomeryshire, suggests a similar pattern, and in fact we know that it contained separate churches of Tysilio and Gwyddfarch, to which a church of the Virgin Mary was added in 1156. At very many sites, the patron saint was buried or enshrined in a separate grave-chapel. Such chapels survive, though rebuilt, at Holyhead and Llaneilian in Anglesey and Clynnog Fawr in Caernarfonshire, and they are known from descriptions in many other places, such as Abergele, Denbighshire and Eglwyswrw, Pembrokeshire.

From the twelfth century, church buildings became larger and more complex. They could now include side chapels, transepts and double naves, so that gradually a single building swallowed up the liturgical life of the whole site. This was linked to the rise of stone building. From the end of the Roman period, churches in Wales were built of timber, wood or other perishable materials like turf. Stone churches were rare or unknown: it is not certain that even the largest sites had them before the twelfth century. Wood was more practical than stone in many ways, being easier to obtain, work and repair, and it was very widely used for churches throughout Britain and Ireland. Wales was not unique, then, but it was perhaps unusually resistant to using stone in churches until quite late. This was not simply a matter of skills lost after the Roman period: masonry building was reintroduced into England in the seventh century and Welsh people would have encountered it. Nor will poverty do as an explanation: far more marginal regions in the west of Ireland, the Scottish islands and the Isle of Man built dry-stone churches. The skilful handling of wood had a cultural significance. Here is the hagiographer Jocelyn of Furness describing how St Kentigern founded the church of Llanelwy in north Wales:[12]

> Some were clearing the space and levelling it, others were laying foundations on the levelled soil. Some cutting timbers,

some carrying them, some putting them together, they were beginning to build a church and the other buildings, after the manner of the Britons, from smoothly polished timbers, just as their father [Kentigern] had laid down and measured; for they could not yet build in stone and were not accustomed to do so.

Tomás Ó Carragáin, writing about Ireland, where wooden churches were similarly far commoner than stone ones, suggests that communities lovingly rebuilt them down the centuries out of reverence for their founder-saints, who had built the first ones.[13] Not until the twelfth century would Welsh communities change their minds about this deeply ingrained cultural habit and accept the superiority of stone for building the house of God.

The consequence is, of course, unfortunate for us: no early medieval church building survives in Wales (apart from some possible Anglo-Saxon stonework at Presteigne), and that severely limits what we can know about actual buildings. Churches will have been small, with one or two chambers at most, not large enough to house much of a congregation. This changed only slowly, and the earliest stone churches were probably also small. We have a description of Llandaf's old church before it was rebuilt in 1120: it was 28 feet long, 15 feet wide, had two very small aisles and a porticus (?side-chapel) 12 feet long with an apse. Bishop Urban thought that this was quite inadequate, and set about having it replaced, but as a bishop's seat it must have been one of the most elaborate of Welsh churches in its time. Llandaf was doubtless already in stone; if it had still been wooden, Urban would surely have complained about that as well.[14]

Very few of the treasures of these churches have survived. Stone sculpture is reasonably durable, and these centuries are notable for some fine high crosses. One of the most impressive stands at Nevern in Pembrokeshire. Crosses with Scandinavian-style decoration are found at Llanbadarn Fawr and Penmon, among other places. At Llanilltud Fawr some of the monuments are inscribed with memorials to kings and abbots. Metalwork survives very poorly but there are a few handbells such as the damaged one that hangs in the parish church of Dolwyddelan, Caernarfonshire. Many similar bells are preserved in Ireland. Shrines and church vessels have, sadly, not been preserved so early. The other treasures to note are books, which will be discussed later.

Large churches were headed by abbots (Welsh *abad*). The remaining members were *claswyr*, 'men of the *clas*'. The Llandaf documents give good evidence for the personnel of the great houses of Llanilltud Fawr, Llancarfan and Llandough. They regularly mention the *sacerdos*, or priest, in addition to the abbot, and the church scholar, who goes under various names – *doctor, lector* – and who was in charge of the school and scriptorium. Twelfth-century poetry mentions the *segynnab*, from *secundus abbas* – a prior, or second-in-command. The larger churches look like cenobitic monasteries that went secular, an impression reinforced by the use of monastic terms like *abad/abbas* and *monasterium*. In this view, the members of the *clas* were originally monks, but over time their discipline lapsed and they were given individual shares of the income and allowed to live apart. There are signs that secularization went even further: shares became hereditary and passed to laymen, who took control of church property and even became abbots. Gerald of Wales, admittedly a biased observer, was scandalized when he visited Llanbadarn Fawr in 1188:

> It is a remarkable fact that this church, like so many others in Ireland and Wales, has a layman as what is called its abbot . . . An old man called Ednywain ap Gweithfoed, who had grown grey in iniquity, was usurping the office of abbot, while his sons officiated at the altar.[15]

The idea that the early Welsh 'monasteries' declined needs to be treated cautiously, however. Probably only a minority were ever wholly monastic in the strict sense. In the previous chapter I noted how the common use of terms like *monasterium* and *abbas* in early medieval sources led scholars to think that the early Welsh and Irish churches suffered a kind of monastic takeover, as if monasteries proliferated at the expense of the secular church and abbots usurped the powers of bishops. But the same words were widely used across early medieval Europe to describe churches and their leaders. They reflect the deep penetration of the whole church by monastic ideals, but a clear division between the secular and the regular clergy was not normal before the tenth-century Benedictine reform (which did not reach Wales). Early medieval *monasteria* would contain some clergy who lived by rule, alongside others who did not. Welsh *clas* churches were multi-purpose institutions that conducted worship, provided pastoral care and ran schools. Historians' views of the early church in Wales, as in Ireland, have been too biased towards monasticism and they have not paid enough attention to pastoral care. It is, for instance, still debated whether churches provided pastoral supervision for local communities or only for their own clergy, and perhaps their tenants as well. Though the evidence from early medieval Wales is too poor in itself to resolve this question, the accumulation of lands and privileges by the churches represents such a gigantic transfer of resources from lay society that it must represent a striving for universal pastoral care, even if the ideal could not be met. At no time were *monasteria* separate from the societies around them, nor free from the need to run estates, administer justice or deal with neighbouring kings and aristocrats. As to the intrusion of laymen into church office, the rationale, at least to start with, was to separate the secular business of running church properties from religious duties at the altar. Observers like Gerald, committed to the all-powerful church of the Gregorian ideal, might hate the idea that clerics should not sully their hands with estate management, but separating out this function was an arrangement for which support could be found in early interpretation of the Bible.[16] Ordained clergy continued to perform divine service under the lay abbots, as Gerald had to admit.

It may be that the regular life did decline after its sixth-century heyday; that would not be surprising, since monastic fervour is hard to maintain over many generations. Gerald of Wales, however, tells us that there were ascetics at some churches, called Culdees – an Irish term, *céli Dé*, that means 'clients of God' – and links them to others well known from Ireland. Hermits and anchorites were common too. Welsh law mentions the *diofrydog*, someone who has taken a vow of abstinence. There was a particular tradition of retreating to offshore islands as a substitute for the deserts in which Christian monasticism had begun.[17] Llancarfan had hermitages on Barry Island and Flatholm, while Ramsey – *Ynys Dewi* – was probably attached to St Davids, and Llangenydd in Gower also had its own offshore island, as did Penmon, which controlled Ynys Seiriol (Puffin Island). The most famous of these island hermitages was Bardsey, attached to the *clas* church of Aberdaron until it became independent around 1200.

The story of one dweller in the desert of the ocean has been left to us. Elgar (Ælfgar), an Englishman from Devon, was seized by Irish pirates and taken into slavery. In Ireland he became executioner for Ruairí Ó Conchobuir, king of Connacht. This was a hateful and demeaning job that no free man would touch, and thus it is understandable that it fell to a slave. Eventually Elgar bought his freedom and returned to Britain, but his ship was driven to Bardsey, where he decided to remain as a hermit to atone for his bloody past. He spent at least fourteen years there, and when he died, his body was found by some sailors and buried in his own little church. We know about Elgar only because he was visited by a learned cleric, called Caradog, to whom he told his story. In 1120, a mission came from Llandaf to translate the bones of St Dyfrig from Bardsey. When the Llandaf clerics learned about Elgar they took some of his teeth back with them and wrote up his *Life*, using Caradog's testimony, in their Book of Llandaf.[18]

Bardsey's tradition was old when Elgar arrived: a monk of Bardsey called Iarddur died in 1012 according to the Welsh chronicles, while its cemetery can be traced back much earlier still. The island is very exposed, and bones emerging from its cemetery after storms doubtless formed the basis for the legend that it housed the remains of saints, a story that is told for the first time in the Book of Llandaf. Already by then Bardsey was called the 'Rome of Britain', both because it was so hard to get to and because so many saints were buried there. Its monastic tradition may be very old indeed if it was connected with a nearby site on the mainland, Capel Anelog, which has two probably sixth-century inscriptions. But by 1100 the link was rather with Aberdaron. The evidence for early medieval Bardsey is frustratingly patchy, but enough survives to suggest a long and rich tradition of monastic life.

The cult of saints

In the early Middle Ages, saints were recognized by their own communities, and there was no concept of canonization, so a saint's cult depended on the collective memory. The earliest stages of memorialization in Wales are lost to us. We saw in Chapter 2 how little of our documentation goes back to the age of the great church founders themselves: really only the writings of Patrick and Gildas, and a few short texts of synodal decisions and penitentials. We do not know, therefore, whether men such as David or Illtud were thought to be saints already in their lifetimes, or how soon after they died their followers began to venerate them. The first document that really allows us an insight is the oldest *Life of St Samson*, written perhaps less than a century after Samson's death. It is the only portrait that we have of a Brittonic saint's cult at such an early stage. It leaves little doubt that Samson was revered as a holy man even when alive, and that his memory was treasured in his various churches. After the *Life of St Samson*, the record is scanty till the ninth century. Documents noted down in the margins of the gospel book of Llandeilo Fawr *c.*800 show how the cults of founder saints had taken hold.[19] Property given to Llandeilo is said to be given 'to God and St Teilo', even centuries after the saint had died. Similarly, 'Teilo' bears witness to a legal judgement contemporary with the manuscript. The bishop of Llandeilo is 'Teilo's bishop', its priest is 'Teilo's priest'. The church was the legal and moral heir of St Teilo and remained under his protection as he looked down on it unceasingly from heaven.

Saints would be remembered on their feast days, which marked their deaths, or 'births into heaven'. We have no early calendars or martyrologies from Wales, but a few Welsh saints are mentioned in the Irish *Martyrology of Tallaght*, made near Dublin at the beginning of the ninth century: David, Beuno and Deiniol.[20] The early saints were buried in their own churches or cemeteries, and their presence encouraged others to seek burial there as well, as we saw above (Chapter 3). Early Irish saints' *Lives* attach a great deal of importance to the idea of the 'place of resurrection': a predetermined final resting place, to which a saint would be guided by an angel and where he or she would lie to await the resurrection and Last

Judgement. Anyone else buried alongside had a high chance, perhaps the certainty, of reaching heaven as well. The same idea certainly operated in Wales though it is rarely expressed so clearly. In the *Life of St David*, for instance, David is inspired to leave his place of apprenticeship when an angel warns him that less than one in a hundred of those buried there would reach heaven: instead, he founds a holier site, the future St Davids.[21]

In England, and on the Continent, saints were moved from their graves into more prominent shrines, usually beside or behind the altar of their church. This process, known as translation, allowed easier access to the precious relics. It was not customary everywhere. At Rome, the early popes were very reluctant to disturb their saints; they left tombs unopened but built altars and churches above them. Likewise, the popes usually refused to break up holy bodies and distribute the relics, as was by now happening widely in Gaul. Instead, they offered contact relics, generally pieces of cloth that had been laid on the tombs to absorb the holy power, though to very privileged people they might give tiny secondary relics, such as filings from the chains of St Peter. It seems that churchmen in Wales felt the same way, for we have no certain proof of any translation before the Norman period. We do hear of a few shrines of very prominent saints. The shrine of David was despoiled by Vikings in 1089 and broken up outside the church, while the shrine of Cadog was seized by English raiders *c*.1022, though a miracle stopped them from wrecking it.[22] Shrines were an obvious target because they were covered in precious gold and silver and gemstones. It is not certain that these Welsh shrines contained the bones of the saints rather than some other kind of relic, and we know that some tombs remained unopened. In the twelfth century Brynach of Nevern, Pembrokeshire, still remained under the east wall of his own church, while Gwynllyw of Newport and Tathan of Caerwent were buried 'in the floor' of their churches.[23] The first translation we know about was the moving of St Dyfrig from Bardsey to Llandaf in 1120. It required major negotiations involving the archbishop of Canterbury, the bishop of Bangor and Gruffydd ap Cynan, king of Gwynedd.[24] The translation of St Gwenfrewi (Winefride) to Shrewsbury abbey in 1138 was even more complex. She lay, along with other saints, in a cemetery at Gwytherin,

Denbighshire. Some of the reverence that surrounded the graves of these saints can be perceived. They were buried apart, in their own cemetery; no one dared enter it except to pray. Above Gwenfrewi's grave stood a little wooden church, to which the sick and diseased flocked in the hope of a cure. 'No dumb animal, no beast of any kind is allowed to enter the cemetery and live; no sooner does it start to graze the grass that grows above the holy bodies than it falls down dead.' No wonder the Shrewsbury monks had to use a great deal of persuasion to get hold of Gwenfrewi's body. Most of the locals were eventually pacified by some visions that made clear God's support for the translation, but one particularly angry opponent had to be bribed to switch sides, as the Shrewsbury prior tells us in his frank and fascinating account.[25]

The reverential fear of disturbing saints' graves, and the tight link between the saint's tomb and 'place of resurrection', diverted Welsh devotion away from bones and onto secondary relics. A famous passage in Gerald of Wales's *Itinerary through Wales* noted that the Welsh, Irish and Scots revered the bells and croziers of the saints as especially powerful relics.[26] There is plenty of evidence to support his observation. St Cybi of Holyhead had his 'multi-coloured finger-bell', presumably one covered in both gold and silver. St Cadog owned a bell allegedly made by Gildas. Croziers are attested at Llanbadarn Fawr, Cardiganshire and St Harmon's, Radnorshire. An Old Welsh poem celebrates the staff of St Padarn, the *Cyrwen* ('blessed point').[27] To these we can add the saints' gospel books. We have already met St Teilo's Gospels, now at Lichfield cathedral. Llancarfan owned gospels supposedly in the hand of Gildas, which survived being lost at sea, unlike two luckless clerics who were carrying them, while Clynnog Fawr's miraculous *Tiboeth* or Book of St Beuno was unscathed by fire.[28] People sought to have their names entered in the saint's gospel book in exchange for some gift or service to the church, hoping that the saint would read out their names on Judgement Day. Gospel books became repositories for legal records and charters. In due course they were enshrined as relics; the books of David and Beuno had richly decorated metal covers. Other relics were more unusual. At Merthyr Cynog there was a celebrated torque or gold necklace, with a dog-head terminal appropriate for a saint whose name refers to hounds.[29] Some churches had miraculous altars. David received an altar that flew all the way from Jerusalem. It was housed in his church of Llangyfelach, Gower, and was considered so holy that none dared uncover it. Cadfan of Tywyn surpassed even that by receiving an altar that descended from heaven. Landscape features also bore the names of saints. Many are only recorded very late, but there are early examples. At Llancarfan, what was probably an old hill-fort was known as *Castell Cadog*. Holy wells are very common in Wales, but usually it is impossible to know how far back their use extends. One very famous well that certainly predates the Norman conquest is St Gwenfrewi's well at Holywell. A miracle recorded in her twelfth-century *Life* is set 'in the time of the Danes in Tegeingl'. Vikings did settle around the area, as is clear from the famous Maen Achwyfan, a carved stone cross with Scandinavian features at Whitford.[30] Further back than the tenth or eleventh centuries, however, we are in the realm of legend.

Intellectual life and spirituality

After the collapse of Roman rule around 400, writing for practical and official purposes would have gone into a steep decline. The ideal that rulers should be literate and educated clung on as late as Gildas's time, but the bureaucratic state with its record-keeping was no more. Yet, paradoxically, the same period must have seen an enormous proliferation of books and libraries in Wales, for one reason: the spread of Christianity. Churches needed the Bible, especially the psalter, gospels and epistles that were used for divine service; canon law; church fathers for theological study; and, not to forget, the vital grammars of Latin, without which no one could learn to read. All this means that there were hundreds, maybe thousands, of books at any one time in early medieval Wales, but they have suffered utter devastation. In fact we have none at all before *c*.800, and from then until *c*.1200 only about twenty. Every single one of the survivors left Wales early on, or else they would have been lost too.

Few though they are, the surviving books give us a fascinating view of the intellectual world of the early Welsh churches. The most impressive is the Lichfield Gospels, beautifully written and decorated, and similar to, though not as fine as, the famous Lindisfarne Gospels and the Book of Kells. The book was at Llandeilo Fawr about 800, but it was not made there, for a note in it tells us that a certain Gelhi bought the gospels for the price of his best cow and presented them to the church. It is possible that the book was made in England; certainly it was lost, somehow, to Lichfield in the tenth century. In the margins are the oldest specimens of Welsh prose: the *Surexit* Memorandum, recording the settling of a legal case; a note about the freeing of a slave called Bleiddudd son of Sulien; a record of a gift of land near Llandybïe. The Lichfield Gospels are a treasure-trove for early Welsh history and for the early recording of the Welsh language.

In Oxford, there is a book stitched together out of pieces of older books that were owned by the English Saint Dunstan in the tenth century. Two of Dunstan's booklets came from Wales. One is a remarkable miscellany of learned texts about the calendar, the date of Easter, weights and measures, and the liturgy, with some texts in Greek. Scholars examining the liturgical texts have made the remarkable discovery that they seem to reflect a Roman rite older even than the time of Pope Gregory the Great, *c.*600; if true, it suggests that the Welsh church was extremely conservative in some of its rituals, as its long adherence to the older Easter dating might also suggest.[31] The other Welsh part of Dunstan's manuscript is – in startling contrast – a copy of the 'Art of Love', a cynical and humorous guide to seduction by the Roman poet Ovid. In spite of his very unchristian subject, Ovid was read in early medieval monasteries as a teaching text for students grappling with advanced Latin. This copy has notes between the lines and in the margins, mostly in Latin, but some in Welsh. The Welsh notes are aimed at young learners of Latin, explaining confusing grammatical forms in the text.[32] Another manuscript, this time in Cambridge, contains the work of Juvencus, a Christian poet of the time of Constantine, who wrote an epic poem retelling the gospel story. Juvencus became a favourite school text in the Middle Ages. This copy contains notes in Welsh and Irish, and two famous Old Welsh poems: one seems to be a lament by a warrior who has lost all his companions except for one hired man, with whom he is too proud to talk, while the other is a religious poem of nine stanzas, of which I give one here:

Gur dicones remedaut elbid
anguorit anguoraut
ni guor gnim molim trintaut.

[He who made the wonder of the world
will save us, has saved us:
it is not too great toil to praise the Trinity.][33]

The notes in the margins and between the lines of early manuscripts – scholars' term for these notes is 'glosses' – provide more precious samples of Welsh at an early stage of its development. It is curious that some manuscripts have glosses in Cornish and Breton next to ones in Welsh. Evidently churchmen moved between the three regions, and the languages were still so close that people thought of them as a single British language. Some churches attracted Irish scholars as well, as the Juvencus manuscript reveals.

Latin was now long dead as a native language in Wales, and young Welsh scholars would have to begin their education by learning it from scratch. With their teacher, they would work through the book of Psalms along with one or other Latin grammar. After that, they might read some Roman literature like Ovid, so as to learn how to deal with literary language, imagery and interpretation; and finally they progressed to the Scriptures and theology. A fascinating glimpse of how people learned Latin is given by the colloquy *De raris fabulis*. This is a teaching book, a bit like a modern phrase-book, giving the kind of Latin you would need to live and work in a church or monastery. The book follows the daily routine from daybreak onwards. A short extract will give a flavour of it:

'Listen, boy!'
'What do you want, my master?'
'I want you to go to my horses, and fetch us two of them, one for me and one for you, so that we can ride to the next farmstead to get beer.'

'Here you are. I have brought the horses just as you ordered/said/commanded.'
'Good. Put the reins around their jaws and the bits in their mouths, and put saddles on both.'

A *sella* is a man's saddle; a woman's is called a *sambulla*.[34]

One thing that emerges incidentally from these colourful dialogues is that young schoolboys had a heavy load of chores. *De raris fabulis* includes glosses in both Cornish and Welsh and is found in a tenth-century manuscript, probably from Cornwall.

More ambitious original texts were also composed. In the 770s, or a little later, a chronicle began to be kept at St Davids, the *Annales Cambriae*. This is the first time that we have contemporary records of events in Wales. Though skimpy, it does record the deaths of bishops of St Davids, among many battles and other events. Around 829 or 830, in Gwynedd, an anonymous author compiled the 'History of the Britons' (*Historia Brittonum*), the first attempt since Gildas to tell the story of the British people down to the English conquests. As there was so little material to work with, the author had to string together very uneven and inadequate sources of different kinds. Despite his best efforts, his story is fragmentary. He found different, and rival, explanations of where the British, Irish and Picts all came from. After that, he collected references for the Roman period, mainly to the visits of Roman emperors to Britain; and then for Christian times he turned to the saints. He had a *Life of St Germanus*, and another of St Patrick from Ireland. He also had some knowledge of Arthur – he is the first author definitely to mention him – and some English material, mainly king-lists, and even a document from northern Britain that contained a little information about the battles of the Britons and the Angles there. Finally, he included a list of Britain's marvels (*mirabilia*), some natural like the Severn Bore, others relating to the saints. One of the marvels was to be seen in a church in Gower: an altar hung in mid-air above the tomb of a saint, held up by the will of God. A suspicious king passed a rod underneath it to test whether there was some hidden support, and though the marvel passed the test, the king died for his lack of faith within a month.

Historia Brittonum is an intelligent and thorough attempt at an impossible task, for even by 829 there was hardly any material left for a historian to work with. For us, it provides precious information about the early cult of saints in Wales. It makes clear that saints' *Lives* were composed here, even though no full ones survive so early. The miracle of the Gower altar comes from one such *Life*, but the stories of St Germanus are richer still. What little we know of Germanus' visit to Britain in 429 was told above, in Chapter 2. By the ninth century he had become the object of myth-making in Wales that far overstepped the modest historical data. Several Welsh churches claimed Germanus as their founder, like Llanarmon-yn-Iâl in Denbighshire or St Harmons in Radnorshire, both of which contributed material to the fantastic story in *Historia Brittonum*. The *Historia* recounts how in Iâl Germanus destroyed the wicked king Benlli and his fort (Foel Fenlli in the Clwydian Hills), and then raised a slave, Cadell, to be the first king of Powys. Germanus also persecuted the villainous Vortigern, finally cornering him at Craig Gwrtheyrn near the River Teifi in Carmarthenshire; like Benlli, Vortigern and his fort were struck by lightning and immolated. It was almost inevitable that medieval Welsh churchmen would seize on St Germanus as a significant figure: here was a prestigious international saint who had actually been in Britain and reformed the British church. Naturally they developed an attachment to him, elaborated new stories about him that linked him to Wales, and founded churches in his honour: there is no need to think, as some modern scholars do, that the various 'Llanarmon' churches were founded by a separate, native saint called Garmon who was only later confused with Germanus of Auxerre.

Germanus helped medieval Welsh churchmen to deal with the poisoned chalice left to them by earlier writers, Prosper and Bede, who had accused the Britons of Pelagianism, and Gildas who attacked them as sinners. Since it was a matter of record that Germanus had saved the Britons from heresy, Welsh churchmen could point to him as evidence that their church was now orthodox and fully Christian. So much weight was attached to Germanus that he even came to be seen as a new apostle who brought the Welsh from the darkness of heresy into the light of pure Christianity. A Welsh bishop, Marcus, who retired to Gaul in the ninth century, told people at Auxerre that Germanus was 'the apostle of his nation'.[35]

At the end of our period a remarkable learned family lived and worked at Llanbadarn Fawr, near modern Aberystwyth. Sulien (1011–91) studied in Scotland and Ireland and was twice bishop of St Davids. His son Rhygyfarch wrote the *Life of St David*, and poetry. Another son, Ieuan ap Sulien, copied and decorated a beautiful copy of the psalter, now kept in Dublin; it is one of the last Insular-style books from Wales. Ieuan too was a poet, who wrote a verse life of his father Sulien. From their works we can reconstruct some of Llanbadarn's library: there were classical poets like Virgil and Ovid, Christian ones like Juvencus and Prudentius, the philosopher Boethius, and many more besides. Rhygyfarch, who died in 1099, lived to experience the conquest of his native Ceredigion by the Normans. He responded with a Latin poem, the *Planctus* or 'Lament':

Now the labours of earlier days lie despised;
The people and the priest are despised
by the word, heart and work of the Normans.
For they increase our taxes and burn our properties.
One vile Norman intimidates a hundred natives with his
    command,
And terrifies them with his look.[36]

By 1070, the Welsh church had existed for over five centuries. Though it lacked a metropolitan, great institutions like Llancarfan or Clynnog Fawr upheld its distinct identity as the earthly church of the Britons. Equally, the Welsh saints – David, Teilo, Cadog, Beuno and the rest – formed a heavenly church who looked down on and protected their own British people, a concept that would eventually be embodied in the catalogue of saints' genealogies known as *Bonedd y Saint*. The Welsh church was still independent, but links with England were close, especially in the south-east, where churchmen like Herewald of Llandaf and Lifris, the author of the *Life of St Cadog*, bore English names, and a Welsh bishop, Tryferin, could move from Glasbury to Hereford. But as the Normans tightened their grip on the country, all of this looked suddenly precarious. In the face of calamity, Rhygyfarch of Llanbadarn Fawr turned to the same answers as Gildas had found five hundred years earlier: the British people must be weighed down by a burden of sins that prevented them from raising their weapons against the enemy. The Britons had been deserted by God; there remained only the slender hope that Rhygyfarch himself might find a way between the hardships of oppression on one side, and the sweet temptations of sin on the other:

> Let it not be either the left or the right way,
> But a royal way between the two,
> Whereby I might ascend to the heavenly kingdom.[37]

Notes

[1]   Mark Redknap and John M. Lewis, *A Corpus of Early Medieval Inscribed Stones and Stone Sculpture in Wales*, vol. 1: *South-East Wales and the English Border* (Cardiff: University of Wales Press, 2007), no. G39. On Joseph, Llandaf and the cult of Teilo, see John Reuben Davies, *The Book of Llandaf and the Norman Church in Wales* (Woodbridge: The Boydell Press, 2003), pp. 16–18.

[2]   Charles-Edwards, *Wales and the Britons 350–1063*, pp. 596–8.

[3]   Richard Sharpe and John Reuben Davies (edited and translated), 'Rhygyfarch's *Life* of St David', in *St David of Wales*, edited by Evans and Wooding, pp. 146–7.

[4]   *Descriptio Kambriae*, i.18, *ecclesiae vero majores, quibus majorem antiquitas reverentiam exhibuit*, my translation. Published translations convey that it was the greater antiquity of the churches that gave rise to their status, but *antiquitas* often means 'people of former times' and the perfect *exhibuit* conveys a decision made in the past.

[5]   *mam eglwys*: Llyfr Iorwerth, *A Critical Text of the Venedotian Code of Medieval Welsh Law*, edited by Aled Rhys Wiliam (Cardiff: University of Wales Press, 1960), §43, l. 20; *praecipuis . . . ecclesiis, Vita Griffini Filii Conani: The Medieval Latin Life of Gruffudd ap Cynan*, edited by Paul Russell (Cardiff: University of Wales Press, 2005), §34.

[6]   The poet Gwynfardd Brycheiniog lists David churches in his poem in honour of the saint; see *www.seintiaucymru.ac.uk*. That Llandaf had a right to Teilo churches is an important idea in the Book of Llandaf;

see Davies, *The Book of Llandaf*, pp. 70–5.

[7] For Llancarfan's charters, see *Vitae Sanctorum Britanniae et Genealogiae*, edited by A.W.Wade-Evans (Cardiff: University of Wales Press, 1944), pp. 124–35 (*Life of St Cadog*, §§55–68).

[8] B. L. Olson and O. J. Padel, 'A Tenth-Century List of Cornish Parochial Saints', *Cambridge Medieval Celtic Studies*, 12 (Winter 1986), 33–71; Richard Sharpe, 'Churches and communities in early medieval Ireland: towards a pastoral model', in *Pastoral Care Before the Parish*, edited by John Blair and Richard Sharpe (Leicester: Leicester University Press, 1992), pp. 90–1.

[9] Wade-Evans, *Vitae Sanctorum Britanniae*, pp. 118–23 (§§48–52).

[10] Wade-Evans, *Vitae Sanctorum Britanniae*, pp. 124–7 (§55).

[11] *The Text of the Book of Llan Dâv*, edited by J. G. Evans and J. Rhys (Oxford: privately published, 1893), charter 156. The grant to Llandaf is fictitious but the terms may reflect Llandogo's status before it passed into Llandaf's hands.

[12] Jocelyn: see *Lives of S. Ninian and S. Kentigern Compiled in the Twelfth Century*, edited by A. P. Forbes (Edinburgh: Edmonston and Douglas, 1874), p. 203. My own translation, see Jocelyn, *Lives of S. Ninian*, p. 77 for Forbes's version.

[13] Tomás Ó Carragáin, *Churches in Early Medieval Ireland: Architecture, Ritual and Memory* (New Haven: Yale University Press), pp. 46–7.

[14] Evans and Rhys, *The Text of the Book of Llan Dâv*, p. 86.

[15] Gerald of Wales, *Itinerarium Kambriae*, ii.5, in *Gerald of Wales: The Journey through Wales / The Description of Wales*, translated by Lewis Thorpe (London: Penguin, 1978), p. 180.

[16] Compare Jean-Michel Picard, '*Princeps* and *principatus* in the early Irish Church: a reassessment', in *Seanchas: Studies in Early and Medieval Irish Archaeology, History, and Literature in Honour of Francis J. Byrne*, edited by Alfred P. Smyth (Dublin: Four Courts Press, 2000), pp. 146–60.

[17] Jonathan Wooding, 'Island and coastal churches in medieval Ireland and Wales', in *Ireland and Wales in the Middle Ages*, edited by K. Jankulak and J. M. Wooding (Dublin: Four Courts Press, 2007), pp. 201–28.

[18] For the *Life*, see Karen Jankulak and Jonathan M. Wooding, 'The Life of St Elgar of Ynys Enlli', *Trivium*, 39 (2010), 15–47.

[19] Dafydd Jenkins and Morfydd E. Owen, 'The Welsh Marginalia in the Lichfield Gospels, Part 1', *Cambridge Medieval Celtic Studies*, 5 (Summer 1983), 37–66.

[20] *The Martyrology of Tallaght*, edited by R. I . Best and H. J. Lawlor (London: Henry Bradshaw Society, 1929), pp. 20, 35, 70.

[21] Sharpe and Davies, 'Rhygyfarch's *Life* of St David', pp. 120–1 (§14).

22 John Reuben Davies, 'Church, Property, and Conflict in Wales, AD 600–1100', *Welsh History Review*, 18 (1996–7), 400.

23 Wade-Evans, *Vitae Sanctorum Britanniae*, pp. 14–15 (§16), 180–1 (§10), 286–7 (§17).

24 Rhys and Evans, *Text of the Book of Llan Dâv*, pp. 84–5.

25 *Vita secunda Sanctae Wenefredae et ejusdem translatio*, in *Acta Sanctorum*, November, vol. 1, p. 729.

26 *Itinerarium Kambriae*, i.2, in *Gerald of Wales*, translated by Thorpe, p. 87.

27 Paul Russell, 'The *Englyn* to St Padarn Revisited', *Cambrian Medieval Celtic Studies*, 63 (Summer 2012), 1–14.

28 Gospels of Gildas: Wade-Evans, *Vitae Sanctorum Britanniae*, pp. 90–3 (§29). *Tiboeth*: Patrick Sims-Williams, *The Book of Llandaf as a Historical Source* (Woodbridge: The Boydell Press, 2019), pp. 12–13.

29 *Medieval Welsh Poems to Saints and Shrines*, edited by Barry J. Lewis (Dublin: Dublin Institute for Advanced Studies, 2015), nos 14 and 15. *Cyn-* in *Cynog* means 'hound'.

30 Edwards, *Corpus 3*, no. F12.

31 Michael Lapidge, 'Latin learning in Dark Age Wales: some prolegomena', *Proceedings of the Seventh International Congress of Celtic Studies, Oxford, 1983*, edited by D. E. Evans et al. (Oxford: D. Ellis Evans, 1986), pp. 91–107.

32 Paul Russell, *Reading Ovid in Medieval Wales* (Columbus: Ohio State University Press, 2017).

33 Ifor Williams, *The Beginnings of Welsh Poetry*, edited by Rachel Bromwich (Cardiff: University of Wales Press, 1980), pp. 101–2.

34 *Early Scholastic Colloquies*, edited by W. H. Stevenson (Oxford: Clarendon Press, 1929), p. 2; my translation.

35 Heiric of Auxerre, *De Miraculis S. Germani*, i.80, edited by J.-P. Migne, *Patrologia Latina*, vol. CCIV, cols 1207C–1272D (at col. 1245).

36 Michael Lapidge, 'The Welsh-Latin Poetry of Sulien's Family', *Studia Celtica*, 8/9 (1973–4), 88–93.

37 Lapidge, 'The Welsh-Latin Poetry', pp. 92–3.

Chapter 5

The Age of Definition and Hierarchy, c.1066–c.1200

MADELEINE GRAY

The Norman conquest has traditionally been seen as opening a new chapter in the history of Wales and the Welsh church. The Normans clearly brought with them the ideas of reform which were current in the later eleventh-century church: attacks on lay control of ecclesiastical appointments, reform of the Benedictine religious order and a renewed emphasis on clerical celibacy, probably as a way of removing the church from the structures of secular society. The pope had blessed their invasion of England and sent William a papal banner. In a more practical sense, the power of the church meant they had to bring ecclesiastical organization under their control as part of the process of conquest. They were not simply pragmatists, though. Rhys Davies's description of Robert of Rhuddlan, 'combining the most ruthless butchery with the most conventional piety', could be applied to most of them.[1]

After a slow start, the Normans swept across the lowlands of north and south Wales, reaching Pembroke, Cardigan and Anglesey by the 1090s and building castles there and in mid-Wales. Hugh, earl of Chester, even gave two manors in Anglesey to his newly founded abbey of St Werburgh in Chester, though the abbey did not retain them for long.[2] At this point, though, it seemed that Wales would be overwhelmed. The scholar and priest Rhygyfarch ap

Sulien of Llanbadarn Fawr wrote despairingly of the ignominy of conquest and the atrocities committed by the Normans. 'Alas that the present time led us into this state of things, where a cruel power threatens to drive away by its authority those who are duly reading (this poem) ... Our limbs are cut off, we are lacerated, our necks condemned to death, and chains are put on our arms.' For Rhygyfarch, this was God's punishment for the wickedness of the Welsh: 'These things I, Rhygyfarch, sadly lament; and, weeping over the losses of a miserable people, I have carefully tried to depict the penalties for sins.'[3]

Thereafter, though, the history of relations between Norman incomers and Welsh rulers becomes more complex. Rhigyfarch's lament notwithstanding, it had never been a straightforward picture of conflict. Recent research on settlement and castle building in Gwent suggests that Normans and local rulers allied against other local rulers: to the Welsh, the Norman incomers were just one more factor in a complex web of local power struggles, potential allies as much as opponents. By the end of the eleventh century, Welsh rulers were being accepted as clients of Norman lords. Thereafter, Welsh resurgences in the twelfth century pushed the Normans back in north and west Wales, leaving Norman lords in control of a strip of land on the borders and the lowlands of the south, with a more uncertain overlordship of a zone to the west of that. The process of conquest, reconquest and compromise created a region known as the March – neither Welsh nor English, with its own diverse customs and values.

With regard to the church, too, the picture is more complex than might at first appear. The features of the Welsh church which the Normans criticised (clerical marriage, the inheritance of church office) were commonplace across eleventh-century Europe: it was precisely these features which the Gregorian reforms were designed to address. Nor was Wales the only country in which these reforms failed to gain traction. In much of the European periphery, for example, parish priests and even some of the higher clergy continued to marry: this was the only practical way of running a household in a subsistence farming economy.

Meanwhile, the Welsh church became part of the process of Norman incursion into Ireland. The Tironian abbey of St Dogmael's had a daughter house at Glascarrig (Co. Wexford). Cistercian foundations also had daughter houses in Ireland: Tintern at Tintern (Co. Wexford), and Whitland at Tracton (Co. Cork). Margam had close links with Monasteranenagh and Holycross and with Monasteranenagh's daughter house at Abbeydorney. Possibly the most significant, though, in terms of their Irish influence, were the Augustinian canons of Llanthony. Hugh de Lacy granted them extensive lands at Colpe and Duleek (Co. Meath), variously described as granges and dependent priories, and another priory at Greatconnell (Co. Kildare). They also held a number of churches in Meath, Westmeath, Longford and Offaly. Here, Hugh was doing the same as his family had done at Llanthony, introducing trusted churchmen into a frontier region. However, the independent adoption of the Arrouasian reform movement in Ireland, the movement to which Llanthony belonged, helped the integration of canons from Llanthony into local society.

Religious Reform

These new religious orders had come to Wales following the first wave of conquest; eventually they were followed by the orders of friars. They brought with them new ideas on devotional life, a new emphasis on Christ's humanity and a piety focused on empathetic identification with his sufferings. The experience of Ireland, though, suggests that these influences would surely have reached Wales independently of the Normans. Indeed, change had been taking place in religious life in Wales before the Normans arrived. The Llancarfan monk Lifris's life of St Cadog, written probably in the 1090s, describes the organization of Cadog's monastery in terms which suggest the late first millennium *clas* (or possibly the comfortable life of a cathedral prebendary).[4] The thirty-six canons (this must have been a nominal figure) each had an *atrium*, an independent residence, supported by a landed estate with gardeners and tenants. Rhigyfarch's life of St David, by contrast, describes a monastery with a lifestyle of extreme simplicity and austerity. The monks labour in the fields, dragging the ploughs themselves rather than using draught animals. They wear rough clothes, eat only bread and vegetables and drink only water. The rule of silence is kept, and much of the night is spent in prayer.[5]

Rhygyfarch may have been quoting from a lost fragment of David's own monastic rule of life.[6] He presents the austerity of David's community as a traditional ideal; however, it also suggests the simplicity and self-sufficiency which would be the guiding principles of the Cistercian order. Rhygyfarch may have been writing a little before Lifris, and almost certainly before the foundation of the Cistercian order in 1098, though he may have been inspired by other slightly earlier monastic reform movements such as the Carthusians and Grandmontines.

What Rhigyfarch's depiction of life in St David's monastery suggests is that ideas of change and reform were already reaching Wales independently of the Normans. Rhygyfarch was himself rooted in the culture and values of the eleventh-century Welsh church. The son of Sulien of Llanbadarn Fawr, bishop of St Davids, he was a priest (and even possibly succeeded his father as bishop of St Davids); but he was also a father. His son, another Sulien, became a leading academic at Llanbadarn Fawr. The unease about human sexuality in Rhygyfarch's life of St David did not prevent him from openly acknowledging his own family life.

Wales was emphatically not on the periphery of western Christendom: it was part of a cultural world linked by the Irish Sea and trading routes to western Europe. Nor was it a cultural backwater. Bishop Sulien had been educated in Scotland and Ireland as well as Wales. The scriptorium of his religious community at Llanbadarn produced beautifully written manuscripts with intricate decoration.[7] Rhygyfarch and his brother Ieuan were educated entirely by their father, and their poetry demonstrates the breadth of their reading in classical and early Christian Latin. Llanbadarn must have had a well-stocked library. Their writing was also rooted in a knowledge of the Bible: in his life of St David, Rhygyfarch used scriptural quotations, allusions and resonances to construct an image of David as a man of scriptural holiness. Biblical language shaped and permeated his own style.[8] The second half of the eleventh century was in many ways a period of revival after the difficulties of the earlier part of the century.

Ecclesiastical reorganization

Ideas on ecclesiastical organization were also reaching Wales independently of the Normans. While the Welsh church had always been led by bishops, the Normans encountered a church whose organization was already changing: territorial dioceses were coalescing, their boundaries becoming fixed. The pattern of mother churches and subordinate churches was fragmenting into a structure of independent parishes. As the Normans pushed across south Wales, the relationship between their new towns and the parochial structure changed. In Gwent, they could establish parish churches in Chepstow, Monmouth and Abergavenny. By the time they reached the Vale of Glamorgan, they encountered a system of rural parishes with established boundaries and rights. Thus, at Cowbridge, for example, the church of the Norman town had to be a chapel of ease of the parish church of Llanblethian. The same happened at Bridgend, Neath and in some cases further west. Further north, the process was probably slower and responded to initiatives by a succession of bishops, supported by secular rulers. The tradition which attributes parish formation in Gwynedd to Gruffydd ap Cynan is a simplification but it seems to have been during his reign that the process took hold.

For all these indigenous developments, the spread of Norman control over much of the better agricultural land in south Wales and the borders made change inevitable: even if change was on its way, under the Normans it became both more rapid and more thorough. The expropriation of Welsh ecclesiastical property could be justified as introducing necessary reform, but it was clearly part of the process of conquest and control. The early conquests in Gwent were pegged down with castles and planned boroughs, most of them incorporating Benedictine priories dependent on one or other of the great abbeys in Normandy. William FitzOsbern's wholesale diversion of the ecclesiastical wealth of eastern Gwent to the Norman abbeys of Lire and Cormeilles created long-term funding problems for the church at parochial level. Further west, the wording of Robert de la Hay's grant of the lands and subordinate churches of the great minster church of Basaleg to Glastonbury made it clear that much of the land covered by the grant was not (yet) in his control. The same process of expropriation changed the ecclesiastical geography of southern Glamorgan and Gower. The estates of the great monastic community at Llancarfan were divided between the abbey of St Peter's, Gloucester, and the new Cistercian foundation at Margam. Further north, though, the process was different, possibly simply because the terrain was less attractive, or less obviously suited to Norman settlement and farming patterns.

The Norman assertion of control began at the top. However, this should not be seen in purely ethnic terms. It is unclear how far the Welsh church had ever accepted the authority of Canterbury. Our only evidence is some retrospective assertions from Llandaf. At Canterbury, Stigand's replacement by Lanfranc in 1070 simply replaced an Anglo-Saxon archbishop of rather ambiguous status with a Norman archbishop of much clearer legitimacy. The first Norman appointment to a Welsh bishopric was Hervé, one of William Rufus' chaplains, appointed to Bangor in 1092. He was soon forced out by the Welsh, but his eventual replacement, David, known as 'the Scot' (though he may in fact have been Welsh), was clearly appointed from Canterbury. The bishop of Llandaf at that point was Herewald. Apparently Welsh in spite of his Anglo-Saxon name, like most Welsh clergy he was married and he may have been the father of Lifris, the hagiographer of Llancarfan. Herewald's successor Urban is generally regarded as a Norman appointment, but he too was Welsh (Urban is a Latinization of Gwrgan), and connected to the ecclesiastical family of Llancarfan. He was trained at Worcester, though, and brought new ideas to his diocese.

It was probably Herewald's predecessor Joseph who established the centre of the diocese in the relatively unimportant *clas* church of Llandaf, though it was not until Urban's time that the bishops were described as 'of Llandaf' (rather than 'of Glamorgan' or even earlier 'of Teilo'). Herewald ruled a diocese stretching from Carmarthen to western Herefordshire, but his control was dependent on the power of the king of Glamorgan. Urban spent much of his career trying to establish this rather loosely organized accumulation of *clas* churches into a territorial diocese with fixed boundaries and an administrative structure. To that end he assembled what he claimed was a collection of charters granting land and churches across south Wales and into Herefordshire to his predecessors as bishops of Llandaf. This collection, now known as the 'Book of Llandaf', has been the subject of lengthy debates among Welsh historians and there is still no consensus about its contents. Are the charters which purport to describe the property of the diocese authentic (though with some rewording); are they complete forgeries; or are they based on original deeds but 'improved' and with some outright fabrication?

Urban struggled to establish the extended bounds of his diocese against the claims of Norman invaders on the one hand and his brother bishops of St Davids and Hereford on the other. He reached an agreement with Robert, earl of Gloucester and lord of Glamorgan: this may explain why there are so few charters in the 'Book of Llandaf' relating to the core of the diocese. He had less success in claiming outlying parishes and estates, and died in 1134 on a final mission to Rome to try to win the pope's support.

Meanwhile, the diocese of St Davids had been caught between Viking pirates to the west and Norman incursions from the east. Bishop Sulien resigned in 1085 and was succeeded by Wilfrid, who may have had Anglo-Saxon ancestry but was clearly regarded by the chroniclers as Welsh. Archbishop Anselm briefly suspended both Wilfred and Herewald of Llandaf, in order to establish his power over them. Wilfrid was succeeded in 1115 by a clearly Norman bishop, Bernard, chaplain of Henry I's wife Matilda. In spite of his Norman origins and court background, Bernard was an energetic defender of the rights of his see and campaigned hard to raise it to metropolitan status.

Llandaf had never been an important monastic settlement and Urban had to create a cathedral chapter virtually *de novo*. The cathedral *clas* at St Davids was well established and powerful; it was not replaced but converted into a cathedral chapter on the continental model. Gradually the Welsh dioceses developed administrative hierarchies on the Norman model, with cathedral officials, archdeacons and rural deans.

Church buildings

The Normans brought with them the tradition of church building in stone, and the areas they conquered in the south and east were soon dotted with impressive stone churches. Much of the Romanesque architecture of the twelfth century has been obscured or replaced by later buildings but there are still good examples to be seen. The *clas* church of St Gwynllyw in Newport was given to Gloucester Abbey, and a new church was built there in *c*.1135–50. Now St Woolos cathedral, the nave still has its drum pillars and round arches, and the archway from the western chapel has elaborate chevron decoration and intriguing praying figures on the capitals. Some of Bishop Urban's cathedral at Llandaf survives: the chancel arch and the repositioned north and south nave doorways. At parish level, and further north and west, there are churches with Romanesque elements and fragments of decorative carving.

However, the same enthusiasm for building in stone soon reached independent Wales (if it had not already done so independently of the Normans). Bangor Cathedral was rebuilt in stone with an apsidal east end in 1120, only to be rebuilt again in the early thirteenth century. *Historia Gruffudd vab Kenan* describes the peace and prosperity of Gwynedd in the later years of Gruffydd's reign: 'and the people began to build churches in every part therein ... Gwynedd glittered then with lime-washed churches, like the firmament with the stars.'[9] Gruffudd ap Cynan's own church-building activities in Gwynedd may have been responsible for the rebuilding of the *clas* church at Penmon (Anglesey), where his son Idwal was abbot, though the famous south door tympanum may be earlier than Gruffydd's rebuilding as it was reset into the wall with additional blocks to raise and level it. The earliest stone fabric at nearby Llangwyfan is also early twelfth century, and there is a Romanesque arch at Aberffraw (also Anglesey) with chevron mouldings and animal heads which may have led to a west tower. Llywelyn Fardd's praise poem for St Cadfan at Tywyn (Meirionethshire) suggests that the stone church there had already been built by that date.

Some of the furnishings of these churches were of high quality. The best surviving example is the great stone reliquary of St

Melangell at Pennant Melangell. Preserved at the Reformation by being built into the fabric of the church, it has now been reconstructed. On a smaller scale, many churches have fonts dating from the twelfth and early thirteenth centuries with Romanesque arcading or fish-scale decoration. It is hard to say what this may be telling us about changing baptismal practices.

Some of the most spectacular stone churches were of course monastic. The priory church at Chepstow had one of the earliest high vaults in Britain, though it has been lost to nineteenth-century remodelling. Ewenny still has much of its Romanesque architecture, probably because the focus of the founding de Londres family's estates shifted westwards and there was no money for extensive rebuilding. Tintern's early church was completely rebuilt in the late thirteenth and early fourteenth centuries, but Margam still has its 'Bernardine' nave, austere in its absolute simplicity. The Welsh rulers were keen to endow Cistercian houses with the resources to build on a large scale. Strata Florida was rebuilt on a new site when Rhys ap Gruffydd of Deheubarth reconquered that part of Ceredigion. Cwm-hir's nave of fourteen bays was longer than Canterbury Cathedral's, but the east end was never completed.

The saints: cults and traditions

The late eleventh century also saw a revival of interest in the lives of the Welsh saints. It would be easy to assume that Rhygyfarch and Lifris were writing the lives of the patron saints of their communities as a reaction against the destruction of their culture. In fact, they were leading a revival in Welsh hagiographic writing which would come to full fruit in the twelfth century and which reflects the developing sense of identity and definition of the church in Wales. Far from being hostile to Welsh traditions, Anglo-Norman clergy shared in the collection and rewriting of Welsh saints' lives. Early Norman bishops like Bernard of St Davids and Urban of Llandaff were keen to promote the cults of Welsh saints who could add to the prestige of their dioceses. One collection now in the British Library was probably copied out in about 1200, at or for the Benedictine priory of Monmouth (though Brecon has also been suggested) and also includes material from Gloucester Abbey.[10] As well as Lifris's *Life of St Cadoc*, the life of Cadog's father Gwynllyw and a version of Rhigyfarch's *Life of St David*, it includes the *Lives* of Sts Illtud, Teilo, Dyfrig, Brynach, Padarn, Clydog, Cybi, Tathan, Carannog, Aedh and Brendan.[11] Most of these are Welsh saints, the majority of them from south-east Wales. The manuscript also contains pedigrees of several saintly families, a liturgical calendar and a Latin–Old Cornish glossary. The Lives copied into this manuscript were written at various dates in the twelfth century, but it seems likely that some were written by Caradog, a scholar and hagiographer from Llancarfan who lived in the first half of the twelfth century and also wrote a *Life* of St Gildas and another *Life* of Cadog.

Caradog in turn may have been the brother of Bishop Urban of Llandaf, who is credited with the other major collection of saints' Lives in twelfth-century Wales. As well as the charters, the 'Book of Llandaf' contains the Lives of a number of saints whose cult centres and property Bishop Urban was trying to claim. This collection of saints' Lives was therefore probably assembled by Urban as part of his defence of the property boundaries of his diocese (and written or rewritten to his instructions). As part of his strategies for establishing and expanding his diocese, Urban secured the relics of St Dyfrig from Bardsey and installed them with great ceremony at Llandaf. It is likely that he commissioned the writing of Dyfrig's *Life* with its emphasis on the saint's primacy as a spiritual leader: in his version, it is Dyfrig who teaches Samson and Teilo, ordains Samson and supervises the affairs of Illtud's monastery at Llanilltud Fawr. There are also a number of references to grants of land to the saint, land which Urban wanted to claim, extending the boundaries of the diocese into what is now Herefordshire.

Nevertheless, the story as told in the *Liber Landavensis* is reminiscent of themes in earlier Welsh tradition. Dyfrig is the son of Eurdil or Efrddyl, and is either miraculously fatherless or illegitimate. There are parallels here with the stories of some other saints but also with the stories of Lleu Llaw Gyffes (in Math fab Mathonwy, the fourth branch of the Mabinogi) and of course of King Arthur. Efrddyl's father, King Peibio, tries to have her killed but she and the baby are miraculously saved, and Dyfrig heals his grandfather of an embarrassing ailment that caused the older man to drivel and foam at the mouth. Dyfrig is then guided to the place of his monastic settlement by a white sow, another familiar theme in early Welsh and Irish legend.

The story of Dyfrig as told in both the 'Book of Llandaf' and the Cotton Vespasian collection is surprisingly lacking in miracles, and particularly in revenge miracles. The other Welsh saints were notoriously vindictive. Lifris reported with every sign of approval several stories which show Cadog in a particularly unforgiving light. He blinded King Rhun of Gwynedd, who had tried to burn one of Cadog's barns. At his command the earth opened and swallowed Sawyl Benuchel, who had plundered the monastery at Llancarfan, and some soldiers who had demanded food from him with menaces. St Gildas came to stay with him in Llancarfan, bringing with him a particularly fine bell. Cadog wanted the bell, Gildas refused to part with it, but the bell then refused to sound until he handed it over.

Tradition also presented Cadog as being harsh in the extreme to his own disciples. According to Lifris, after establishing a monastic community at what is now Llancarfan, he left to study and teach in Ireland. When he returned three years later, he found the monastery in ruins. Furious, he forced the monks back to manual labour, dragging timber from the woods to begin the work of reconstruction. Two stags came out of the forest to help them, which is said to be why the stream running past the monastery is called the Nant Carfan, the Stag Valley. One Lent he took two of his disciples from Llancarfan on a retreat to Ynys Echni, the island now known as Flatholm. From there they went to Barry, where the students realised they had left Cadog's prayer book behind. He sent them back to get it, in a storm, then watched from the headland as their little ship foundered and they were drowned, but the book was saved. Cadog even managed to cheat King Arthur. A soldier who had killed three of Arthur's knights claimed sanctuary in one of Cadog's churches. Arthur tried to threaten Cadog, but was afraid to attack him. Eventually they reached a compromise: Cadog would keep the soldier and give Arthur a herd of cattle as compensation. But when Arthur's followers took the cattle and tried to drive them across the river Usk, the cattle turned into bundles of fern.

Most of the revenge miracles in these stories have to do with the demonstration of the saint's power and the defence of the community's property and privileges. Like the wizards Math fab Mathonwy and Gwydion in the Mabinogion, though, the saints are represented as having powers which extend over the natural world. We have to assume that Cadog could have quelled the storm and rescued his pupils: he chose not to.

There are other smaller collections and single Lives of saints in various manuscript sources. Of particular interest are the (admittedly very few) Lives of female saints. Non, mother of St David, appears in the early parts of his *Life*, variously described as a young noblewoman or a nun. She becomes pregnant with David as a result of rape by the local king, and is celibate before and after the birth: the rape story thus brings her as near to a virgin birth as is possible. There are miracles during her pregnancy and the drama of David's birth, out in the fields, with standing stones which appear to protect her modesty. Thereafter, she fades out of the narrative.[12] It is a strange story, and in Rhygyfarch's version there are many puzzling elements, most notably the fact that David's father is presented as holy in name and nature, and receives the prophecy of David's birth a full thirty years before the event, but is still responsible for raping Non. It is possible that Rhygyfarch, although he was himself a married priest, was influenced by the increasing unease about human sexuality at the beginning of the second millennium. Is what we have here a story of a holy family which has been darkened into a story of rape in order to keep Non as near to the status of a chaste virgin as possible?

In the case of Gwenfrewi (Winefride in English-language versions of her life) we have two versions of the story, both written around the 1130s. The first anonymous version presents Gwenfrewi as a tough-minded young woman with some of the duties of a priest; in the second, written by Robert Pennant, prior of Shrewsbury Abbey, she is an innocent. In both versions, though, she is assaulted by a neighbouring prince, Caradog, who beheads her when she will not submit to his advances. She is then healed by her spiritual mentor Beuno and becomes a nun. In the anonymous version of her *Life*, she travels to Rome, reforms religious life in Britain and founds a religious community. In Robert Pennant's version, after Beuno's death she travels to find another male mentor and finally settles in a religious community founded by a man, St Eleri. This reworking of a saint's life encapsulates much of the changed thinking on gender in the early part of the second millennium.[13]

Women and the church

In spite of these changes, women were still able to use the church for the power of independent action that they were often denied in secular culture. Women founded churches: according to an inscribed stone at Llanfihangel-y-traethau in Harlech, the church was built by 'Gwleder, mother of Hoedliw' in the middle of the twelfth century. Towards the end of the thirteenth century, it was Efa ferch Maredudd, a descendant of the royal house of Deheubarth, who commissioned the Welsh translation of the theologically complex Athanasian creed 'for her spiritual benefit and comfort'.[14]

However, there is no denying the fact that opportunities for religious life for women were becoming more restricted. In place of the flexible communities of the Welsh tradition, the Normans introduced priories of the reformed Benedictine order, dependent first on the great abbeys of Normandy then on abbeys with which they had links in England. Thus, Chepstow was a subordinate priory of Cormeilles, Goldcliff of Bec, Monmouth, of St Florent near Saumur, and Abergavenny of St Vincent le Mans. Further west, Ewenny was a priory of Gloucester and Pembroke of St Martin, Séez, while Brecon was dependent on Battle Abbey. These were 'conventual' priories, ideally with communities of twelve monks and the prior. Monks could be recruited locally but the prior was appointed by the mother house. These were all communities for men: Wales's only Benedictine community for women was the one at Usk, founded at some point in the late twelfth or early thirteenth century and possibly originating in an informal community of women from Usk Castle who wanted to lead lives of devotion and seclusion.

There have been many attempts to explain the lack of provision for religious women in medieval Wales. On the one hand, women had a stronger position in society and may have felt less need to retreat behind the convent wall. On the other hand, Welsh land law did not give women the right to hold land, so it was more difficult for them to endow religious communities. There is also a sense in the poetry of the period that this was not a society that valued celibacy in women. Women were praised for more domestic virtues: hospitality, charity, healing, religious devotion in the home. Ultimately, the answer may lie in the politics of conquest. Religious houses were often founded on boundaries, to control conquered territories or to protect against further conquest. Houses for women were perceived as vulnerable, less able to protect the land they held and more in need of protection themselves.

The religious orders

Establishing the reformed Benedictine communities was almost always part of the political process of conquest. Most were in the new boroughs, planned round a castle and with the priory to provide for the spiritual needs of what was effectively an enterprise zone. They were also part of the process of religious reform. Some, like Monmouth and Ewenny, were on land which had belonged to earlier Welsh monastic communities, and all were given oversight of (and funded by) the parish churches of the surrounding area. This was partly because recent ideas on reform made marcher lords reluctant to hold spiritual income such as tithes, but there is no doubt that it was also a cheap way of endowing a religious community. The diversion of so much parochial revenue would cause serious financial problems for the church in the centuries to come. There was nevertheless a more spiritual side to the foundation of religious communities. They were above all powerhouses of prayer. This was their work, their contribution to the community. It would be easy to see the foundation of religious houses by marcher lords and Welsh rulers alike in transactional terms: *do ut des*, I endow your community so that you pray for me; but this is unduly cynical. They were part of the 'economy of salvation', but that has to be seen in the wider context of the spiritual community.

There was also a number of short-lived foundations and 'cells', with smaller groups of monks managing land and tithes given to the mother abbey. Glastonbury was given all the churches of a Welsh kingdom stretching from the Wentloog levels to the head of the Sirhowy and Ebbw valleys and founded a short-lived priory on the site of the old minster church at Basaleg, but the monks were soon withdrawn to Glastonbury and much of the endowment of the priory was leased to the diocese of Llandaf. There was a similarly short-lived foundation at Cardiff. It is even possible that either Robert fitzHamo or Robert de la Hay had intended to found a priory in Newport when they transferred the property of the *clas* church of St Gwynllyw to Gloucester Abbey in the 1090s. Later surveys suggest that the land belonging to the church extended into several of the surrounding parishes; it looks very much like the core endowment of a pre-Norman monastic foundation.[15] This in turn might explain the very high quality of the Romanesque carving in what is now St Woolos cathedral.

Some of the short-lived Norman foundations were in areas reclaimed by the Welsh. Gilbert Fitz Richard gave the property of the *clas* at Llanbadarn Fawr to Gloucester Abbey to found a priory, but the area was reclaimed by the Welsh and the monks were forced to return to Gloucester. Similarly, Richard Fitz Pons gave the *clas* church of St Paulinus at Llanfair-ar-y-bryn (Llandovery) to found a priory cell of Great Malvern. When Rhys ap Gruffydd reclaimed the area he expelled the monks, accusing them of immoral behaviour, though this may have been a pretext.

Pre-Norman religious communities did survive, though sometimes with a change of identity. The Llancarfan community was still there well into the twelfth century as tenants of the abbey of Gloucester. In north Wales the communities at Bardsey, St Tudwal's Island, Beddgelert, Penmon and Ynys Lannog (Puffin Island) became Augustinian canonries in the course of the thirteenth century. Interestingly, it was the austere hermit communities on the islands rather than the more liberal *clas* communities on the mainland which took the lead in this process. There were other Augustinian houses in Wales. Llanthony was on the traditional site of a hermitage connected with St David. Carmarthen had been a *clas* church which was converted into a

Benedictine priory, then refounded by Bernard, bishop of St Davids, as an Augustinian house. There is no evidence of continuity with the *clas* community, but the house had Welsh canons and played a key role in the transmission of Welsh culture. It was here that the 'Black Book of Carmarthen' was written, an early thirteenth-century collection including religious and praise poetry and prophecies connected with Merlin. St Kynemark's (Monmouthshire) and Haverfordwest (Pembrokeshire) were both on new sites. St Kynemark's was endowed with churches on and near the lands of Tintern Abbey, and it has been suggested that the Augustinians were placed there by a bishop of Llandaf to prevent the Cistercians from taking over and closing the churches (as they had done elsewhere).

The tradition of the wandering hermit also survived into the Norman period. Elgar, originally from Devon, was taken as a captive to Ireland. Having obtained his release, he travelled to Bardsey, where he lived first as part of the monastic community there and latterly as a hermit, dying in the early twelfth century. He was sufficiently venerated there for Urban to take his relics to Llandaf in 1120.[16] Caradog, a former member of the household of the king of Deheubarth, was tonsured by Bishop Herewald in Llandaf, travelled to Llangenydd in Gŵyr where he built himself an oratory and on to St Davids, where he was ordained a priest. After a time on the 'island of Arry' (possibly Ynys Barry, on the coast north-east of St Davids) he was driven out by pirates and moved to another hermitage near what is now Haroldston. Though he is described as a hermit, he was not alone in his wanderings and may have established a small community of hermits at Llangenydd.[17] Hermits were engaged in the religious politics of the period. Meilyr, a hermit active in the uplands of Gwent and Glamorgan, facilitated the establishment of a short-lived Cistercian abbey at 'Pendar' in the upper Taff or Rhondda valleys, and was also involved in Hywel ab Iorwerth's foundation of Llantarnam Abbey.

Wales had its share of reformed religious orders. Religious life at the French abbey of Cluny had developed in a way which ran counter to much of the new thinking on religious life at the beginning of the second millennium. Instead of simplifying, the community at Cluny and its dependencies developed the *opus Dei*, the performance of the liturgy, to the point at which it was virtually their only activity. There was a small Cluniac community at Malpas near Newport (Monmouthshire), a dependent priory of Montacute, but with only two or three monks it is unlikely that they were able to maintain such high standards of worship. There was a similarly small (and rather troubled) community at St Clears, though the splendour of its Romanesque church suggests that a larger establishment was originally planned there.

The hermit monks of Tiron and Savigny also attracted foundations in Wales. Robert FitzMartin, lord of Cemais, established a Tironian community subsequently known as St Dogmael's on the site of the old *clas* of Llandudoch. His mother Geva established a priory of St Dogmael's on the site of another early church on Caldey Island. Here again, impressive buildings belied the small size of the community. St Dogmael's had another cell at Pill, near Milford Haven, as well as its priory at Glascarrig in Ireland. The Savignac order was very similar to the Cistercians and was eventually absorbed into the larger organization, but the Savignacs reached Wales before the Cistercians did, possibly because Savigny itself was on the borders of Normandy and Brittany. Richard de Granville established Savignac monks on the west bank of the Neath in 1130, apparently placing them on the frontier of his conquests. There were Savignac monks at Basingwerk by 1132 (and possibly a few years earlier). They may have aimed to associate themselves with the nearby shrine and holy well of St Gwenfrewi. However, their foundation owes a lot to the desire of Ranulf de Gernons, earl of Chester, to establish his authority in the Welsh region of Tegeingl.

The order of choice, though, in medieval Wales, was the Cistercians. It is difficult to establish a reason for this. The Cistercian ethos, with its austerity and hard physical work, clearly resonated with Welsh traditions of the Age of the Saints. Like so much else, though, it may also have been associated with the politics of conquest and Welsh revival. The Cistercians, like the Benedictines and the other reformed orders, arrived in Wales as Norman implants. Tintern and Margam were both Norman foundations, though the Welsh rulers of Afan and Senghenydd associated themselves with grants to Margam and the establishment of its short-lived daughter house at Pendar. Whitland and Strata Florida, too, were initially Norman foundations. When Rhys ap Gruffydd reconquered that part of Deheubarth, he evicted the Benedictine monks from Llandovery. However, he clearly saw the advantages in retaining the support of a powerful international organization such as the Cistercian order. Both Whitland and Strata Florida were given new sites, funds for extensive building programmes and further endowments of land. From Whitland the order spread across Wales with the support of virtually every dynasty of Welsh rulers. Doubt has been cast on Llywelyn ab Iorwerth's grant to Aberconwy of extensive lands and rights in the Conwy and Alwen valleys, Llŷn and Anglesey and the mountains around Snowdon. It seems, though, that the surviving text of the grant (in a confirmation by Edward III) may have been assembled by the monks after their move to Maenan and 'improved', but that it reflects authentic charters from Llywelyn to the abbey.[18]

Cistercian abbeys were supposed to be on remote and uncultivated sites, though recent research is suggesting that some at least were on or near earlier spiritual or political centres. Excavation at Strata Florida has identified an earlier building on a slightly different axis from the abbey church. The earlier building incorporated a well and sat within a burial ground, suggesting a previous ecclesiastical foundation. Valle Crucis, north of Llangollen, takes its name from the Pillar of Eliseg, a ninth-century cross less than half a kilometre up the valley. Placed on a Bronze Age burial mound, the pillar records the lineage of the rulers of Powys and may have marked a place of royal inauguration and assembly. Tomb carvings at Valle Crucis and Strata Florida may predate the abbeys in which they now sit. Margam has a famous collection of early carved stones, though there is no documentary evidence for a church or *clas* community there before the arrival of the Cistercians.

Clearer evidence for the establishment of religious houses on sites of earlier religious settlement comes from the two houses for Cistercian women. The position of women in Cistercian monasticism was ambivalent. There were Cistercian houses for women from the earliest days of the order, and recent scholarship has challenged the idea that the Cistercians were hostile to women. Nevertheless, as the structures of the order became more formalised in the later twelfth century, the position of the women's houses became increasingly subordinate. They were placed under the supervision of male houses, and Cistercian nuns had to observe strict enclosure, making the self-sufficient lifestyle of the men's houses virtually impossible. Cistercian houses for women were more likely than the men's houses to be existing communities adopting the Cistercian rule rather than new foundations, and this may well have been what happened at Llanllŷr and Llanllugan.

Both have 'llan' place names, suggesting earlier churches on the site. Llanllŷr, in the Aeron valley in Ceredigion, was founded by Rhys ap Gruffydd on a site which had been a hermitage. An inscribed stone there records the grant of a 'tesquitus' (a small waste place, but with the sense of a desert or monastic retreat) to one Madomnauc, probably the Irish saint Mo Domnóc who appears in Rhigyfarch's *Life of St David*.[19] Llanllugan (Montgomeryshire) was founded by Maredudd ap Rhobert, lord of Cydewain, at some point in the early thirteenth century. Like some English houses for women, its 'foundation' may have been a process whereby an informal community of women was reorganized into a more structured religious house. The name 'Llanllugan' and the church of Llanwyddelan across the valley suggest there may have been an earlier community there dedicated to the Irish saint Lorcan Wyddel.

The self-sufficiency and stress on hard physical work which were the guiding principles of the Cistercian order clearly appealed to the Welsh. The Cistercians were fortunate in that their arrival coincided with a period of climate improvement. Instead of letting their land to tenants, they established grange farms where the bulk of the work was done by lay brothers. These were men recruited from local peasant families who lacked the education for life in the monastery, but who had the skills needed for farming. Over much of Wales, the first point of contact with the Cistercians was through one of these grange farms. Lay brothers were able to take over rough pasture and woodland and bring it into cultivation. Fields which they laid out can still be seen on the Crugwyllt ridge above Margam and the Rhyswg ridge above Abercarn (Monmouthshire). Further into the mountains, the Cistercians had extensive pasture for sheep, and by the thirteenth century they were exporting wool on a large scale to Flanders and Italy.

There were early links between the Cistercians and the military orders, in spite of their radically different objectives. Bernard of Clairvaux was a personal friend of Hugh de Payens, one of the founders of the Knights Templar, and wrote in support of the order, seeing it as the answer to the conflict between Christian and military ideals. These links may have become less significant after Bernard's death, and were of little importance in Wales. Here, the Templars had profitable estates administered from their centres at Llanmadoc in Gower and just over the border at Garway (Herefordshire), but there is no evidence that members of the order were ever resident at Llanmadoc. Their presence was almost entirely in Anglo-Norman areas, and they received few donations from the Welsh, possibly because they were so closely associated with English royal patronage.

The Knights Hospitaller, on the other hand, were more explicitly charged with hospitality to pilgrims and other travellers, and had a strong presence in Wales. Like the Templars, they received most of their endowment from Anglo-Norman lords, but Rhys ap Gruffydd of Deheubarth confirmed their holdings when he reconquered Ceredigion. It is possible that Llywelyn ab Iorwerth granted the church at Ellesmere (Salop) to the Hospitallers of Dolgynwal or Ysbyty Ifan, though the authenticity of the surviving charter claiming this is questionable.[20] It has been suggested that in Wales it was the Hospitallers who were more closely linked with the Cistercians. Their estates adjoined around Strata Florida and in the upper Conwy valley, but this may have been coincidence. There were hospices for travellers on their estates at Slebech (Pembrokeshire) and Ysbyty Ifan (Gwynedd), and possibly at Gwanas near Dolgellau and Ystrad Meurig (Ceredigion), which may have been geared to pilgrimage routes to St Davids, Strata Florida and Bardsey.

Wales was ideal territory for monks and nuns who wanted to live remote from the world. It was less ideal for the orders of friars, who usually gravitated towards towns where they could preach and be supported by the local community. Llywelyn ab Iorwerth's introduction of Franciscan friars to Llanfaes in Anglesey in 1237 was ostensibly to provide a burial place for his wife Siwan, but could also be seen as part of a programme of urbanization and economic development. Wales had two other Franciscan communities (Carmarthen and Cardiff), five Dominican houses (Cardiff again,

Haverfordwest, Bangor, Rhuddlan and Brecon), and one each of the Carmelites (Denbigh) and Augustinian friars (Newport). It is hard to quantify their impact, but the spread of religious knowledge in secular society in the thirteenth century must have been at least in part due to their work.

It was usually monastic houses, and above all the Cistercian abbeys, that Welsh rulers chose for their burial places. Choice of a burial location made a powerful statement about power in this world, but was also an effective strategy for ensuring the intercessory prayer of the monks and their support at the resurrection of the dead. Successive members of the royal house of Gwynedd were buried at Aberconwy. Margam was an Anglo-Norman foundation but many of the Welsh rulers of Afan left their bodies for burial there. Princes of Powys were buried at Valle Crucis, and many of the royal house of Deheubarth were buried at Strata Florida, though Rhys ap Gruffydd and two of his sons were buried in St Davids Cathedral.[21] Some Welsh rulers, though, chose religious houses in what is now England: princes of Gwynedd at Haughmond, princes of Powys at Wombridge. Gruffydd ap Cynan made deathbed gifts to the Benedictine abbeys of Chester and Shrewsbury in 1137 but chose to be buried in Bangor Cathedral.[22] Some Anglo-Norman lords chose Cistercian burial places (the Marshal earls and countesses at Tintern) but they were equally likely to choose Benedictine priories with which they were associated. Women were less likely to be buried in Cistercian abbeys, though Matilda de Breos, wife of Gruffydd son of the Lord Rhys, was allowed to take the Cistercian habit with her husband at Strata Florida and buried there. Llywelyn ab Iorwerth established the Franciscan friary at Llanfaes to enshrine the grave of his wife Siwan, and his grandson Llywelyn ap Gruffydd's wife Eleanor de Montfort was also buried there.

Relics and relic cults

Gruffydd ap Cynan's links with Shrewsbury and Chester may have something to do with negotiations for the translation of the relics of St Gwenfrewi, which were taken to Shrewsbury with Chester's help. This eventually took place in the year after Gruffydd's death, with the approval of his son Owain. Like the translation of Dyfrig's relics from Bardsey to Llandaf, this signalled a considerable cultural shift. Early medieval Wales did not share the passion of continental churches for the collection and dispersal of bodily relics, though there is some evidence for the acceptance of relics from outside. The relics which were venerated were the property of the saints: books, bells, croziers. The bodies of the saints were supposed to stay where they had lived, died and were buried: in some senses the whole landscape associated with them became a massive contact relic. This unease is reflected in Robert of Shrewsbury's account of his search for Gwenfrewi's relics, the care that he took to secure the permission of both the bishop and the lay ruler, the extent of local opposition and his explanation of how he managed to overcome it.[23]

There is some evidence for changing Welsh attitudes to bodily relics in the twelfth and thirteenth centuries. The monks of Shrewsbury were able to return to Gwytherin and take the relics of St Eleri, who was according to Robert Pennant the founder of the religious community in which Gwenfrewi ended her days. At Pennant Melangell, a small separate church, the *cell y bedd* ('the cell of the grave') had been built over St Melangell's burial place. This has been rebuilt and incorporated into the present church, but Melangell's relics were translated into a magnificent stone sarcophagus in the twelfth century. It is possible that the relics of St David (unusually for Wales) had been translated to a shrine by the end of the eleventh century and reading between the lines of the *Annales Cambriae* it seems more than likely that they were stolen during a Viking raid.[24] Rhygyfarch described them rather vaguely as being buried somewhere in the grounds of his monastery, 'in sua sepelitur civitate'. By the thirteenth century the monks of Glastonbury were claiming that a relic of St David had reached their monastery in 962, but the evidence for this is uncertain. Leominster claimed a relic of his arm and the priory at Ewenny claimed to have discovered his body outside the south door of the church. Somehow those remains were acquired by the cathedral at St Davids but they were subsequently plundered by Edward I and others. Cadog may also have been translated to a shrine in the eleventh century, but his body remained whole and in the location where he died.[25]

Wales and the wider world: Crusades and pilgrimage

Welsh participation in the Crusades has often been downplayed and even ignored by historians. While it has to be admitted that not that many Welshmen made their way to the Holy Land as soldiers (more went, later, as pilgrims), there were Welshmen in the troop led by the lord of Thouars in 1096, possibly recruited through the connection of the lords of Thouars with the abbey of St Florent près Saumur and its priory in Monmouth.[26] In 1188, Henry II sent Archbishop Baldwin on a preaching tour of Wales to enlist support for the third crusade. According to Gerald of Wales, who accompanied him, over three thousand Welsh and Marcher men took the cross, though in the event only a few of them actually made it overseas.[27] Some may have been overwhelmed by the excitement of the great preaching meetings and have subsequently thought better of their vows, but for many it seems that taking the cross meant a willingness to support the crusade in some other way rather than a promise of actual active service.

The underlying problem was, of course, that both Welsh and Anglo-Normans had plenty of scope for their fighting abilities nearer home. The willingness of both Welsh and Marcher recruits to go on Crusade seems to have been linked very closely to the state of affairs in Wales. The comparative peace of the later part of Henry II's reign undoubtedly encouraged Welsh participation in the third crusade. Stories about a Welsh bowman at the siege of Acre (1291) suggest that Welsh archers were sufficiently common to be regarded as stock figures. Good relations between Gwynedd and Chester in the early thirteenth century meant that a number of Welsh recruits accompanied Earl Ranulf of Chester on the fifth crusade. There were several notable Welshmen who went on crusade: it is even possible that Llywelyn ap Gruffydd took part in the crusade led by Richard of Cornwall in 1240.[28]

It is difficult to distinguish between Welsh crusaders and pilgrims in the twelfth and thirteenth centuries: indeed, it may not be a valid distinction. The terms for 'crusader', 'pilgrim' and 'christian' in the *Brut y Tywysogion* are often interchangeable.[29] There are a couple of clear references to non-combatant pilgrims to the 'Holy Land' in the *Brut y Tywysogion*. In 1125, Morgan ap Cadwgan went on pilgrimage as penance for killing his brother, and died on the way back; and in 1144, a group of Welsh pilgrims was drowned in the Mediterranean on their way to Jerusalem. This may underestimate the number of pilgrims: others may have returned safely and not been considered worthy of recording. Pilgrimage was certainly part of the Welsh tradition. The lives of the Welsh saints include almost as a matter of course pilgrimages to Rome and to the 'Holy Land'. Nor are their journeys described as difficult or dangerous: the focus is rather on their experiences at the destination and their validation by the pope and the patriarch. This does not, of course, prove anything about pilgrimage in the sixth century but it does suggest that it was considered commonplace in the twelfth. There was nevertheless awareness of the hardship of travel: an anonymous early thirteenth-century religious poem put into the mouth of a pilgrim describes the laborious journey to the sites mentioned in the Bible.[30]

There is a sense in early Irish and Anglo-Saxon literature that pilgrimage had to involve travel across the sea to a foreign country.[31] The same feeling is reflected in the 'Lament of the Pilgrim', which speaks of choosing exile for the sake of God: 'Can mynnwys er Duw ddifröedd – arnaw' ('Since he desired for God's sake to suffer exile'). By the eleventh century, the definition of pilgrimage had widened, so that William the Conqueror's journey to St Davids in 1081 could optimistically be described in the *Brut y Tywysogion* as a pilgrimage (*causa orationis*).[32] In 1123 Pope Callixtus II made St Davids one of the key pilgrimage destinations in Europe with a declaration that two pilgrimages to St Davids were to be considered the equivalent of one to Rome and three the equivalent of one to the Holy Land. This was ostensibly in response to a petition by Bishop Bernard, but it was also linked to Callixtus' vision of a western church bound together by pilgrimage routes. It was Callixtus who also promoted the pilgrimage to Compostela in northern Spain.

Wales had other shrines, though much of the evidence for their existence and for pilgrimage to them dates from the later medieval period. Margam had a relic of the True Cross by the thirteenth century which must have attracted pilgrims. The life of St Elgar in the *Book of Llandaf* described Bardsey as 'the Rome of Britain, on account of the duration and danger of travel to [it]', implying that it was a focus for pilgrimage.[33] The lives of St Gwenfrewi both contain collections of miracles at the saint's shrine in Holywell, and in some cases those who are healed are described as having travelled there, but there is seldom anything to suggest a formal pilgrimage. The Welsh also travelled to shrines in England: a thirteenth-century addition to William of Malmesbury's *De Antiquitate Glastoniensis Ecclesiae* ('On the Antiquity of the Church of Glastonbury') describes the 'frequent prayers' of Welsh pilgrims at Glastonbury, which claimed relics of St David and of other saints.[34] At the beginning of the thirteenth century Wales was emphatically part of western Christendom, though increasingly challenging relations with England had their impact on the church as much as on secular life.

Notes

[1] R. R. Davies, *Conquest, Co–existence and Change: Wales, 1063–1415* (Oxford: Clarendon Press, 1987), p. 31.

[2] *A History of the County of Chester*, vol. 3, edited by C. R. Elrington and B. E. Harris (Oxford: Oxford University Press for the Institute of Historical Research, 1980), pp. 132–46.

[3] Michael Lapidge, 'The Welsh-Latin Poetry of Sulien's Family', *Studia Celtica*, 8/9 (1973–4), 88–93 (lines 1–3, 37–8, 81–3 of the poem).

[4] A. W. Wade-Evans, *Vitae Sanctorum Britanniae et Genealogiae* (Cardiff: University of Wales Press, 1944), pp. 24–141. On the dating of this and Rhigyfarch's life of St David, see Davies, *The Book of Llandaf and the Norman Church in Wales*, p. 76 n. 2, and 'The Saints of South Wales and the Welsh church', in *Local Saints and Local Churches in the Early Medieval West*, edited by Thacker and Sharpe, pp. 387–90.

[5] Sharpe and Davies (edited and translated), 'Rhigyfarch's *Life* of St David', in *St David of Wales: Cult, Church and Nation*, edited by Evans and Wooding, pp.107–55, description of the life of the monastery on pp. 124–9.

[6] David N. Dumville, *Saint David of Wales* (Cambridge: Cambridge University Press, 2001), pp. 12–14.

[7] Gillian L. Conway, 'Towards a cultural context for the eleventh-

century Llanbadarn manuscripts', *Ceredigion*, 13/1 (1997), 9–28.

[8] Thomas O'Loughlin, 'Rhigyfarch's *Vita Davidis:* An *Apparatus Biblicus'*, *Studia Celtica*, 32. (1998), 179–88.

[9] D. Simon Evans, *A Medieval Prince of Wales: The Life of Gruffudd ap Cynan* (Burnham-on-Sea: Llanerch Press, 1990), pp. 82–3.

[10] British Library MS Cotton Vespasian A.xiv.

[11] Most are edited and translated in Wade-Evans, *Vitae Sanctorum Britanniae*.

[12] James, *Rhigyfarch's Life of St David*, pp. 3–5, 30–2.

[13] *Two Mediaeval Lives of Saint Winefride*, edited and translated by Ronald Pepin and Hugh Feiss (Toronto: Peregrina, 2000).

[14] Henry Lewis, 'Credo Athanasius Sant', *Bulletin of the Board of Celtic Studies*, 5 (1929–31), 195–6.

[15] The National Archives, London: E112/107/64/8.

[16] Karen Jankulak and Jonathan Wooding, 'The Life of St Elgar of Ynys Enlli', in *Solitaries, Pastors and 20,000 Saints: Studies in the Religious History of Bardsey Island (Ynys Enlli)*, edited by Jonathan Wooding, *Trivium*, 39 (2010), 15–47.

[17] *Nova Legenda Anglie*, edited by Carl Horstman (Oxford: Clarendon Press, 1901), vol. 1, pp. 174–7.

[18] *The Acts of Welsh Rulers 1120–1283*, edited by Huw Pryce (Cardiff: University of Wales Press, 2005), pp. 348–63.

[19] James, *Rhigyfarch's Life of St David*, pp. 18, 41.

[20] *The Acts of Welsh Rulers*, edited by Pryce, pp. 419–21.

[21] The tombs traditionally identified as theirs are fourteenth-century, but may be retrospective monuments near actual graves.

[22] Evans, *A Medieval Prince of Wales*, pp. 51–2, 82–3.

[23] Pepin and Feiss, *Two Medieval Lives of St Winefride*, pp. 77–89.

[24] F. Cowley, 'The relics of St David', in *St David of Wales: Cult, Church and Nation*, pp. 274–9.

[25] Wade-Evans, Vitae Sanctorum, pp. 110–11.

[26] *The Canso d'Antioca:Aan Occitan Epic Chronicle of the First Crusade*, edited by Carol Sweetenham and Linda M. Pateson (Farnham:Ashgate, 2003), pp. 109, 227.

[27] Giraldus Cambrensis, *The Journey through Wales/The Description of Wales*, translated by L.Thorpe (Harmondsworth: Penguin, 1978), p. 204.

[28] Evidence for this in the Lanercost Chronicle is discussed in Kathryn Hurlock, *Wales and the Crusades c. 1095–1291* (Cardiff: University of Wales Press, 2011), pp. 110–11.

[29] *Brut y Tywysogion: Peniarth MS. 20*, edited by Thomas Jones (Cardiff: University of Wales Press, 1941), pp. 179–80; *Brut y Tywysogion or The*

Chronicle of the Princes, edited and translated by Thomas Jones (Cardiff: University of Wales Press, 1952), pp. 96–7.

[30] *Gwaith Dafydd Benfras ac Eraill o Feirdd Hanner Cyntaf y Drydded Ganrif ar Ddeg*, Beirdd y Tywysogion VI, edited by N. G. Costigan (Cardiff: University of Wales Press, 1995), pp. 565–70.

[31] T. M. Charles–Edwards, 'The Social Background to Irish *Peregrinatio*', *Celtica*, 11 (1976), 43–59.

[32] *Brut y Tywysogion*, edited by Jones, p. 23

[33] *Solitaries, Pastors and 20,000 Saints*, edited by Wooding, pp. 39, 43.

[34] John Scott, *The Early History of Glastonbury: An Edition, Translation and Study of William of Malmesbury's* De Antiquitate Glastonie Ecclesie (Woodbridge: Boydell Press, 1981), pp. 64–7, and I. G. Thomas, 'The cult of saints' relics in Anglo–Saxon England' (unpublished Ph.D. thesis, University of London, 1974), 171–2, referencing thirteenth-century interpolations in William of Malmesbury's *De Antiquitate Glastoniensis Ecclesiae*); G. H. Doble, 'The Celtic saints in the Glastonbury relic lists', *Somerset and Dorset Notes and Queries*, 24 (1944–6), 86–9.

Chapter 6

Conquest and Apocalypse, c.1200–c.1420

MADELEINE GRAY

For the later twelfth century, the leaders of independent Wales were members of the royal house of Deheubarth. By the beginning of the thirteenth century, though, the focus had shifted back to Gwynedd. Llywelyn ab Iorwerth, 'the Great' (1173–1240), succeeded in uniting much of north Wales under his rule and exercised a looser dominance over the smaller kingdoms further south. Increasingly, though, Welsh independence had to be negotiated in the context of an increasingly powerful and aggressive neighbour. Llywelyn had secured a peace treaty with King John and married John's illegitimate but acknowledged daughter Joan (Siwan in Welsh). Their son Dafydd struggled to assert his authority against the challenge of his older brother Gruffydd, son of Llywelyn ab Iorwerth by a previous relationship. In turn, Gruffydd's son Llywelyn came close to re-establishing his grandfather's hegemony but was eventually defeated by Edward I of England. Part of the problem was the Welsh law of succession. While there was room for debate, this could be interpreted as requiring the division of the kingdom among all of a ruler's sons, possibly even including sons who were born out of wedlock but acknowledged. Even more challenging was the fact that there was little sense of Welsh national identity: lesser rulers often preferred alliance with a distant English king to acknowledging the overlordship of another Welsh ruler.

The support of leading churchmen was a key element in the political strategies of Welsh rulers in the struggle to preserve Welsh independence. Their landholding alone made them powerful, and many came from leading families, both Welsh and Anglo-Norman. While the rulers of England could usually call on the backing of the archbishop of Canterbury, Welsh rulers could hope to counter this with declarations of support from Welsh bishops. Acting as diplomats and advocates, bishops and abbots could persuade the pope to support the Welsh cause. The church also provided vital services for the development of state administration: the clergy served as administrators and bureaucrats for the Welsh kings in the increasingly bureaucratic and professionalized administration of the twelfth and thirteenth centuries. The church provided not just personnel but safe storage for documents and regalia. Cistercian abbeys had space and buildings which could provide accommodation and a theoretically neutral base for great assemblies. When Llywelyn ab Iorwerth summoned the other Welsh rulers to swear fealty to his son Dafydd in 1238, it was at Strata Florida that they met. The church was thus called on to validate his increasingly ambitious claims of overlordship. The Welsh rulers in turn could reward support with gifts of land and privileges. However, the hostility of the church was always a potential problem. Caught between the financial demands of increasingly pressured Welsh rulers and the claims of obedience from Canterbury, it was tempting for senior Welsh clergy to turn to England for support.

While Llywelyn ab Iorwerth succeeded in maintaining good relations with his church leaders, his successors were not so fortunate (or so able). Llywelyn had also used the papacy in his political framework, placing his younger son and heir Dafydd under the pope's protection. Dafydd was able to use this to stave off Henry III's demands in 1244 (though there is some debate over whether he actually tried to become a vassal of the pope).[1] However, Dafydd ap Llywelyn fell out with Richard, bishop of Bangor, possibly because Dafydd seized his half-brother Gruffydd at a parley under Bishop Richard's protection.

Tensions between prince and bishops continued into Llywelyn ap Gruffydd's reign. Llywelyn had allies in the chapters of both Bangor and St Asaph cathedrals, and he had every reason to suppose that Richard's successor Anian, and Anian II of St Asaph, would be at least amenable to his rule. However, there were recurring disputes over the rights of bishops and clergy and their tenants. This was made worse by the financial pressures of Llywelyn's agreements with the English Crown: needing to raise money, Llywelyn was tempted to trespass on episcopal rights. However, it was not always the princes who were at fault: the bishops were sensitive to any perceived threat to their position. From their point of view, of course, the defence of their privileges was as much a sacred duty as a practical one. Land and rights had been given to the saint. Failure to defend them could incur the anger of the saint; and the Welsh saints were known for their miracles of revenge and punishment as well as miracles of help and healing.

Anian of Bangor was constrained by his position in the heartland of Gwynedd and the fact that his cathedral chapter generally supported Llywelyn. Anian of St Asaph, with a base nearer the English border, had more freedom of action and was able to call on the pope and the archbishop of Canterbury for support. After his defeat in 1277 (and possibly because of that defeat) Llywelyn began to lose control of the Bangor chapter. This freed the bishop to appeal to Edward I against what he claimed were Llywelyn's unjustified exactions. There is still debate over the interpretation of the opaque reference in one version of the *Brut y Tywysogion* to a plot against Llywelyn in Bangor cathedral – 'and then was done the betrayal of Llywelyn in the belfry of Bangor by his own men.'[2] However, it seems likely that the conspiracy involved some at least of the leading churchmen of the cathedral and diocese.

Possibly because of their uncertain relations with the bishops, successive rulers of Gwynedd relied more on the heads of religious houses for support. They were not always prepared to oblige: the Cistercians, as an international order, could have wider loyalties. The abbot of Strata Marcella, in a difficult position on the border, sided with the bishops of Bangor and St Asaph, supporting

Gruffydd ap Gwenwynwyn against Llywelyn ap Gruffydd. The other Cistercian abbots, though, wrote to the pope in support of Llywelyn ap Gruffydd in his dispute with Anian of St Asaph. However, the history of strained relations between princes and bishops clearly contributed to the problems of the Gwynedd regime.

The politics of conquest could even influence hagiographic literature. A story in the collection of miracles of St Thomas Cantilupe of Hereford described an incident in Conwy in 1303. A small child fell into the castle ditch and was thought to be dead. According to some of the subsequent depositions, a burgess of the town vowed to St Thomas that if the child recovered he would go on pilgrimage to St Thomas's tomb in Hereford. Immediately the boy recovered. But an alternative version of the same story credited his recovery to the Holy Cross of the church of Conwy 'for which God very often works miracles in the town'. The Holy Cross of Conwy may have been one of Wales's many miracle-working rood carvings, though it is surprising that no poetry mentioning it survives. Alternatively, it could be a memory of the Croes Naid, the relic of the True Cross that was one of the most sacred items in the regalia of Gwynedd, seized by Edward I in 1283. The miracle story could recall either its time at Aberconwy Abbey or its return to Wales on one of Edward's visits. The last of those visits, though, was in the spring of 1295. By 1303 the Croes was back in England. It is still possible, though, that what Conwy had was a contact relic, possibly something that had housed the Croes and still retained some of its power.[3]

The same saint was credited with one of the more bizarre and political miracles in medieval Wales. After an uprising at Oystermouth in the summer of 1287, one of the participants, William ap Rhys or 'Cragh', was sentenced to be hanged in Swansea. At the first attempt, the crossbeam of the gallows broke. He was hanged again and thought to be dead. His body was taken to a nearby house, where he was 'measured' to the saint: the length of his body was measured with string which was then folded to make the wick of a candle. His friends prayed to Thomas Cantilupe and he revived.[4]

Morality and spirituality

It is difficult to know how much credit to give to outside criticism of the Welsh church at this period. Archbishop Pecham's fulminations against lax clerical morals have more to do with the surviving tradition of clerical marriage. His attack on the linked problems of poverty and lack of education reflects 'the exacting standards of a highly-educated Franciscan committed to reforming the Church throughout the province of Canterbury.'[5] He placed the blame squarely on the bishops, who were responsible for failing to implement reforming decrees from Canterbury. The problem of poverty in south Wales had much to do with the diversion of parochial income to support numerous small religious houses. In north Wales it was more the result of the pattern of portionary churches, in which income was diverted to members of local families. Pecham suggested that portions should be gradually abolished on the deaths of existing portion-holders, but nothing seems to have become of this.

Pecham also criticized lay society in Wales for immorality, notably for the acceptance under Welsh law of the rights of children born outside marriage, or in marriages of close relatives. Here, as in so many other aspects of medieval Welsh history, Wales was not unique. Concepts of illegitimacy and church control of marriage were developing across Europe in the thirteenth century, and the worst that can be said for Wales is that change took place a little more slowly than elsewhere. Ironically, it was Edward I's settlement which fossilized Welsh civil law.

On the other hand, by the twelfth and thirteenth centuries we have an increasing amount of evidence for the spirituality of lay people. Much of this comes from poetry composed at the courts of the princes of Gwynedd and reflects the values of a society ruled by a warrior elite. God and the saints are praised for their heroic virtues: there is little room here for 'gentle Jesus, meek and mild'. God the Father is 'Duw dofydd', but also 'gwledig', ruler of a 'gwlad' or land, and 'priodawr', the lawful claimant. Like the good earthly ruler, he is generous, the support and protector of his people. He is just in his judging but also vengeful: 'Gwae a goddwy Duw', according to one poem sometimes attributed to Meilyr ap

Gwalchmai 'woe to the one who angers God.'[6] Even when pleading for forgiveness for sin, the poets used language reminiscent of the *dadolwch* genre, poems pleading for reconciliation with an estranged patron. Speaking of the assurance of divine forgiveness, Gwalchmai ap Meilyr asserted:

Edifeiriawg da, Duw a'i ceinmyn:
Ef caiff carennydd o'i ffydd ffechyn

[God will honour the contrite and good:
He will obtain reconciliation because of his ardent faith][7]

and Gwalchmai's son Meilyr ap Gwalchmai pleaded

Carennydd Dofydd beunydd a'm bo.

[May I have the Lord's friendship always.][8]

The word *carennydd* is precisely the word used in secular praise poetry to describe the reconciliation of two parties when all outstanding disputes between them have been settled.

Much of this language could have been drawn from the Psalms, with which the poets would have been familiar from their attendance at the canonical hours and the Mass. However, the closeness of the language of their religious poetry to the language of praise poems to earthly rulers suggests that it should also be seen in that tradition. Praise of God was part of the poet's duty, alongside and even before praise of the royal patron. According to one version of the traditional Welsh law texts, the 'Book of Blegywryd', 'When the king desires to listen to poems, let the *pencerdd* present to him two poems . . . one about God and the other about kings.'[9] God was actually spoken of as the poet's patron, rewarding him for his poetry: 'Duw a'm rhydd, o'm rheiddun ofan, Rhwydd obaith o waith y winllan', sang Cynddelw, 'God will give me, because of my gift of craftsmanship, great confidence from labour in the vineyard.'[10]

Christ, too, was seen in heroic terms, *Christus victor* as much as *Christus patiens*. 'Duw a fedd o'i fuddugoliaeth', according to Elidir Sais in his *marwnad* for Rhodri ab Owain, 'God governs by virtue of his victory.'[11] Cynddelw spoke of the 'gwrhydri', the 'heroism' of the Incarnation and Einion ap Gwalchmai described Christ as 'arwr', a hero.[12] According to Gwalchmai ap Meilyr, Heaven is 'tin rhygymyrth Crist o groes edwyn cethri', 'the land that Christ seized by the painful cross of nails'.[13] It is probably this emphasis on Christ the hero that led to the very vivid descriptions of the Harrowing of Hell in so many of these poems. According to Dafydd Benfras,

> oed eu lle llu wrth syllyaw
> Dyd y kymerth Crist croc yn eidaw:
> Yg gwaelawt uffern, affleu vraw – einyoes . . .
> Pan dyuu y Mab Rat, oed reit wrthaw.

> [Confused was the situation of the host looking on,
> The day Christ took up the cross as his own,
> In the depth of hell, in the grip of a terror-stricken existence . . .
> When the Son of Grace came, there was need for him.][14]

With regard to the saints, too, the praise of the poets sometimes echoes secular praise poetry. Like the lives of the saints, the poetry presents them in the same terms as secular heroes. Cadfan's church at Tywyn is full of good things:

> Nyd oes eissyoes eisseu yndi,
> Namyn heirt a beirt a bartoni
> Namyn het, a met y mewn llestri

> [There is never want there,
> But beautiful things, and poets, and poetry,
> Peace, and mead in vessels][15]

and Cynddelw describes St Tysilio as

> Post Powys, pergig kedernyt
> pobyl argledyr arglwyd diergryt.

> [Pillar of Powys, spear of strength,
> Support of the people, fearless lord.][16]

This was poetry composed for performance at court, in the king's great hall and therefore with a wide audience. The 'Book of Blegywryd' explicitly says the poetry is to be performed 'yg cynted y neuad', where the king sits in the hall.[17] The language and inspiration of the poets suggests the breadth of their knowledge, but also the breadth of knowledge that they expected in their listeners. Some of the court poets were clearly able to read Latin and would have understood the biblical texts read and sung as part of the liturgy of the Mass. Other aspects of the liturgy may also have influenced their writing. Gruffydd ab yr Ynad Coch's poem invoking the aid of saints and angels as well as the Trinity belongs in the tradition of the early medieval Irish church, but must also have been influenced by the Litany of the Saints that was part of the Easter vigil as well as other services.[18]

For many others, the extent of their biblical and theological knowledge suggests that they were able to learn from sermons in Welsh or from other forms of personal instruction. The poets had clearly been instructed in the basic confession of faith, the Apostles' Creed. The structure of the creed, with its twelve articles of faith – creation of the world by God the Father, Jesus as his divine son, the incarnation, crucifixion, resurrection, ascension and second coming, the Holy Spirit, the communion of saints, the forgiveness of sins, bodily resurrection and eternal life – is reflected in the structure of a number of poems praising God. Einion ap Gwalchmai's *Awdl i Dduw* praises the generosity of the creation and the redemptive sacrifice, then takes us through the Harrowing of Hell, when Christ 'dug anrhaith uffern yn ei afflau', 'seized Hell's booty in his grip' (this is mentioned in the Apostles' Creed but not in the more detailed and theologically sophisticated Nicene Creed which was part of the liturgy of the Mass), resurrection, ascension, saints, forgiveness and 'gorfod gorffowys baradwys bau' ('the reward of a resting place in the land of paradise').[19]

The style of much of the poetry, too, suggests influences from contemporary sermons – which in turn suggests that, although we do not have surviving Welsh versions of books of advice for preachers before the fourteenth century, either they did exist or the Latin and French books of advice were sufficiently understood and used. It was indeed a Welsh friar, the Franciscan John of Wales, who wrote one of the most popular books of advice, in *c*.1275. In this he set out the art of preaching 'dividendo, subdividendo et concordando propositi thematis', by division, subdivision and concordance.[20] This is exactly what books of sermon exemplars did, using lists like the Seven Deadly Sins, the Ten Commandments and the seven petitions of the Lord's Prayer as mnemonics.

Gruffydd ab yr Ynad Coch made powerful use of this in a poem addressed to Christ as 'y gŵr a'n rhoddes rhiniau ar dafawd', the hero who gave us spoken mysteries. In a series of lines using *cymeriad*, rhetorical repetition, beginning 'Gwae . . .', 'Woe to', he enumerates the Seven Deadly Sins (plus five more for good measure, including some from the Ten Commandments), and mentions without details the seven petitions of the Lord's Prayer, the seven virtues and the seven words of Christ on the cross. Clearly he expected the audience to know these without being told. He then moves on to a terrifying description of the torments of Hell which may have been inspired by sermons or similar literature:

> Ydd oedd yn berwi, wb o'r bârau
> Saith canmil peiriaid o eneidiau,
> A glaweir ac ôd a seirff a llewod,
> A phawb heb annod yn ei boenau . . .

> [There were boiling, alas for the afflictions,
> Seven hundred thousand cauldronfuls of souls
> And sleet and snow and serpents and lions
> And each without respite in his agonies . . .][21]

The poets' allusions to theological concepts and to episodes in the lives of the saints suggest that they expected their audience to be equally well informed. They clearly did not see it as their duty to supplement the education provided by the clergy. They assumed that implicit references to biblical stories and the use of language with scriptural resonances would be picked up and understood. They were more concerned to express religious sensibility than to expound dogma. In general, though, they display understanding of some of the more difficult theological concepts: with regard to the Trinity, for example, most of them negotiate with remarkable skill the complexities of the relationship between Father, Son and Holy Spirit, three persons but one God. Gwalchmai ap Meilyr clearly knew the most complex of the creeds, the Athanasian, with its enumeration of the relationships between the three persons:

> Pwyll a'm cyfeiryd o'r Creawdr, o'r cŷd
> O'r Mab, o'r Ysbryd, o'r iawnfryd fri
> O'r Drindawd, undawd undras â mi;
> Undra drugaredd, unwedd ofri,
> Undeg tair person uwch archengylion,
> Unddonion neifion nerth heb trengi,
> Undanc fwynt wrthyf wrth Eu moli;
> Un Duw ŷnt wyntau a diau dri.

> [The wisdom will guide me of the Creator, of the union
> Of the Son and of the Spirit, of the right-minded authority
> Of the Trinity, unity of the same lineage as I;
> Alike in great mercy, similarly noble,
> Equally fair are the three persons above archangels,
> Equally able are the heavenly ones of unfailing strength,
> Equally peaceable may they be toward me for praising them;
> One God are they, and undoubted three.][22]

Gwalchmai ap Meilyr also alluded to a paradox based on the theology of the Trinity, that Mary was daughter of God the Father and thus both daughter of and sister to her son and ultimately mother to her father:

> Hi yn vam wy thad, hi hy wyry heb wad . . .
> Hi yn verch wy mab y mot yssyt,
> Hi yn chwaer y Duw o dwywawl fyt.

> [She is mother to her father, she is virgin without denial . . .
> She is daughter to her son, it is her privilege,
> She is sister to God from holy faith.][23]

Elidir Sais came perilously close to the Patripassian heresy (the idea that God the Father actually suffered at the Crucifixion) when he spoke of 'Gwener, bu crai, bu creulyd Crog ein Tad' ['Friday, it was harsh, bloody was the Cross of our Father'][24]: it would be interesting to know whether Elidir really knew what he was saying here. In general, though, references to Father and Son are entirely in line with the accepted understanding of the Trinity. There are few references, though, to the Holy Spirit other than those in the context of the Trinity.

The accepted teaching of the twelfth-century church followed the thinking of St Augustine and the church fathers: humanity was essentially depraved, and we are incapable of living virtuously or even desiring repentance without the gift of God's grace. This is reflected in the writing of the earlier *Gogynfeirdd* poets: according to Gwalchmai ap Meilyr,

> Truan a anian inni o amwyll
> Tra charu present pres cynhywyll . . .
> Trugarawg Ddofydd, treiha fy ngherydd!

> [Wretched is our nature because of the foolishness
> Of excessive love of this world of gloomy haste . . .
> Merciful Lord, lessen my sin!][25]

Gwalchmai's son Meilyr prayed 'Defawd ddibechawd im a bucho' ('May he choose sinless ways for me').[26]

Towards the end of the thirteenth century, though, and possibly under the influence of sermons and homiletic literature urging individuals to take responsibility for their own moral behaviour, the poets placed more emphasis on the need to avoid sin. At the end of the poem in which he listed the Seven Deadly Sins and mentioned the seven virtues and the seven petitions of the Lord's Prayer, Gruffydd ab yr Ynad Coch begged

> Ni bwyf lwth ddiawg, ni bwyf lesg ofnawg,
> Ni bwyf weithredawg cam weithredau,
> Ni bwyf gyhuddgar, ni bwyf ymladdgar,
> Ni bwyf anhygar yn hogi gau,
> Ni bwyf hoedl gywall o weithred arall,
> Ni bwyf ŵr angall erbyn angau.

[May I not be greedy and lazy, may I not be faint and fearful,
May I not be a doer of evil deeds,
May I not be accusing, may I not be pugnacious,
May I not be malign, honing lies,
May I not be faulty of life because of any other deed,
May I not be a foolish man in the face of death.][27]

It is worth remembering, though, that these are petitions, not
declarations: Gruffydd was aware that he could not fulfil these
intentions without God's help.

From this it is clear that the poets reflect developments in
spirituality during the twelfth and thirteenth centuries. Writing in
the late eleventh century, Anselm had insisted on Christ's humanity
as a counterweight to the excessive stress (as he saw it) on his divine
nature. Bernard of Clairvaux used human emotion, love for the very
human Jesus, as a way of leading lay people as well as monks towards
spiritual love of (and eventual union with) God. St Francis built on
this with an emphasis on the human aspects of the story – the birth
in the stable, the humble upbringing, the physical pain of the
Crucifixion. The Franciscans thus encouraged a personal and deeply
felt engagement with Christ's humanity. While the Cistercians did
not generally preach or minister to the laity, they gave hospitality
to travellers and kept the Welsh chronicles. It is likely, therefore, that
poets could have encountered Cistercian spirituality while
travelling, possibly with their princely patrons. The Franciscans, by
contrast, saw it as their mission to preach to ordinary people. They
only had three bases in Wales, but their ideas must have influenced
the preaching and teaching of other members of the clergy. From
this developed devotion to various aspects of Christ's humanity –
his wounds, the Instruments of the Passion – and an emotional
identification with his sufferings. Gruffyd ab yr Ynad Coch has
perhaps the most powerful reflection on these:

Ai ddwylaw ar lled wedyr llidiaw
A'r gwaed yn ffrydiau ynghylch Ei fronnau
A'i holl welïau heb elïaw,
A'i goron yn ddrain ac Yntau'n gelain,
A'i ben yn anghrain wedy'r greiniaw,

Ag ôl ffrowyllau ar Ei ystlysau
Er gwneuthur angau a phoen iddaw.

[With His hands stretched out, inflamed,
With the blood in streams around His paps,
With all His wounds unanointed,
With His crown of thorns and Himself a corpse,
With His head hanging down, fallen,
With the mark of the scourges on His sides,
To cause Him death and pain.][28]

This, though, was at the very end of the thirteenth century: it took some time for the image of the suffering Christ to take priority over the image of the victorious hero. The same tendency is found in the visual sources. The carving of the crucifixion at Cwm-iou cannot be earlier than the thirteenth century, but it shows Christ crowned and triumphant on the cross. Gruffydd was also picturing the Man of Sorrows as he would appear on the Day of Judgement, 'yn barawd i'n diburiaw / A'r gwaed yn gired â'r dydd y croged' ('ready to purify us' / 'With the blood as fresh as the day He was crucified').[29] It is a terrifying and guilt-inducing image, but also a reassuring one: thanks to this suffering, we will be purified.

St Francis was keen to encourage devotion to the earlier parts of the story as well. Madog ap Gwallter was almost certainly a Franciscan friar, though from the style of his writing he had also been trained as a bard. His simple but powerful retelling of the nativity story invites the audience to share in the human experience, to travel with the shepherds and the kings:

I'r tŷ ydd ânt, heb ddôr, heb gant, gwynnawg ddrysau;
Y Mab ydoedd, a anydoedd dan ei nodau,
A'i fam ar lawr, a'i bron werthfawr wrth Ei enau.

[To the house they went without a door, without a fence, its entrances exposed to the wind,
The Son was there, who had been born beneath its protection,

And His mother on the ground, with her precious breast at
His mouth.][30]

Elsewhere in the poetry of the period, though, there is little about
the nativity story. As with the later visual evidence, it seems the
Welsh were less concerned with the emotional response to a
vulnerable baby and more concerned with God the powerful
creator, redeemer and judge.

It may also have been the friars who brought to Wales the
increased emphasis on mystical experience and eventual union with
God which characterized thirteenth- and fourteenth-century piety.
Ymborth yr Enaid ('The Sustenance of the Soul') is a text written
by a Dominican friar, probably in the middle of the thirteenth
century.[31] Beginning with an invocation of the Trinity and some
basic advice on sins to avoid and virtues to cultivate, it moves on to
a discussion of the difference between affectionate and foolish love
and a practical guide to achieving mystical visions and ecstasies. The
author was clearly well-read and a trained theologian. He knew the
work of the twelfth-century theologian Hugo of St Victor and the
descriptions of mystical experiences in Gerardus de Fracheto's *Vitae
Fratrum Ordinis Predicatorum* ('Lives of the Friars of the Order of
Preachers'). He had some distinctive ideas on the equating of
human and divine love which may have been inspired by the
Dominican theologian Richard Fishacre. Intriguingly, from the
short passages of poetry in the work, he was also a trained bard:
could he have joined the Dominicans as a mature adult after
training as a poet? *Ymborth yr Enaid* stands alone as a guide to the
mystical life, but it was intended as part of a bigger work, *Y Cysegrlan
Fuchedd* ('The Consecrated Life'), which has not survived and may
never even have been completed. Written in Welsh, it seems to have
been intended as an introductory guide for novices in the author's
community (possibly Bangor) but its appearance in the mid-
fourteenth-century manuscript of the Anchorite of Llanddewi-brefi
suggests that it rapidly became available to devout lay people as well.

The Cistercians have been credited with inspiring the
heightened focus on the Virgin Mary in thirteenth-century
religious thinking, but this was always implicit in the emphasis on
Christ's humanity and earthly life. It was reflected in the liturgy,

with hymns like the Stabat Mater, a meditation on Mary's grief at the foot of the cross. There was always a danger that this would tip over into what has been called 'Mariolatry', worship of Mary as if she were herself divine. In general, this is something the poets were able to steer away from. They evidently saw Mary as a powerful advocate for their souls but were clear that she could only intercede. Einion ap Gwalchmai prayed:

A'm eiriolwy Mair ar ei mabgwas . . .
Na'm gado rhên rhy'n deg prynas
Yn rhewin Cäin gan Sathanas.

[May Mary intercede for me with her son . . .
That the Lord who fairly redeemed us not leave me
In Cain's ruination with Satan.][32]

They were similarly aware of the ability of the saints to intercede, but only to intercede. Gwynfardd Brycheiniog asserted:' Dewi, a Drwy eirioled Duw a uet' ['Through the intercession of David, and God who governs].[33]

We do also have some surviving poetry written by the clergy themselves. As well as Madog ap Gwallter, there were several anonymous or unidentifiable poets whose work appears in the 'Black Book of Carmarthen' and the 'Book of Taliesin', and who were probably monastic or secular clergy. Their work is similar to that of the court poets – praise of God, reflection on Christ's sufferings and the Day of Judgement, numerical schemes – but they show a higher level of biblical learning, and in particular knowledge of the Old Testament. One poem in the 'Book of Taliesin', *Llath Moesen* ('The Rod of Moses'), reflects on God's dealings with the Jewish people from Abel to the Incarnation.[34] Madog's other surviving poems are an ode to God and one to St Michael, patron saint of his home parish, Llanfihangel Glyn Myfyr. He may also have been responsible for a verse reworking of Geoffrey of Monmouth's *Historia Regum Britanniae*.[35]

Throughout the medieval period, Welsh religious poetry is generally characterized by a comparatively optimistic belief in God's ultimate mercy. The poets bewail their sins and pray for forgiveness, but in general they are confident that forgiveness will be given. Meilyr ap Gwalchmai spoke of his terror of judgement and hell and begged:

Mechdeÿrn caeroedd, na cherydd fi,
Can ni wn na'm ffordd na'm ffurf arni,

[Citadel's sovereign, do not chastise me,
For I know neither my road nor my way upon it]

but ultimately declared that 'Credwn i'r rhëen rhy'n bendigas' ['We believe the king who has blessed us'].[36] This is partly because we are looking at the work of the court poets, for whom God was the generous patron, 'hywydd, rhwydd, rhinwedawg' according to Llywarch ap Llywelyn, ready, generous and virtuous.[37] Nevertheless, it is possible that this confidence reflects a more general spiritual tradition.

Towards the second half of the thirteenth century, though, there was a darker note in some of the poems. Dafydd Benfras's elegy poems are usually optimistic about the fate of the soul. One poem, however (possibly written after the deaths of Llywelyn ab Iorwerth and his sons Gruffydd and Dafydd) is a very bleak meditation on the brevity of human life: the earth which nourishes us, consumes us, and we will all come to the cold grave.[38] While this is in no way as graphic as the macabre imagery of Dafydd Ddu Hiraddug and Sion Cent, it anticipates the *memento mori* tradition of the later Middle Ages. And on a late thirteenth-century tomb in Chirk is a Latin inscription which also anticipates the cadaver tombs and the *memento mori* tradition of the fifteenth century:

Qwis eris qui trancieris, sta, perlege, plora
Sum quod eris, furam quod es, pro me precor ora paternoster.

[Whoever you are who pass by, stop, read and weep;
I am what you will be, I was what you are, please say the 'Our Father' for me.][39]

For the poet, as for the person responsible for this tomb carving, the crisis of the fourteenth century had a long foreshadowing.

Famine, plague and war

The fourteenth century was a difficult time for Wales, and for the Welsh church. The final defeat of the princes of Gwynedd was followed by a harsh settlement: high taxation, legal change and the imposition of English administrators. Edward III's wars with France may have offered opportunities for Welsh mercenary soldiers, but they meant repeated demands for taxation, from the church as much as from lay landowners. Rising population in the thirteenth century had led to overfarming and soil exhaustion in the uplands. The deteriorating climate in the early fourteenth century bore particularly harshly on a country most of whose agricultural land was at best marginal. Successive outbreaks of epidemic diseases in animals damaged the pastoral economy. The Black Death was less cataclysmic in its effects in Wales than in lowland England and continental Europe, presumably because of the limitations on trade and travel, but was still devastating, particularly in the lowlands.

These problems may have contributed to a series of uprisings in the fourteenth century. Finally, in 1400, Owain Glyndŵr, a north Wales landowner and heir to the royal houses of Powys and Deheubarth, led a rising which came near to reclaiming Welsh independence for a short time. As with the princes of Gwynedd, the church was a crucial factor in his political strategies. The Cistercians were particularly strong supporters of his, and suffered for it. John ap Hywel, abbot of Llantarnam, heard the confessions of Glyndŵr's troops before the battle of Usk in 1405 and was killed on the battlefield. Fighting during Glyndŵr's campaign and its suppression resulted in large-scale destruction of buildings and damage to land.

The most severe impacts of the demographic crisis were felt by the religious houses. The Benedictines, and other orders whose revenue was largely dependent on parish revenues, rents and manorial income, found it increasingly difficult to secure tenants. Tithes were worth less, and labourers demanded ever higher wages. Meanwhile, there was a recruitment crisis among the monks. The Cistercians found it particularly difficult to recruit lay brothers, or to control those they had. No longer able to farm their large estates themselves, they had to resort to letting their land to tenants, at a time when tenants had the upper hand in negotiations.

This was the period when many upland settlements on marginal land shrank or were completely deserted and their churches fell into ruins. Upland parishes could be huge, served by several chapels of ease and parochial chapelries. A string of lost chapelries runs along the edge of the mountain zone in the valleys of south-east Wales: Manmoel in Monmouthshire, Capel Gwladus and Coly Chapel in Gelli-gaer, Glamorgan, Capel y Fan and a possible two others in Merthyr Tydfil, Glamorgan. The same picture can even be found in the lowland zone: this is probably when the chapelries in outlying hamlets of parishes like Llancarfan and St Athan fell into decay. Even parish churches like Cwmcidi and Uchelolau (all Glamorgan) struggled, though these two were not finally abandoned until the sixteenth century.

The parish clergy also suffered. The poet-priest Tudur ap Gwyn Hagr complained ruefully that his graveyard was a wilderness, there was no one left to pay burial fees or tithes, and the job of consoling the bereaved was hard, but he carried on stoically.[40] Being in close contact with the dead and dying, parish priests were of course the most vulnerable to infection, and registers of ordinations and appointments suggest that the death rate was high. Inevitably, standards were lowered.

The numbers of parish priests recovered remarkably quickly, but the problems of the religious houses were more deep-seated. While they seem to have retained the respect of their local communities, they were no longer at the leading edge of devotional life. Apart from the very late foundation of Carmelite friars in Denbigh, there were no new foundations of religious houses in Wales after the mid-thirteenth century.[41] The Carthusians were given land around Llangiwa in north-east Monmouthshire, but apart from this the more recent monastic reforms passed Wales by. The leaders of local society were now the gentry, and few would have the resources to establish a new monastic community. Instead, they moved on to establishing chantries and other private endowments for priests to say Mass in parish churches, cathedrals and free chapels.

Problems with recruitment and funding do seem in some cases to have led to deterioration in monastic morale. The scandal at

Abergavenny Priory in the early fourteenth century is perhaps an extreme example of this. Even before the demographic crisis, numbers had declined and there were seldom more than five monks. They were accused of wandering outside the priory, consorting with prostitutes, and enacting bizarre and obscene parodies of the crucifixion for the entertainment of their friends. Some of these accusations may have been exaggerated, but the lord of Abergavenny, John de Hastings, took immediate action. The bishop of Hereford conducted a visitation and the prior was replaced.[42] The reputation of the priory recovered rapidly: John de Hastings was buried there in 1324, as were several of his family. Other visitation returns suggest problems with both morale and governance at other houses as well. Nevertheless, monasteries and friaries continued to receive bequests in wills, and they were still popular places for burial.

Lay spirituality: belief and practice

Much of lay devotion was structured around the lives of the saints, and poetry dedicated to them. After the revival of Welsh hagiographic writing in the late eleventh and early twelfth centuries, there was a steady stream of saints' *Lives* written in both Latin and Welsh. Some of the earliest translations into Welsh were of the lives of the virgin martyr saints Katherine and Margaret, but there were also thirteenth-century translations of the *Life* of Mary Magdalene and her sister Martha. These last two include detail of the extra-biblical legends of their time in France, Mary as a hermit and Martha at Tarascon. There were also Welsh *Lives* of David and Beuno written about this time.

It would be easy to view devotion to saints, offerings and pilgrimages to statues and wells as 'popular' religion in the pejorative sense, little more than superstition. Even the simplest paintings of the saints could have surprisingly complex thinking behind them. A fragmentary thirteenth-century wall painting of Mary Magdalene at Llanilltud Fawr (Glamorgan) shows her with her vessel of precious ointment and one hand raised in witness. Medieval stories about Mary Magdalene meshed together several of the women called Mary in the Gospels and identified her as a reformed prostitute. She was usually identified by the jar of precious ointment, with which according to some biblical accounts she had anointed Christ's feet, before washing them with her tears and wiping them with her hair. This made her a powerful image of repentance and forgiveness. However, her anointing of Christ's feet could be seen as prefiguring the final sacrament of extreme unction. According to the gospels of Mark and John, Mary Magdalene was the first to see Christ after the resurrection, and it was she who brought the news to his other followers. For this reason, she was called by some medieval writers the *apostola apostolorum*, the apostle to the apostles. This gave her the status of a preacher and was a challenge to other thinking on the role of women in the church. All this is encapsulated in the one wall painting.

Rising standards of literacy are reflected in the increased availability of devotional literature from the fourteenth century onwards. Most of the work of translation seems to have been done by members of religious orders, particularly the friars. Some were working for the benefit of less well educated colleagues, producing books with translations and paraphrases of key texts. The best-known of these began 'Yn y mod hwnn y dysgir y dyn py delw y dyly credu y duw . . .' ['In this way a man is taught how he should believe in God and love God and keep the Ten Commandments and guard against the Seven Deadly Sins and receive with honour the seven sacraments of the Church'].[43] It contained a paraphrase of the Creed, a translation and commentary on the commandments and lists of the seven corporal works of mercy as well as the sins and the sacraments. These were the basics of the faith which Archbishop Pecham ordered all priests to teach their congregations. Translations such as 'Yn y mod hwnn' and the English 'Lay-folk's Catechism' suggest that key texts were learned first in the vernacular and then in Latin. On the one hand, such a basic manual of instruction could imply that the clergy had not been well taught themselves. On the other hand, they do seem to have educated their parishioners, and copies of 'Yn y mod hwnn' also appear in collections apparently intended for lay readership. Popular poetry assumes familiarity with biblical texts as well as with these key teachings.

Religious texts were also commissioned by lay people. It was Gruffydd ap Llywelyn ap Phylip ap Trahaearn of Cantref Mawr in south-west Wales who commissioned the anchorite of Llanddewi-brefi to write the collection named after its scribe. This remarkable book gives us an overview of the devotional reading of an educated layman. It begins with a translation of the *Elucidarium* of Honorius Augustodunensis, a work in question-and-answer form covering world history, questions about sin and the end of the world. The *Hystoria Adrian ac Ipotis* is another work in dialogue form, this time on Christian doctrine. As well as several saints' lives and episodes from the life of the Virgin Mary, the *Book of the Anchorite* includes versions of the translation of the Athanasian Creed and 'Yn y mod hwnn', and the famous mystical text 'Ymborth yr Enaid' or 'Cysegrlan Fuchedd'.[44]

While there was no complete translation of the Bible into Welsh before the sixteenth century, there were translations and paraphrases of extracts. The text known as *Y Bibyl Ynghymraec* was not a translation of the whole text but an adaptation of a Latin summary of the historical texts in the Old Testament. Originally intended for students, it must have spread to a lay readership, as there are twenty surviving Welsh copies. Other translations included the story of the Annunciation from Luke's gospel, the crucifixion story from Matthew's gospel and the prologue of John's gospel. There were also translations of apocryphal texts including the 'Gospel of Nicodemus' with its account of the trial of Jesus, the Harrowing of Hell and the resurrection, and the 'Ystoria Addaf', the symbolic story of the wood of the cross that grew from the three seeds planted on Adam's grave. The public services of the church were, of course, in Latin but there were Welsh translations of some of the prayers and liturgies, the most popular being the Office of the Blessed Virgin Mary. These were presumably for lay use.

It is difficult to be sure how widely these texts were known, but there is some evidence by implication in slightly later poetry. A series of prayers meditating on Christ's wounds and the mystery of salvation traditionally linked to Brigid of Sweden, the 'Fifteen Oes' (named because each section of the meditation begins with the invocation 'O . . .'), survives in several Welsh manuscripts. The prayers are mainly focused on the contrasts between Jesus' human sufferings and his divine powers. The final prayer links biblical references and eucharistic imagery with a focus on the saving power of his wounds, more emphatic in the surviving Welsh translations than in the Latin equivalent:

O Iesu, y wir winwydhen, ffrwythlonaf o daeoni, copha di y cyflawnder elhyngedigaeth lhifeiriaint o waet, yr hwnn oedh yn rhedec o'th weiliaû di megys y rhet y gwin o'r bagadaû, yr amser yr oedhut ti yn traûaelû ar yr hoelion ar y Groes. Bit y'th gof di adel brathû dy ystlys di a gwaew y marchoc dalh hyt pann holhtes dy galonn di a gelhwng ffrwt o waed drosom ni a dwfr yn ehelaeth . . .

[O Jesus, true vine, most fruitful of goodness, remember the fullness of absolution from the outpouring of your blood, which flowed from your wounds as wine flows from a cluster of grapes when you laboured on the nails of the cross. Remember how you allowed your side to be pierced by the spear of the blind knight until your heart was split and poured a stream of blood on us, and water in abundance . . .][45]

The whole text was clearly well known by the later Middle Ages. In a poem addressed to the Welsh St Brigid of St Bride's Major (Glamorgan), Iorwerth Fynglwyd deliberately conflated the various saints of that name, partly in order to be able to refer to the Oes: but he only referred to them in passing, and clearly assumed that his audience would be familiar with them. This poem is, of course, later than 1420 but it reflects the growth and complexity of lay spirituality in what has often been seen as a period of unrelieved crisis.

Notes

[1]   Michael Richter, 'David ap Llywelyn, the first prince of Wales', *Welsh History Review*, 5 (1970–1), 205–19; Benedict G. E. Wiedemann, '"Fooling the Court of the Lord Pope": Dafydd Ap Llywelyn's Petition

to the Curia in 1244', *Welsh History Review*, 28/2 (December 2016), 209–32.

2   *Brut y Tywysogion Peniarth 20*, edited by Jones (1941), p. 228; *Brut y Tywysogion Peniarth 20* (1952), p. 120.

3   Susan Ridyard and Jeremy Ashbee, 'The resuscitation of Roger of Conwy: a Cantilupe miracle and the society of Edwardian north Wales', *Journal of Medieval History*, 41 (2015), 309–24.

4   The depositions and analysis are at *http://www.medievalswansea.ac.uk/ en/the-story/the-twice-hanged-william-cragh/#ref-51* (accessed 27 May 2017). For a detailed analysis, see *Power, Identity and Miracles on a Medieval Frontier*, edited by C. A. M. Clarke (Abingdon: Routledge, 2017).

5   Huw Pryce, 'The Medieval Church', in *History of Merioneth*, II: *The Middle Ages*, edited by J. Beverley Smith and Llinos Beverley Smith (Cardiff: University of Wales Press for the Merioneth Historical and Record Society, 2001), pp. 270–1.

6   N. G. Costigan, *Defining the Divinity: Medieval Perceptions in Welsh Court Poetry* (Aberystwyth: University of Wales Centre for Advanced Welsh and Celtic Studies, 2002), pp. 49, 169.

7   *The Medieval Welsh Religious Lyric: Poems of the Gogynfeirdd, 1137–1282*, edited by Catherine A. McKenna (Belmont, MA: Ford & Baillie, 1991), pp. 160–1.

8   *The Medieval Welsh Religious Lyric*, edited by McKenna, pp. 172–3.

9   *Cyfreithiau Hywel Dda yn ôl Llyfr Blegywryd*, edited by Stephen J. Williams and J. Enoch Powell (Cardiff: University of Wales Press, 1942), p. 25.

10   Costigan, *Defining the Divinity*, p. 176.

11   Costigan, *Defining the Divinity*, p. 170.

12   *The Medieval Welsh Religious Lyric*, edited by McKenna, pp. 24–5.

13   *The Medieval Welsh Religious Lyric*, edited by McKenna, pp. 160–1.

14   *Gwaith Dafydd Benfras*, edited by Costigan, pp. 388–9; Costigan, *Defining the Divinity*, pp. 74–5.

15   *Gwaith Llywelyn Fardd I*, edited by Kathleen Ann Bramley (Cardiff: University of Wales Press, 1994), p. 15; *The Medieval Welsh Religious Lyric*, edited by McKenna, p. 30.

16   *Gwaith Cynddelw Brydydd Mawr I*, edited by Nerys Ann Jones and Ann Parry Owen (Cardiff: University of Wales Press, 1991), p. 26; *The Medieval Welsh Religious Lyric*, edited by McKenna, p. 31.

17   *Llyfr Blegywryd*, edited by Williams and Powell, p. 25

18   *The Medieval Welsh Religious Lyric*, edited by McKenna, pp. 58–9, 212–15.

19   *The Medieval Welsh Religious Lyric*, edited by McKenna, pp. 194–7.

20   Margaret Jennings, 'The "Ars componendi sermones" of Ranulph

Higden', in *Medieval Eloquence: Studies in the Theory and Practice of Medieval Rhetoric*, edited by J. J. Murphy (Berkeley: University of California Press, 1978), p. 114.

[21] *The Medieval Welsh Religious Lyric*, edited by McKenna, pp. 216–17.

[22] *The Medieval Welsh Religious Lyric*, edited by McKenna, pp. 156–9.

[23] Andrew Breeze, *The Mary of the Celts* (Leominster: Gracewing, 2008), p. 7.

[24] Costigan, *Defining the Divinity*, p. 189.

[25] *The Medieval Welsh Religious Lyric*, edited by McKenna, pp. 158–9.

[26] *The Medieval Welsh Religious Lyric*, edited by McKenna, pp. 172–3.

[27] *The Medieval Welsh Religious Lyric*, edited by McKenna, pp. 218–19.

[28] *The Medieval Welsh Religious Lyric*, edited by McKenna, pp. 30–1.

[29] *The Medieval Welsh Religious Lyric*, edited by McKenna, pp. 206–7.

[30] Text in *Welsh Court Poems*, edited by Rhian M. Andrews (Cardiff: University of Wales Press, 2007), p. 42; translation in *The Medieval Welsh Religious Lyric*, edited by McKenna, p. 48.

[31] *Ymborth yr Enaid*, edited by R. Iestyn Daniel (Cardiff: University of Wales Press, 1995); R. Iestyn Daniel, *A Medieval Welsh Mystical Treatise* (Aberystwyth: Centre for Advanced Welsh and Celtic Studies, 1997).

[32] *The Medieval Welsh Religious Lyric*, edited by McKenna, pp. 184–5

[33] *Gwaith Llywelyn Fardd I ac eraill o feirdd y ddeuddegfed ganrif*, Cyfres Beirdd y Tywysogion II, edited by K. A. Bramley and R. Geraint Gruffydd (Cardiff: University of Wales Press, 1994) p. 448 (l. 291).

[34] *The Medieval Welsh Religious Lyric*, edited by McKenna, p. 75.

[35] *Welsh Court Poems*, edited by Andrews, pp. xxxv–xxxvi, 41–2; *Gwaith Bleddyn Fardd a beirdd eraill ail hanner y drydedd ganrif ar ddeg*, edited by Rhian M. Andrews (Cardiff: University of Wales Press, 1996), pp. 347–92.

[36] *The Medieval Welsh Religious Lyric*, edited by McKenna, pp. 178–9, 184–5.

[37] Costigan, *Defining the Divinity* p. 173.

[38] *Welsh Court Poems*, edited by Andrews, pp. 36, 139–40; *Gwaith Dafydd Benfras*, edited by Costigan, pp. 491–6.

[39] Colin Gresham, *Medieval Stone Carving in North Wales* (Cardiff: University of Wales Press, 1968), pp. 77–9. Unfortunately, we only have Colin Gresham's drawing as evidence for this stone: it was sold by the owners of Chirk Castle in the early years of the twenty-first century, and its present whereabouts are unknown.

[40] *Gwaith Dafydd y Coed a Beirdd Eraill o Lyfr Coch Hergest*, edited by R. Iestyn Daniel (Aberystwyth: Centre for Advanced Welsh and Celtic Studies, 2002), p. 191.

41 Denbigh Friary was traditionally said to have been founded before 1289, but David Williams has argued for a date in the 1340s: 'The Carmelites in Medieval Wales', *Archaeologia Cambrensis*, 167 (2018), 257–78.

42 The bishop's report is in *Registrum Ade de Orleton, episcopi Herefordensis*, vol. 5, edited by A. T. Bannister (London: Canterbury and York Society, 1908), pp. 151–3.

43 Glanmor Williams, *The Welsh Church from Conquest to Reformation* (Cardiff: University of Wales Press, 1976), p. 93.

44 Idris Foster, 'The Book of the Anchorite', *Proceedings of the British Academy*, 36 (1950), 197–226. On the 'Cysegrlan Fuchedd' see above, p. 137.

45 B. F. Roberts, 'Pymtheg Gweddi San Ffraid a'r Pardwn', *Bulletin of the Board of Celtic Studies*, 16 (1954–6), 254–68.

Chapter 7

Y Ganrif Fawr:
Christianity in Late Medieval Wales,
c.1420–c.1530

MADELEINE GRAY

ᳵ

The suppression of the Glyndŵr uprising was followed by a programme of savage repression. Many historians have seen this as a period of crisis and disorder. The presence of outlaws like the notorious 'Red Bandits of Dinas Mawddwy' has been explained as a result of social and political dislocation. Paradoxically, though, the demographic crisis of the fourteenth century and the trauma of defeat left the indigenous Welsh tenants in a stronger position. There was money in the local economy, and there was also enthusiasm for spending that money to the greater glory of God. This was the period that Saunders Lewis described as 'Y Ganrif Fawr', the great century, a period of religious and cultural flowering.[1]

Church building and rebuilding

Lay devotion found its most obvious expression in the rebuilding and redecoration of so many Welsh churches in the later medieval period. The need for reconstruction does in some cases reflect an earlier period of neglect and decay during the famines and plagues of the fourteenth century, though rebuilding in some areas began during those years of crisis. It is also difficult to disentangle motivations. Local politics and community pride could stimulate church-building projects quite as effectively as piety. Nevertheless, the fact that these were articulated through the fabric of the church indicates how fundamental religion was to the worldview.

In some cases it was the local elite who initiated building projects. The descendants of Llywelyn ab Iorwerth's seneschal, Ednyfed Fychan, have been credited with work on the churches at Penmynydd, Llandyfrydog and Llanddyfnan. These were all rebuilt around 1400. Ednyfed's descendants, the ancestors of the Tudor family of Penmynydd, were key promoters of the Glyndŵr uprising, raising the possibility that their church-building projects may have been connected with their political strategies. Later in the fifteenth century, the Stanley family (and Thomas Stanley's wife Lady Margaret Beaufort, mother of Henry VII) have been credited with the complete rebuilding of churches in north-east Wales including Hope and Mold in Flintshire and (most spectacularly) Gresford in Denbighshire.

Nevertheless, it is clear that in many cases the rebuilding and redecoration of the parish church was a communal effort. Even at Gresford, where the initiative seems to have come from the Stanley family, more was needed. Funds were being raised for the tower in 1512, and stained glass was given by John ap Madoc Vaughan and his wife Margaret in 1498, Ralph Davenport of Chester in 1505 and the rector, William Roden, in 1506. Elsewhere, there were clearly local fund-raising campaigns. Work on the well chapel at Holywell has traditionally been credited to Lady Margaret Beaufort and the Stanley family, but Tudur Aled's *cywydd* to St Gwenfrewi is an open pitch for contributions.[2] Comparatively small sums of money were sometimes left in wills towards windows, towers and bells, in some cases specifying that the money was to be handed over when work was in progress, suggesting long-term projects.

By the end of the fifteenth century, many Welsh churches had invested in stained glass. Most of what survives is in the north and may be the work of craftsmen from the York workshops. There are spectacular collections in the churches of Flintshire and the Vale of Clwyd, but there is work of high quality even in remote country churches in the mountains to the west. The little church at Llanrhychwyn, high above the Conwy valley, has fragments of a sequence which must once have filled all the windows. Above the altar is the crucifixion with two saints, one with a crozier and identified as St David, the other with a pilgrim staff, possibly St Rhychwyn. In the east window of the south aisle is a sensitive depiction of the Trinity, God the Father holding his crucified son in his arms while the dove of the Holy Spirit hovers over them. God the Father looks at his son (himself) with tender compassion but cannot share his suffering: that would be heresy. Above them is a fragment of the Virgin and Child, the infant Jesus in his mother's hands. Unusually, this depicts Jesus as a small and vulnerable baby. In general, medieval artists preferred to depict Jesus, even in nativity scenes, as a miniature adult. They were less interested in sentimental portrayals of a tiny infant and more interested in a Godhead with which they could engage.

Religious foundations, chantries and colleges

Wales had only a few of the perpetual chantries which were such a feature of late medieval devotional life in England, and most were of fairly late foundation. Establishing a perpetual chantry was cheaper than founding a monastery, but it still necessitated setting aside land worth at least the clerical minimum stipend (£5 a year by the early sixteenth century) and making arrangements for its administration. In Newport (Monmouthshire) it was the mayor and burgesses who held the land of Jenkin Clark's chantry, leased it out to tenants and presumably nominated the chantry priest.[3] Similar arrangements may have prevailed in other boroughs. Wales also had just over eighty less formal endowed services and stipendiary priests. There were some larger foundations – the colleges of St Peter's Ruthin (Denbighshire), Clynnog Fawr (Caernarfonshire), Holyhead (Anglesey), St Davids (Pembrokeshire), Brecon, and Kidwelly and Llanddewi-brefi (Carmarthenshire); a much larger number of free chapels, some of them with endowed priests; a few hospitals and charitable foundations; and a number of lesser endowments for occasional prayers and masses. Chantries were usually endowed for the recently dead but could also be explicitly for those whose identity was no longer known. Brecon had an endowment to pay a priest to say the mass of St Michael in the town charnel house.[4]

There may also have been less formal establishments that have escaped record. Rhisiart ap Rhys's elegy to Elspeth Matthew of Radur near Cardiff centres around her devotion to the shrine of the Virgin Mary at Penrhys. His claim that

Parlwr gan fŵr niferoedd
i fêls draw fal ostri oedd[5]

is difficult to translate, but she was clearly offering more than the hospitality expected of a gentlewoman. The poet goes on to describe her generosity to the shrine, but does not say that she ever went there. It seems likely that she was accommodating pilgrims, and she may have considered herself to have taken informal vows. Her house may even have been an establishment like the small informal *maisons Dieu* documented by Gilchrist and Oliva in wealthier areas of England.

To some extent, the religious houses had been left behind by changing patterns of devotion, but they were still important in local society. Evidence for this is provided by the numbers of the elite who still chose burial in a religious house rather than in the parish church or cathedral. The alabaster tombs of the Herbert family in Abergavenny Priory are justly famous. There has been some debate about the date and original location of the Gruffydd and Tudur tombs in north-west Wales. The Gruffydd tomb is now in the parish church at Llandygái and the tomb of Gronw Fychan (d. 1382) and his wife Myfanwy is at Penmynydd, but poetic evidence suggests both were originally in the friary church at Llanfaes (or possibly in the case of the Gruffydd tomb in the Dominican friary in Bangor). Religious houses still had moral authority and political power. Richard, Duke of York, was lord of Cydewain through his mother Anne Mortimer. In 1453, during his struggle with Henry VI, he gave a suite of stained glass windows to the Cistercian nuns of Llanllugan (Montgomeryshire). The community there was small and poverty-stricken, but their prayers and moral support were clearly worth having.

The focus of devotional life, though, had moved on. Widening educational opportunities led to an increase in literacy, for women as well as men. Education had traditionally been provided by the monastic communities, but the household was also a place for learning, particularly for women. Some of the chantry foundations also provided basic teaching. By the sixteenth century, the David Mathew service in Llandaf Cathedral paid a priest £5 14s. 10d a year to teach twenty poor children. The north Wales chantry certificates in 1548 even give us a little detail about the curriculum these priests were expected to teach. The trustees of the fraternity of our Lady at Montgomery paid a priest to keep a free school in the town. He was expected to teach the children Latin grammar as well as reading, writing and singing.

Saints, shrines and pilgrimage

The cults of the saints were still an important part of devotional life. In the late fifteenth and early sixteenth centuries there was another burst of hagiographic writing, this time mainly in Welsh, with lives of some very local saints like Ieuan Gwas Padrig, Llawddoc and Curig. A 'Life of St Gwenfrewi' was adapted from the Robert of Shrewsbury's Latin *Life*, and there were translations of the *Lives* of the apostles and other saints from the Latin.

Poetry dedicated to the saints was mainly geared to their shrines and the churches dedicated to them. Some seem to have been commissioned by the incumbents of those churches. Gwilym Gwyn's poem in praise of St Eilian gives a detailed account of the saint's life and miracles (raising the dead, sailing on a stone) before praising Niclas ab Elis, rector of Llaneilian (Anglesey) and clearly the poem's patron.[6] Other poems, though, were commissioned by lay patrons, possibly for performance on the saint's feast day. Lewys Glyn Cothi spoke of feasting on St Llawddog's Day with landowners who lived in a parish dedicated to the saint and had presumably asked him to compose the poem.[7] There were also poems which seem to have been composed out of straightforward devotion by the poet on his own initiative. Some of Lewys

Morgannwg's pleas to the Virgin Mary, though connected with her shrine at Penrhys, resonate with personal concern:

Mair, mam, unair am enaid,
Mair, wrthfawr air wrth fy raid!

[Mary, mother, one word for a soul's sake,
Mary, a powerful word at my hour of need!][8]

Lay devotion was also reflected in the increased popularity of pilgrimage. Welsh pilgrims continued to go to what Lewys Glyn Cothi called the 'tair ffynnon gwynion i'r drugaredd' ['the three blessed fountains of mercy']: Rome, Santiago and the Holy Land. Huw Cae Llwyd took his young son with him to Rome, and they were amazed by the city's treasures. If you wanted to count the relics there, he said, you might just as well try to count the pebbles of the sea. The Welsh poets who went on pilgrimage to Rome in the fifteenth century all commented on the relics that they saw there, including the pillar where Christ was tied to be scourged, nine thorns from the crown of thorns, the vernicle, the sponge, and a piece of the True Cross. Hywel Dafi went to Santiago on the traditional Welsh route, sailing from Tenby to Coruña with a group of pilgrims from south-west Wales. The brass monument of Sir Hugh Johnys and his wife Maud in the church of St Mary, Swansea, recorded with pride that he was 'made knight at the holy sepulcre of our lord ihū crist in the city of Jerusalem the xiiii day of August the yere of oure lord gode MCCCCxlj'.

By the fifteenth century, though we have evidence for an increasing number of shrines within Wales. Some, like Holywell, St Davids and Penrhys, attracted pilgrims from England and possibly from even further afield. Lewys Morgannwg's claim that pilgrims came to Penrhys *hyd môr a thir*, 'over sea and land'[9] may mean no more than that the shrine attracted the devout of the west of England as well as Wales, but the image there was sufficiently important for its destruction to be a national priority in 1538. It has been suggested that shrines like Penrhys could have functioned as stopping places on the route to St Davids: this would be in line with better-documented pilgrimages like the routes to Santiago, where pilgrims could take in other shrines like those of St Martin at Tours or St Mary Magdalene at Vézélay.

There was also a network of shrines of more local importance. These could be focused on the actual burial place of a local saint, on their possessions (the gold torc of St Cynog at Merthyr Cynog, Breconshire, the bell of St Dwynwen at Llanddwyn, Anglesey), on a holy well (Gwenfrewi's well at Holywell is the prime example, but there were numerous others) or even on a painting or carving. The most famous (and in general the most popular) of these were the statues of the Virgin Mary. Usually these seem to have depicted her with the infant Jesus in her arms. Poetry to these statues made it clear that they exemplified the mystery of the incarnation and the virgin birth: writing about the statue at Penrhys, Gwilym Tew spoke of 'forwyn a sy famaeth', the virgin who is a nurse.[10] But there were many others, of native Welsh saints and saints from the international tradition. The great statue of St Derfel with his 'horse' (more likely a stag) at Llandderfel (Merionethshire) attracted as many as six hundred people on the saint's day in 1538. The chapel of St Leonard of Limoges in the parish church at Cwm-iou had an image of the saint which was worth 6s. 8d a year in offerings to the monks of Llanthony.

The greater shrines remained popular throughout the medieval period, but lesser shrines could go in and out of fashion. A papal bull of 1405 described how 'a multitude both of English and Welsh' were resorting to the little island chapel of St Twrog near Beachley, now just on the Gloucestershire side of the border but then within the Welsh march. Offerings at the chapel were valued at £10 in 1400, but in 1535 it was described as worth nothing 'because it stands in the sea', though the following year a diocesan survey valued it at 26s. 8d.[11]

The motivation for pilgrimage was sometimes penance, sometimes pure devotion, but in many (probably most) cases a need for healing or to give thanks for healing received. Dafydd Epynt begged St Cathen of Llangathen to cure him of ague, and an anonymous poet offered candles and song to St Curig of Llangurig in the hope that it would restore his sight. When Anne, wife of Gruffydd ap Rhys of Branas in Llandrillo (Merioneth), commissioned Lewys Glyn Cothi to compose a poem praying for her husband's safe return from Santiago, the poet concluded by saying 'I'w dau gorff gras Duw a gaid' ['God's grace was obtained for their two bodies']. The implication of this may be that they had both been healed through the intercession of St James, and Gruffydd's pilgrimage was to give thanks for that healing.[12]

Miracle stories like those of Thomas Cantilupe described in Chapter 6 were collected into dossiers which were sent to the Vatican as part of the evidence for canonization. Other English shrines made collections of miracles for their own publicity purposes. There are very few such collections in Wales, possibly because so few saints were formally canonized. However, later medieval poems to the saints and their shrines are full of miracle stories, some of which seem to refer to specific events. Lewys Morgannwg's account in one of his poems to the shrine of the Virgin Mary at Penrhys,

> O daw byddar at arall
> Fe glyw llef o glwyf y llall,[13]

> [If a deaf man came up to another
> He would hear a cry from the wound of the other]

seems a bizarre image but he may be referring to an actual miracle story. The motif of a speaking wound is a familiar one from other miracle stories. It occurs in Chaucer's Prioress's Tale: a pious little boy learned the Marian antiphon *Alma Redemptoris Mater* ('Loving Mother of our Saviour'). He sang it daily on his way to school until his neighbours, incited by the devil, killed him. His throat was cut but his wounds opened to allow him to sing his song. The story behind Lewys Morgannwg's poem seems to be a specific event: a deaf man's condition is cured *and* he hears a cry coming from someone else's wounds. The way the story is alluded to, without any narrative detail, suggests that the story was too well known to need repeating, and it is at least possible that Lewys was referring to a recorded miracle story from the shrine.

The beliefs behind church decoration

It is too easy to view these stories of saints and miracles as mere superstition. The same could be said of the late medieval enthusiasm for church decoration. As the poets make clear, though, there was much more complex thinking behind these practices. Much of the art of the later medieval period was squarely focused on the key doctrines of the incarnation and the redemptive sacrifice. There were few depictions of the actual nativity scene: much more common was the Annunciation, the real beginning of the story of human salvation. This was depicted in alabaster tombs and stained glass and even on one of the choir stalls at Gresford.

The great east window at Gresford, the gift of Thomas Stanley, is a complex meditation on the incarnation and Mary's relationship with the Trinity. Much of what is there now is eighteenth- and nineteenth-century restoration, but this does seem to reflect the original. The panels at the top of the main lights depict the three persons of the Trinity, Father, Son and Holy Spirit, and Mary in her relationship with each of them. In the panel depicting Christ the Son, she is shown as a diminutive figure on his knee, symbolizing her complex identity as his mother and (Christ being God) his daughter and bride. The key is in the figure of St John the Evangelist, there to trigger reflection on the opening words of his gospel, 'In the beginning was the Word, and the Word was with God, and the Word was God.' The tracery at the top of the window once contained a tree of Jesse, again reflecting the humanity and the human ancestry of the divine Word. This was complex theology, but below it was a visual representation of the 'Te Deum', the great hymn of praise of the church. The orders of angels, the apostles, the prophets and the martyrs, all join in praising the mystery; the viewers, even if they do not fully understand, can praise.

Elsewhere, the stained glass at Gresford told the apocryphal stories of Mary's life, death and assumption, and the lives of numerous saints. Unusually, there is no surviving depiction of Christ's death. However, the crucifixion formed the centrepiece of most sets of stained glass windows. The emphasis is usually on contemplation rather than narrative. The figure of Christ is often accompanied by motifs which comment on the significance of the story and may link to Bible readings or elements of the liturgy. At Llangadwaladr (Anglesey) the central figure of Christ is flanked by angels who collect his blood in chalices; this will become the wine of the eucharist.

The figure of Christ at Llangadwaladr is thin to emaciation, with the bones showing through the skin. This may have been intended as a pointer to Psalm 22, the 'crucifixion psalm' whose first line Christ quoted on the cross – 'My God, my God, why have you forsaken me':

> I am poured out like water
> and all my bones are out of joint . . .
> a company of evildoers encircle me;
> they have pierced my hands and feet –
> I can count all my bones –
> they stare and gloat over me;
> they divide my garments among them
> and for my raiment they cast lots.

This would have been familiar from the Palm Sunday liturgy. John Mirk mentioned it in his Good Friday sermon, one of those for which there was a Welsh paraphrase with much more detail of Christ's sufferings.[14]

Like many depictions of the crucifixion, the one at Llangadwaladr shows Christ with blood streaming not just from hands, feet and side but all over his body. This probably derives from the story of the woman 'solitary and recluse' who saw Christ in a vision and was told by him that the number of his wounds – from scourge, thorns, nails and spear – equalled the number of fifteen paternosters said daily for a year. An increasingly generous series of indulgences was offered to those repeating the paternoster in this way.

The crucifixion story was also reflected in the almost ubiquitous device of the Arma Christi, shields with the emblematic representation of the pierced hands, feet and heart and the actual implements of Christ's suffering. In their fullest form, these are almost an archaeology of the whole story of the week before the crucifixion. They could include the palms of his triumphal entry into Jerusalem, the lantern from his arrest in the garden at Gethsemane, the pillar and whip of his scourging and the crown of thorns, as well as the nails and cross of the actual crucifixion. They were depicted in stained glass and wall paintings, carved on rood screens and tombs. The little brass plaque to Richard Foxwist, a Caernarfon scrivener, in the old parish church of Llanbeblig, shows him on his deathbed holding a shield with the five wounds clearly displayed. The inscription makes their importance clear: *tenet expirans vulnera quinque tua,* 'while dying he holds your five wounds.'

A more detailed representation of Christ's wounds was found in the Image of Pity, Christ seated on (or rising from) his tomb and pointing to the wound in his side. This may have been based on a Byzantine icon in the church of Santa Croce in Rome. There was a legend that Pope Gregory, celebrating Mass in the church, had a vision of Christ showing his wounds and surrounded by the Instruments of the Passion. This too was depicted all over late medieval churches, in stained glass and wall paintings and on tombs. In the wall painting from the church at Llandeilo Talybont, it was surrounded by prayers including the very popular late medieval prayer 'Jesu mercy, Lady help'.

This emphasis in visual representation and devotional writing on the physicality of the crucifixion and particularly on Christ's blood and the loving enumeration of his wounds is one of the more challenging aspects of late medieval piety for a modern audience. The focus on graphic descriptions of repeated episodes of torture makes for difficult reading and even more difficult viewing. This approach was however very much part of the mystical tradition of the *devotio moderna*. Popular prayers in the later medieval tradition encouraged worshippers to concentrate on each wound in turn and to consider its relevance to their own sins and difficulties. The point was to inspire not guilt and terror but hope: the wounds guaranteed salvation. While Guto'r Glyn at the end of his life spoke powerfully of his fear of the judgement day and of the reproach of Christ's wounds,

Ofn y grog o fewn Ei grys
A'r iawnfarn ar yr enfys . . .
Ofn y loes a fu'n Ei ladd

[Fear of the Rood within its veil
And the true judgement upon the rainbow . . .
Fear of the wound which caused His death],

he still placed his hope in the redemptive sacrifice:

Wrth y Mab a'i wyrthiau maith
Ym mrig aberth mae'r gobaith.

[My hope is in the Son and His great miracles
At the apex of His sacrifice.][15]

Other poets echoed this. In a poem mainly geared to praise of the statue of the Virgin Mary at Penrhys and asking for her help at the day of judgement, it was ultimately to the wounds that Lewys Morgannwg turned:

Ofn y frawd gan fy Nuw fry
Mi archaf i'w bum archoll.

[I fear the judgement of my God above.
I petition his five wounds.][16]

An anonymous poem sometimes attributed to Iolo Goch probably refers to the schematic visual depiction of the wounds:

Pum archoll i'n arfoll ni,
Pum aelod y pum weli.

[Five wounds to receive us,
The five members of the five wounds.][17]

Roods and rood screens

The most striking furnishing of most medieval Welsh churches was the rood screen. This separated the people's part of the church from the chancel, but its main function was as support for the rood, the great carving of the crucifixion. The screen did to some extent obscure the view of the Mass being celebrated at the far side, but it also framed it with significant imagery. Screens were decorated with vine trails, reminders of the wine of the eucharist and of Jesus's description of himself as 'the true vine'. The decoration could also include corn sheaves and oak leaves and acorns. Many of the poets described the beads of the rosary as acorns. Thanking Rhisiart Cyffin ab Ieuan Llwyd for the gift of a rosary, Guto'r Glyn spoke of 'Mes Duw ar fy mys deau', God's acorns on my right finger.[18] The screen at Llanrwst (Denbighshire) had the Instruments of the Passion carved in its tracery, and the screen at Llanengan (Caernarfonshire) had the five wounds on one of its panels.

Some of the most spectacular surviving screens are in remote churches in the mountains and the far west: at Llanengan (Caernarfonshire), Llanegryn (Merionethshire), Llananno (Radnorshire) and Partrishow (Breconshire). Welsh rood screens are different in style from English ones, being more sturdily constructed and boxy, with a virtually flat ceiling under the loft. This meant they could be bigger and capable of accommodating numbers of people. Windows to illuminate the actual loft space, squints through the chancel arch and pierced panelling to the east of the loft suggest use as part of the liturgy. To judge from the surviving corbels, the loft at Llancarfan (Glamorgan) was about nine feet wide, and it may have incorporated a rood altar. Squints through the chancel arch at the level of the rood loft at Colwinston, Llanfrynach and Llangynwyd (all Glamorgan) may also indicate the location of altars. Side altars under the screen survive at Partrishow, and painting on the chancel arch suggests similar altars in the church from Llandeilo Talybont (Glamorgan), now rebuilt at the National History Museum in St Fagans.

All this suggests that for some churches the construction of a substantial rood screen was a way of providing additional side altars, for use on different days or for private services of prayer for the souls of the dead. Altars under the screen would have been in the people's part of the church, and masses celebrated there were almost tangible. The screen did not completely obstruct the view of the high altar, either. Welsh screens had low panels at the base, often pierced with tracery, so that the altar could easily be seen through them. All this was done very much in the context of the carving of the crucifixion above the screen.

Some of the roods were sufficiently famous to attract pilgrims, and there are poems to several of them. The most popular Welsh roods, to judge by the quantity of surviving poetry, were those at Llangynwyd and Brecon. Even more poetry survives to the rood at Chester, near enough to north Wales for a short pilgrimage but with something of the allure of the foreign. Gruffydd ap Maredudd ap Dafydd's poem to the Chester rood sums up much medieval thinking about the history of human sin and redemption. He pulls together the localized carving at Chester, the legends of the True Cross and the physical reality of the body of the crucified Christ in a complex web of literary allusion. Like most of the other poems to roods in Wales, it is meditative rather than descriptive, though Tomas ab Ieuan ap Rhys's poem to the rood at Llangynwyd has been described as 'a compressed crucifixion narrative';[19] it includes Christ's washing of his disciples' feet, Judas' kiss, the nailing to the cross, the offer of vinegar and the piercing of Christ's side. Hywel ap Dafydd ap Ieuan ap Rhys took a similar approach at Brecon. Other poets, though, have a tighter focus on the actual fabric of the cross and Christ's body, the wounds and the outstretched arms. As Bleddyn Fardd said,

> Bei meddyliai dyn a'i feddyliaw
> A fu o ddolur ar Ei ddwylaw
> Gan gethri parawd yn cythruddiaw – cnawd,
> Ef ni wnâi bechawd na'i rybuchaw.

> [If man thought and pondered
> How much pain [Christ's] hands suffered
> From willing nails torturing his flesh,
> He would do no sin nor wish to.][20]

Gruffydd Fain's poem to the rood at Llanbeblig (the old parish church of Caernarfon) also spoke of Christ on the rainbow, judging the world. This, and Guto'r Glyn's description of 'Ofn y Grog o fewn Ei grys, A'r iawnfarn ar yr enfys' ['the Rood within its veil and the true judgement upon the rainbow'], probably refer to paintings of the last judgement on the chancel arch.[21] The surviving doom painting at Wrexham (Denbighshire) and the simpler version on the panels of the rood screen at Llanelian-yn-Rhos (also Denbighshire) give an indication of what would have been visible behind the crucifix in virtually every church. It was a terrifying scene, with bodies coming out of their graves, some being welcomed up to heaven and some pitchforked into the jaws of hell. There was reassurance, though, in the painting and in its position. Christ was usually depicted in the red robes of a judge but showing his wounds, and behind him there could be angels with placards of the Instruments of the Passion, the implements which caused those wounds. The symbolism of the whole sequence of carving and painting was also ultimately one of hope. The nave symbolized earth, the chancel heaven: but it was a very familiar heaven, near at hand and visible. It could be reached by going through the suffering and through the judgement.

Wall paintings

Wall paintings were, of all forms of church decoration, the most 'popular', though the term 'popular religion' is not always helpful. It implies a simple and credulous approach to religious devotion which is not borne out by the evidence. In Wales, for example, some of the most extravagantly apocryphal stories of the Virgin Mary and the martyrs are depicted in churches under the patronage of the devout and aristocratic Margaret Beaufort, cousin and mother of kings. Meanwhile, wall paintings and carvings in remote country churches present complex and sophisticated ideas on Christ's redemptive sacrifice and the eucharist. But wall paintings were 'popular' in the sense that they were comparatively cheap, could be paid for and therefore presumably commissioned by the ordinary parishioners, and had to be painted *in situ*, usually by local craftsmen. Here, if anywhere, we could expect churches to be adorned with the legends of the saints. There are surprisingly few depictions of Welsh saints on church walls, possibly because they were already represented by three-dimensional votive carvings. The three figures on the north wall of the north chapel of Llandeilo Talybont may have been St Teilo with Sts Dewi and Padarn, his companions on his pilgrimage to Rome, but they are very unusual. There are far more of the saints of the international tradition. Many churches would have been dominated by a huge wall painting of St Christopher facing the door. The giant who carried the Christ child across a river, he was the saint who brought Christ to the dying. The promise was that those who saw his picture would not die an evil death that day.

Wall paintings could also echo the meditative focus on Christ's wounds and the story of the redemptive sacrifice. The wall paintings at Llandeilo Talybont included, as well as a St Christopher, St Margaret stabbing the devil with her cross staff and St Roche with his plague sore. The main sequence of paintings, though, seems to have been designed as a meditation on the story of the crucifixion told through the Instruments of the Passion. The wall paintings, furthermore, incorporated a surprising amount of text. As well as captions and speech scrolls, a sequence of prayers functioned as a litany, guiding the viewer around an early version of the stations of the cross. The fact that the majority of those who saw the paintings (and who presumably raised the money for their installation) could not read the texts without help does not seem to have been seen as a problem.

Even the simplest stories of the saints could be freighted with deeper meaning. The story of St Christopher, the giant who wanted to serve the most powerful ruler on earth, reads like pure fantasy. However, the idea of his role at the time of death reflects the medieval belief that death was something to be prepared for. Books of advice were available, with the Latin title *Ars Moriendi*, the art of dying. Often written in Latin, they were illustrated with woodcuts for those who could not read. The Flintshire priest Richard Whitford first wrote his *Dayly Exercise and Experyence of Death* at the request of the Bridgettine community of Syon, but it was published as late as 1537 for a wider lay audience. In particular, Whitford was aware of the temptation to last-minute despair. The Devil would 'come in before you ... and assayle you in many sondry wyse' – by clinging to this world, relying on good deeds rather that the merits of Christ, or falling into despair because of the weight of sinfulness. The reader was encouraged to practise resisting these temptations and to rely on Christ's 'precyous blode with his bytter passyon and his most cruel and shamefull deth'.[22] For this you might need the support which St Christopher would give you.

The *Ars Moriendi* also promised the help of saints who had sinned and been forgiven: Peter, who betrayed Christ; Mary Magdalene, the reformed prostitute; Paul, who persecuted the early Christians; and the good thief, who was promised, 'This day you will be with me in Paradise' (Luke 23:43). Poetry to the roods at Brecon and Llangynwyd suggests that they may have had carvings of the thieves as well as Christ, John and Mary. A group of tombstones with triple crosses in the western Vale of Glamorgan may be based on the design of the Llangynwyd rood or may be additional evidence of the importance of the good thief in encouraging the dying.

The art of the macabre

Wall paintings may also have reflected what seems at times to have been a late medieval obsession with the physicality of death and the decay of the body. Recent discoveries at the parish church of Llancarfan in the Vale of Glamorgan have included a gruesome death figure, a rotting corpse complete with worms and a toad, dragging a fashionably dressed young man into the window embrasure and presumably out into the graveyard. Wales has no surviving examples of the complete dance of death which was so popular in the later Middle Ages, though poetry suggests that the dance at Old St Paul's in London was well known. There are also hints in some of the poetry that there may have been Welsh versions of the dance which have been lost. Describing the dance, Lewys Môn said

Diriaid ydyw'r aderyn
Dwyn sy fyw i'r dawns a fyn ...

[Terrible is the bird,
taking the living into the dance ...],[23]

and Dafydd Trefor described death 'dwyn'r emprwr o dwr 'i dad' ['stealing the emperor from his father's tower]'.[24] These images of a bird and of death dragging someone from a tower cannot be found in any surviving representation of the dance. Both poets were working in Anglesey and they may have been inspired by a painting of the dance on the island, possibly in the Franciscan friary at Llanfaes (the friars made much use of the dance in their preaching). Lewys Môn's *marwnad* to Sir Thomas Salisbury asked, 'Pa loes Angau Powls yngod?' ['What agony the death of Paul's nearby?').[25] If it was 'nearby', close to Sir Thomas Salisbury's home, this may suggest another dance in the Dominican friary at Rhuddlan. Finally, there are vivid images in the poetry of death playing games with humanity. Lewys Morgannwg saw death as a kind of celestial footballer:

Chwarae'r bêl y mae gelyn
Nos a dydd am einioes dyn.
Chwarae ag angau nid gwiw.

[The enemy plays the ball
Day and night for the lifetime of a man.
Playing with death is not worthy.][26]

Wales also had a few examples of the cadaver tombs which were popular in the fifteenth and sixteenth centuries, though none of the particularly gruesome ones with lizards and worms which can be found in continental Europe. It would be easy to view these tombs as yet another example of the obsession with death and decay which seems to characterize the later Middle Ages – what Huizinga famously called 'the mingling of the smell of blood and roses'.[27] However, reminders of the imminence and omnipresence of death also had a positive side: like the wall paintings of St Christopher, they speak to a concern with the 'good death' which is in many ways surprisingly modern.

A case study: the stained glass at Llandyrnog

How was all this pulled together into a coherent worldview? The surviving medieval stained glass at Llandyrnog (Denbighshire) has been assembled into the east window but it contains elements which must have filled windows in other parts of the church. What survives gives us a remarkable compendium of late medieval devotion. Here are the saints of the Welsh tradition: Asaph and David, Gwenfrewi and Marchell. Intriguingly, David is presented as an archbishop, with pallium and cross-staff: was someone making a political point? Gwenfrewi is shown with the sword of her decapitation and the scar which she was said to have borne for the rest of her life, but her status and learning are also indicated. She carries a large book in her left hand. Marchell is one of the early medieval Welsh saints about whom we know nothing certain. According to tradition she was a hermit, the sister of St Tyrnog, to whom Llandyrnog was dedicated, and the nearby parish church of Whitchurch or Eglwyswen was dedicated to her. The stained glass constructs an identity for her, based on the same design as the other female saints in the window: she carries the palm of her 'white martyrdom' (a life of sacrifice and self-abnegation) in her right hand, and in her left, through a fold of her cope, she holds a book.

In the same part of the tracery are saints from the English and international traditions, Catherine and Frideswide. Catherine is one of the most popular and frequently depicted saints in the medieval tradition, but Frideswide is more of an oddity. She was the patron saint of Oxford University: was the rector when the stained glass was installed a former student there? She also appears in Welsh poetry and seems to have been assimilated into the Welsh company of saints: Lewys Glyn Cothi described his patron's wife Gwenhwyfar as 'Saint Ffriswydd Meirionydd wen' – she is the St Frideswide of Merioneth.[28] It is also worth remembering that Catherine was the patron saint of students and scholars. It is seldom possible to work out who was actually responsible for the design of stained glass windows and wall paintings, but it seems reasonable to assume that the parish priest would have had some input.

The window also has episodes from the life of the Virgin Mary. The scene of the Annunciation shows her at a prayer desk with an open book in front of her and with the customary lily between her and the angel. The other scene shows her coronation by her son as queen of heaven. These may be all that survive of a sequence telling her life story, similar to the sequence at Gresford and the much more fragmentary one which must have existed at Hope (Flintshire). Veneration of the Virgin Mary is one of the more problematic aspects of late medieval piety and it could overstep the dividing line between veneration and worship. When Rhisiart ap Rhys, writing about the shrine at Penrhys, claimed,

Delw Fair nid dilafurach
no Mair o nef am roi'n iach

[The image of Mary has no less efficacy
than Mary of heaven to heal],[29]

he had clearly gone too far. However, the distinction between God's power to forgive and Mary's power to intercede was one which the poets usually managed with more skill. The popular late medieval prayer 'Jesu mercy, Lady help', found on a tombstone at Tintern and on the painting of the Image of Pity at Llandeilo Talybont, summed up the orthodox teaching of the church.

Depiction of Mary also had implications for gender identities. On the one hand, she was shown as an obedient and submissive handmaid to God's will. On the other hand, she was allowed to be shown as a woman of learning: as well as the books which appear in virtually all depictions of the Annunciation, her early life was often illustrated by a picture of her mother teaching her to read. Her assumption into heaven and her coronation were equally complex. On the one hand this part of the story recognized her unique status as the virginal mother of the Godhead. On the other hand, it was hard not to depict her as a figure of power.

There was a surprising amount of text in medieval stained glass and even on wall paintings. The Annunciation usually included the words of Gabriel's greeting to Mary, 'Ave Maria, gratia plena, dominus tecum', in a speech scroll from the angel's mouth. This was the opening of one of the prayers that every medieval person was supposed to learn, first in their own vernacular then in Latin. For

Guto'r Glyn it was the 'anrheg o'r Chwegair', the gift of those six words, which began the story of human salvation.[30] Visual depiction of the Annunciation could serve as a reminder of this. Without what we would describe as literacy, the ability to decode unfamiliar text, the medieval viewer could probably learn to recognize the A. and M. of the Ave Maria (the letters often picked out in red) and would be reminded to repeat the prayer. The windows at Llandyrnog once included another of the core texts that the medieval parishioner was expected to learn, the Apostles' Creed. The simplest of the church's statements of belief, this was believed to have been written by the apostles themselves. They were usually depicted with their own clauses of the creed, on speech scrolls or banners. As with the Ave Maria, the viewer would know the clauses of the creed by the apostles associated with them rather than the other way around.

At the heart of the window, as it was at the heart of late medieval piety, is the figure of the crucified Christ. Blood streams from his wounds, but the angels hovering at the bottom of the picture have empty chalices. Instead, the blood becomes ribbons of scarlet leading to panels depicting the seven sacraments of the Catholic church. Not all the depictions of the sacraments survive. A few fragments may come from the scenes of penance and the eucharist. Baptism and confirmation are missing, but marriage, ordination and extreme unction are virtually complete. The scenes of marriage and extreme unction are particularly touching in their humanity. Marriage shows a young couple in their best clothes, surrounded by friends and the officiating priests. The stream of blood extends down to the young woman's heart. In the scene of ordination, the blood touches the hands of the ordaining bishop. Extreme unction shows a sick man in bed, naked except for a nightcap, with the priest holding his hand. In the foreground is a commode, a piece of furniture which often appears in these scenes to signify a sickroom. The priest has brought chalice, paten and holy oil, and a small crucifix. This was not to terrify but to comfort. The *Order for the Visitation of the Sick* directed the priest to hold the cross before the dying person's eyes 'that in the image they may adore their redeemer and have in mind his passion, which he endured for their sins'.[31] Like Richard Foxwist's plaque with the five wounds, this was to inspire not so much guilt as reassurance.

———

The church on the eve of the Reformation

It is tempting to see the early sixteenth century merely as a preparation for the events of the 1530s and the long process of change in the British church. Historians have judged regions of England and Wales by how ready they were for those changes, or how determinedly they resisted them. We need to set this aside and consider the Welsh church in the early Tudor period without the distorting lens of hindsight. From this perspective it is clear that it was a period of revival, economic as well as spiritual, after the famines and plagues of the fourteenth century and the trauma of the Glyndŵr uprising and its suppression. Even for the religious houses, traditionally regarded as virtually obsolete by this time, there are clear signs of recovery. This can be seen most clearly in evidence of rebuilding. Neath and Llantarnam were both given money for glazing their windows, and Tintern received several bequests specifically for building work. A rebuilding programme at the Carmelite friary in Denbigh had barely started when the house was closed in 1538. In some cases, of course, rebuilding was evidence of previous neglect. As late as 1528, Abbot John ap Rhys of Strata Marcella issued an indulgence to raise funds for the rebuilding of his abbey, the 'greater part' of which was 'broken down'.[32]

Some of the rebuilding reflects the diminished size and changing role of the communities: the monastic dormitory at Valle Crucis, for example, was converted into accommodation for the abbot and his guests. There was also a desire for more physical comfort (fireplaces, panelling) and for privacy. These have been seen as evidence of deteriorating standards, but Anne Müller has recently made the point that they also reflect a move towards interiority in line with the development of the *devotio moderna* in lay society: '[T]he individual cell was to become an important place for the monk to build on his inner landscape so that he could encounter God.'[33]

Monastic churches were redecorated and furnished with carvings and choir stalls. Some of this is evidence for local patronage. The magnificent wooden Jesse at Abergavenny is all that remains of what must have been a staggering piece of carving, richly painted and gilded. It was probably funded by Richard Herbert of Ewyas, whose tomb can still be seen in the church. The choir stalls, too, and the lost rood screen, may have been provided by the Herberts. Some of the decorative detail – pomegranates, Prince of Wales feathers – could suggest royal patronage, but they are more likely a local celebration of the marriage of Prince Arthur and Catherine of Aragon in 1501.

Some of the rebuilding, though, must have been funded by improvements in monastic administration and estate management. Traditionally, historians have interpreted the evidence for monastic leasing patterns in the sixteenth century as bordering on corruption, an attempt to tie up lands for short-term profit in anticipation of the Dissolution. Where we have full collections of monastic leases (as opposed to post-Suppression records), the picture is often more complex. Late sixteenth-century surveys of Llantarnam's former granges in the hills of north-west Monmouthshire suggest a determined strategy of leasing farmsteads for long terms from the end of the fifteenth century.[34] This surely responded to the very gradual rise in population and the possibility of securing tenants for deserted copyhold land, and indicates a prudent desire to tie up tenancies for as long as possible.

As well as providing accommodation and patronage for the poets, monastic communities took a more active role in the cultural developments of the period. Guto'r Glyn praised Abbot Dafydd of Valle Crucis as a poet as well as a leader, 'thrwy'r gerdd athro', a teacher through poetry.[35] Dafydd ab Owain of Margam (where he may have been prior) was praised for writing an 'antem i Fair mewn tôn', probably a setting of the *Salve Regina* and possibly polyphonic (in spite of the fact that the Cistercians had earlier been opposed to musical elaboration).[36] Dafydd Nanmor described polyphony at Strata Florida – 'sŵn byrdwn lle bo / Trebl a mên' ['the sound of burden where there is treble and mean'].[37] Lewys Glyn Cothi's *marwnad* for Gwladys ferch Dafydd Gam, wife of Sir Wiliam ap Tomos of Raglan, spoke of her funeral liturgy at Abergavenny Priory, with 'organau oll hyd frig nef ag arianllais, gôr unllef' ['organs the whole length of heaven on high and silver voices, a choir in one voice'], suggesting simpler singing but accompanied by organ music.[38] Hywel Dafi mentioned an organ at the Dominican friary in Brecon, and the Cistercians of Strata Marcella, Neath, Valle Crucis and Cwm-hir all had organs by the 1520s.

There were some obvious targets for criticism, in the secular church as well as in the religious houses. The secular church was desperately underfunded, partly as a result of the agricultural poverty of the country, but mainly because so much parochial income in the south and east was diverted to religious houses. Partly as a result, clerical standards of education were low. There were very few graduates, though this does not seem to have prevented the parish clergy from teaching their congregations the basics of the faith. For the parish ministry, university education would have been of limited value. Teaching at Oxford and Cambridge was in Latin, and the culture of the universities was English: this would have left young men ill-prepared for the task of communicating with a Welsh-speaking congregation.

The Welsh dioceses were the poorest in the province. Most bishops were absentees, many of them heads of religious houses in England. Diocesan administration was weak: neither Llandaf nor St Davids cathedrals had a dean. Instead, the precentor presided over the running of the cathedral. This did however make it easier for Welsh clergy to take positions of authority. All the precentors of St Davids were Welsh after 1437, and so were most of the chancellors. St Asaph also had a succession of Welsh deans and chancellors. At Llandaf the clergy associated with the cathedral in the earlier part of the sixteenth century included Hugh Jones, the future bishop, and Henry Morgan, younger son of the Tredegar family. Both these men had studied at Oxford, and there is some evidence to suggest that their influence spread through the diocese. As well as their positions at the cathedral, some of these educated men had parish connections and responsibilities. Jones was rector of Tredynog (Monmouthshire). In his will in 1543, Henry Morgan left his Bible commentary and all his divinity books to Edward David, the vicar of Usk. (It is worth noting that David was not a graduate, but he was clearly capable of reading and valuing academic books.) Morgan's copy of Polydore Virgil's *Historia* and all his other books went to his former colleague Hugh Jones.[39]

Robert ap Rhys of Plas Iolyn in Ysbyty Ifan (Denbighshire), younger son of one of the heroes of the battle of Bosworth in 1485, was an ordained priest, chancellor and vicar-general of his home diocese of St Asaph and Thomas Wolsey's personal chaplain. He was also married and had at least sixteen children. Two of his sons were successive abbots of Conwy (and one may have been married while he was abbot), and a third was abbot of Strata Marcella. To regard this as corruption, though, may be to miss the point. They were a powerful local family, and this seems to have been what was expected of them. The poets of north Wales praised Robert for both 'dysg a nerth', learning and power.[40] Lewis Môn even claimed 'Iaith Ebryw i'th fyw o'th fin', 'the Hebrew language is alive on your lips'.[41] If true (and it is probably poetic exaggeration), this would make him a pioneer of Renaissance learning in Wales.

The revival of monastic life was paralleled by a revival in the production of devotional literature for a lay readership. As well as the huge corpus of devotional poetry, there was prose like Huw Pennant's translation of the *Life* of St Ursula and Gutun Owain's diligent transcriptions of saints' *Lives* and other texts. Churches were also accumulating collections of books. Some were liturgical books (including a printed Mass book left by John Morgan, bishop of St Davids, to the parish church at Llandyfaelog, Breconshire, in 1504), but others were of more general interest. William Geffery's bequest of a rather eclectic collection – the *Polychronicon*, *The Fall of Princes*, *Dives and Pauper* and the *Liber Sancte Terre* – was to be chained in the parish church of Swansea 'in such place as the warden thinks best'.[42] This was the beginnings of a public library.

There is little or no suggestion of any desire for religious change in early sixteenth-century Wales. All the evidence of surviving buildings, wills and poetry suggests contentment with what the late medieval church was offering. Virtually all the wills of landowners and leading townsmen alike left money for prayer for their souls. Even those who did not leave money explicitly for prayer for their souls usually left other bequests to the church, and it is reasonable to assume that they expected these to be rewarded by prayer. Another Anglesey man, Hugh Bulkeley of Beaumaris, left nothing for prayer for his soul but made several bequests to the rebuilding of Beaumaris church and to the friars of Llanfaes and provided for the education of an apparently unrelated young man as a priest.[43] Much more common, though, were simple bequests of money for prayer for the soul for a year or so. Five pounds a year for this seems to have been the standard rate. There is almost a sense of tranquillity in these Welsh wills;[44] while bequests for intercessory prayer are almost universal, they are less generous than those in (for example) Bristol. This may even link to the more optimistic attitudes to the fate of the soul in some (though not all) of the Welsh poetry of the period.

Work on rebuilding and redecorating churches continued into the early sixteenth century and even beyond. The wall paintings from the church at Llandeilo Talybont, imaginatively recreated at the National History Museum in St Fagans, date from the 1520s. Work on the well and chapel at Holywell may have been begun by Lady Margaret Beaufort or her Stanley relatives, but the dendrochronology of the roof timbers suggests that work continued into the late 1520s, possibly under the patronage of the nearby Basingwerk Abbey. The tower at Cwmcarfan (Monmouthshire) is dated to 1525 or later by the will of Thomas ab Iorwerth ap Hopkin of Monmouth, who left ten marks towards its building.

For all their apparent contentment with the late medieval church, though, the people of Wales offered very little resistance to the great changes of the sixteenth century. Part of the explanation may lie with pragmatic politics: the gentry, whose leadership was crucial to any resistance, benefited so much from the first of the 'Acts of Union' and were clearly reluctant to abandon what they had gained. David Williams's judgement that 'men will abandon so lightly only what they lightly hold'[45] clearly underestimates the depth of popular piety in the early sixteenth century. The problem may have lain with the nature of that piety. It was essentially reflective and meditative rather than argumentative, and left its adherents without the resources to debate and challenge new ideas. Nevertheless, the Welsh response to the Reformation remains one of the great puzzles of our history.

Notes

1   Saunders Lewis, *Braslun o Hanes Llenyddiaeth Gymraeg* (Cardiff: University of Wales Press, 1932), ch. 7.
2   *Gwaith Tudur Aled*, edited by T. Gwynn Jones (Cardiff: University of

Wales Press, 1926), vol. 2, pp. 523–6.

[3] London, TNA, E112/107/48/6.

[4] TNA, E178/3503.

[5] *Gwaith Rhys Brydydd a Rhisiart ap Rhys*, edited by Morgan Williams and Eurys I. Rowlands (Cardiff: University of Wales Press, 1976), p. 51.

[6] Barry Lewis, *Medieval Welsh Poems to Saints and Shrines* (Dublin: Institute for Advanced Studies, 2015), pp. 73–5, 344–6.

[7] *Gwaith Lewys Glyn Cothi*, edited by Dafydd Johnston (Cardiff: University of Wales Press, 1995), p. 141.

[8] Lewis, *Medieval Welsh Poems to Saints and Shrines*, pp. 125–7, 396–8.

[9] *Gwaith Lewys Morgannwg*, edited by A. Cynfael Lake (Aberystwyth: Canolfan Uwchefrydiau Cymreig a Cheltaidd, 2004), vol. 2, p. 503.

[10] Anne Elizabeth Jones, 'Gwilym Tew: astudiaeth destunol a chymharol o'i lawysgrif, Peniarth 51, ynghyd ag ymdriniaeth â'i farddoniaeth' (unpublished Ph.D. thesis, University of Wales, 1980), 448.

[11] *Calendar of Inquisitions Post Mortem . . . vol. xviii, 1–6: Henry IV (1399–1405)*, edited by J. L. Kirby (London: HMSO, 1987), p. 77; *Valor Ecclesiasticus Temp. Henricus VIII Auctoritate Regia Institutus,* edited by J. Caley and J. Hunter (6 vols, London: Record Commission, 1810–34), vol. 2 (1814), p. 501; *The Register of Charles Bothe, Bishop of Hereford (1516–1535),* edited by A. T. Bannister (Hereford: Cantilupe Society, 1921), p. 367.

[12] Lewis, *Medieval Welsh Poems to Saints and Shrines*, pp. 95–7, 366–8.

[13] *Lewys Morgannwg*, edited by Lake, vol. 2, p. 504.

[14] Henry Lewis, 'Darn o'r Ffestival', *Transactions of the Honourable Society of Cymmrodorion, 1923–4: Supplementary Volume* (London: Honourable Society of Cymmrodorion, 1925), p. 60.

[15] *http://www.gutorglyn.net/gutorglyn/poem/?poem–selection=118* (accessed 30 March 2020).

[16] *Lewys Morgannwg*, edited by Lake, vol. 2, p. 508. Lewis, *Medieval Welsh Poems to Saints and Shrines* pp. 127, 398, has a slightly different reading.

[17] *Cywyddau Iolo Goch ac Eraill*, edited by Henry Lewis, Thomas Richards and Ifor Williams (Cardiff: University of Wales Press, 1972), p. 98.

[18] *http://www.gutorglyn.net/gutorglyn/poem/?poem–selection=059* (accessed 30 March 2020).

[19] Christine James, '"Y grog ddoluriog loywrwm": golwg ar y canu i Grog Llangynwyd', *Llên Cymru*, 29 (2006), 89–90.

[20] Lewis, *Welsh Poetry and English Pilgrimage*, p. 3.

[21] Jones, *Celtic Britain*, pp. 557–8, *http://www.gutorglyn.net/gutorglyn/poem/?poem–selection=118* (accessed 30 March 2020); James, '"Y grog

ddoluriog loywrym'".

22 Richard Whitford, *A Werke for Householders: A Dayly Exercyse and Experyence of Death*, edited by J. Hogg (Salzburg: Anglo-American Institute, 1979), pp. 93–4.

23 *Gwaith Lewys Môn*, edited by E. I. Rowlands (Cardiff: University of Wales Press, 1975), p. 298.

24 Irene George, 'The Poems of Syr Dafydd Trefor', *Transactions of the Anglesey Antiquarian Society* (1935), 102.

25 *Lewys Môn*, edited by Rowlands, no. 59 (lines 1–2), p. 208.

26 *Lewys Morgannwg*, edited by Lake, vol. 2, no. 76 (lines 49–51), p. 420, translation by David Hale (to whom I am grateful for this reference). For further discussion of this theme see Madeleine Gray and David Hale, 'Dancing and Dicing with Death: literary evidence for some lost wall paintings in Wales', *Transactions of the Ancient Monuments Society*, 65 (2021), 7–19.

27 Johann Huizinga, *The Autumn of the Middle Ages*, translated by Rodney J. Payton and Ulrich Mammitzsch (Chicago: University of Chicago Press, 1996), p. 24.

28 *Lewys Glyn Cothi*, edited by Johnston, p. 507.

29 *Gwaith Rhys Brydydd a Rhisiart ap Rhys*, edited by J. M. Williams and E. I. Rowlands (Cardiff: University of Wales Press, 1976), p. 14.

30 *http://www.gutorglyn.net/gutorglyn/poem/?poem–selection=118* (accessed 30 March 2020).

31 Quoted in Eamon Duffy, *The Stripping of the Altars: Traditional Religion in England, 1400–1580* (New Haven: Yale University Press, 1992), p. 314.

32 David H. Williams, *The Welsh Cistercians* (Leominster: Gracewing, 2001), pp. 68–9. Two copies survive: BL Egerton 2410 f. 4 and NLW Printed Books W.s. 1528.

33 Anne Müller, 'Interpretations of Claustral Spaces with Special Reference to Dormitories', in *Monastic Wales: New Approaches*, edited by Janet Burton and Karen Stöber (Cardiff: University of Wales Press, 2013), p. 240.

34 NLW MS 17008D, calendared with introduction in Madeleine Gray, 'Henry, earl of Pembroke's Survey of the Manor of Mynyddislwyn in 1570', *National Library of Wales Journal*, 30/2 (Winter 1997), 171–96.

35 *http://www.gutorglyn.net/gutorglyn/poem/?poem–selection=118* (accessed 30 March 2020).

36 BL Cotton Domitian A iv, f. 242r–v, discussed in Ann Parry Owen, 'Cywydd gofyn cloc gan Ddafydd ab Owain o Fargam ar ran Morys o ardal Y Fenni', *Llên Cymru*, 35 (2012), 3–18.

[37] Thomas Roberts and Ifor Williams, *The Poetical Works of Dafydd Nanmor* (Cardiff: University of Wales Press, 1923), p. 73.

[38] *Lewys Glyn Cothi*, edited by Johnston, p. 248.

[39] TNA, PROB 11/29/270.

[40] *Gwaith Tudur Aled*, vol. 1, edited by T. Gwynn Jones (Cardiff: University of Wales Press, 1926), p. 203.

[41] *Lewys Môn*, edited by Rowlands, p. 179.

[42] TNA PROB 11/14/333.

[43] TNA PROB 11/15/255.

[44] The term is Rhianydd Biebrach's, in a lecture to the Bangor Conference of Celtic Studies, July 2012.

[45] David Williams, *A History of Modern Wales* (London: Murray, 1950), p. 46.

Chapter 8

Reformation Wales, 1530–1603

DAVID CERI JONES

While there may have been little evidence of dissatisfaction with the performance of the late medieval church in early sixteenth-century Wales, and few signs of sympathy with the revolutionary evangelical theological opinions emanating from Martin Luther's Wittenberg around 1517, the Welsh accepted Henry VIII's separation from the Roman Catholic church in the early 1530s with a deafening lack of complaint. Yet this is not to claim that the Welsh, at least in any great numbers, immediately became enthusiastic Protestants. Acceptance of royal policy and enthusiasm for sweeping religious change were not necessarily the same thing. Recent historians of the Reformation have become reluctant to view the religious changes of the mid-sixteenth century in isolation from longer–term developments. Some argue that they were part of a profound renegotiation of the role of the church within western European society, and another development in the insatiable quest for purer expressions of faith between the fourteenth and the eighteenth centuries. In Wales, the religious disruptions of the 1530s were just the beginning of a long journey by which evangelicals, as the early Protestants were most commonly known, sought to transform Wales and the Welsh into a nation of Protestants. It was to be a tortuous process with many false dawns, and did not begin to be realised until the evangelical revivals of the middle decades of the eighteenth century – the moment when, as Glanmor Williams so strikingly commented, 'the Reformation came of age in Wales'.[1]

Henry VIII and the break with Rome

The uncoupling of the English church from the authority of the Roman Catholic church was not something precipitated by any spiritual epiphany on the part of an English theologian, but rather emanated from the political and marital difficulties of Henry VIII. Needing to secure a male heir, Henry, with the assistance of his chief minister Thomas Cromwell, separated the English church from the oversight of the bishop of Rome in 1533, installing himself as 'Supreme Head of the Church of England'. Once Henry had married his new love Anne Boleyn in secret in 1532, Thomas Cranmer, the archbishop of Canterbury, was free to declare Henry's marriage to his brother's widow, Catherine of Aragon, null and void, and his new marriage to Anne entirely legitimate. Thus over a thousand years of papal authority in England and Wales came to an abrupt end. However, Henry was no Protestant, at least in theological terms, having recently been granted the title of 'Defender of the Faith' by the Pope for his denunciation of Martin Luther's theological innovations in 1527. Yet there were some within the royal court, most notably Anne herself as well as Thomas Cromwell, who sought to further the cause of Protestant reform clandestinely, being careful not to arouse the suspicions of the unpredictable and volatile Henry. For them the cause of Protestant reform proved to be a case of one step forwards followed by two steps back. All the same, the direction of travel was unmistakable.

In Wales these events were barely noticed by the majority of people. Remote from the main centres of power and lacking many of the institutions that were necessary for Protestant ideas to take root, not least larger towns and cities and well-connected universities, Wales proved unsurprisingly conservative in religious matters. Henry's initial break with Rome registered barely a murmur of opposition. The poet Lewys Morganwg was a notable exception: for him the split from Rome was nothing less than an act of treachery, Henry having being duped by his new wife Anne:

Gwall Lloegr oedd golli i Gred
Gwae'r ynys pan goroned.

[England's error was losing its Faith;
Woe the island when she was crowned.][2]

For most the first real indication of dramatic religious change occurred when Henry closed down the monasteries. As has been shown in earlier chapters, these religious houses had been at the centre of Welsh spiritual, intellectual and cultural life for many centuries, and some have seen their forced closure as an act of wanton destruction: 'an orgy of licensed vandalism worthy of the Taliban at worst'.[3] Yet, in reality, by the mid-1530s the Welsh monasteries were a pale reflection of what they had once been. There had been some efforts at rebuilding, not least following the destruction that accompanied the Glyndŵr rebellion at the beginning of the fifteenth century, but by the time that Cromwell's inspectors visited, the Welsh monastic houses were poor, chronically undermanned and in many cases dilapidated too. The survey they produced, the *Valor Ecclesiasticus* (1535) did not major in prurient detail on the moral failings of some of the inhabitants of the monasteries, but argued instead that the poverty of the Welsh religious houses made it impossible for them to function effectively any longer.

Consequently, in March 1536 all forty-seven religious houses in Wales with an income of less than £200 a year were dissolved. Just three houses were temporarily spared, Strata Florida, Neath and Whitland, and the majority of the 250 monks, friars and nuns in Wales slipped into relative obscurity, many with comfortable state pensions.[4] Within a few years the few surviving houses had also been closed. There was little resistance, and few if any voices were raised in protest. In one stroke Henry had successfully removed one of the potential sources of opposition to his religious settlement. But he had also done much more than that; he had tapped into an important source of revenue, and in carefully disposing of monastic assets he was able to purchase the loyalty of those who became the chief beneficiaries of one of the largest disposals of land and property England and Wales had ever seen.

Many of the Welsh gentry were able to snap up monastic lands and buildings, acquiring in the process a powerful reason to remain loyal to the king. In the sprawling St Davids diocese, the eighteen religious houses were easy pickings for well-resourced and politically well-connected individuals. In Pembrokeshire, John Bradshaw, originally from Radnorshire, acquired St Dogmaels and its dependent priory at Caldey, property he soon augmented with the addition of other lands in the county.[5] Further north in Cardiganshire Richard Devereux had acquired Strata Florida after its suppression in 1539, and from his base at the former bishop's palace at Lamphey near Pembroke, became an important patron of Protestantism, especially in the southern parts of the St Davids diocese.[6] In Monmouthshire the imposing Tintern Abbey was leased in perpetuity to the earl of Worcester, while other monastic sites were leased to entrepreneurial local landowners.[7] In Glamorgan, the county in which were to be found some of the best-endowed religious houses in the whole of Wales, a small group of leading families were able to cement their position by the acquisition of prime real estate. Among the most successful was Sir Rice Mansell who, over a seventeen-year period, managed to acquire the bulk of the land that had been attached to Margam abbey, and Sir Edward Carne who took possession of Ewenni priory in the fertile vale of Glamorgan.[8]

If the dissolution enhanced the economic prestige of the Welsh gentry, Henry's desire to shore up the security of his realm, not least because of the threat of a Spanish invasion designed to drag England back into the Catholic fold, led to the strengthening of their political position also. The so-called 'Acts of Union' of 1536 and 1543 completed the long-overdue incorporation of Wales into the governmental structures of the English state, a process which had been gradually taking place since at least the Conquest in 1282 if not before. Passed, as the preamble to the 1536 act declared, out of Henry's 'singular zeal, love and favour'[9] towards the Welsh people, the act swept away the still quasi-independent marcher lordships and extended English county government to the whole of Wales. The Welsh gained twenty-seven members of Parliament, representing the new shires and boroughs of the country, and English common law became the norm, displacing the ancient native laws of Hywel Dda. The successful implementation of this new system of government was dependent on the active cooperation of the Welsh gentry, acting as the Crown's servants in Wales. Welsh loyalty to Henry, something that could be traced back to his father, Henry Tudor's deliberate emphasising of his Welsh ancestry as he made his bid for the throne in 1485, ensured that the twists and turns of Tudor royal policy, not least in religious matters, were accepted with little opposition in Wales. The Welsh regarded the Tudor monarchs as their own, and as rulers who had their best interests at heart.

Yet the response to the initial efforts to introduce a more overt Protestantism into Wales in the middle decades of the sixteenth century was a mixture of bewilderment and confusion. For the Welsh man or woman in the pew the clamp-down on certain religious practices in the first and second Royal Injunctions of 1536 and 1538 was the moment when the radical nature of the new religious settlement was brought home to them with real force. These documents, which in effect represented guidance to the clergy over what was acceptable and what was not, forbade such commonplace practices as pilgrimages, the offering of money and candles to images and relics, and the use of beads in prayer.[10] Some of the most frequented Welsh pilgrimage sites were also destroyed. These included the shrine to the Virgin Mary at Penrhys in the Rhondda,[11] and at Llandderfel in Merioneth the wooden statue of Derfel Gadarn, the sixth-century monk who, according to legend, had been a warrior in the armies of King Arthur.[12] Here was the deliberate removal of much that had been familiar and comforting for reasons that were not always fully understood.[13]

The arrival in Wales of committed champions of Protestantism could not but make an impact. The election of William Barlow, a radical Protestant and close confidant of Cromwell, first to the priory of Haverfordwest in 1534, and then as bishop of St Davids from 1536, represented the first real effort to advance Protestantism in Wales. Barlow repeatedly denounced the clergy of his diocese. Not one of them he wrote 'sincerely preacheth God's word', while the inhabitants of the diocese were characterized by 'enormous vices . . . misordered living and heathen idolatry'.[14] Barlow's reforming programme was uncompromising. In an attempt to weaken the hold of what he regarded as Catholic superstition he proposed moving the focus of the see of St David's to Carmarthen, thereby ending the cathedral, 'a delicate daughter of Rome, naturally resembling the mother in shameless confusion',[15] as a site of pilgrimage and veneration. The second element of his programme was the endowment of a number of grammar schools and the provision of Protestant preachers, financed by some of the resources released after the suppression of religious houses in the diocese. It was a radical, perhaps even visionary, plan that faced in two directions: on the one hand it sought the entire eradication of the surviving remnants of Roman Catholicism, and on the other its replacement with a literate Bible-based Protestantism. With the protection and support of Cromwell, and Henry's own desire to weaken any hankering after the pope throughout his realm, Barlow was able to attempt a root-and-branch reform of his diocese.

However, fierce resistance from the conservative cathedral chapter dogged Barlow's episcopate, frustrating his efforts at every turn. When royal policy tacked in a more conservative direction after the fall of Cromwell in 1540, Barlow found himself exposed, and forced to act more circumspectly. There is no doubt that many of Barlow's innovations were deeply unpopular; outside some Pembrokeshire coastal towns there were few of the literate middling sorts of people necessary for the effective spread of the Protestant message after all. For most, radical Protestantism was both alien and unintelligible. While Barlow's Welsh career revealed the difficulties which reformers faced in converting more than a tiny minority to the new faith, his so-called 'Protestant experiment',[16] did point to some of the strategies that would need to be adopted if Welsh Protestants were to be more successful in the future. In this respect, Barlow was a genuine pioneer.

For Barlow the chief barrier to the reception of Protestantism was 'the hungry famine of heryng the worde of God and desolate scarcite of true preachers'.[17] But that was only part of the problem. When many of the early Protestants attempted to preach sermons in Wales, they did so in a language which was, with the exception of the more Anglicized areas of southern Pembrokeshire and the border counties, incomprehensible to the monoglot Welsh-speaking population. All too easily the new faith came to be regarded in the minds of many as alien, as the *ffydd Saeson* (the 'English faith'). There were, however, some bishops who recognized the problem of this misconception, none more so than Arthur Bulkeley, who became bishop of Bangor in 1541. He actively promoted the use of the vernacular in his diocese, calling on all the clergy under his care to learn the Creed, the Ten Commandments, the Ave Maria and the Paternoster in Welsh.[18] It was to be leadership of this nature that encouraged some in Wales to begin the process of translating parts of the Bible into Welsh. An anonymous south Walian scholar, using the Latin Vulgate and William Tyndale's recent English translation, had begun the task of rendering some parts of Scripture in Welsh, albeit it seems solely for his own personal use.[19] In the closing months of Henry VIII's reign, Sir John Price of Brecon criticized the Welsh clergy for their many failures, and lamented the fact that 'the great part of my nation the Welsh are in incalculable darkness for want of knowledge of God and His commandments'.[20] His answer was the first Welsh-language printed book, *Yny lhyvyr hwnn* ('In this book') (1546), containing translations of some of the best-known passages from the New Testament.[21] It was a small step, but a critical one in terms of the indigenization of the Protestant faith in Wales.

The Edwardian radical Reformation

The reign of Edward VI (1547–53) witnessed an intensification of the Reformation in England and therefore in Wales too. It represented, in the words of Diarmaid MacCulloch, a genuine 'religious revolution' as a small but militant Protestant leadership transformed the church into the envy of European Protestantism.[22] If Protestant reformers had proceeded gingerly under the unpredictable gaze of Edward's father, they were given free rein during the rules of the Duke of Somerset (1547–9) and the Duke of Northumberland (1550–3), in turn the leaders of the regency council who oversaw the realm on Edward's behalf, who of course died before he reached an age to rule alone.

The Edwardian programme of religious reform had two facets. There was firstly, the continued destruction of still more aspects of the medieval religious inheritance. This included the further confiscation of church property by means of the Chantries Act (1547). Chantries were chapels, often privately endowed, and sometimes purpose-built, in which prayers for the departed could be offered in perpetuity. Although there were relatively few of them in Wales by the middle of the sixteenth century, the suppression of those that still functioned not only further undermined belief in purgatory, but also provided the Crown with much-needed additional revenue, and another opportunity to cement support in the localities through the sale of the land and property attached to them.[23] Alongside was the continued clamp-down on Roman Catholic ceremonies, the banning of the observance of many saints' days, the destruction of images and the tearing down of altars. But there was also the creation of something new, a fully Reformed Church of England. Priests were soon allowed to marry, indeed encouraged to do so. The Latin Mass was replaced by a vernacular communion service, and the laity were allowed to partake of both the bread and the wine. Yet in Wales the English-language service was even more incomprehensible than its Latin predecessor which at least had the virtue of familiarity. Cranmer, the archbishop of Canterbury, fortified and emboldened by an influx of European Protestants, rewrote the liturgy of the English church, publishing his first 'Book of Common Prayer' in March 1549. It was superseded a few years later by a replacement prayer book, shorn of some of the ambiguous language of the first, and buttressed by Cranmer's 'Forty–Two Articles', a summary of the doctrinal position of the new church, coloured at this point by Cranmer's preference for a Calvinistic understanding of the doctrines of salvation.

For many in Wales, this was the moment when the full ramifications of the adoption of Protestantism became apparent. Much that had been commonplace and reassuring for centuries was lost for good. Gauging responses to these changes is notoriously difficult. Much weight is placed by historians on the output of a small number of prominent Welsh poets, but the evidence of their work can be difficult to read since they often wrote in support of the opinions of their patrons. Having said this, during the reign of Edward some common themes are detectable. Siôn Brwynog, a deeply conservative voice and perhaps one of the most prolific of the mid-sixteenth-century bards, gave expression to the sense of bewilderment which many in Wales felt at the pace of religious change. He lamented the confusion brought about by the new English-speaking clergy and an English-language liturgy:

> Wrth y bwrdd o nerth ei ben
> A bregetha brygawthen . . .
> On'd oedd dost, un dydd a dau,
> I'r llawr fwrw'r allorau?

> [By the table in full voice
> He preaches in jabbering sort . . .
> Was it not a bitter blow to have cast down the altars
> To the ground within a day or two?][24]

Among the consequences of these religious changes was, in his view, a marked lowering of the spiritual temperature throughout Wales:

> Oerder yn yn amswer ni,
> Yr iâ glas yw'r eglwysi . . .
> Côr ni bydd cŵyr yn y byd
> Na channwyll yn iach ennyd.

> Yr eglwys a'i haroglau
> Yn wych oedd ein hiachau.
> Yr oedd gynt arwydd a gaid
> Olew yn eli enaid.

> [There is a coldness in our times,
> the churches are as cold as ice . . .
> There is no wax nor a single candle
> for a moment in the chancel of any church.

> The church that with its incense
> well healed us.
> There was once oil as a symbol of
> balm for the soul.][25]

While some lamented the disappearance of the 'Old Faith', few in Wales publicly opposed the religious changes. Despite the bishop of St Davids, Robert Ferrar's, 'fear of tumult'[26] at the pace of religious change, no prominent Welsh figures were spurred into action by the conservative Prayer Book, the Western rebellion in Devon and Cornwall, or the Kett rebellion in Norfolk in the summer of 1549. Rather, Welsh loyalties to the Crown overrode any misgivings that some might have privately harboured about such root-and-branch change. Many of the gentry had benefited so splendidly from the religious changes that had occurred during Henry's reign that their loyalty to Edward was all but guaranteed.

There were others for whom Edward's reign represented the opportunity for which they had long been waiting. Small in number they may have been, but there were some in Wales of more radical Protestant views. However, with the exception of Robert Ferrar, they were not be found sitting on the bench of bishops. Most of the Welsh bishops were conservative figures, happy to support the royal supremacy and administer their dioceses with some care, but less keen on championing radical religious reform.[27] Ferrar, who had replaced William Barlow at St Davids in September 1548, arrived in his diocese determined to inject new energy into the stalled reform programme of his predecessor. He set about rooting out the remaining vestiges of Catholic religious practice, tried to ensure that copies of the English Bible were available throughout his diocese and committed himself to regular and systematic preaching. Yet he quickly became embroiled in bitter conflict with his cathedral chapter, and his energies were dissipated. As a result, the cause of Protestant reform in the diocese became bogged–down in petty arguments and rivalries.[28] Yet there were other corners of Wales in which Protestant ideas received a warmer reception. The determining factor tended to be the presence of a significant English-speaking population, able to take advantage of inexpensive copies of the Bible and the Prayer Book. Towns like Haverfordwest, Pembroke, Cardiff and Wrexham all had vocal Protestant communities, but it was in Carmarthen, the largest town in Wales at the time, that perhaps the greatest progress in the cause of reform had been made. Having said this, it is important not to overstate the significance of these developments. Numbers remained small, and early Welsh Protestants found the evangelistic task confronting them almost insurmountable. When preaching at Abergwili on the outskirts of Carmarthen, Robert Ferrar found that there were 'scarce three or four who understood him'.[29] His frustration revealed the biggest challenge faced by radical Protestants in Wales; the Protestant faith seemed alien and was often unintelligible. The overwhelming majority remained largely unmoved by the passionate efforts of the early Welsh Protestants.

It was this fact that inspired and motivated William Salesbury. A native of Llansannan in Denbighshire, Salesbury had been educated in the latest Renaissance humanist learning while a student at Oxford, where he had also converted to Protestantism after encountering some of the works of Martin Luther.[30] Salesbury was quick to grasp that if his fellow Welsh men and women were to be won over to anything other than a nominal Protestantism, the evangelical faith had to be made accessible to them in their own language. In an introductory letter to *Oll Synnwyr Pen Kembero Ygyd* ('The Sum of a Welshman's Wisdom') (1547), Salesbury urged his fellow Welshmen to 'make pilgrimage, barefoot, to the King's majesty and his Council to solicit to have leave for the Holy Scripture in your language, for the sake of those of you who are neither able nor likely to learn English'.[31] Salesbury became the unofficial interpreter of the religious changes of these years, publishing a bilingual tract justifying the marrying of priests and a striking appeal advocating the tearing down of altars in 1550,[32] but he was quick to realize that if the Welsh were to have the Scriptures and prayer book available to them in their own language he would need to provide them himself. Almost as a stopgap, in 1551 Salesbury published *Kynniver Llith A Ban* ('So Many Lessons and Verses'), a book containing translations into Welsh of those passages from the Gospels and Epistles that were appointed to be read throughout the liturgical year in the Book of Common Prayer. While this was, of course, short of being a translation of the whole Bible into Welsh, it did ensure that worshippers in Wales enjoyed the startling and revelatory experience of hearing the words of Christ in their mother tongue for the first time. It was a crucial moment in the indigenization of Protestantism.

Mary's Counter-Reformation

Given the cool reception afforded Protestantism by many in Wales up to this point, particularly the radical variety that became the Crown's preferred option during Edward's reign, one might have expected the Welsh to have breathed a collective sigh of relief at the accession to the throne of the Roman Catholic Mary – Henry's daughter by his first wife, Catherine of Aragon – in 1553. And in some respects they did, not least when many features of the 'Old Faith', including the Latin Mass, were quickly restored. At a national level, leading figures in the Edwardian reform movement were soon imprisoned, including Cranmer, and in her first Parliament in October 1553, the Edwardian religious laws were abolished and the Church of England returned to the position it had occupied towards the end of Mary's father's reign. However, this was but the first step. The following year Henry's religious laws were also repealed, and by the end of that year papal supremacy had been restored over the English church, leaving Mary free to carry out the brutal suppression of English Protestantism by means of hastily erected funeral pyres in many parts of the country.

The poet Siôn Brwynog rejoiced at this turn of events:

Wele fraint y sain yn neshau – eilwaith
Wele'r hen 'fferennau'
Wele Dduw a'i law ddehau
Yn gallu oll ein gwellhau.

[Behold once more the privilege of the saints draws near,
behold the old masses;
behold God making us whole
with his right hand.][33]

However, many among the clergy were less enthusiastic, not because they had become committed Protestants, but because they had taken full advantage of many of the opportunities presented to them by the Edwardian religious changes, chief among which was the chance to marry.

There were some notable immediate casualties. Robert Ferrar was deprived of his bishopric in March 1554; his successor oversaw the deprivation of at least 115 married clerics in the diocese between April 1554 and the following March.[34] A similar number lost their livings in Bangor diocese, but the evidence for the other Welsh dioceses is fragmentary and incomplete.[35] Needless to say the upheaval was considerable, leaving the church crippled by a lack of clergy in some parts of the country. However, the numbers of burnings for heresy in Wales were few. Robert Ferrar, kept in prison for most of Mary's reign, was finally burned at the stake in the market square at Carmarthen in March 1555. The late twentieth-century Irish poet, Ted Hughes, a distant relative of Ferrar's, evocatively captured the scene:

> [...] out of his eyes,
> Out of his mouth, fire like a glory broke,
> And smoke burned his sermon into the skies.[36]

By contrast, Rawlins White was a humble and probably illiterate fisherman from Cardiff. According to John Foxe's 'Book of Martyrs', White had committed much of the Bible to heart after hearing it read to him by one of his sons. He soon began to preach, and probably led a small Bible study group in the town during Edward's reign. He became a virulent critic of the bishop of Llandaf who soon had him imprisoned. The end came relatively quickly, and he was burned at the stake in the town wearing his wedding outfit on the same day as Ferrar met his fate in Carmarthen sixty miles to the west. Legend has it that White even helped the executioner pile straw around the pyre, before telling him to 'knocke the chaine fast, for it may be that the flesh would striue mightily'.[37] Comparatively little is known of the third Marian martyr, William Nichol from Haverfordwest. Foxe referred to him as 'so simple and good a soul that many esteemed him half foolish',[38] but he must have been a person of some local significance to warrant public execution. He was unfortunate to be burned at the stake just six months before Mary's death.

The three Welsh martyrs were merely a small proportion of the almost three hundred executed in England during Mary's reign.

There were a few Welsh Protestants who chose the path of exile on the Continent, perhaps a dozen or so out of the over eight hundred who found refuge in cities such as Geneva, Strasbourg and Frankfurt.[39] Among their number was Richard Davies, later to be appointed bishop of St Davids. Although he sided with the more conservative faction, holding to the Prayer Book liturgy, during his exile in Frankfurt, he would nevertheless instigate radical reform within his diocese following his return to Wales after the accession of Elizabeth. For the majority, the advent of Mary and the return to Catholicism proved to be both bewildering and dispiriting. This was not helped by Mary's unpopular marriage to Philip II of Spain in 1554, a development that seemed destined to relegate England to the position of a vassal state within the Spanish empire. When Mary lost Calais, England's last continental territorial possession, to the French in January 1558, the sense that England had become a diminished power seemed to be confirmed.

Within Wales, many who had benefited so richly from the disposal of monastic lands during the previous two decades sat tight and said as little as possible, nervous of what any full-scale revival of Roman Catholicism might mean for both their power and their wallets. They were unlikely, with a few notable exceptions, to stump up the money necessary to invest in the restoration of some of the outward trappings of Catholic worship.[40] However, recent scholarship has suggested that focusing on the repressive nature of the Marian regime alone has tended to blind historians to some of the positive reforming achievements of her reign. Eamon Duffy, for example, has argued that Cardinal Reginald Pole, who became archbishop of Canterbury in 1556, attempted to bring the English church in line with the reforming agenda of the Council of Trent.[41] Pole had significant Welsh connections, and seems to have taken a particular interest in the affairs of the Welsh church. Some of the bishops appointed to the Welsh dioceses reflected this. Thomas Goldwell, appointed to St Asaph in 1556, set about injecting a healthy dose of discipline into the clergy under his charge,[42] and in the appointment of Morys Clynnog as bishop elect of Bangor and Gruffydd Robert as archdeacon of Anglesey, the Welsh church gained two senior clergy who were committed to revivifying a reformed Catholicism in the Welsh language.[43] They were to become the focal point of clandestine Welsh Roman Catholic resistance to Elizabeth in the second half of the sixteenth century, and responsible for the survival of a Welsh Catholic community. However, many of these efforts were cut drastically short by the death of Mary in November 1558. Whether, with more time, England and Wales might have been won back to a more enthusiastic embrace of Counter-Reformation Catholicism is impossible to tell. What seems certain is that despite a lack of enthusiasm for full-throated Protestantism in Wales, there were too many by the end of Mary's reign who had a vested interest in the success of a royal supremacy free from papal control. Despite Mary's earnest efforts, dragging the nation back to the pre-1530s position was doomed to failure.

Wales and the Elizabethan religious settlement

The response of the Welsh to the accession of Elizabeth I in November 1558 was muted. There had been simply too much upheaval and too many switches of religious direction to regard the dawn of the reign of the daughter of Henry VIII and Anne Boleyn with anything other than trepidation. Elizabeth's personal religious views have long been something of an enigma. Although she seems to have stuck fairly closely to some of her father's religious preferences, when her religious settlement installed her as the 'Supreme Governor' of the Church of England rather than 'Supreme Head', out of deference to those who felt that it was not fitting for a woman to be the head of the church, her allegiance to the Protestant cause was plain to see. In her Act of Uniformity (1558) she took the Church of England back to 1552, parking it precisely at the point when radical Protestants felt they had secured their most decisive victory with the publication of the second Edwardian Prayer Book, a more explicitly Reformed version of the simplified liturgy that Cranmer had prepared in 1549. Yet plenty of elements of the old faith remained untouched, leading some to argue that Elizabeth's church was a sort of compromise, a *via media*, charting a middle way between the extremes of Catholicism and more radical Protestantism. However, more recently historians have questioned that position, and now tend to agree with Patrick Collinson's view, 'that the Church of England was putting down its anchors in the outer roads of the broad harbour of the Calvinist or (better) Reformed Tradition'.[44]

This is not to say that either Elizabeth or the majority of people in the country had suddenly become Calvinists, but it is to argue that the leadership of the Church of England was firmly in the hands of those of a Reformed theological persuasion. However, among the bishops Elizabeth inherited in Wales such views were rare; two of them, Thomas Goldwell at St Asaph and Henry Morgan at St Davids, refused to swear the Oath of Supremacy, Bangor was vacant, and only Anthony Kitchen at Llandaf, 'a timeserver who would doubtless have become a Hindu ... provided he was allowed to hold on to the see of Llandaff",[45] eventually signed. Some of the Catholics that Mary had appointed to prominent positions in the Welsh church fled abroad while they still could, with Morys Clynnog even calling on his fellow countrymen to look for ways to support the overthrow of Elizabeth, preferring them to 'attain eternal blessedness under a foreign lord than to be cast into the nethermost hell'.[46] Among the wider clergy there were few who refused the oath in the royal visitation of the dioceses in the summer of 1559, and Wales largely escaped the worst excesses of the fresh wave of iconoclasm that was unleashed by them. While there was a groundswell of loyalty to Elizabeth herself, there was as yet little detectable enthusiasm for full-blown Protestantism.

To secure loyalty to the new settlement in Wales, effective leadership was essential, and Elizabeth's choice of bishops to fill the vacant sees was a masterstroke. Those she appointed were convinced Protestants, and two had just returned from exile on the Continent. Richard Davies became bishop of St Asaph, and Rowland Merrick accepted the see of Bangor. Thomas Young was briefly appointed to St Davids, but following his translation to York in 1561 was replaced by Davies. Crucially, all three were Welshmen, an early indication of the Crown's awareness of the peculiar spiritual needs of the country. It was a pattern that would be maintained throughout Elizabeth's reign; thirteen of the sixteen bishops appointed were of Welsh origin and the majority were committed in varying degrees to the cause of reform.[47] One of the major achievements of the Reformation in Wales was the vastly improved quality of leadership at the very top of the church.

However, the state of the dioceses that the new bishops inherited was anything but encouraging. The Welsh church remained chronically poor, indeed the resources available to the bishops to make improvements had if anything become still more limited throughout the course of the sixteenth century. Much of the property of the church, and the resulting revenues, had fallen into the hands of laymen. The damage caused by these impropriators was severe. The rights to present clergy to livings rested in their hands, and more often than not they were more interested in maximizing their income than investing in high-quality clergy, especially those with a university education. Sermons, the main evangelistic tool of sixteenth-century Protestants, remained rare occurrences. There were numerous vacant parishes, with many clergy having to serve more than one just to make ends meet.[48] Not for nothing did Richard Davies call these lay impropriators 'insatiable cormorants', 'greedy for church spoils and contemptuously intolerant of the church's rulers'.[49] The consequence of all this was plain to see. In 1567 Nicholas Robinson, bishop of Bangor, reported that the people of his diocese were still characterized by ignorance with many 'in the dregs of superstition . . . images and altars standing in the churches undefaced, lewd and indecent vigils and watches observed, much pilgrimage-going, many candles set up to the honour of the saints, some relics yet carried, and all the country full of beads and knots'.[50] Further south in St Davids the situation was little different: in 1570 Richard Davies bemoaned the fact that 'a great number' were still 'slow and cold in the true service of God; some careless for any religion; and some that wish the romish religion again'.[51] Driving up basic standards was difficult enough, turning the Welsh into ardent Protestants an enormous challenge.

Important as the literary activities of William Salesbury had been during the reign of Edward, at the start of Elizabeth's reign the Welsh still lacked the basic texts of the Protestant faith in their mother tongue. Without them, the queen's newly appointed Welsh bishops knew that their labours would be largely in vain. It was at this point that Salesbury's earlier entreaties that the Crown make provision for the translation of the Bible into Welsh finally came to fruition. Working closely with Richard Davies, in 1561 Salesbury wrote an impassioned appeal to members of the Privy Council urging them to:

> consult together what may be thought most expedient, & what remedie most present for the expulsment of sooch miserable darkness for the lack of shynyng light of Christe's Gospell as yet styll remayneth among the inhabitants of the same principalitie . . . that then it may please your good lordships to wyll and require and com'aund the learned men to traducte the boke of the Lordes Testament into the vulgare walsh tong . . .[52]

With the assistance of Humphrey Lhuyd, the member of Parliament for Denbigh, a bill was drafted in 1563 calling for the 'whole Bible, containing the New Testament and the Old, with the Book of Common Prayer and Administration of the Sacraments . . . be truly and exactly translated into the British or WELSH Tongue'. [53] It stipulated that the task had to be completed within five years, by 1 March 1567, and laid the responsibility for its delivery squarely at the door of the Welsh bishops, although it remained silent on who exactly was responsible for the funding of the project. At the heart of the Act passed by Parliament was the recognition that the language of worship in Wales should be Welsh.

For almost two years Salesbury took up residence in the bishop's palace at Abergwili near Carmarthen, and worked with Davies, by this time bishop of St Davids, on the translation of the Prayer Book and the New Testament.[54] Although he was not solely responsible for its production, the Welsh translation of the New Testament when it was published in October 1567 bore his unmistakable imprint. He translated all except the pastoral epistles of 1 Timothy, James, 1 and 2 Peter and the letter to the Hebrews, which were completed by Davies, and the book of Revelation, completed by Thomas Huet, the precentor at St Davids cathedral. It was a work of remarkable Renaissance scholarship, based as it was on Salesbury's close familiarity with the latest editions of the texts that made up the Scriptures in their original languages. Salesbury's translation deserves to stand alongside the landmark vernacular translations of Tyndale and Luther, not just for its high level of textual accuracy, but for its crucial role in bringing the words of Jesus, Paul, Peter and John to its readers and listeners in their mother tongue, often for the first time.

The translation was prefaced by Richard Davies's 'Epistol at y Cembru' ('Letter to the Welsh'), in which Davies defended Protestantism against the charge of being new, alien and perhaps most damagingly of all the *ffydd Saeson*. Davies argued that the Protestant and, more specifically, the Reformed faith was a renewal of the ancient Celtic church which had supposedly been established in these islands by Joseph of Arimathea in the immediate post-Apostolic age.[55] This purer version of the Christian faith, he argued, had been corrupted following the arrival of Augustine of Canterbury in the seventh century and the takeover of the indigenous 'British' church by the Roman Catholic. After centuries of ignorance and superstition, he wrote, the Welsh now had the opportunity to return to the true faith, the faith they had once experienced in its purity, in their own language. He urged them to

> Take it [the Welsh New Testament] in thy hand, grasp it and read it. Here shalt thou see thy former condition, here wilt thou acquaint thyself with thy old faith, and the praiseworthy Christianity thou hadst before. Here wilt thou find the faith thou didst defend unto fire and sword, and for which thy religious and thy learned men were martyred long ago in the persecution.[56]

As earlier chapters in this book have shown, there was little truth in the claim of an ancient, purer and independent 'British' church, but in a sense that didn't matter. By harnessing the Welsh sense of themselves as different and distinct, Davies was able to present the Reformed faith not just as more faithful to Scripture, but also more in tune with the religious instincts of his fellow countrymen and women.[57] Being Protestant, he seemed to be suggesting, was being more fully and authentically Welsh.

It is hard to overstate the importance of the publication of Salesbury's New Testament. When used alongside his translation of the Prayer Book, which had been published six months earlier and contained his translations of the book of Psalms as well,[58] the worship in Welsh parish churches was transformed almost overnight. It was a moment of genuine religious awakening. Yet Salesbury's translation was not without its problems. Salesbury was primarily a Humanist scholar, and while he certainly wished to present the New Testament in language accessible to the widest possible readership, there were times when his decision not to render Welsh words phonetically and his preference for Latinized, rather than more familiar Welsh renderings, led him to use words and phrases which sounded archaic and were not immediately familiar to the average reader or indeed listener.[59] Salesbury did not have William Tyndale's ear for a telling phrase, and did not share his empathy for the language of the humble ploughboy, the qualities that had made Tyndale's translation so resonant and enduring.

Important as this new translation of the New Testament was, there was much still to do, and Salesbury and Davies ploughed on with the task of translating the rest of the Bible. However, their working relationship broke down in 1575, apparently after a disagreement over the translation of a single word, and both died in the early 1580s, before much progress had been made on the Old Testament.[60] Their mantle was taken up by William Morgan, who since 1578 had been vicar at Llanrhaeadr-ym-Mochnant in Montgomeryshire. Morgan had been educated at Cambridge, the hotbed of English Puritanism, and had excelled in the study of the biblical languages, especially Hebrew. Admirably well qualified for the task of translating the Old Testament into Welsh, Morgan was appointed successor to Davies and Salesbury after a sample of his work had been approved by the bishops of Bangor and St Asaph.[61] Compelled by the conviction that his fellow countrymen and women should not 'be suffered to perish from the hunger of the word',[62] Morgan laboured tirelessly until the herculean task was complete. Remarkably, by 1587 he had finished both his translation of the Old Testament, and a revision of Salesbury's New Testament, replacing his awkward orthography with a more natural and vibrant Welsh style. Perhaps as much as a quarter of Salesbury's New Testament was overhauled in the process.

Morgan spent almost a year in London overseeing his Bible through the press. When the large and lavishly produced, though slightly unwieldy, volume appeared, it was a magnificent achievement, and a fitting testimony to the quarter of a century's labour that had gone into its production. Each thousand-page volume cost £1, a very substantial sum, and the initial print run of 1,000 copies was quickly exhausted following the Privy Council's instructions that the four Welsh bishops were to ensure that each parish in Wales purchased its own copy for its own use.[63] While its publication did not have quite the same impact as the 1567 New Testament, it proved to be a no less important moment. Morgan had a greater affinity with the Welsh literary and bardic tradition, and the Welsh he used was both more polished and vivid than Salesbury's. It set the standard for written Welsh for generations to come, but more importantly it rendered the Protestant faith intelligible to the people of Wales in an idiom and style that was genuinely their own. George Owen of Henllys, the antiquarian, a few years after the appearance of the new Bible famously wrote:

> we have had the light of the gospel, yea the whole Bible, in our native tongue, which in short time must needs work great good inwardly in the hearts of the people, whereas the service and the sacraments in the English tongue was as strange to many or most of the simplest sort as the mass in the time of blindness was to the rest of England.[64]

No longer could Protestantism be cavalierly dismissed as the faith of the English.

Welsh Catholics

Those in Wales who maintained their preference for *yr Hen Ffydd* ('the Old Faith') lived a perilous existence during Elizabeth's reign. As had been the case with some Protestants a few years earlier, the accession of Elizabeth saw a number of Catholic priests flee almost immediately to the Continent for refuge. For a time, there were enough Marian priests in Wales to sustain the sacramental life of the dwindling remnant of Roman Catholics, but as these priests began to die out so the fortunes of the Welsh Catholics became more precarious. Critical to the survival of Catholic witness in Wales was a regular supply of priests, prepared to work in secret and often at considerable risk to shore up the beleaguered faithful. The founding of a number of missionary colleges by William Allen, first at Douai in France in 1568, and then in 1576 at Rome, led briefly by the less than popular Morys Clynnog before being taken over by the Jesuits a few years later,[65] proved crucial in providing a steady supply. Allen's vision was for nothing less than the reconversion of England and Wales, and his seminary was intended to train enough missionary priests to bring that about. Of the fifty-one students in residence at Douai between 1574 and 1578 eleven were Welsh.[66] When Edmund Campion and Robert Persons launched their Jesuit mission to England and Wales in 1580, they singled out Wales for particular attention, assuming that there was a groundswell of support and loyalty to the Catholic faith among the Welsh.[67]

Among the cohort of students of Welsh origin at Douai was Robert Gwyn. In 1576 he had returned to his native Caernarfonshire, where he heroically devoted himself to the production of Catholic literature in the Welsh language. He is thought to have been the author of three or four books, including probably *Y Drych Christianogawl* ('The Christian Mirror') (1586–7), the first Welsh-language book actually printed on Welsh soil, produced clandestinely in a cave on the Little Orme near Llandudno. Despite not being an original work – it drew heavily on Robert Persons's *The Christian Directory* (1582)[68] – Gwyn bemoaned the fact that there were too many places in Wales that only 'retain the name of Christ in their memory, knowing hardly anything more of what Christ is than animals do.'[69] The publication of the book, and the existence of a printing press on Welsh soil dedicated to producing Catholic literature, sent panic throughout the country, coinciding as it did with the Jesuit mission and increased tensions over a possible Spanish invasion.

Estimating the number of Catholics in Wales during Elizabeth's reign is an imprecise exercise. The first list of Welsh recusants – that is, those who refused to take communion in the Church of England – was produced in 1574. It revealed just eighty-eight recusants in the whole of the country,[70] probably the tip of the iceberg in terms of those who still hankered after the 'Old Faith', but a sign that there were very few prepared publicly to question Elizabeth's religious settlement. At times of increased political tension, not least in the 1580s, the numbers of recusants uncovered increased sharply, revealing perhaps more about the extent of the government's nervousness than the actual number of Catholics. Nonetheless, there were some high-profile casualties especially in the 1580s, following the passing of an act making it treason for Catholics to proselytize. The brief furore surrounding the visions of the thirteen-year-old Elizabeth Orton, who railed against 'the Religion of Protestauntes' and 'their wicked and accurse churche' as 'moste abominable in God's sight' caused no little consternation in north–east Wales, and led to Orton being investigated before the dean of Chester cathedral.[71] In the spate of Catholic repression during these months, the poet and schoolteacher Richard Gwyn was arrested and tried for treason, before being executed in Wrexham in 1584.[72] Those who frequented Mass now faced imprisonment, a heavy fine of £20 for their recusancy, and severe curtailments on their freedom of movement. Unsurprisingly, there was a spike in the numbers prosecuted for recusancy in the 1580s. However, the defeat of the Spanish Armada in 1588, ending the possibility of a successful Catholic invasion, was perhaps the most damaging blow dealt to Catholics in England and Wales, putting paid to any realistic chance of the reconversion of the country, at least in the short term.

Catholics in Wales went underground in the later years of Elizabeth's reign. There was still a scattering of missionary priests working in the country, enjoying the protection of local Catholic gentry families like the earls of Worcester, who were thought to keep Catholic priests at Raglan,[73] the Herberts at Powis Castle near Welshpool or individuals like John Barlow at Slebech in Pembrokeshire, whose home was 'seldom without Jesuits and traitorous seminaries'.[74] However, by the closing years of Elizabeth's reign the number of recusants had passed its peak. In the dioceses of Bangor and St Davids they were few and far between; only in St Asaph in north-east Wales,[75] and in Monmouthshire in the diocese of Llandaf did there remain surprisingly persistent pockets of recusant activity.[76] There might have been considerable fondness for the familiar routines of the 'Old Faith' in Wales, but there was little appetite for either a return to full-blown Catholicism or for the sort of secret and hazardous existence which continued loyalty to Rome now demanded.

Puritans and Preachers

The presence of recusants and the stubborn persistence of Catholic ritual in some places was enough to worry some earnest Welsh Protestants, none more so than John Penry. Originally from Breconshire, Penry had been converted to a radical form of Puritanism, possibly even Presbyterianism, while at Cambridge. Although he rarely returned to Wales, he used the experience of his homeland as an illustration of the failures of the Elizabethan Church of England to bring about the conversion of the country to anything more than a nominal profession of the Protestant faith. In three pamphlets, the *Aequity of an Humble Supplication*, the *Exhortation unto the Governors and people . . . of Wales*, and the *Supplication unto the High Court of Parliament* published in quick succession in 1586–7 he set out his case for the more effective conversion of the 'perishing souls' of Wales.[77] Most of 'our people', he wrote are either 'such as neuer think of anie religion true or false, plainly meere Atheists or stark blinded with superstition'. There are hardly any, he wrote, 'in some score of our parishes, that hath a sauing knowledge'.[78] He laid the blame for this squarely at the door of the Welsh bishops for appointing 'swarmes of yngodlie ministers' who kept out 'a learned and godlie ministerie'[79] with the result that there were people in Wales who 'think it sufficient to heare one sermon perhaps in al their life."[80] His remedy for these ills was for the Queen – that is, the civil rather than the religious authority – to 'speedie prouiding vuto vs such pastors, as may feede vs with the food of life, the pure worde of God, and bring vs home vnto the only Lord of pastors, & sheepeheards, the Lord Iesus'.[81] However, his virulent and sustained criticism of the bishops soon caught up with him, and at the age of just thirty-one he was executed for sedition in London.

There was a sense in which some of what Penry was calling for was already beginning to happen, albeit on a small and somewhat unco-ordinated scale. Penry has tended to be regarded as one of Wales's first Puritans, one of those who felt that the progress of the Reformation had been too slow, and that reform was far from complete. However, Penry's separatist views were hardly mainstream, even within the wider English Puritan movement. Far more representative were those prominent voices within the Church of England who had not yet given up on the Established Church as an effective driver of religious change and who, far from being part of the 'encrease of sinnefull men, risen up in steed of their father the idolatrous Monkes and Fryars'[82] of Penry's vituperative prose, worked tirelessly at the task of reform. While it would probably be an exaggeration to label these figures Puritans, or even that they represented a Welsh Puritan movement, their literary endeavours were crucial in explaining both the nature of the Church of England, and the Reformed faith, to the people of Wales in their own language. At the heart of these endeavours was William Morgan, who in 1595 had become bishop of Llandaf. In 1599 he saw through the press a new Welsh version of the Book of Common Prayer which replaced the 1567 version's reliance on Salesbury's translations with Morgan's own livelier rendering of the Scriptures. He also worked tirelessly to encourage his clergy to preach regularly, and his efforts to recruit more graduates to serve in his diocese, despite it being the poorest in Wales, bore some fruit. There is plenty of evidence to suggest that sermons had become more frequent in Wales by the early seventeenth century.[83] These were small gains, but Penry's lonely voice was not being entirely ignored.

At the same time the number of Welsh-language theological works coming off the London presses began to increase. Maurice Kyffin published a translation of Bishop John Jewel's *Apologia Ecclesiae Anglicanae* (1562) in 1594, a defence of the Church of England that stressed its Reformed character.[84] Others contributed further to the production of Calvinistic theological texts in Welsh. Huw Lewys produced a translation of Miles Coverdale's *A Spiritual and Most Precious Pearl* (1550), perhaps the first work of practical divinity to be published in Welsh.[85] Of more importance, though, were the efforts of Robert Holland, a Cambridge educated Puritan who translated many of the writings of the leading English Puritan

William Perkins while serving parishes in Pembrokeshire and Carmarthenshire.[86] Perkins had developed an intricate Calvinistic theological system, learned from Theodore Beza, John Calvin's successor at Geneva. The covenantal Calvinism of Perkins, mediated through Holland's translations, was to have a profound effect in Wales in the centuries which followed. Taken together these theological works became the foundations of a Welsh Reformed theological tradition of quite remarkable sophistication.

Yet this was pretty rarefied stuff, and beyond the reach of most churchgoers in late sixteenth-century Wales. By Elizabeth's death in 1603 few could remember anything other than the Protestant Church of England. The Welsh had supported the church out of loyalty to the Tudor monarchs, and while there were plenty of ardent Protestants, the lack of preaching and the illiteracy prevalent throughout the country meant that few could read the Bible for themselves. On the ground, popular religious practice remained a mix of different elements, a combination of deference to the Church of England, a hankering after traditional religious practices like pilgrimages, the frequenting of relics and holy wells where they remained intact, and a variety of superstitious and magical beliefs and practices.[87] There is no reason to think that Bishop Middleton's (of St Davids) instruction to his clergy to desist from any practices that 'doth retain a memory of the idolatrous mass'[88] would have been any less relevant in 1603 than it had been when first issued twenty years earlier.

Christopher Haigh famously wrote that by 1603 England was a Protestant nation, but the English were not a nation of Protestants.[89] The same might be said of Wales and the Welsh. Wales had undoubtedly experienced a Reformation. The connection with Rome had been severed and there was considerable loyalty, perhaps even affection, for the Church of England and great pride in the Welsh translation of the Bible. But the number of fervent and committed Protestants in Wales by the end of the sixteenth century remained stubbornly small. Perhaps this should come as no surprise. In the words of Ethan Shagan, the Reformation had made the idea of belief more difficult, as rival churches redefined it 'as a privileged condition, a rarefied status unavailable to many or even most people'.[90] To belong was difficult, there were formidable hurdles to be overcome before one could be regarded as an authentic Protestant. Maybe we should think, therefore, not about how slow the progress of the Reformation had been in Wales, but rather how much had been achieved in such a short space of time. A solid foundation had been laid; the need to construct an edifice that was strong enough to endure remained.

Notes

1 Glanmor Williams, *Welsh Reformation Essays* (Cardiff: University of Wales Press, 1967), p. 30.
2 Quoted in David Hale, 'The Henrician Reformation: the perspective of one South Wales poet', *Morganwg*, LXII (2018), 15.
3 Geraint H. Jenkins, *A Concise History of Wales* (Cambridge: Cambridge University Press, 2007), p. 153.
4 Glanmor Williams, *Renewal and Reformation: Wales, c.1415–1642* (Oxford: Oxford University Press, 1987), pp. 284–5.
5 David Walker, 'Religious Change, 1536–1642', in *Pembrokeshire County History*, vol. III: *Early Modern Pembrokeshire, 1536–1815*, edited by Brian Howells (Haverfordwest: Pembrokeshire History Society, 1987), p. 103.
6 John Morgan-Guy, 'The Diocese of St Davids in the Reformation Era, I: From Rebellion to Reaction, 1485–1553', in *Religion and Society in the Diocese of St Davids, 1484–2011*, edited by William Gibson and John Morgan-Guy (Farnham: Ashgate, 2015), p. 28.
7 Madeleine Gray, 'Religion and Belief, 1530–1642', in *The Gwent County History*, vol. III: *The Making of Monmouthshire, 1536–1780*, edited by Madeleine Gray and Prys Morgan (Cardiff: University of Wales Press, 2009), p. 64.
8 Glanmor Williams, 'The Ecclesiastical History of Glamorgan, 1527–1642', in *Glamorgan County History*, vol. IV: *Early Modern Glamorgan*, edited by Glanmor Williams (Cardiff: Glamorgan County History Trust, 1974), p. 210.
9 Hugh Thomas, *A History of Wales, 1485–1660* (Cardiff: University of Wales Press, 1972), p. 45.
10 'The First Royal Injunctions of Henry VIII, 1536' and 'The Second Royal Injunctions of Henry VIII, 1538', in *The Reformation in England to the Accession of Elizabeth I*, edited by A. G. Dickens and A. D. Carr

(London: Hodder Arnold, 1967), pp. 77–85.

[11] Madeleine Gray, 'Penrhys: the archaeology of a pilgrimage', *Morganwg*, 40 (1996), 10–32.

[12] See W. J. Evans, 'Derfel Gadarn: a celebrated victim of the Reformation', *Journal of the Merionethshire Historical and Record Society*, 11 (1991), 137–51.

[13] Katherine Olsen, 'Religion, Politics, and the Parish in Tudor England and Wales: A View from the Marches of Wales, 1534–1553', *Recusant History*, 30/4 (2011), 527–36.

[14] Quoted in Williams, *Welsh Reformation Essays*, p. 113.

[15] William Barlow to Thomas Cromwell (1739), in Richard Fenton, *A Historical Tour through Pembrokeshire* (London: Longman, 1811), Appendix 8, p. 32.

[16] Quoted in Williams, *Welsh Reformation Essays*, p. 111.

[17] Quoted in J. Gwynfor Jones, *Aspects of Religious Life in Wales, c.1536–1660: Leadership, Opinion and the Local Community* (Aberystwyth: Centre for Educational Studies, 2003), p. 127.

[18] Nia M. W. Powell, 'Arthur Bulkeley: Reformation Bishop of Bangor, 1541–1552/3', *The Journal of Welsh Religious History*, 3 (2003), p. 35.

[19] R. Geraint Gruffydd, 'Dau destun Protestannaidd o Lawysgrif Hafod 22', *Trivium*, I (1966), 56–66; Williams, *Wales and the Reformation*, p. 146.

[20] Quoted in, Glanmor Williams, 'Unity of Religion or Unity of Language? Protestants and Catholics and the Welsh Language 1536–1660', in *The Welsh Language before the Industrial Revolution*, edited by Geraint H. Jenkins (Cardiff: University of Wales Press, 1997), p. 208.

[21] For its contents, see R. Geraint Gruffydd, '*Yny lhyvyr hwnn* (1546): The Earliest Welsh Printed Book', *Bulletin of the Board of Celtic Studies*, XXIII, part 2 (1969), 105–16.

[22] Diarmaid MacCulloch, *Tudor Church Militant: Edward VI and the Protestant Reformation* (London: Penguin, 2001).

[23] Williams, *Wales and the Reformation*, pp. 159–61.

[24] Quoted in (including translation), Jones, *Aspects of Religious Life in Wales, c.1536–1660*, p. 141.

[25] Quoted in (including translation), Jones, *Aspects of Religious Life in Wales, c.1536–1660*, pp. 146–7.

[26] Quoted in *Tudor Wales*, edited by Trevor Herbert and Gareth Elwyn Jones (Cardiff: University of Wales Press, 1988), p. 122.

[27] Williams, *Wales and the Reformation*, p. 171. For examples of such bishops, see Madeleine Gray, 'The Cloister and the Hearth: Anthony Kitchin and Hugh Jones, two Reformation bishops of Llandaff',

Journal of Welsh Religious History, III (1995), 15–34.

[28] Andrew J. Brown, *Robert Ferrar:Yorkshire Monk, Reformation Bishop and Martyr in Wales* (London: Inscriptor Imprints, 1997).

[29] Quoted in Williams, *Welsh Reformation Essays*, p. 134.

[30] D. Densil Morgan, 'Diosg yr Allorau: William Salesbury a'i *Baterie of the Popes Botereulx*', *Y Traethodydd*, CLXXII (October 2018), 215–20.

[31] Quoted in R. Brinley Jones, *William Salesbury* (Cardiff: University of Wales Press, 1994), p. 21.

[32] *Ban Wedy I Dynny Air Yngair Allan o Hen Gyfreith Howel Dda* (London, 1550), and *The Baterie of the Popes Botereulx, commonly called the High Altare* (London, 1550).

[33] Quoted (with translation) in *Tudor Wales*, edited by Herbert and Jones, p. 122.

[34] Glanmor Williams, 'The episcopal registers of St David's, 1554–65', *Bulletin of the Board of Celtic Studies*, XIV (1950), 45–54.

[35] Williams, *Wales and the Reformation*, pp. 197–8.

[36] 'The martyrdom of Bishop Ferrar' (1957), in Ted Hughes, *The Hawk in the Rain* (London: Faber and Faber, 1968), pp. 60–1.

[37] John Foxe, *The Unabridged Acts and Monuments Online* (1570 edition) (Sheffield: The Digital Humanities Institute, 2011). Available from: *http//www.dhi.ac.uk/foxe* (accessed 23 December 2020). See also Nia M. W. Powell, 'Rawling White, Cardiff and the early Reformation in Wales', in *Clergy, Church and Society in England and Wales, c.1200–1800*, edited by Rosemary C. E. Hayes and William J. Shiels (York: Borthwick Institute, 2013), pp. 121–37.

[38] Foxe, *The Unabridged Acts and Monuments Online* (1583 edition).

[39] Williams, *Wales and the Reformation*, p. 208.

[40] Madeleine Gray, *Images of Piety:The Iconography of Traditional Religion in Late Medieval Wales* (Oxford: Archaeopress, 2002), p. 78.

[41] Eamon Duffy, *Reformation Divided: Catholics, Protestants and the Conversion of England* (London: Bloomsbury, 2017), ch. 4.

[42] T. F. Mayer, 'Thomas Goldwell (d.1585)', *Oxford Dictionary of National Biography* (Oxford: Oxford University Press, 2004).

[43] R. Geraint Gruffydd, 'The Renaissance and Welsh literature', in *The Celts and the Renaissance: Tradition and Innovation*, edited by Glanmor Williams and Robert Owen Jones (Cardiff: University of Wales Press, 1990), p. 25.

[44] Patrick Collinson, 'England and International Calvinism, 1558–1640', in *International Calvinism, 1541–1715*, edited by Menna Prestwich (Oxford: Clarendon Press, 1985), p. 215.

[45] Eamon Duffy, *Fires of Faith: Catholic England under Mary Tudor* (New

Haven: Yale University Press, 2009), p. 23.

[46] Quoted in Williams, *Wales and the Reformation*, p. 221.

[47] Jones, *Aspects of Religious life in Wales*, pp. 33–40.

[48] For a more detailed picture of the state of the Welsh dioceses at this point, see Madeleine Gray, 'The diocese of St Asaph in 1563', *Journal of Welsh Religious History*, 1 (1993), 1–40; 'The diocese of Llandaff in 1563', *JWRH*, 2 (1994), 31–95; 'The diocese of St Davids in 1563', *JWRH*, 5 (1997), 29–56.

[49] Quoted in Williams, *Wales and the Reformation*, p. 330.

[50] David Mathew, 'Some Elizabethan Documents', *Bulletin of the Board of Celtic Studies*, VI (1933), 77–8.

[51] Katherine K. Olson, '"Slow and Cold in the True Service of God": Popular Beliefs and Practices, Conformity and Reformation in Wales, *c.*1530–*c.*1600', in *Christianities in the Early Modern Celtic World*, edited by Robert Armstrong and Tadhg Ó hAnnracháin (Basingstoke: Palgrave Macmillan, 2014), p. 92.

[52] Quoted in Jones, *William Salesbury*, p. 51.

[53] 'Act for the translation of the Bible, 1563', in *Tudor Wales*, edited by Herbert and Jones, p. 126.

[54] Gruffydd Aled William, '"Ail Dewi Menew": Golwg ar Richard Davies', *Y Traethodydd*, CLXXIV (Ebrill 2019), 94–112.

[55] Glanmor Williams, *Reformation Views of Church History* (London: Lutterworth Press, 1980), pp. 63–4.

[56] Translation in Albert Owen Evans, *A Memorandum on the Legality of the Welsh Bible and the Welsh Version of the Book of Common Prayer* (Cardiff: William Lewis, 1925), p. 103.

[57] Lloyd Bowen, 'The Battle of Britain: History and Reformation in Early Modern Wales', in *Christianities in the Early Modern Celtic World*, edited by Armstrong and Ó hAnnracháin, pp. 140–2.

[58] R. Geraint Gruffydd, 'The Welsh Book of Common Prayer', *Journal of the Historical Society of the Church in Wales*, 17 (1967), 43–55.

[59] For a defence of Salesbury's approach to translation, see James Pierce, *The Life and Work of William Salesbury: A Rare Scholar* (Aberystwyth: Y Lolfa, 2016), ch. 20.

[60] Williams, *Wales and the Reformation*, p. 339.

[61] Isaac Thomas, *William Morgan and his Bible* (Cardiff: University of Wales Press, 1988), pp. 43–5.

[62] These are words from Morgan's dedication to his new Welsh Bible, quoted in *Tudor Wales*, edited Herbert and Jones, p. 126.

[63] Glanmor Williams, 'Bishop William Morgan and the first Welsh Bible', in *The Welsh and their Religion: Historical Essays* (Cardiff: University of

Wales Press, 1991), p. 192.

[64] George Owen, *Dialogue of the Government of Wales (1594): Updated Text and Commentary*, edited by John Gwynfor Jones (Cardiff: University of Wales Press, 2010), pp. 96–7.

[65] Jason A. Nice, 'Being "British" in Rome: The Welsh at the English College, 1578–84', *Catholic Historical Review*, 92/1 (January 2006), 1–24.

[66] Williams, *Wales and the Reformation*, p. 251.

[67] John Bossy, *The English Catholic Community, 1570–1850* (London: Darton, Longman and Todd, 1975), pp. 15–24.

[68] Geraint Bowen, 'Roman Catholic Prose and its background', in *A Guide to Welsh Literature, c.1530–1700*, edited by R. Geraint Gruffydd (Cardiff: University of Wales Press, 1997), pp. 226–7.

[69] Translated in *Tudor Wales*, edited by Herbert and Jones, p. 123.

[70] Williams, *Wales and the Reformation*, p. 263.

[71] Alexandra Walsham, 'The Holy Maid of Wales: Visions, Imposture and Catholicism in Elizabethan Britain', *English Historical Review*, 132/555 (2017), 250–85.

[72] D. Aneurin Thomas, *The Welsh Elizabethan Catholic Martyrs* (Cardiff: University of Wales Press, 1971), pp. 51–4.

[73] Gray, 'Religion and Belief, 1530–1642', in *The Gwent County History*, vol. 3, edited by Gray and Morgan, p. 71.

[74] Walker, 'Religious Change, 1536–1642', in *Pembrokeshire County History*, vol. III, edited by Howells, p. 114.

[75] E. Gwynne Jones, 'Catholic Recusancy in the Counties of Denbigh, Flint and Montgomery', *Transactions of the Honourable Society of Cymmrodorion* (1945), 114–33.

[76] F. H. Pugh, 'Glamorgan Recusants, 1577–1611: A Selection from the Returns in the Public Record Office', *South Wales and Monmouthshire Record Society*, 3 (1954), 49–72.

[77] J. Gwynfor Jones, 'John Penry: Government, Order and the "Perishing Souls" of Wales', *Transactions of the Honourable Society of Cymmrodorion* (1993), 47–81.

[78] John Penry, 'A treatise containing the aeqvity of an humble supplication' (1587), in *Three Treatises Concerning Wales*, edited by David Williams (Cardiff: University of Wales Press, 1960), p. 32.

[79] Penry, 'A treatise containing the aeqvity', in *Three Treatises*, p. 27.

[80] Penry, 'A treatise containing the aeqvity', in *Three Treatises*, p. 7.

[81] Penry, 'A treatise containing the aeqvity', in *Three Treatises*, p. 12.

[82] John Penry, 'A viewe of some part of such publick wants & disorders as are in the service of God, within her Maiesties countrie of Wales,

together with an humble Petition, unto this high Court of Parliament for their speedy redresse' (1588), in *Three Treatises*, p. 124.

[83] Williams, *Wales and the Reformation*, pp. 390–2.

[84] Maurice Kyffin, *Deffynniad Ffydd Eglwys Loegr* (1595).

[85] Huw Lewys, *Perl Mewn Adfyd* (1595).

[86] D. Densil Morgan, *Theologia Cambrensis: Protestant Religion and Theology in Wales*, I: *From Reformation to Revival, 1588–1760* (Cardiff: University of Wales Press, 2018), pp. 11–34.

[87] Olsen, '"Slow and Cold in the True Service of God"', pp. 100–5.

[88] Quoted in Williams, *Wales and the Reformation*, p. 285.

[89] Christopher Haigh, *English Reformations: Religion, Politics and Society under the Tudors* (Oxford: Oxford University Press, 1993), p. 280.

[90] Ethan H. Shagan, *The Birth of Modern Belief: Faith and Judgement from the Middle Ages to the Enlightenment* (Princeton: Princeton University Press, 2018), p. 4.

Chapter 9

Securing a Protestant Wales, 1603–1760

DAVID CERI JONES

Like all buildings designed to stand the test of time, constructing a lasting edifice on the foundations laid by the sixteenth-century Welsh Protestants was an enterprise that demanded skill, patience and no little heroism. The appeal of Protestantism had been limited for much of the sixteenth century, at least until the appearance of the Welsh-language translation of the Bible in 1588. While progress winning over the Welsh to a more committed loyalty to Protestantism was often laborious, by the end of the period covered in this chapter a profound religious change had taken place. After a revolutionary civil war, and an experiment in Puritan republican government, Wales and the Welsh gradually became literate and were drawn in large numbers to an energetic and popular form of evangelical Protestantism. It proved to be a 'Great Awakening', transforming many of the Nonconformist denominations that had emerged during the seventeenth century into dynamic forces of religious, social and cultural change in the late eighteenth century and beyond.

Puritanism and the birth of Nonconformity

The accession of James I in 1603 was greeted with neither enthusiasm nor major complaint in Wales. Welsh support for the new Stuart king remained as solid and unequivocal as it had been for his Tudor predecessors. Indeed, there is evidence to suggest that James envied the seamless and successful English assimilation of Wales that had taken place in 1536 and used it as a model as he sought a similarly harmonious merger of the Crowns of England and Scotland.[1] James's reign has tended to be regarded as a period of relative quiet and consolidation, not least when compared with the turbulence of the reign of his son. In Wales, the Jacobean church witnessed significant further, if incremental, improvement. While Elizabeth had prioritized appointing Welshmen as bishops, the Stuarts did not see this as the overriding consideration in their choice of candidates for Welsh sees, and this has sometimes got in the way of a proper assessment of the quality of the men appointed at the beginning of the seventeenth century. In reality, most of the Jacobean bishops were marked by godliness and scholarly acumen, broadly Calvinist as was the case with the majority of James's other episcopal appointments, and – most importantly – committed to the ongoing reform of their dioceses.[2] The Welsh church benefited in these years from a moderate Puritanism, as both scholars and religious figures worked within the confines of the Established Church, rather than in competition with it or indeed opposition to it.

Some of the impetus for further reform came from the circle of scholars that had gathered around Bishop William Morgan. One of their number, Edward James of Cadoxton near Neath, published a Welsh translation of the Book of Homilies in 1606,[3] a real boon to hard-pressed clergy trying to craft effective sermons week after week with such meagre resources. The translation was highly significant, ensuring that parishioners throughout Wales were exposed to unequivocally Reformed theology on a regular basis. One of the great achievements of James's reign in religious terms was the production of the magisterial Authorized Version of the Bible in 1611, a development that would mould the religious lives of English-speaking Christians in Wales in profound ways. The majestic prose of the Authorized Version forced Welsh scholars back to the 1588 Welsh translation of the Bible, and in 1620 a new revised edition was produced. Largely the work of Dr John Davies of Mallwyd, assisted by his brother-in-law and bishop of St Asaph, Richard Parry, up to a third of Morgan's translation was revised. Reflecting the latest biblical and textual scholarship, the new edition smoothed out some of Morgan's colloquialisms, and a more polished prose emerged in its place, making it at least the equal of the magisterial King James Bible. A similar revision of the Book of Common Prayer took place the following year.[4] In both instances, the versions that were finalized following these improvements became the settled texts which were to become so familiar and beloved by subsequent generations of Welsh Christians. The production of the relatively inexpensive *Y Beibl Bach* a little later in 1630 ensured that the words of the Scriptures reached a wider audience in Wales than ever before.[5] The production of these texts firmly 'embedded Protestantism in the national fabric of Wales'.[6]

The 'Puritanism' of these decades was an uncontentious and attractive Anglican piety,[7] and reformers dedicated themselves to explaining and commending the faith to their Welsh parishioners. The production of an edition of the Psalms, the church's hymnbook, in simple Welsh metre and homely language by Edmund Prys in 1621, proved to be a landmark moment in the worshipping life of the church in Wales.[8] The ability of song to reach places where the spoken and written word made only slow progress was something grasped by the vicar of Llandovery, Rhys Prichard. Using well-known verse forms and popular tunes, Prichard produced over 250 poems containing a mixture of snippets of Scripture, basic doctrinal instruction and practical moral teachings. Transmitted largely by word of mouth, the poems were not collected and published in their entirety until 1681,[9] when they proved to be a popular and effective means of teaching the Reformed faith in rural Welsh-speaking communities,[10] not least in areas which often lacked enough preachers to communicate the faith through the favoured Puritan means of the sermon.

This is not to say that the traditional means of communication were overlooked; two books in particular, published in these decades, popularized some of the best examples of English Puritan spirituality in Wales. Lewis Bayly, who served as bishop of Bangor from 1616 until 1631, had originally published his *The Practice of Piety* in 1611. A work of Puritan practical divinity, a Welsh translation was published in 1630.[11] The second book, a Welsh translation of Arthur Dent's *The Plain Man's Pathway to Heaven* (1601),[12] was a fictional work in which Dent invented four characters to depict the different attitudes to the gospel that existed in the church and wider community. Both books provided readers not only with a summary of Calvinist doctrine, but in characteristic Puritan style, practical advice and counsel for each stage of life, and in the case of Bayly's work detailed guidance on how to parcel up each day in order to live effectively to the glory of God.[13] While the Church of England in Wales during James's reign still laboured under many of the same weaknesses as it had under his Tudor predecessors, not least its endemic poverty and the shortage of preachers, it nonetheless became a genuinely Reformed institution during these decades.

Having said this, by the time of the appearance of both these works of practical Puritan spirituality, the kind of moderate conformist Puritanism which they represented was beginning to fall out of favour. In 1625 James I had been replaced by his son Charles. Where James had worked patiently with his parliament, Charles lacked both his father's patience and his political skills, and tensions quickly mounted as Charles sought to raise ever more taxes to fund his European military adventures in the interminable Thirty Years War (1618–48). Yet, it was Charles's support of anti-Calvinist, or Arminian, factions within the Church of England that increased tensions still further. While Arminian was a theological term denoting (unlike Calvinism) the unfettered use of free will in the process of salvation, in practice it came to indicate the restoration of quasi-Catholic liturgy, ritual, ornamentation and sacramental worship within the Church of England.

In Wales the earliest evidence of this move towards 'High Church' ceremonial had been William Laud's refashioning of his private chapel during his relatively brief sojourn as bishop of St Davids between 1621 and 1626.[14] By the time Laud had become archbishop of Canterbury in 1633, Charles had dispensed with parliament entirely, and with Laud at his right hand began to effect a major change in the direction of the church. When Laud began to utilize the newly revived Court of High Commission to enforce these changes, their wish to expunge Reformed Protestantism from the church was plain for all to see. The success of their programme to restore the 'beauty of holiness' to churches all over the land depended on episcopal compliance, and during the 1630s bishops sympathetic to these views and prepared to enforce the new rubrics were parachuted into each of the Welsh sees. Paradoxically, one of the consequences of this diocesan resolution was to reveal the existence of a larger number of more radical Welsh Puritans than had been previously assumed, many of whom were not prepared to acquiesce in the new regime. Some suspected that the incredibly hard-won gains of the Reformation itself were under threat.

When Benjamin Rudyard complained in the House of Commons in 1628 that 'Wales was scarce in Christendom',[15] he was undoubtedly being too pessimistic. Some ambitious evangelization initiatives had been launched, and some important advances in a Puritan direction had been made. In Wrexham, Haverfordwest, Carmarthen and Swansea, towns which had influential English-speaking populations, lectureships funded by local boroughs had been established to supplement the lack of adequate preaching from the resident clergy. These were a gifted and dedicated group, though not all were of the calibre of Walter Cradock, who in the eleven months he spent in Wrexham in 1635–6 saw such success that local publicans tried to drive him out of the town.[16] The inhabitants of Wrexham quickly gained a reputation for 'gadding to sermons',[17] something that could also have been said about the residents of Cardiff, some of whom had responded with enthusiasm to the preaching of William Erbery.[18] A thirst for evangelical preaching certainly existed in some parts of Wales. Cradock was perhaps the earliest example of the kind of itinerant preacher who would do so much over the next century and more to transform the spiritual complexion of Wales. Among those converted under his Wrexham ministry was a young Morgan Llwyd; a Welsh Puritan movement was beginning to take shape.

What galvanized many of these men was the determination of William Murray, the bishop of Llandaf, to clamp down on Puritan activity in his diocese. The pretext for doing so was the enforcement of the 'Book of Sports', guidance drawn up during James's reign, advising which games and recreations were permitted on Sundays. No Puritan worth his salt was likely to read out such a liberal interpretation of the Sabbath to his parishioners, and when William Wroth, vicar of Llanfaches near Newport, and William Erbury, vicar of St Mary's in Cardiff, refused to read it or to wear a surplice when leading worship, one of the most tangible signs of the attempt to re-Catholicise the worship of the Church of England, they found themselves summoned before the Court of High Commission. Erbury, together with Cradock, his curate, were accused by their bishop of preaching 'very schismatically and dangerously', while Wroth was suspected of leading 'away many simple people' from the church.[19] Their options were few: they could either fall into line, something Wroth did initially, resign from the church altogether, an option taken by Erbury and Cradock, or leave the country for friendlier climes. This latter solution was the one taken by Marmaduke Matthews, vicar of Penmaen on the Gower, who was accused by the bishop of St Davids of 'preaching against the keeping of all holy days' and other 'profane opinions'.[20] He fled Wales for the more congenial environment of Puritan New England in 1638.

Although emigration to the American colonies was not a realistic option for most, New England Puritanism nonetheless had an important influence in Wales. Although there is no conclusive evidence that Wroth actually resigned his living, by late 1639 he had become the pastor of an Independent church at Llanfaches. The church was a gathered community, a voluntary association of believers who covenanted together to elect their own officers and pastors, free of outside influence and interference. They were largely modelled after the Congregationalism of the 'New England Way',[21] and the Llanfaches congregation drew its members from a wide area. It was likened by some to Antioch, the first Gentile congregation in the New Testament. 'All was Spirit and life',[22] Erbury wrote of Llanfaches, and as befitted 'the mother church in that Gentile country' of south Wales,[23] it inspired the founding of other congregations at Cardiff under the oversight of Erbury, possibly a church in Merthyr, though the evidence for its existence is not conclusive, and another in Swansea under the direction of

Ambrose Mostyn.[24] Although the Llanfaches congregation proved short-lived on account of the dispersal of many of the Welsh Puritans at the outbreak of the civil war in 1642, it nonetheless represents an important milestone in the Welsh Christian story. Religious communities outside the control of the state, those that would become known as Dissenting or Nonconformist churches, were soon to become one of the distinguishing features of the Welsh Christian tradition.

Civil war and religious revolution

Yet by 1640 the tide was beginning to turn, and Charles I's difficulties enforcing an Anglican prayer book on the Presbyterian Church of Scotland necessitated the recall of parliament after an eleven-year hiatus. The Puritan-dominated Long Parliament seized the opportunity to check the power of Laud and his bishops, and before the end of the year Erbury had penned *The Humble Petition* (1640), imploring parliament to turn its attentions towards Wales. He bemoaned the lack of preachers in Wales, calling the clergy 'blind guides' and 'dumb doggs'; Erbury called for nothing less than a 'seconde reformacon', by which he meant the removal of the bishops and the outlawing of the Prayer Book altogether.[25] The outbreak of civil war in August 1642 was initially a moment of crisis for the small communities of Welsh Puritans. Wales came out strongly in support of Charles I, and although Wales did not witness much actual fighting, royalist Wales remained no place for those who challenged the king. The Llanfaches congregation, the hub of the Welsh Puritan movement, was disbanded and its members and leaders scattered. Some found their way to Bristol others to London, while Cradock, Vavasor Powell and Morgan Llwyd preached on behalf of the parliamentary cause. But their fortunes soon changed, and by the end of the first civil war in 1646 it was clear that with Charles fatally weakened the opportunity to cajole parliament into making provision for the religious needs of Wales was too good to let pass.

In a sense the Welsh Puritans were pushing at a door that was already ajar. The Long Parliament had been sufficiently concerned about the persistence of loyalty for the king in Wales to support efforts to bring the light of the gospel to what they dubbed one of the darkest of the many 'dark corners of the land'.[26] A Committee for Plundered Ministers had been established in late 1642 charged with examining poorly performing clergy, and where necessary removing them from their parishes. In Wales, 35 clergymen had been removed in Glamorgan, while 18 had lost their parishes in neighbouring Monmouthshire. In their place, between 1644 and 1649 around 130 ministers were settled in parishes in various parts of Wales.[27] This was a considerable way short of the root-and-branch second Reformation many hoped for, but there were some real advances. The committee recognised the need for more preaching in Wales and appointed itinerant preachers who they hoped would be able, by their energy and charisma, to make up for the shortfall in the number of godly clergy they had been able to send into Wales. In north Wales, Vavasor Powell and Morgan Llwyd were among those commissioned, while in the south similar provision was made. In many respects these years were something of a golden age for the Welsh Puritans; given licence to roam across the country, some like Walter Cradock witnessed genuine religious revival. He proclaimed with some jubilation that 'the gospel is run over the mountains between Breconshire and Monmouthshire . . . as the fire in the thatch'.[28]

Even so, much remained to be done; the final defeat and execution of the king in January 1649, and with his departure the overthrow of the Church of England, gifted the Puritans a gilt-edged opportunity for more radical and far-reaching initiatives. The Rump Parliament, the fifty or so members that remained at Westminster after Colonel Pride's purge of royalist sympathizers in December 1648, quickly responded to the demands of those who had been pressing the claims of Wales. Among those voices was John Lewis, whose *Contemplations upon the Times* (1646) had presented parliament's cause to the Welsh, assuring them that parliament minded 'our happiness more than we do our selves' and was determined to 'presently purge Church and State' in order to 'introduce the Gospel among us'.[29] The solution when it eventually came was the Act for the Better Propagation and Preaching of the Gospel in Wales. Passed in February 1650, it made possible the seizure of Church of England assets to fund a preaching ministry in Wales.[30] Seventy-one commissioners were appointed, forty-three for the south and twenty-eight for the north, and under the leadership of Major-General Thomas Harrison they enthusiastically began inspecting serving clergy in communities all over Wales, turfing out those they deemed immoral, incompetent or not sufficiently evangelical. During the three-year duration of the act the devolved commissioners expelled 278 clergymen from parishes throughout Wales. However, this figure does not tell the whole story; there had been earlier clear-outs, and many clergy, reading the signs of the times, had jumped before being pushed.[31] The number of Welsh parishes lacking an effective ministry might therefore have been far higher than these figures suggest. These months quite literally witnessed a 'purgation of the temple'.[32]

The task of finding suitable replacements for those who had been ejected proved a far tougher challenge. A committee of twenty-five of the most prominent Puritans was set-up, but despite their best endeavours the Approvers were only able to recruit 135 'godly and painful men of approved conversation . . . to preach the Gospel in Welsh'.[33] Once again they were forced to fall back on the efforts of itinerants. Although precise numbers are difficult to pin down with absolute certainty, it has been estimated that there may have been as many as ninety itinerants active in Wales between 1650 and 1653.[34] Among their number were some familiar faces; none were as tireless as Vavasor Powell who preached in 'two or three places a day', and was 'seldom two days in a week throughout the year out of the Pulpit', preaching

> in every place where he might have admission both day and night, if he passed through any Fair, or Market, or near any great concourse of People (so great was his love to Souls) he would take the opportunity in his Journey to preach Christ, yea his whole life was a continual preaching.[35]

Much that is written on these years tends to stress both the limitations of what was achieved by the propagators, and its foreign character, that it was an essentially English effort at the evangelization of Wales by a parliament bent on the centralization of political power. But this is to overlook the very real achievements of these years; many of those appointed by the Propagators were of Welsh origin, and a good number were also Welsh-speakers. For close on a century Welsh Protestants had repeatedly called for a concerted effort to bring the gospel to Wales; during the 1650s communities were exposed to gospel preaching on a scale hitherto unheard of, and responsibility for the governing of Wales was delegated to the hands of those with local knowledge and experience. It was this that led the historian David Williams to suggest that the Propagation 'constitutes the only attempt made throughout the centuries to grant Wales a measure of self-government'.[36] Home rule or not, these proved to be months and years of very real spiritual awakening.

The biggest weakness of the Propagation Act was that it was so short-lived. When the Rump Parliament failed to renew it in 1653 the grand experiment in godly self-government came to an abrupt end. The Rump was replaced with the 'Barebones' Parliament, a hand-picked assembly consisting of a large number of Fifth Monarchists, millenarian Puritans who were determined to create a new political system in preparation for the return of Christ and the start of his millennial reign. Yet by this time the Puritan cause was beginning to fragment. In frustration, Cromwell dismissed Barebones and assumed the role of Protector of the Realm at the end of 1653. He remained personally committed to the evangelization of Wales,[37] with the result that the Commission for the Approbation of Publicque Preachers, better known as the 'Triers', was set up. Its thirty-eight members were based in London; highly centralized, it contained few Welsh members, and its remit was to settle ministers in Welsh parishes, rather than fund a system of itinerant preachers. It was a short-sighted approach, as once again there were simply not enough godly ministers to plug the gaps.[38]

The Welsh Puritans had become polarized by this time as well. Some like Cradock and Llwyd remained loyal to Cromwell, though Llwyd turned inwards towards more mystical views and withdrew from public life altogether.[39] In contrast, Erbery refused to accept a stipend from the state for preaching, and died in 1654 racked with doubts about the divinity of Christ and the doctrine of the Trinity.[40] Powell turned bitterly against Cromwell and spent much of the rest of the decade fomenting rebellion among his followers along the Welsh border. Finding himself at odds with his fellow Welsh Puritans, and in and out of prison on account of suspected sedition, Powell tried with increasing desperation to rally the dwindling millennial hopes of the saints still under his sway.[41] From the pens of each of them flowed works of sophisticated theological reflection, some of which repackaged the riches of the Reformed tradition for a Welsh readership.[42] There were other groups in Wales that flourished during these years too, united by their repudiation of any state control over their affairs. In 1649 John Myles established the first Baptist cause at Ilston on the Gower, and in the years that followed knitted together an Association of Calvinistic Baptist congregations across south Wales.[43] The Quakers, who not only repudiated any involvement of the state, but also the institutional apparatus of the church as well, began to put down roots in some parts of Wales following the evangelistic efforts of the Quaker founder, George Fox, and his Welsh disciple John ap John in 1654 and 1655. Soon there were Quakers in the main English-speaking urban communities in Wales, though they often attracted suspicion and sometimes violence and persecution as well.[44]

The 1650s were an enormously exciting decade in the Welsh Christian story. While there was considerable disruption and no little frustrated ambition, these were years of renewal, sophisticated theological reflection and creative new initiatives. Vavasor Powell claimed that by 1660 there were more than twenty Puritan congregations in Wales numbering 'in some two, in some three, some four hundred members'.[45] These were small but far from insignificant numbers, and Dissenting congregations began to put down deep roots in Welsh soil. Their pioneering efforts would in time bear ample fruit, and their direct spiritual descendants would go on to play an influential role in shaping Christian witness in Wales. Yet the death of Cromwell in 1658, and the return of the monarchy in 1660 in the shape of Charles I's exiled son, led many Welsh Puritans to approach the new political reality with foreboding, wondering if they had much of a future at all.

Anglicans and Dissenters

They were right to be fearful. Although Charles II's arrival at Dover in May 1660 was greeted with widespread relief, even enthusiasm, in some parts of Wales, the re-establishment of the Church of England, and with it the return of many of those who had been forced from its ranks during the Commonwealth, meant that a time of reckoning was at hand. For many churchmen the efforts of the Propagators to spread the gospel in Wales had resulted in nothing but chaos, turning the world upside down, with unqualified and sometimes uneducated itinerants holding sway, often backed up by the military might of Cromwell's Major-Generals. Many were, therefore, keen for the return of what the Welsh poets called 'the way of the old Welsh'.[46] And they largely got their wish. With the return of the Church of England, and by return was meant a reversion to the situation that had existed in 1642, came a slew of new episcopal appointments, and an attempt to enforce conformity to the Established Church by means of an Act of Uniformity (1662), which required all clergymen to pledge their allegiance to the newly revised Book of Common Prayer.[47] By the time the act was enforced on St Bartholemew's Day (24 August), ninety-five Welsh clerics had already resigned their benefices; a further thirty-five refused to publicly proclaim their allegiance to the new church and were ejected, many joining the ranks of Dissent.[48] Most of those deprived were in south Wales and some of the Welsh border counties, and they now found themselves subjected to a set of laws that sought to deprive them of their civil and religious liberties. This 'Clarendon Code' stipulated that all religious gatherings of more than five people had to use the liturgy of the Church of England, that those who had refused to swear allegiance to the church were not allowed to preach within five miles of a town, and that all local government officials had to be regular Anglican communicants. It was hugely restrictive, designed to stifle any opportunity for the growth of Dissenting congregations, and was backed up by punitive fines, and even the threat of imprisonment and exile.[49]

For some this was the point of no return; John Myles took the majority of his Ilston congregation with him to the American

---

colonies, where he founded a new Baptist community, first at Rehoboth, and then in an entirely new settlement called Swansey in Massachusetts. However, for most Welsh Dissenters or Nonconformists such a drastic course of action was not possible. Vavasor Powell lost his liberty entirely, spending much of the 1660s in prison, before dying in custody in 1670.[50] Others were forced underground, becoming adept at evading detection, holding services in remote spots far away from the prying eyes of local magistrates or clerics thirsty for revenge. Still others took on secular employment, providing them with useful cover to serve their scattered flocks on the side. Although the period between the Restoration and 1689, when Dissenters were finally granted a measure of religious toleration, are often referred to as the 'heroic age' of Welsh Dissent, in truth the force with which the local authorities pursued Dissenters ebbed and flowed. For much of the time they were able to worship in relative peace. Served by leaders of inexhaustible energy and uncommon ability in the pulpit, these scattered communities of Dissenters not only survived the experience of persecution and repression, but some actually experienced a modicum of growth.

In Breconshire, Henry Maurice picked up Vavasor Powell's mantle, serving the Independent congregation at Llanigon near Hay-on-Wye from 1671, and by his itinerating throughout south-east Wales knitted together a network of Congregationalist believers.[51] In north Wales, Hugh Owen followed in the footsteps of Morgan Llwyd, itinerating throughout the north from his base at the Independent congregation at Wrexham.[52] In north-west Wales though it was the Quakers who made the greatest inroads during the 1660s and 1670s, especially in Merionethshire, before the trauma of persecution forced over two thousand of them to look still further west and establish their own community in the newly established Pennsylvania colony.[53] The Baptists survived the trauma of the loss of Myles's leadership after 1663, and under the guidance of William Jones, who founded a Baptist congregation at Rhydwilym in Pembrokeshire in 1667, began to sink deeper roots.[54] However, few were as tireless in their evangelism or as wide in their sympathies as Stephen Hughes, sometimes known as the 'apostle of Carmarthenshire'. Having served as rector of Meidrim during the early 1650s, Hughes was among those ejected in 1662. Resettling in Swansea he served a network of local congregations, not exclusively among the Independents, there being a measure of denominational cross-pollination during these years, and his forays into Carmarthenshire and Pembrokeshire led to the establishment of at least eight congregations.[55]

These were years of pioneering evangelism and church planting, yet getting an accurate sense of the number of Dissenters in Wales in these decades is not straightforward. As already mentioned, Dissenters often lurked in the shadows, with many being reluctant to identify themselves publicly for obvious reasons. Nonetheless a census taken in 1676 revealed that there were 4,193 Dissenters in Wales, that most were to be found in the diocese of St Davids, and that the Independents far outnumbered those from the other denominations.[56] These were small numbers, though far from insignificant: in the generation that followed each of the Welsh Dissenting denominations experienced further growth, albeit of a fairly modest kind. By the time of the next assessment of Dissenting numbers between 1715 and 1718 there were eighty-nine separate congregations in Wales accounting for the care of around 17,700 souls. The figures also revealed that there were many more Dissenters in south Wales than in the north, and that the Independents still remained by far the largest body.[57] Yet these were still relatively small numbers; despite some important developments, Dissenters remained a smaller proportion of the Welsh population. However, in some places, particularly in growing urban communities like Swansea and Wrexham, they could appear far more prominent; appealing to craftsmen, professionals and merchants, the kinds of middling sorts of people who were beginning to play an increasingly prominent role in shaping their local communities, Dissenters became allied with forces of profound change in late seventeenth- and early eighteenth-century Wales. This meant that Dissenters were often far more influential than the number of members in individual congregations alone might suggest.

While the granting of religious toleration in 1689 came as an obvious relief, and allowed Dissenters to worship freely, albeit in registered meeting houses, by this point they had become less fearful for their survival, and their attentions turned to questions of

_____

theological identity, evangelism and expansion. Welsh Dissent gradually became more confident and diverse. With the exception of those influenced by Erbury and Llwyd, most Welsh Dissenters tended to be broadly Calvinist in theological outlook, but by the early years of the eighteenth century a wider range of theological voices can be detected. Among the Independents and Presbyterians High or hyper-Calvinist views emerged. Bringing to the foreground the divine decrees of election and reprobation and magnifying the role of sovereign free grace in the process of human salvation, High Calvinists provoked heated debate in various parts of Wales. At Wrexham a division took place in the town's Independent congregation when some of its members began to champion more moderate Calvinist views,[58] while at Henllan in Carmarthenshire a bitter and protracted dispute took place between those who advocated stricter and those who preferred moderate versions of Calvinism, a division which not even a major ministerial synod at Pencader could entirely resolve.[59] Among the Baptists too there were new theological currents; some repudiated Calvinism altogether in favour of Arminianism, while others moderated some of the more deterministic elements of Calvinism in an evangelical direction combining a belief in predestination with a wider understanding of the extent of the atonement, freeing them to evangelize widely and indiscriminately. The influence of the Bristol Academy, where the majority of Welsh Baptist ministers received their training,[60] ensured that a moderate evangelical Calvinism remained in the ascendancy in Wales. It would become the default position of Calvinists in Wales, well beyond the narrow confines of the Baptist churches alone.

Education and literacy

When it came to evangelism, some Dissenters were willing to work in tandem with sympathetic churchmen, especially in the cause of education and the publication and distribution of godly evangelical literature. Few were more committed to this endeavour than Stephen Hughes. During the 1670s he worked in close partnership with Thomas Gouge, a London-based Dissenter who had established the Welsh Trust in 1674, a charitable body that united Anglicans and Dissenters in the cause of the evangelization of Wales. The Trust set about its work with no little vigour, and within a year it had set up over eighty schools in south Wales.[61] For Hughes the Trust was primarily a vehicle for evangelism through literature, not least those works he had himself produced. His edition of Vicar Prichard's verse, *Canwyll y Cymry* had appeared in 1672, and his editions of some of the classic texts of English Puritanism had been translated into Welsh, most notably John Bunyan's *The Pilgrim's Progress* (1678), ensuring that the growing Welsh Dissenting communities were furnished with a body of literature in Welsh that was unequivocally Calvinist in ethos. Yet Hughes's biggest achievement was undoubtedly his production of a new and inexpensive edition of the Welsh Bible in 1678, eight thousand copies of which were disseminated by the Trust in the months that followed.[62] Although the active life of the Trust was relatively short, being wound up following the death of Gouge in 1681, well over five thousand theological and devotional books were distributed in Wales.[63] More people suddenly had access to both the Scriptures and good books than ever before.

The work of the Welsh Trust was taken up on the eve of the eighteenth century by the Anglican Society for Promoting Christian Knowledge. Founded in 1699, the SPCK was one of a series of voluntary societies designed to foster moral and spiritual renewal. The granting of toleration to the Dissenters had as profound an effect on Anglicans as it did on the Dissenters; having lost its religious monopoly, the Established Church now found itself having to adapt and to win worshippers through persuasion and inducement rather than relying on its privileged position as the default option for those with spiritual concerns. Throughout much of the country Anglicans had made relatively little headway in securing the conversion of their members to anything more than a nominal loyalty to the Protestant faith.[64] As this chapter has shown, for Protestants more generally this had been a perennial problem; with its reliance on reading and understanding the Bible for oneself and listening to sermons, Protestantism faced an uphill task establishing itself in communities where comparatively few were able to read, and where preaching was practically unheard of.

In the later decades of the seventeenth century a number of individuals and groups sprang up within established state churches throughout Europe intent on developing new techniques to secure a deeper attachment to Protestantism. Among the most influential of these were the Lutheran Pietists in Germany who championed a religion of the heart, the conviction that only personal spiritual transformation through the new birth and a life of continual holiness and charity would bring about renewal and the conversion of large numbers of the only nominally Christian. Philipp Jakob Spener developed what he called the *collegia pietatis*, small groups in which people could meet together for Bible study, prayer and more intense fellowship, while August Hermann Francke at Halle taught the Bible, founded small prayer groups, opened orphanages, established schools, built printing presses and sent out missionaries to far distant lands.[65] He successfully demonstrated that it was possible to turn nominal Christians into white-hot believers.

Many of those involved in the work of the SPCK had been influenced by the example of Francke. Its sister organizations, the Society for the Reformation of Manners (1691), and the Society for the Propagation of the Gospel in Foreign Parts (1701) spoke volumes about its ambition to bring about a far-reaching 'moral revolution'.[66] In Wales, the SPCK had a transformative effect, thanks largely to the leadership of patrons like Sir John Philipps of Picton Castle in Pembrokeshire. It initially concerned itself with establishing charity schools, and ninety-six of them were opened during its first forty years.[67] Philipps himself set up twenty-two schools in Pembrokeshire alone, paying for their accommodation, equipment and the salaries of their teachers.[68] Yet the appeal of the schools was not as wide as it might have been. Most were to be found in south Wales's small and widely scattered market towns, and the language of instruction, as in the Welsh Trust schools a few decades earlier, was predominantly English.

Far more effective, and of longer-term consequence, was the SPCK's support for the dissemination of godly literature. A network of corresponding members was used to distribute these books, and lending libraries were set up in each of the Welsh dioceses so that books could be borrowed by the less affluent.[69] While much of this literature consisted of reprints of Puritan works, there was also a stress on books from the 'High Church' Anglican tradition. This body of work, often influenced by patristic writers from the first five centuries of the church, championed a religious devotion based on unrelenting self-examination, regular fasting, the routines of Prayer Book worship, and the frequent partaking of the Eucharist. Its classic text was Richard Allestree's *The Whole Duty of Man* (1657), translated into Welsh as *Holl Ddledswydd Dyn* by John Langford, rector of Efnechtyd in Denbighshire, in 1672. Consisting of seventeen chapters, it outlined in practical terms what it meant to love God and one's neighbour as oneself. Interspersed with written prayers, it was intended to be used as a devotional manual and read and reread alongside the Bible and the Book of Common Prayer over and over again. It proved to be as much of a best-seller in Wales as elsewhere.[70] It was no accident either that one of the most popular books which the SPCK distributed in Wales at this time was a Welsh translation of Archbishop Tillotson's *Persuasive to Frequent Communion* (1696), perhaps the most influential single work from within the 'holy living' tradition, and emblematic of one of its main emphases. Some five thousand copies were distributed in Carmarthenshire alone.[71] The Anglican 'holy living' tradition represented a demanding piety; at its best it approached the Christian life with seriousness and rigour, but it could sometimes have a tendency to lead to a moralistic religious observance rather than a joyful faith. It proved to be a phase through which many of the leaders of what became the evangelical revival in the 1730s and beyond were to pass.

That there was an almost insatiable demand for books in early eighteenth-century Wales can also be seen by the rate at which the bibles printed by the SPCK were eagerly snapped up. In 1718, ten thousand copies of a new edition of the Welsh translation of the Bible were printed, a thousand of which were given away free to the poor.[72] The SPCK's commitment to Bible printing and distribution continued unabated throughout much of the century, with some fifty thousand copies of various editions being marshalled through the presses by the early 1750s.[73] Taken together with the 545 Welsh titles that were published between 1660 and 1730, a fivefold increase in the number of items published in the decades before that,[74] this represented a profound shift as Wales began to move from being a society in which the spoken word was dominant to one in which the printed word was becoming more important.[75] But by this stage, perhaps a still more important development was under way: the Welsh were being taught to read, and on a grand scale.

It was a task undertaken by perhaps one of the most visionary Welshmen, Griffith Jones. Jones was an Anglican clergyman in southern Carmarthenshire who had begun attracting unusually large congregations in 1713, first as a humble curate, and then as rector at Llanddowror. He was passionately concerned that many of the 'poor ignorant people' under his care were dropping into the 'dreadful Abyss of Eternity',[76] and became vehemently critical of his fellow Anglican clergy for their spiritual indolence and lack of gospel preaching. With a thronging multitude breaking down the doors of one church and crowds being turned away from others, Jones ventured into the open air, preaching both beyond the bounds of his own parish and at locations where it was convenient for large crowds to gather.[77] These were nothing short of local religious revivals of a kind that would become increasingly common.

Despite his obvious preaching gifts, Jones quickly came to the conclusion that the effectiveness of his ministry was hampered by the illiteracy of those to whom he preached. It was one thing for the number of books to be increasing, quite another to furnish people with the skills to be able to read them. Jones addressed the problem by coming up with a system of peripatetic or circulating schools. Meeting at times that fitted in with the rhythms of the farming year, and in locations that were accessible to the largest number of people, Jones's schools first opened their doors in 1731 to men and women, adults and children without discrimination. Unlike previous initiatives, Jones's schools used both the English and Welsh language depending on local linguistic patterns, and deployed the Welsh-language Bible and the Anglican Prayer Book as their main textbooks. Jones claimed to be able to teach a person to read in little more than six weeks, and regular updates on his achievements appeared in the pages of *The Welch Piety*, a publication that was both an annual report on progress and a marketing tool aimed at drumming up financial support from well-heeled benefactors in Wales and beyond. In the thirty years of their existence it is estimated that Jones's schools taught between 250,000 and 300,000 people – well in excess of half the population – to read.[78] Almost overnight the words of the Bible sprang into life as people throughout Wales were able to read the words of Christ for themselves for the first time. It created a spiritual hunger which the many godly books printed by the SPCK and others during these decades, not least those in the 'holy living' tradition, could not fully satisfy.

Revival!

During Easter 1735 one of Griffith Jones's schoolmasters, Howell Harris, from Trefeca, a small hamlet in Breconshire, found himself in the agonizing throes of an evangelical conversion experience. He was far from alone. In many parts of Europe and North America it seemed that the incidence of startling conversions was on the rise. In 1727, for example, a religious revival had taken place among a group of Moravians on the estate of Nicholas, Count von Zinzendorf at Herrnhut in Saxony after four young girls were born again, while in Northampton, Massachusetts in late 1734, a Congregational minister, Jonathan Edwards, had been caught up in a powerful revival in his church following a number of conversions among the young people in the local community.[79] News of these revivals spread quickly, whether through the forced migration west of European Protestants like the Moravians, or the publication networks that criss-crossed the Atlantic, ensuring that when Jonathan Edwards wrote his account of the Northampton revival it was devoured by those who had already been spiritually awakened.

Harris's Easter conversion was followed a few weeks later by a still more dramatic experience. What he called his 'baptism with fire' occurred as he was praying in the tower of his parish church: it was an experience which convinced him that God was calling him to some form of public ministry.[80] He found an immediate outlet for his energies by visiting the homes of his neighbours, enquiring after their spiritual well-being, reading the Bible or other evangelistic books, and pressing on them the need for a personal faith in Christ. Remarkably the number of people he visited began to increase until he had a small network of families under his pastoral care. As his confidence grew, he relied less on reading from other people's books and began preaching himself, or as he preferred to call it 'exhorting'. Yet Harris faced a dilemma: his activities were clearly bearing fruit, but the more successful he became, the more he attracted the disapproval of local clergy. Encouraged by the support of Griffith Jones and a few well-disposed Dissenting ministers, Harris carried on, increasingly viewing the Church of England 'as a mission field'.[81] By the end of 1736, with the number of conversions increasing, Harris began to sort his converts into small religious communities for Bible study, prayer and fellowship: within a few years he had oversight of over fifty of these societies in the south-eastern corner of Wales.[82] There had been a spiritual awakening, and the societies that Harris established, though ostensibly within the Anglican church, soon looked suspiciously like an alternative to it.

At roughly the same time a Church of England curate at Llangeitho in Cardiganshire was passing through a similar experience as Harris. Not unusually, Daniel Rowland had been ordained some time before he showed any sign of saving faith, but while listening to Griffith Jones preach one day he experienced new birth.[83] Unlike Harris, Rowland had a pulpit from which to preach, and after an initial period preaching judgement and God's wrath, he came to understand more fully the gospel of grace, and to preach it with a new urgency and winsomeness. Soon many began to wind their way to Llangeitho to listen to Rowland, and to receive Communion from the friendly hands of an evangelical clergyman. In a sense both Harris and Rowland preached nothing more than their own experiences during these formative years. Neither was an especially profound or original theological thinker, both took the Protestant message of justification by faith alone, and preached that salvation was available immediately and instantaneously through an experience of new birth. That experience, they believed, came most often in response to the preaching of the gospel, and might be accompanied with intense emotion as converts fell down or wept under the weight of conviction of sin, and shouted out or even laughed with inexpressible joy as they moved from spiritual darkness to light.

Historians have suggested many reasons for the appeal of Methodism in the late 1730s, though few have focused on the evangelical spiritual dynamic that motivated Harris and Rowland and gripped the lives of their many converts.[84]

Initially, there were two independent religious awakenings in south Wales, one in the east the other in the west, sparked into life apparently independently of each other. The one factor common to both was Griffith Jones, but alarmed at Harris and Rowland's often cavalier attitude to parish boundaries, the loyally Anglican Jones quietly distanced himself from his young protégés in order to safeguard the reputation of his schools. It was not until August 1737 that Harris and Rowland met each other for the first time, a meeting at which they exchanged stories about their recent exploits, and talked about the small groups for new converts they had been setting up. They agreed to pool their resources and meet on a regular basis, effectively fusing their two awakenings into a single renewal movement.[85] Significantly, they also discussed the newly published British edition of Jonathan Edwards's *A Narrative of Surprising Conversions* (1737), his account of the Northampton awakening two years earlier, and both concluded that 'surely the time here now is like New England'.[86] Edwards helped them to understand that such startling responses to their preaching were the result of a fresh outpouring of the Holy Spirit, and that God had set in motion 'a glorious work in the world'.[87] From the outset, the Welsh Methodists were conscious that they were part of an internationally resurgent evangelical movement, fuelled by a new move of the Spirit of God.

In the months that followed, Harris and Rowland redoubled their efforts, and by the beginning of 1739 Harris could report in a letter to George Whitefield, the leader of the parallel English awakening, that there was a 'great revival' under way in Cardiganshire, a 'sweet prospect' in Breconshire and Monmouthshire and some 'well-wishers to the cause of God in Montgomeryshire and Glamorgan'.[88] Having just returned from the first of many extended visits to America, Whitefield sped west to Wales, and after meeting Harris and visiting his societies, declared that the Welsh seemed 'much readier to receive the Gospel than … England'[89] and that he wished to catch 'some of [Harris's] fire'.[90] Whitefield became an increasingly familiar sight in Wales in the months and years that followed, preaching back-to-back sermons alongside Harris, one in English and the other in Welsh, and becoming part of the Welsh revival's inner circle.[91] Harris also started to spend increasing amounts of time in London where he encountered John and Charles Wesley and the Moravian societies, and began to shoulder an increasing amount of the responsibility for the leading of Whitefield's Tabernacle Society, especially after the English revival had splintered along Moravian, Wesleyan and Calvinist lines by 1741.[92]

By the early 1740s Harris's preaching had won two significant converts to the growing Methodist movement. William Williams was born again listening to Harris preach from the top of a gravestone in the churchyard at Talgarth, and quickly left his medical studies for ordination in the Church of England.[93] The exquisite hymns which he began writing soon after gave vivid expression to the experiences at the heart of the Methodist movement, while his prose writings combined Calvinist theology and experiential piety in harmonious and rare balance. Howell Davies, a schoolmaster at Talgarth, was ordained under Griffith Jones's guidance, and went on to occupy a number of parishes in Pembrokeshire.[94] United by their Calvinism and knit together by shared experiences of God's grace, these four Anglicans, three ordained and one lay, set about the task of evangelizing Wales with unrelenting vigour.

Roughly responsible for different parts of south Wales they slowly extended the frontiers of Methodism. As they did so, Harris and Rowland, with the help of Whitefield, inched their way towards an administrative system for the network of societies that had been established by 1742. A connexional system slowly evolved: at the local level the societies were gathered into groups of five or six with each society given a designated leader. Society leaders were instructed to meet monthly to coordinate their activities, and there was a further bi-monthly meeting at which society leaders in neighbouring counties were also to meet. The country was also divided into a number of circuits, each placed under the oversight of a superintendent who met quarterly and oversaw the examination and appointment of individuals to roles throughout the movement. An all-Wales body, the Public Society, was also established, becoming the main decision-making body of the revival.[95] Harris was the dominant figure in the development of this structure, and his energies infused the whole with the required dynamism and vigour.

Harris continued to divide his time between England and Wales, assisting in the development of a structure to oversee the Calvinist societies that looked to Whitefield for leadership. In January 1743 at a meeting held at Watford near Caerphilly, attended by the leaders of the Welsh revival and the English Calvinists Whitefield and John Cennick, a formal merger of the two movements took place with the founding of the Joint Association of English and Welsh Calvinistic Methodism. Whitefield was appointed Moderator, Harris his deputy with a roving brief in Wales and increased responsibilities at the headquarters of what had become English Calvinistic Methodism at Whitefield's Tabernacle in London.[96] At the same time as John Wesley had been busy establishing his own English Methodist movement, a Calvinist alternative had taken shape. For a time more extensive than Wesley's network of societies, the significance of these developments has tended to be lost because of the subsequent histories of both movements, not least the eclipse of the Calvinistic societies in England due to Whitefield's protracted absences in the American colonies.

Some have suggested that it would be a mistake to assume that the Welsh revival was yet making as profound an impact on Wales as the traditional description of it as a 'great awakening' might suggest. In the early 1740s, numbers certainly remained relatively modest. Within the roughly seventy or so societies that existed, there were perhaps no more than 1,500 members, and they were widely scattered, an indication of the regional nature of early Methodism. While there were pockets of strength in most of the south Wales counties, Methodism had yet to make inroads into north Wales. Indeed when Harris preached at Machynlleth in February 1740 he was rounded on by a mob and beat a hasty retreat, while at Bala the following year he was severely beaten by another crowd armed with sticks and stones.[97] Yet Methodism grew, and by the end of the decade the number of societies had increased to 420,[98] an indication that the committed members of the Methodist movement in Wales might have numbered around ten to twelve thousand by this stage. This figure does not do justice to the countless individuals who would have heard Harris or Rowland preach, but did not necessarily take the formal step of joining one of the Methodist societies, returning instead with a new commitment to their parish church or Dissenting meeting house. Judging the effect of Methodism by statistics alone can blunt our appreciation of its impact. There can be little doubt that many thousands heard the gospel communicated with conviction and power in an easily understandable form from the mouths of Methodist preachers, many even for the first time. It was little wonder that William Williams likened the coming of Methodism to a 'glorious morn' and the rising of the sun in full splendour on Wales.[99] Perhaps there had been a 'great awakening' after all.

Sadly, from the mid-1740s the Welsh revival began to run into problems as relations between Harris and Rowland broke down. Having repeatedly failed to secure Anglican ordination, Harris resorted to reminding his colleagues that he had been 'the first of all the Brethren'[100] and should therefore be accorded pre-eminence. His demands became increasingly insistent by the late 1740s when the toll of over a decade's travelling and the burden of leading the revivals in England as well as Wales brought him perilously close to breaking point. In addition, there were two further developments of still greater threat. Harris had grown close to the Moravians. Some suspected that he had actually joined them, not least once he started giving undue prominence to the spiritual power of the physical blood and wounds of Christ, and making confusing statements about the doctrine of the Trinity, suggesting at one point that it had been God the Father who had suffered and died on the cross in the form of God the Son.[101]

However, it was his highly compromising relationship with a married woman, Mrs Sidney Griffith, that proved the final straw. Referring to her as a prophetess, Harris became convinced that God communicated directly with him through Mrs Griffith. He appears to have become infatuated with her, and once he began demanding that she be included within the revival's inner circle, action had to be taken.[102] Whitefield expelled Harris from the London Tabernacle in January 1750, and shortly after a division took place in Wales that saw the revival split between Harris's and Rowland's people. The latter group was far larger, and there is a sense in which Rowland had been preparing for this moment for some time. With the assistance of William Williams, Rowland took control of the revival, securing the loyalty of most of the Methodists. For his part Harris retreated to Trefeca with a small rump of supporters where he set about creating a religious community which he named 'The Family'.[103] After the intensity and excitement of the previous fifteen years, the 1750s proved to be a far less fruitful decade and the Welsh revival was effectively mothballed. While Rowland was able to keep the societies largely together, further advance proved difficult without the charismatic and inspirational Harris in full harness.

The Methodist revival during the late 1730s and 1740s represented a profound change, and a definite raising of the spiritual temperature in Wales. By 1760 many in Wales had been taught to read at Griffith Jones's schools, and discovered that the answers to their spiritual needs were to be found in the pages of the Bible as explained and applied in the preaching of Harris, Rowland and others, brought to fruition in an experience of the new birth, and nurtured in the warm and comforting embrace of religious revival. Evangelical religion of this flavour was to transform Wales in the decades that followed.

Notes

[1]   G. Dyfnallt Owen, *Wales in the Reign of James I* (London: The Boydell Press, 1988), p. 8.

[2]   Glanmor Williams, William Jacob, Nigel Yates and Francis Knight, *The Welsh Church from Reformation to Disestablishment, 1603–1920* (Cardiff: University of Wales Press, 2007), pp. 9–12

[3]   *Pregethau a osodwyd allan . . . i'w darllein ymhob Eglwys blwfy* (1606).

[4]   Gwilym H. Jones, 'John Davies and Welsh translations of the Bible and Book of Common Prayer', in *Dr John Davies of Mallwyd: Welsh Renaissance Scholar*, edited by Ceri Davies (Cardiff: University of Wales Press, 2004), pp. 208–25.

[5]   Eryn M. White, *The Welsh Bible* (Stroud: Tempus, 2007), pp. 43–4.

[6]   Gruffydd Aled Williams, 'Bibles and Bards in Tudor and Early Stuart Wales', in *The Cambridge History of Welsh Literature*, edited by Geraint

Evans and Helen Fulton (Cambridge: Cambridge University Press, 2019), p. 239.

[7] Glanmor Williams, 'Religion and Welsh Literature in the Age of the Reformation', in *The Welsh and their Religion: Historical Essays* (Cardiff: University of Wales Press, 1991), p. 161.

[8] Edmund Prys, *Llyfr y Psalmau* (1621).

[9] *Canwyll y Cymry sef, Gwaith Mr. Rees Prichard, gynt Ficer Llanymddyfri* (1681).

[10] R. Brinley Jones, *'A lanterne to their feete': Remembering Rhys Prichard, 1579–1644, vicar of Llandovery* (Lanwrda: Drovers Press, 1994).

[11] Lewis Bayly, *Yr Ymarfer o Dduwioldeb*, translated by Rowland Vaughan (1630).

[12] Arthur Dent, *Llwybr Hyffordd . . . i'r Nefoedd*, translated by Robert Llwyd (1630).

[13] The content and significance of both books is discussed in detail in Morgan, *Theologia Cambrensis: Protestant Religion and Theology in Wales*, vol 1, pp. 45–51.

[14] John Morgan-Guy, 'The Diocese of St Davids in the Reformation Era II: From Reaction to Restoration, 1553–1660', in *Religion and Society in the Diocese of St Davids,* edited by Gibson and Morgan-Guy, pp. 54–7.

[15] Quoted in Christopher Hill, *Society and Puritanism in Pre-Revolutionary England* (Harmondsworth: Penguin, 1991), p. 58.

[16] Geoffrey F. Nuttall, *The Welsh Saints, 1640–1660: Walter Cradock, Vavasor Powell, Morgan Llwyd* (Cardiff: University of Wales Press, 1957), ch. 2.

[17] Williams, Jacob, Yates and Knight, *The Welsh Church*, p. 32.

[18] John I. Morgans, *The Honest Heretique: The Life and Work of William Erbery (1604–54)* (Tal-y-bont: Y Lolfa, 2012), pp. 18–20.

[19] 'Glanmor Williams, 'The Ecclesiastical History of Glamorgan, 1527–1642', in *Glamorgan County History*, vol. 4, edited by Williams, pp. 254–5.

[20] Thomas Richards, *The Puritan Movement in Wales, 1639 to 1653* (London: National Eisteddfod Association, 1920), p. 27.

[21] David D. Hall, *The Puritans: A Transatlantic History* (Princeton: Princeton University Press, 2019), pp. 229–32.

[22] Quoted in Geraint H. Jenkins, *Protestant Dissenters in Wales, 1639–1689* (Cardiff: University of Wales Press, 1992), p. 74.

[23] R. Geraint Gruffydd, *'In that Gentile Country': The Beginnings of Protestant Nonconformity in Wales* (Bridgend: Evangelical Library of Wales, 1976).

[24] Williams, Jacob, Yates and Knight, *The Welsh Church*, p. 32.

25 Lloyd Bowen, 'Wales and Religious Reform in the Long Parliament, 1640–42', *Transactions of the Honourable Society of Cymmrodorion*, 12 (2005), 42.

26 Christopher Hill, 'Puritans and the "dark corners of the land"', *Transactions of the Royal Historical Society*, 13 (December 1963), 77.

27 Geraint H. Jenkins, *The Foundations of Modern Wales, 1642–1789* (Oxford: Oxford University Press, 1987), p. 47.

28 Quoted in C. Hill, 'Propagating the Gospel', in *Historical Essays, 1600–1750*, edited by H. E. Bell and R. L. Ollard (London: Adam & Charles Black, 1963), p. 42.

29 John Lewis, *Contemplations upon these Times, or the Parliament Explained to Wales* (London, 1646), p. 32.

30 Stephen K. Roberts, 'Propagating the gospel in Wales: the making of the 1650 act', *Transactions of the Honourable Society of Cymmrodorion*, new series 9 (2004), 57–75.

31 David Walker, 'The Reformation in Wales', in *A History of the Church in Wales*, edited by David Walker (Penarth: Church in Wales Publications, 1976), pp. 75–6

32 Quoted in Jenkins, *Protestant Dissenters in Wales*, p. 17.

33 Quoted in Williams, Jacob, Knight and Yates, *The Welsh Church*, p. 40.

34 A. M. Johnson, 'Wales during the Commonwealth and Protectorate', in *Puritans and Revolutionaries: Essays in Seventeenth-Century History Presented to Christopher Hill*, edited by D. H. Pennington and K. V. Thomas (Oxford: Clarendon Press, 1978), p. 238.

35 Edward Bagshaw, *The Life and Death of Mr Vavasor Powell* (1671), p. 107, quoted in Jenkins, *Protestant Dissenters in Wales*, p. 79.

36 David Williams, *A History of Modern Wales* (London: John Murray, 1951), p. 115.

37 Lloyd Bowen, 'Oliver Cromwell (*alias* Williams) and Wales', in *Oliver Cromwell: New Perspectives*, edited by Patrick Little (Houndmills: Palgrave Macmillan, 2009), pp. 178–9.

38 Lloyd Bowen, '"This murmuring and unthankful Peevish Land": Wales and the Protectorate', in *The Cromwellian Protectorate*, edited by Patrick Little (Woodbridge: Boydell and Brewer, 2007), pp. 144–64.

39 R. Tudur Jones, 'The Healing Herb and the Rose of Love: the piety of two Welsh Puritans', in *Reformation, Conformity and Dissent: Essays in Honour of Geoffrey F. Nuttall*, edited by R. Buick Knox (London: Epworth Press, 1978), pp. 154–9.

40 Morgan, *The Honest Heretique*, pp. 27–30.

41 Nuttall, *The Welsh Saints, 1640–1660*, ch. 3.

42 Morgan, *Theologia Cambrensis*, vol. 1, pp. 85–132.

_____

43 D. Densil Morgan, 'John Myles and the Future of Ilston's Past', in *Wales and the Word: Historical Perspectives on Welsh Identity and Religion*, edited by D. Densil Morgan (Cardiff: University of Wales Press, 2008), pp. 7–8.

44 Richard C. Allen, *Quaker Communities in Early Modern Wales: From Resistance to Respectability* (Cardiff: University of Wales, 2007), ch. 1.

45 Quoted in Bowen, 'Wales, 1587–1689', in *The Oxford History of Protestant Dissenting Traditions*, vol. 1: *The Post-Reformation Era, 1559–1689*, edited by John Coffey (Oxford: Oxford University Press, 2020), p. 234.

46 Quoted in Jenkins, *The Foundations of Modern Wales*, p. 174.

47 John Spurr, *English Puritanism, 1603–1689* (Houndmills: Palgrave Macmillan, 1998), pp. 131–2.

48 John Gwynfor Jones, 'The growth of Puritanism, c.1559–1662', in *The Great Ejectment of 1662: Its Antecedents, Aftermath, and Ecumenical Significance*, edited by Alan P. F. Sell (Eugene, OR: Pickwick Publications, 2012), p. 61.

49 Michael Watts, *The Dissenters: From the Reformation to the French Revolution* (Oxford: Clarendon Press, 1978), pp. 221–7.

50 R. Tudur Jones, 'The sufferings of Vavasor', in *Welsh Baptist Studies*, edited by Mansel John (Cardiff: South Wales Baptist College, 1976), pp. 77–91.

51 R. Tudur Jones, 'Religion in Post-Restoration Brecknockshire, 1660–1668', *Brycheiniog*, 8 (1962), 41–6.

52 R. Tudur Jones, *Congregationalism in Wales*, edited by Robert Pope (Cardiff: University of Wales Press, 2004), p. 77.

53 Richard Allen, 'In search of a New Jerusalem: A preliminary investigation into the cause and impact of Welsh emigration to Pennsylvania, c.1660–1750', *Quaker Studies*, 9 (2004), 31–53.

54 B. G. Owens, 'Rhydwilym Church, 1668–89: A Study of West Wales Baptists', in *Welsh Baptist Studies*, edited by John, pp. 92–107.

55 Glanmor Williams, 'Stephen Hughes (1622–1688): "Apostol Sir Gâr", the Apostle of Carmarthenshire', *Carmarthenshire Antiquary*, 37 (2001), 25–6.

56 Eryn M. White, 'From Ejectment to Toleration in Wales, 1662–89', in *The Great Ejectment of 1662*, edited by Sell, pp. 140–1.

57 Jenkins, *The Foundations of Modern Wales*, p. 195.

58 Jones, *Congregationalism in Wales*, edited by Pope, pp. 104–5.

59 J. E. Lloyd, *A History of Carmarthenshire*, vol. 2: *From the Act of Union (1536) to 1900* (Cardiff: London Carmarthenshire Society, 1939), pp. 165–70.

60 Roger Hayden, *Continuity and Change: Evangelical Calvinism among*

Eighteenth-century Baptist Ministers Trained at Bristol Academy, 1690–1791 (Milton under Wychwood: Baptist Historical Society, 2006).

[61] Eryn M. White, 'Popular Schooling and the Welsh Language', in *The Welsh Language before the Industrial Revolution*, edited by Geraint H. Jenkins (Cardiff: University of Wales Press, 1997), p. 321.

[62] Brynley F. Roberts, 'Stephen Hughes (1622?–88)', in *Oxford Dictionary of National Biography* (Oxford: Oxford University Press, 2004).

[63] Jenkins, *The Foundations of Modern Wales*, p. 109.

[64] John Spurr, 'The Church, the societies and the moral revolution of 1688', in *The Church of England, c. 1688–c. 1833*, edited by John Walsh, Colin Hayden and Stephen Taylor (Cambridge: Cambridge University Press, 1993), pp. 127–43.

[65] W. R. Ward, *The Protestant Evangelical Awakening* (Cambridge: Cambridge University Press, 1992), ch. 2.

[66] David Ceri Jones, 'Welsh evangelicals, the eighteenth-century British Atlantic world and the creation of a "Christian Republick"', in *Wales and the British Overseas Empire: Interactions and Influences, 1650–1830*, edited by H. V. Bowen (Manchester: Manchester University Press, 2011), pp. 91–6.

[67] Mary Clement, *The SPCK and Wales, 1699–1740* (London: SPCK, 1954), pp. 102–33.

[68] Richard Brinkley, 'Religion and Education, 1660–1815', in *Pembrokeshire County History*, vol. III, edited by Howells, pp. 232–33.

[69] Clement, *The SPCK and Wales*, pp. 42–7.

[70] Morgan, *Theologia Cambrensis*, vol. 1, pp. 176–7.

[71] Geraint H. Jenkins, *Literature, Religion and Society in Wales, 1660–1730* (Cardiff: University of Wales Press, 1978), p. 72.

[72] Jenkins, *Literature, Religion and Society in Wales*, p. 62.

[73] White, 'Popular Schooling and the Welsh Language', p. 324.

[74] Jenkins, *Literature, Religion and Society in Wales*, pp. 34–5.

[75] Richard Suggett and Eryn White, 'Language, literacy and aspects of identity in early modern Wales', in *The Spoken Word: Oral Culture in Britain, 1500–1800*, edited by Adam Fox and Daniel Woolf (Manchester: Manchester University Press, 2003), pp. 67–77.

[76] Quoted in Geraint H. Jenkins, '"An old and much honoured soldier": Griffith Jones, Llanddowror', *Welsh History Review*, 11/4 (1983), 457.

[77] Eifion Evans, *Fire in the Thatch: The True Nature of Religious Revival* (Bridgend: Bryntirion Press, 1996), p. 62.

[78] W. T. R. Pryce, 'The Diffusion of the "Welch" Circulating Charity Schools in Eighteenth-Century Wales', *Welsh History Review*, 25/4 (December 2011), 491.

79 W. R. Ward, 'Evangelical awakenings in the North American world', in *The Cambridge History of Christianity: Enlightenment, Reawakening and Revolution, 1660–1815*, edited by Stewart J. Brown and Timothy Tackett (Cambridge: Cambridge University of Press, 2006), pp. 329–47.

80 Richard Bennett, *The Early Life of Howell Harris* (London: Banner of Truth, 1962), ch. 2.

81 Geraint Tudur, *Howell Harris: From Conversion to Separation, 1735–50* (Cardiff: University of Wales Press, 2000), p. 20.

82 Eifion Evans, *Howell Harris, Evangelist 1714–1773* (Cardiff: University of Wales Press, 1972), p. 22.

83 Eifion Evans, *Daniel Rowland and the Great Evangelical Awakening in Wales* (Edinburgh: Banner of Truth Trust, 1985), ch. 4.

84 For the emergence of evangelical religious forms in the early eighteenth century, see David W. Bebbington, *Evangelicalism in Modern Britain: A History from the 1730s to the 1990s* (London: Unwin Hyman, 1989), chs 1 and 2.

85 David Ceri Jones, Boyd Stanley Schlenther and Eryn Mant White, *The Elect Methodist: Calvinistic Methodism in England and Wales, 1735–1811* (Cardiff: University of Wales Press, 2012), pp. 13–14.

86 David Ceri Jones, '"Sure the time here now is like New England": What happened when the Welsh Calvinistic Methodists read Jonathan Edwards?', in *Jonathan Edwards and Scotland*, edited by Kenneth P. Minkema, Adriaan C. Neele and Kelly Van Andel (Edinburgh: Dunedin Academic Press, 2011), pp. 55–6.

87 David Ceri Jones, *'A Glorious Work in the World': Welsh Methodism and the International Evangelical Revival, 1735–1750* (Cardiff: University of Wales Press, 2004).

88 Howell Harris to George Whitefield (8 January 1739), National Library of Wales, Calvinist Methodist Archive, The Trevecka Letters, no. 136.

89 George Whitefield to Samuel Mason (7 April 1739), in Graham C. G. Thomas, 'George Whitefield and Friends', *National Library of Wales Journal*, 27/2 (Winter 1991), 197.

90 George Whitefield, *A Continuation of the Reverend Mr Whitefield's Journal from his Arrival at London to his Departure from thence on his way to Georgia* (London: James Hutton, 1739), p. 49.

91 Keith Beebe and David Ceri Jones, 'George Whitefield and the "Celtic" revivals', in *George: Life, Whitefield Context and Legacy*, edited by Geordan Hammond and David Ceri Jones (Oxford: Oxford University Press, 2016), pp. 135–7.

92 David Ceri Jones, "'The Lord did give me a particular honour to make [me] a peacemaker": Howel Harris, John Wesley and Methodist Infighting, 1739–1750', *Bulletin of the John Rylands University Library of Manchester*, 82/2–3 (Summer and Autumn 2003), 73–98.

93 Eifion Evans, *Bread of Heaven: The Life and Work of William Williams, Pantycelyn* (Bridgend: Bryntirion Press, 2010), ch. 2.

94 Derec Llwyd Morgan, 'Howell Davies (1717?–1770), Methodist leader', in *Oxford Dictionary of National Biography* (Oxford: Oxford University Press, 2004).

95 W. G. Hughes-Edwards, 'The development and organisation of the Methodist Society in Wales, 1735–50' (unpublished M.A. thesis, University of Wales, 1966).

96 Jones, Schlenther and White, *The Elect Methodists*, pp. 60–3.

97 Tudur, *Howell Harris*, p. 138.

98 Eryn M. White, '"The world, the flesh and the devil" and the early Methodist societies of south west Wales', *Transactions of the Honourable Society of Cymmrodorion* (1990), 60.

99 David Ceri Jones, '"A Glorious Morn": Methodism and the rise of Evangelicalism in Wales, 1735–62', in *British Evangelical Identities Past and Present*, edited by Mark Smith (Milton Keynes: Paternoster, 2008), pp. 101–2.

100 Quoted in Jones, Schlenther and White, *The Elect Methodists*, p. 81.

101 Tudur, *Howell Harris*, pp. 170–3.

102 Tudur, *Howell Harris*, ch. 8.

103 Eryn M. White, 'Women, work and worship in the Trefeca family, 1752–1773', in *Religion, Gender and Industry: Exploring Church and Methodism in a Local Setting*, edited by Peter Forsaith and Geordan Hammond (Eugene, OR: Wipf and Stock, 2011), pp. 109–22.

Chapter 10

Building a Nonconformist Nation, 1760–1890

D. DENSIL MORGAN

In 1760 virtually no one would have foreseen that within half a century Wales was in the process of becoming what the mid-Victorian Henry Richard would describe, memorably, as 'a nation of Nonconformists'.[1] Protestant Nonconformity was a minority faith – Catholic Nonconformity was infinitesimally smaller – while the vast majority of the people cleaved to the Church of England into which they had been born, baptized and confirmed. The largest body within Protestant Dissent were the Congregationalists, staunchly Calvinistic in creed, with their eighty or so churches, followed by the Baptists with their nearly two-score congregations, equally Calvinistic in creed, whose polity included an associational structure binding churches together within county and cross-county limits. Seventeenth-century Presbyterianism had never taken root in Wales, though many of the Presbyterian values – doctrinal exactitude as a requirement for church membership and the prizing of a learned ministry – had been perpetuated among the Congregationalists. It was here during the later part of the century, in mid-Cardiganshire and the northern part of Glamorgan, that a rationalist strain of Arminianism, developing into Arianism,[2] would occur, turning later into full-blown Unitarianism. This, however, would never become a major part of the Welsh religious mix. As for the Quakers, the most radical of the Puritan sects, their strength had been dissipated and presence curtailed, first by the substantial emigration to Pennsylvania three-quarters of a century earlier, and latterly by a curious diminution of spiritual fervour and missionary zeal. Friends' witness would be confined to rural mid-Wales and such industrialized centres as Swansea and Neath.[3]

The impact of the evangelical revival

The most significant aspect of Welsh religious life by 1760, certainly as it would later transpire, had been the inception of the evangelical revival a quarter-century earlier. The establishment of the Methodist movement with its disciplined network of *seiadau* or fellowship meetings bound together by its monthly meetings and association gatherings, had solidified despite severe tensions among the leaders and Howell Harris's withdrawal to supervise the life of his remarkable religious community in 1752.[4] Following a comparatively lean decade, new impetus was injected into the movement's life with the so-called Llangeitho revival of 1762, sparked both by the preaching of Daniel Rowland and the publication early in the year of William Williams of Pantycelyn's *Caniadau y Rhai sydd ar y Môr o Wydr* ('Songs of those who are on the Sea of Glass'), a reference to the words of John the Divine in Revelation 4:6 and 15:2, and the author's finest hymn collection to date. Revivalism, or the deepening of spiritual intensity sometimes (though not always) accompanied by emotionalism and physical manifestations, would become highly significant for the vitality and expansion of popular evangelicalism in nineteenth- and early twentieth-century Wales, and an important factor in the nation's religious self-understanding.

As well as partly inaugurating the Llangeitho revival, that revival itself contributed to the next, and vital, phase in Williams's career. Previously he had been known as a pastoral overseer and hymnist, but not as an author of prose. His first prose works, *Llythyr Martha Philopur* ('The Letter of Martha Philopur') (1762) and *Ateb Philo-Evangelius* ('Philo-Evangelius' Reply') (1763) culminating in his handbook on how to lead a *seiat* or fellowship meeting, *Drws y*

Society Profiad ('Door to the Experience Meeting') (1777), constitute a body of work of high significance not only for the building-up of converts in the faith, but in establishing the identity of the burgeoning Methodist movement and for subsequent Welsh literature generally. The two poles of authority for late eighteenth-century Welsh Calvinistic Methodism were the sermons of Daniel Rowland, published in three volumes: *Tair Pregeth a bregethwyd yn yr Eglwys Newydd, gerllaw Llangeitho* ('Three Sermons preached at the New Church near Llangeitho') (1772), *Pum Pregeth* ('Five Sermons') (1772) and *Tair Pregeth . . . a bregethwyd . . . gan y Parchedig Daniel Rowland, Gweinidog yr Efengyl yn Llangeitho* ('Three Sermons . . . preached . . . by the Reverend Daniel Rowland, Minister of the Gospel in Llangeitho') (1775) along with the hymns and prose works of William Williams. Whereas the sermons, each in the seventeenth-century Puritan style of mainstream Reformed orthodoxy, provided the doctrinal underpinning for the movement's faith, the prose works outlined a philosophy of history and mapped the contours of a religious psychology of exceptional insight and abiding effect. Conscious that revivalistic Methodism on this scale was a new phenomenon in the religious life of Wales, and that it cohered with the powerful spiritual awakenings that were being experienced throughout continental Europe and in America especially, Williams fashioned a theory of history encompassing cycles of renewal and decline into which the Welsh evangelical revival fitted. Along with this, the vivid analysis of the life of the soul as portrayed in the fictional lives of such representative converts as Martha Philopur and her friend Mary, as well as the *dramatis personae* in the remarkable epic poem *Theomemphus* (1764), provided the ever-increasing waves of young men and women who were being added daily to the fellowship meetings with a means of coping with the ecstasies, joys, temptations and pitfalls of their new life in Christ. For the first time in Wales, the female voice was being heard in mainstream religious discourse. By the time of his death in 1791, Williams had produced a body of creative and practical literature in Welsh the like of which had never been seen before.

Williams, along with Howell Harris who had returned to the fellowship of the revivalists in 1763, and Daniel Rowland, were loyal members of the Church of England who never envisaged Methodism as being anything other than a renewal movement within the Established Church. The evangelical revival had broken out not within the neat, sober meeting houses of orthodox Dissent, but in an ecclesiastical communion that many zealous Independents and Baptists would have regarded with suspicion if not considerable disdain. Despite some early cooperation between Harris, the Independent Edmund Jones and the Baptist Miles Harry, both of whom were preachers in Monmouthshire, by 1740 Methodism and Dissent had gone their separate ways. Tensions arising from different ecclesiologies had come to the fore, as had an older Dissenting distrust of 'enthusiasm' or overt emotionalism. Writing in 1764, the Calvinist Thomas Morgan, formerly pastor of the Independent church at Henllan Amgoed, Carmarthenshire, claimed that Methodist practices were 'stark mad', while the movement itself 'was given up to a spirit of delusion to the great disgrace and scandal of Christianity'.[5] Such was the characteristic posture of classic orthodox Dissent. Nevertheless, by the late 1770s a spirit of renewal was breaking through the hard crust of Dissenting rigidity; preaching was becoming more effective, evangelism – always a mainstay in dissenting witness – more potent, and more and more people were being drawn to discipleship and church membership. 'We have reason to believe', lyricized the 1779 letter of the Welsh Baptist Association, 'that the winter is past, the rain is gone, flowers appear in the earth, the time of the singing of birds has come and the voice of the turtle is heard in our land.'[6] 'This year', wrote the Glamorgan Baptist Jonathan Francis in 1785, 'God saw fit to pour out the spirit of revival on many of our members. Many are smitten and convicted to such a degree that they cleave to the godly imploring of them what they must do to be saved.'[7] 'Generally I had more testimonies of conversions under my ministry abroad than at home', declared Morgan John Rhys, minister at the Pen-y-garn church near Pontypool, in 1791; 'I preached as often as I could in dark places if I could find anywhere where no one had preached before.'[8] By then it was patent that the energies of the evangelical revival were being experienced beyond the bounds of the (still nominally Anglican) Methodist movement, and that Dissent itself was being renewed.

One of those who best exemplified this transformation was the Baptist Christmas Evans. Born in Cardiganshire in 1766, he was brought up among the Presbyterians and was converted during a revival at the Llwynrhydowen church in 1784. Drawn towards Baptist convictions, he was baptized through immersion in 1788 and began preaching before being ordained to the ministry on Caernarfonshire's Llŷn Peninsula a year later. By then Methodism was making huge inroads into north Wales, and following the example of the Methodist itinerant, Robert Roberts of Clynnog, he began preaching in a dramatic, awakening way. The results were startling. 'I baptized about fifty during that first year, and we had eighty in fellowship during the second year there.'[9] Older Dissenting fears of enthusiasm were now yielding to more potent realities: 'Great powers accompanied his ministry in those days. His hearers would weep, wail and jump as though the world were igniting round about.'[10] His removal to Anglesey in 1791 coincided with extraordinary revivalistic expansion among the Methodists and Independents as well as the island's Baptists, and by 1800 Dissenting witness everywhere was being revolutionized.

Whatever temporal reasons could be given for this change, in Evans's mind it was due to two indubitable facts: pointed evangelistic preaching and the sovereign work of the Spirit of God. 'There was something exceptional about the preaching of those days', he recollected, 'that it succeeded in turning a nation of Sabbath-breakers and persecutors into a nation who came together to hear the Word of God'.[11] The preaching which had characterized earlier generations had been formal and cerebral:

Many of the old Presbyterians and the Baptists [he claimed] were able preachers but their style was so cold and lifeless that it froze everything that it touched. When Rowlands from Llangeitho, [the Baptist] David Jones, Pontypool, and others like them, began preaching as though fired from heaven, the old [preachers][12] were forced to pack their goods and dismantle their stalls for there was no one left to listen to them in neither fair nor marketplace, between Holyhead and Cardiff.[13]

By the second decade of the century, the situation had been transformed utterly:

> Perhaps there has never been such a nation as the Welsh who have been won over so widely to the hearing of the gospel. Meeting houses have been erected in each corner of the land and the majority of the common people, nearly all of them, crowd in to listen. There is virtually no other nation whose members have, in such numbers, professed the gospel so widely, in both south Wales and the north.[14]

The revolution in the style and effectiveness of preaching had been supplemented by outpourings of the Holy Spirit:

> Showers of blessing fell upon the churches regularly. They often fell quite unexpectedly and when they did, they were invincible. The awakenings would affect some scores of people at a time causing them to shake, weep and cry 'What must I do to be saved?' They would coincide with the spirit of prayer and supplication and a conviction of utter unworthiness and the need for being reconciled by Christ's blood. When these showers fell, hundreds would be added to churches within a year. God's work prospers more in a single Sabbath following these awakenings than from a year's preaching.[15]

Evans was only one of a new generation of remarkably gifted preachers: the Independent William Williams of Wern, near Wrexham, and the Methodist John Elias are inevitably classed together as a triumvirate, but in fact there were now scores if not hundreds of such orators coming to the fore. By then, Nonconformist Wales was coming into its own.

The witness of the Established Church

It has been claimed by recent Anglican historians that 'Methodism in Wales was a result of the pastoral revival of the Established

Church'.[16] It is certainly true, as we have seen, that the Methodist movement began not among the Dissenters but through the exertions and preaching of Howell Harris and Daniel Rowland, and was perpetuated by the labours of Williams Pantycelyn and their colleagues, all of whom were Anglicans, but there were incipient tensions between the revival and the Church from the beginning. The most dynamic force within Welsh Anglicanism had been Griffith Jones, rector of Llanddowror, whose immense endeavours in the cause of biblical literacy had been achieved independently of the hierarchy and with little official support. The Church certainly possessed its strengths and was not devoid of virtues. A quiet, High Church, sacramentalist piety was shared by many of its parish priests and characterized their teaching, and there was general support among the lower clergy for the work of Griffith Jones. In fact, '[b]y the eighteenth century the Anglican Church had become widely accepted in Wales and seems to have been held in some affection.'[17] Nevertheless, even its most committed devotees were aware that there were failings in Church life which needed to be addressed.

According to the historian of Anglican High Churchmanship, Peter Nockles, 'the year 1760 ... marked the dawn of something of a High Church revival'[18] when a cohort of theologically orthodox bishops were raised to the bench. Among them were Charles Moss, bishop of St Davids between 1766 and 1774, John Warren, also at St Davids between 1779 and 1783 before being translated to Bangor where he governed until 1800, and most significantly in terms of the party's impact on the Established Church as a whole, Samuel Horsley who led the diocese of St Davids between 1788 and 1793.

Fresh from St Davids, which had seen significant Methodist activity over the years, in his primary diocesan visitation of 1784, John Warren charged his Bangor clergy to visit the sick, catechize the young and present those who were duly prepared for confirmation, the rite being 'the completion of baptismal grace and a joyful assurance of glory and immortality, if they shall persevere in their faith and their obedience to the end'.[19] They were to preach simply and clearly, leading worship according to the rubrics of the Book of Common Prayer 'in a distinct, earnest and solemn manner so as to fix the attention of your hearers, to kindle their affections and quicken their devotions'.[20] In all, they were instructed to fulfil 'a grave and devout performance of all public affairs of the Church'.[21] Particularly significant was Warren's defence of the parish system and his strictures on Methodist itinerancy:

> Some there are . . . who tell us that the Word of God ought not to be bound, that ministerial duties ought not to be confined within certain districts and that it would be more for the interest of religion if parochial enclosures were thrown open and all had full liberty to exercise their gifts wherever they were called.[22]

Such an opinion was, he claimed, unjustified, 'deserving no more attention than those who are for overthrowing all dominion and property in lands and estate'.[23] The bishop's fear of social disorder would be overcome were the clergy to fulfil their spiritual mission effectively and attract the disaffected back to its ministrations.

A more strident note was struck by Samuel Horsley in his primary charge to the St Davids clergy in 1790. Whereas sound doctrine would never drive a wedge between faith and works, 'the frenzy of the Methodists' at their most pernicious was to do that very thing, there being 'a prevalence of their numbers [he had heard] in these parts'.[24] Like Warren in Bangor, Horsley accepted that many Methodists were sincere in their piety if deluded by a spirit of enthusiasm. 'The great crime and folly of the Methodists consists not so much in heterodoxy', he claimed, 'as in fanaticism, not in perverse doctrine but rather in a disorderly zeal for a propagation of the truth.'[25] Were the clergy to inculcate in the laity the pernicious nature of schism while fulfilling their spiritual obligations conscientiously, the Methodist rift would soon be overcome: 'Nourished with the sincere milk of the Word by their proper pastors, they would refuse a drink of doubtful quality mingled by a stranger. In a word our churches would be thronged, while . . . the field-preacher would bellow unregarded to the wilderness.'[26] It is doubtful whether Horsley realized the spiritual discipline of Welsh Calvinistic Methodism of the time, or the quality of teaching that two generations of its leaders had provided for their followers. As one of the 'Anglo-bishops' (*yr Esgyb Eingl*), he, like the others, was isolated from the religious culture of the common people as well as their language.[27] Rowland, Williams Pantycelyn, Peter Williams and Thomas Charles could hardly be regarded as unlettered tub-thumpers, while many of the unordained Methodist exhorters were men of considerable intelligence and standing within their communities. On the other hand, there were still too many clergymen who had neither the ability nor the inclination to nourish the faithful with the sincere milk of the Word. In responding to the bishop of Llandaf's inquiries as to the prevalence of Dissent in 1763, William Miles, rector of Llanbleddian and Cowbridge in the Vale of Glamorgan, responded with a contempt which did him little credit: 'No Dissenters unless the strolling Methodists may be deemed as such. There is a Methodist meeting house at Aberthin in this parish. Methodists of all trades and denominations, tinkers, thatchers, weavers and other vermin.'[28] If, by 1790, the High Church bishops strove to respect the Methodists' sincerity even if they felt the need to challenge their ecclesiastical discipline and doctrinal views, there were still too many of the clergy who had little understanding of the religious revolution that had taken place around them and even less sympathy. And as we have seen, by these decades that revolution was occurring not only among the Methodists but within the ranks of Protestant Dissent too.

The Calvinistic Methodist secession

By the turn of the century the strains that Welsh Methodism was under had become severe. Daniel Rowland had died in 1790 (Howell Harris had passed away seventeen years earlier, in 1773), and in a famous letter written in May 1790, seven months before his own demise, Williams Pantycelyn charged Thomas Charles (who, after the 1811 secession, along with Thomas Jones of Denbigh, would inherit the movement's leadership) to preserve its orthodoxy. For sixty years the Welsh Calvinistic Methodists had been kept sound in the faith, and whereas a section of Dissent was succumbing to heterodoxy, 'Believe me dear Mr Charles, the antinomian, the Socinian and Arian doctrine[s] get [*sic*] ground daily', Calvinistic orthodoxy was still the mainstay of the movement's faith: 'The Articles of the Church of England, the Nicene, the Athanasian Creeds, the Lesser and Larger Catechism of the Assembly with their Confession of Faith are some of the grandest and most illustrious beauties of the Reformation.' It was these that 'our young exhorters should study . . . over and over', as they constituted 'the good, delicious divine fountain of which the honest Methodist drink[s]'.[29] Doctrinally and indeed constitutionally, its episcopally ordained leaders still saw Methodism as a means of rejuvenating the Church of England, a view which was becoming increasingly difficult to sustain. Even from the beginning, the ambiguities of such a stance had been manifest: Methodist preachers had little compunction about itinerating across parish boundaries while the associations were independent of diocesan structures and society meetings were wholly free of parochial control. Although the sense of intense fellowship engendered within the *seiadau* was meant to supplement the normal round of sacramental worship within the parish churches, in reality it often superseded Prayer Book norms entirely. This had become especially true when parish clergy had little sympathy for either Methodist practice or evangelical truth. Thomas Jones (later of Creaton) who, along with his fellow clergy David Jones, Llangan, David Griffiths of Nevern and Nathaniel Rowland, shared the pre-secession movement's leadership, complained bitterly of clerical opposition: 'The Lord have mercy upon the clergy in North Wales; they are surely at the worst; blinder they cannot be. The people perish for lack of knowledge.'[30] Yet Jones, especially, could never tolerate the idea of turning his back on the establishment. For him Welsh Calvinistic Methodism existed to renew the Established Church. It was left to his namesake, Thomas Jones of Denbigh, not only to show that such a view was no longer feasible, but to initiate the next phase in the movement's history.

Thomas Jones of Denbigh belonged to the first generation of lay leaders whose preaching abilities (or in his case theological acumen) matched and indeed outshone those of the Methodist clergy. Having already secured his reputation as a first-class dogmatician and apologist, it was he who provided the doctrinal rationale for what had become an overwhelming practical inevitability: the secession of the Welsh Calvinistic movement from the Mother Church. By now there were multiple thousands of converts whose only experience of vital Christianity had come not from the ministrations of the establishment but from the preaching of unordained itinerants supported by skilled pastoral care within the fellowship meetings. Owing ever less allegiance to the Church of England, they were asking why they should attend their parish churches to take the sacrament from the hands of clergy who were not only non-Methodist but often anti-Methodist as well. Writing to his brother, William, a cleric in Truro, John Williams, an episcopally ordained clergyman and eldest son of Williams Pantycelyn would write:

> The distance between us and the Established Church is increasing daily, and the young people are taking for granted that the Church is only a kind of civil Christianity. The old people still feel a good deal of prejudice in favour of the Church, but the younger set of us would not grieve if all the clergy were exiled to the other side of the Ganges. But . . . none of us dare, either privately or publicly, say anything disrespectful of the Established Church.[31]

There was little hope, or indeed desire, that the Anglican bishops would ordain a fresh generation of Methodist clergy. Had not the time come to administer the sacrament of baptism and the Lord's Supper within the fellowship meetings instead? Thomas Charles was not yet convinced, yet there was a groundswell of feeling that the movement's clerical leaders were putting the administration of the sacraments (for which ministerial ordination was still required) above the preaching of the gospel. Charles's reply to Ebenezer Morris, the Cardiganshire lay-leader, in an association meeting at Bala in 1809, defused a tense situation, though only for the while: 'What is most important? The preaching of the gospel or the administration of the sacraments?' 'The preaching of the gospel', Charles retorted. 'Then', said Morris, 'we are one.'[32] Had he said, 'the administration of the sacraments was just as essential, and only those who had been episcopally ordained were justified in administering them', the movement would have been irrevocably split. As it was, he agreed with the unordained preachers that it was their work, the preaching of the word, which was both effective for the salvation of the masses and had precedence in the gospel scheme.

He also realized – as they did – that the present anomaly could no longer be sustained. Thomas Jones's letter to Charles, dated 4 January 1810, made the break inevitable:

> I do not recollect seeing a visible church described by any writer but as a congregation of people having the Word of God truly preached, and the sacraments duly administered among them . . . That compelling any of our members to seek for either of the sacraments from without the pale of our own connection is a thing we ought not to be guilty of, as being contrary to the Word of God and to the universal custom of the churches of God in every age and country.[33]

In other words, Jones, the most theologically informed of all Methodist leaders, had come to the conclusion that the Welsh Calvinistic Methodists were no longer a renewal movement within a church but had become a church in their own right. That being the case, it would *not* be schismatic to break away from the Church of England. Rather, they were duty-bound to constitute themselves as a separate church with its own established sacramental ministry. Such a move would be in accord with 'the Word of God and the universal custom of the churches of God in every age and country'. Consequently, and still not without some trepidation, on 19 June 1811 in Bala, Merionethshire, Thomas Charles ordained eight Calvinistic Methodist preachers, and by so doing severed the connection between the Methodist movement and *Yr Hen Fam*, the Mother Church. Two months later, in Llandeilo, Carmarthenshire, he repeated the process by ordaining a further thirteen preachers, under the auspices this time of the south Wales association, thus completing the task of forming a national body, free of the Established Church. Not only had the Calvinistic Methodists become Dissenters, but Nonconformity itself had become the most potent religious force in nineteenth-century Wales.

The Wesleyan mission

The Calvinistic Methodists were not the only Methodist body in Wales, and by the time of Thomas Charles's secession, the Wesleyans were also evangelizing assiduously among the people. During his lifetime, John Wesley, who died in 1791, had agreed to allow Howell Harris and his colleagues free rein in Wales, but in 1800 Wesley's successor, Thomas Coke, a native of Brecon and a zealous missionary leader, persuaded the Methodist Conference to institute a Welsh mission. Preliminary work had already been done by Edward Jones, usually known as 'Edward Jones Bathafarn', in the Ruthin area of the Vale of Clwyd, who was soon joined by three fellow Welsh-speaking itinerants: Owen Davies, John Hughes and John Bryan. A vigorous application of the Arminian message of general redemption or that Christ had died not for the elect but for all of humankind, made an immediate impression and soon there were nearly six thousand converts, served by some forty-nine preachers, in district circuits which had been established at Ruthin, Caernarfonshire, Llanidloes, Aberystwyth and south Wales. Early growth following this frenetic burst of activity was not, however, sustained. Following Coke's death in 1814, the leaders were relocated to English circuits, and although the structures persisted, Welsh Wesleyan Methodism would never attain the same numerical strength or geographical spread as its partners in Dissent, even though it was complemented in the 1820s by evangelists from Hugh Bourne's Primitive Methodist movement and William O'Bryan's Bible Christians. Their ministry was especially attractive to incoming Cornish tin workers and lead miners in mid-Wales and the industrial Valleys, while a Welsh-language renewal movement, *Y Wesle Bach* ('The Minor Wesleyans'), was active in north-west Wales during the 1830s. On the evening of 30 March 1851, according to the statistics collated by Horace Mann in that year's great religious census, as many as 26,509 worshippers attended Wesleyan services in the counties of south Wales and 26,886 in the north, 6,109 attended Primitive Methodist services in south Wales and 666 in the north, along with a total of 1,530 south Wales worshippers in the chapels of the Wesleyan Association, the Wesleyan New Connexion and the Wesleyan Reformers, and 2,104 in the same small communions along with the Bible Christians in north Wales.[34] By mid-century, therefore, some 57,000 worshippers could be accounted as affirming different brands of the Wesleyan Methodist faith in Wales.

Anglicanism in Wales between the secession and mid-century

There is little doubt that the secession of the Calvinistic Methodists damaged the evangelistic and pastoral effectiveness of the Established Church and its claim to represent the bulk of the Welsh faithful. Evangelical witness in the parishes remained, but (apart, perhaps, from David Griffiths and those around him in Pembrokeshire) the gospel clergy were bereft of conspicuous leadership and the effective network which undergirded the strength of the evangelical party beyond Offa's Dyke.[35] The beginnings of the post-Methodist evangelical tradition within the Welsh Anglican church occurred, however, with the decision of William Cleaver, bishop of St Asaph, to ordain spiritually awakened non-graduates within his diocese. Hardly a reforming bishop while at Bangor, whither he had been translated from Chester in 1800, his removal to St Asaph in 1806 signalled a change in his attitude towards episcopal responsibilities. Putting a stop to non-residency in the parishes and ensuring that all his clergy were adequately housed, he was persuaded, not least by John Roberts, vicar of Tremeirchion, that zealous evangelical churchmen were fit to be ordained. Within months of the Methodist secession, a half-dozen native-born young men, imbued with the spirit of the revival, were admitted straight into holy orders.[36] Following Cleaver's death in 1815, John Roberts praised his late diocesan not only for having initiated this policy but for allowing clergy to hold experience meetings, prayer gatherings and preaching services in the Methodist mode: 'We are all now tolerated in the full enjoyment of private means that we may establish . . . and we trust there is some stir among the dry bones.'[37]

A similar occurrence took place in St Davids, initiated by Eliezer Williams, the vicar of Lampeter. Thomas Burgess, who had been inducted to the diocese in 1803, had already launched a vigorous programme of renewal on High Church lines, disseminating tracts, bibles and Prayer Books, establishing clergy libraries and promoting Sunday schools for the children of the poor. Wary, however, of evangelicalism and knowing nothing of the mores of Welsh Calvinism, he was in no position to respond to the crisis which the ordination movement exacted on the Church. Williams had gained renown for the excellence of his grammar school, established in his parish in 1806 and licensed by Burgess for the training of ordinands. Unlike his father, the Calvinistic Methodist biblical expositor Peter Williams, Eliezer was never a Methodist, though he rued the fact that the Church had forfeited the services of many excellent men through its unbending attitudes to that movement: 'It is much to be regretted', he wrote to his brother, Peter Bayley Williams, a north Wales rector, in December 1810, 'that our bishops are strangers to the country and know so little of its temper and disposition, otherwise schisms of this nature might be prevented.'[38] Years later the same sentiment was echoed by his son:

> Had our spiritual rulers given more encouragement to pious ministers, and had they pursued more conciliatory measures towards these men, whose only crime ... was a deadness to the world and a devotedness to their sacred functions, we should not have now to mourn over the prevalence of schism or the emptiness of many of our venerable churches.[39]

Conscious of the need to nurture the evangelical spirit within the diocese, Eliezer persuaded Burgess to allow preaching meetings among the clergy and encouraged capable young men who would otherwise have been drawn to Methodism, to train for ordination: 'Not a few of them have risen to distinguished eminence as preachers', noted his son. 'They have drawn together large congregations and their hearers have continued through life to be consistent and exemplary members of the Church.'[40] It was men like these who would perpetuate the evangelical succession in nineteenth-century Welsh Anglicanism.

Sacramentalism and High Churchmanship, however, remained the norm. In typical fashion Peter Williams (not to be confused with the Methodist leader), archdeacon of Merioneth, stated that true Christianity was a matter of moral striving, 'holy living' and sacramental grace. Believers, he stated, are 'placed by baptism, faith and repentance in a state of salvation, but this state must . . . be maintained afterwards by a holy life'.[41] Regeneration was through baptism: 'Christ himself has made baptism as well as faith necessary for salvation.'[42] The Holy Spirit was effective in that rite and the Lord's Supper, which he referred to as 'the Blessed Sacrament'.[43] This high sacramental doctrine cohered with a stern moralism. True faith and costly obedience were two aspects of the one divine truth, but grace was readily available to all who would come to Christ: 'The benefits guaranteed by the two sacraments ordained by Christ in his church, and given at God's specific command, are regeneration through the waters of the baptismal font and the cleansing of the faithful communicant through the bread and wine of the Lord's Table.'[44] The aim of preaching was to bring people to the Lord's Table where alone the fullness of salvation was to be found.

The policy of appointing Englishmen to Welsh sees persisted, though it was among a section of the native clergy, *yr hen offeiriad llengar* ('the old literary parsons'), that the Welsh cultural renaissance of the early nineteenth century found its focus. Walter Davies ('Gwallter Mechain'), John Jenkins ('Ifor Ceri'), W. J. Rees, of Cascob in Radnorshire, and Thomas Price ('Carnhuanawc') were vital in re-establishing the eisteddfod movement and in preserving Welsh-language scholarship. Historians of Welsh Anglicanism have always pointed to their work as an example of 'the vitality of the Established Church in the early nineteenth century',[45] yet in terms of administrational effectiveness and evangelistic verve, weaknesses prevailed. It was not until mid-century, under the leadership of a new generation of more pastorally aware bishops such as Connop Thirlwall installed at St Davids in 1840, Thomas Vowler Short instituted at St Asaph in 1846, and Alfred Ollivant (formerly professor of divinity at St David's College, Lampeter), inducted to Llandaf in 1849, that the institutional and financial restructuring which was already afoot in the English dioceses impacted the Church of England in Wales. Although the Catholic renewal of the Oxford Movement would begin to register in some Welsh parishes after 1840 while the evangelical clergy remained assiduous in their ministrations, it would not be until the 1870s that the Welsh Church would regain significant ground lost to a vibrant, popular Dissent.

Nonconformist foreign missions, Sunday schools, the Bible and the press

The optimism and ebullience of the evangelical revival had, among other things, created a vision for foreign missions. The post-millennialist impulse so pronounced in the works of Williams Pantycelyn in which a golden age of Christian expansion would lead to the second coming, led many to believe that the process was afoot whereby the world would soon be won for Christ. The first of the missionary societies, the Particular Baptist Society for the Propagation of the Gospel among the Heathen (later the Baptist Missionary Society) had been established by the Northamptonshire shoemaker William Carey in 1792, and was followed three years later by the London Missionary Society (the LMS), a joint venture sponsored by Congregationalists, Presbyterians and evangelical Anglicans. Within Wales the idealistic and politically radical Baptist Morgan John Rhys had fused social commitment with missionary fervour by evangelizing in Paris in the wake of the French Revolution and the fall of the Bastille, while the first Welsh auxiliary of the Baptist Missionary Society was established, in Swansea, in 1814. That of the LMS was formed in Carmarthen a year later. Zeal for foreign missions abounded both then and thereafter, with the Congregationalists, pioneered by their first missionaries David Jones and Thomas Bowen, focusing their work on Madagascar in the Indian Ocean, while following the creation of their own missionary society in 1840, the Calvinistic Methodists experienced much success in their chosen fields of labour, namely the Khasia Hills area of the Assam Province and the Lushai Hills of Mizoram, both in north-east India, and Sylhet in Bengal.

The same motivation contributed to the establishment and rapid growth of the Sunday school movement and of the British and Foreign Bible Society. Although the ever-innovative Morgan John Rhys had already begun forming Sunday schools during the late 1780s in which he inculcated general literacy as well as Bible knowledge among the youth of Glamorgan, it is Thomas Charles who is credited with being the father of the Sunday school movement in Wales. Having inherited the mantle of Griffith Jones, Charles realized that the results of popular revivalism would only be consolidated by rooting converts in biblical truths and sound doctrine. In order for such catechesis to be effective, literacy was essential. Having thrown in his lot with the Calvinistic Methodists in Bala in 1784, within a year he had established a Sunday school in the town on the pattern of Griffith Jones's circulating schools, and soon took upon himself the responsibility of employing, training and supervising a band of teachers. By 1794, at which time Charles was acting as an agent for Robert Raikes's Society for the Support and Encouragement of Sunday Schools, there were some twenty schools throughout Merionethshire and beyond, each teaching basic literacy skills and biblical doctrine in the vernacular, not always meeting on a Sunday but sometimes during weekday evenings as well, with their teachers being paid some twelve pounds per annum. Like the circulating schools, they would be convened mostly during the autumn and winter, when agricultural tasks were at their lightest, and Charles himself would decide where they would be established and whether they should last for three months, six months or a whole year. The first Sunday school specifically for adults was established, at Bala once more, in 1811, by which time they were proliferating throughout the land. During the same year Charles reported thus:

> I am just returned from a fortnight's tour through Caernarvonshire . . . I was most highly delighted with the proficiency which the children and young people had made in reading and catechetical instruction . . . From the age of 5 to 25 or 30, they generally attend schools, and many old people, grey-headed in ignorance, are stirred up by the young to seek for knowledge in the Bible in their old age. They are emerging out of ignorance *en masse*.[46]

By 1813 there were 256 Sunday schools in the six north Wales counties and 186 in south Wales, 442 in all. Two generations later, by the mid-1840s and across the denominations, there were 2,644

Sunday schools in Wales with 296,194 attendees of all ages, served by a phalanx of 19,591 teachers.[47] According to Huw J. Hughes, historian of the Sunday schools, 'They rose from the soil of Wales and the ordinary people of Wales were their beneficiaries.'[48]

The one other aspect of burgeoning evangelistic activity with which Charles is associated is the distribution of bibles. By now the need for cheaply produced bibles in the vernacular had become insatiable, and what became the British and Foreign Bible Society was established in 1804. The story of fifteen-year-old Mary Jones, walking barefoot the twenty-five miles to Bala from her home in Llanfihangel-y-Pennant in 1800 in order to buy her own copy of the Bible from Thomas Charles, has long become part of evangelical folklore.[49] The suggestion of forming a society to supply the wants of needy Bible readers not only at home but in the developing mission fields abroad was broached in a meeting of the Religious Tract Society in 1802, at which Charles was present. The upshot was the establishment of the Bible Society two years later, Charles's contribution to the new organization being vital. It too benefited from the extraordinary revivalistic energy which was being expended at the time, and soon tens of thousands of cheap though sturdy Welsh bibles were being made available for a uniquely appreciative populace.[50] Writing in July 1810 to the officers of the Society, Charles related how this had come about:

> I was continually applied to for Bibles, & much distressed I was (more than I can express) to be forever obliged to say I could not relieve them. The institution of the British & Foreign B[ible] S[ociety] will be to me, & thousand others cause of unspeakable comfort & joy as long as I live. The beneficial effects already produced in our poor country, of the abundant supply of Bibles by the means of it, are incalculable.[51]

In all, by the second decade of the nineteenth century, that 'nation of Nonconformists' remarked upon by mid-century observers, was well on the way to being formed.

By now there were thousands of ordinary people, biblically literate and spiritually keen, who craved for religious knowledge at the expense, sometimes, of more general information. Periodical literature, book production and publishing generally would expand exponentially during the early and mid-nineteenth century, most of which was spiritual and religious in tone. The first Welsh periodical had been Morgan John Rhys's *Cylchgrawn Cymraeg*, five issues of which appeared in 1793 and 1794, followed by Thomas Charles and Thomas Jones's more emphatically devout *Trysorfa Ysprydol* in 1799 and the first Welsh weekly newspaper, *Seren Gomer*, published by the Swansea Baptist minister Joseph Harris in 1814. By 1818 it had been reconfigured as a fortnightly journal with a marked religious content. Thereafter Welsh periodical literature took on a pronounced denominational character. Of the scores, indeed hundreds, of Welsh magazines which flooded the market were the Wesleyans' *Eurgrawn* from 1809, the Calvinistic Methodists' *Goleuad Cymru* and *Y Drysorfa*, the one from 1818 and the other from 1830, the Baptists' *Cyfrinach y Bedyddwyr* and *Greal y Bedyddwyr*, both established in 1827, the one serving south-east Wales and the other the south-west, along with the *Gwir Fedyddiwr* from 1842, the Congregationalists' *Dysgedydd* appearing from 1821, the *Diwygiwr* from 1835 and the north Wales-based *Cronicl* from 1843. The Anglican *Haul* began publishing in 1835 and the Unitarians' *Ymofynnydd* in 1847.[52] The more highbrow *Traethodydd*, established by Lewis Edwards as a literary and philosophical quarterly modelled on *Blackwood's Magazine* and *The Edinburgh Review* first appeared in 1845, but it too was overwhelmingly religious and theological in its nature. In such a (one is tempted to say) suffocating atmosphere, only religious literature could survive. A general interest magazine, *Y Cylchgrawn*, folded in 1837 for want of readers. 'It wanted religious information', complained its editor, 'and consequently excited little interest. The people have not been accustomed to think much upon any but religious topics.'[53] By mid-century presses throughout Wales were churning out innumerable scriptural commentaries, doctrinal treatises, preachers' biographies, moral tracts and temperance literature, often to the detriment of more secular subjects. The claim made by Thomas Rees, the historian of Protestant Dissent, in 1867 was, if anything, understated: 'Welsh literature is remarkable for its religious character and high moral tone.'[54]

Mid-century success

By mid-century, the feeling that Nonconformity had overtaken the Established Church as the premier medium of religious expression among the Welsh was proved to be factually true by the results of the religious census of 1851. On the evening of Sunday 30 March, in the seven south Wales counties of Monmouthshire, Glamorgan, Breconshire, Radnorshire, Carmarthenshire, Cardiganshire and Pembrokeshire, 71,156 worshippers were recorded as having attended services in Independent chapels, 68,334 in Baptist chapels and 52,511 among the Calvinistic Methodists. This does not include the smaller denominations such as the Moravians, the Quakers, Lady Huntingdon's Connexion or the Mormons. In the six north Wales counties of Montgomeryshire, Denbighshire, Flintshire, Merioneth, Caernarfonshire and Anglesey, there were 27,947 Independent worshippers, 13,651 Baptists, not including the 'Scotch' or Sandemanian Baptists, the followers of J. R. Jones of Ramoth,[55] and as many as 69,304 attendees at Calvinistic Methodist churches. In all, therefore, there were 81,984 Baptists, 99,103 Independents and 121,855 Calvinistic Methodists at services on census Sunday. In other words, and if the statistics are to be believed, four-fifths of all worshippers in Wales were outside the pale of the Established Church.[56]

Even earlier Anglicanism was seen to have lost its grip on the Welsh nation. 'The Church spell has lost its charm for the people', remarked a character in the autobiography of Robert Roberts, 'the Wandering Scholar', during the 1840s; 'there is no question about it: they have found out a tune more pleasing to their ears.'[57] The age-old weaknesses of the Church in the four Welsh dioceses – large and unwieldy parishes, dilapidated buildings situated far from the growing centres of population and paltry endowments insufficient to support resident clergy and their families – were starkly revealed in the census returns. Dissent, however, was shown to be genuinely responsive to the needs of the people. The chapels were more numerous, accessible and often more welcoming than old, damp and draughty parish churches. Even when there was no specific animus against the Church, many worshipped in the chapels for pragmatic reasons rather than doctrinal principle. 'Those who attend Church in the morning', reported the vicar of Nevern in Pembrokeshire, 'attend chapels in their different localities in the evening.'[58] 'It is well known', wrote the church warden of the Anglesey parish of Llanfihangel-Ysgeifiog, 'that in Wales those who attend Church at one point of the day generally attend Dissenting places of worship at another.'[59] Sometimes this grated on the clergy. 'Farm servants and labourers indifferent to the solemn services of the Church', complained the vicar of Llandyrnog, Denbighshire, 'reserve themselves for the night meeting [at the Nonconformist chapel in the parish] attracted by strange teachers and other equally unworthy circumstances.'[60] Few, however, were as candid about the weaknesses of the establishment as the vicar of Nevern; he readily admitted that many 'would be living the lives of heathens had not the Dissenters built chapels in different parts of the parish'.[61] And usually those chapels were flourishing. 'As is the case frequently in Wales', stated Michael D. Jones, then minister at Bwlchnewydd, Carmarthenshire, 'the chapel is so crammed occasionally that many more attend than are able to find room to sit and are consequently forced to stand',[62] while in north Wales, a Calvinistic Methodist respondent from Tal-sarn wrote: 'Sometimes our chappel [*sic*] is crowded and though it will hold more than 500 it is too small.'[63] On the whole, Nonconformity was in a thriving state, and the Anglican clergy admitted, often with an air of despondency: 'The people follow Dissent.'[64]

The radical impulse and political Dissent

By the beginning of the nineteenth century political concerns did not loom large in the minds of Welsh Nonconformists. Methodism was inherently conservative, whereas even the older Dissenters, the Independents, Baptists and the emerging Unitarians whose roots were in the upheavals of the Commonwealth period, were on the whole content to accept the position assigned to them following the Toleration Act of 1689. Free to worship according to their own rites, they were required nevertheless to pledge allegiance to the Crown and register their meeting houses, and were barred from holding public office and graduating at the English universities.

They were also obliged to contribute to the Established Church (to which they did not belong) by paying their tithe and church rate. By the 1820s, however, some were beginning to chafe against these civic disabilities and had begun petitioning parliament for their redress. They were jubilant at the repeal of the Test and Corporation Acts in 1828 which lifted the bar to public office, while some Welsh Nonconformists even approved of the Catholic Emancipation Act of 1829, not through any innate sympathy with popery as such, but on the basis of straightforward civic rights. The Great Reform Act of 1832 which granted Wales five additional parliamentary seats including the new industrial centres of Merthyr Tydfil and Swansea, had shown how inequitable the old system had been, and although the slight widening of the franchise did nothing to disturb a status quo in which representation remained in the hands of the same few landed families, change had at least begun. Grievances were now aired in the denominational press, the mainly Baptist *Seren Gomer*, the Independents' *Diwygiwr* under the fiery David Rees of Llanelli, and the north Wales-based *Cronicl* edited by the radical Samuel Roberts, 'S.R.', of Llanbrynmair. Other influential Nonconformist ministers used the popular press to agitate for reform, notably the Independent William Rees ('Gwilym Hiraethog') in the pages of the weekly *Amserau*, and the Methodist Thomas Gee in the *Baner*.

A huge fillip to the awakening political conscience of Nonconformist Wales was the publication in 1847 of the three-volume *Reports of the Commissioners of Inquiry into the State of Education in Wales*, the notorious 'Blue Books'. Although ostensibly an objective account of the status of elementary education in Wales, due to its being authored by three London-based barristers who, although assiduous in their researches had depended wholly on the views of Anglicized landowners and Anglican clergy, the resulting report was highly prejudiced. In it, the Welsh were portrayed as ignorant and immoral, blame being laid primarily at the door of Nonconformity and the Welsh language. The response, led, among others, by the Independents Henry Richard and Evan Jones ('Ieuan Gwynedd'), the Baptist Thomas Price and Lewis Edwards of Bala, was volcanic, deepening the already serious rift between chapel and church, and disabusing the Methodists of their erstwhile quietism.

'The Treason of the Blue Books', as it came to be known, provided a catalyst for a much greater level of political involvement than hitherto, as did the evictions of Nonconformist tenants from their Merionethshire farms for refusing to vote for the sitting member, the Tory W. W. E. Wynne, during the election of 1859. With the further widening of the franchise in the 1867 Representation of the People Act, the stage was set for a wholesale realignment of Welsh politics. All male heads of households were granted the vote, the electorate in Swansea and Cardiff increased threefold, that in Merthyr Tydfil rose tenfold, while that in the whole of Wales of those entitled to vote expanded by over 250 per cent. A later act, of 1884, widened the franchise even more drastically to include labourers and the smaller tenant farmers. This would spell the end of the Tory hegemony in Wales. In the 1868 general election, twenty-one Liberals were returned and only twelve Tories, and among the radicals Henry Richard, formerly a Dissenting minister and London-based champion of the Liberation Society, and his colleague George Osborne Morgan, the one for Merthyr and the other in Denbighshire. In other words, Welsh Dissent, duly radicalized, had found its effective political voice.

The theology of Dissent

The theology of Dissent throughout the years of expansion was Calvinism. The Methodists had inherited theirs from Daniel Rowland and Williams Pantycelyn before being systematized by Thomas Charles and Thomas Jones of Denbigh. Charles's hugely influential catechism, *Yr Hyfforddwr yn Egwyddorion y Grefydd Gristionogol* ('The Instructor in the Principles of the Christian Religion') (1807), paralleled in many ways the equally influential eighteenth-century catechisms of Griffith Jones, Llanddowror, and was issued in as many as ninety impressions, the final one being published in 1909. Along with his *Hyfforddwr*, an even more influential work to come from his pen was the *Geiriadur Ysgrythurol* ('Scriptural Dictionary') (1805–11), an encyclopaedic biblical compendium which furnished its readers with all that they needed to know not only concerning Scripture and doctrine but their application to personal and family life. It too was issued in numerous editions throughout the century and beyond. The Wesleyan mission of 1800 to 1815 had sharpened the Methodists' appreciation for the Calvinistic particulars, and much of the theological polemic of the first quarter of the century had to do with the doctrine of election and atonement theory. Here Thomas Jones of Denbigh came into his own, his learned treatises *Y Drych Athrawiaethol* ('The Doctrinal Mirror') (1806), *Ymddiddanion Crefyddol* ('Religious Dialogues') (1807) and especially the *Ymddiddanion . . . ar Brynedigaeth* ('Discourses . . . on Redemption') (1816 and 1819), strengthening the moderate Calvinist consensus which would continue to characterize the movement despite pressures from the Wesleyans, on the one hand, to abandon the concept of particular atonement totally, and by his fellow Calvinist John Elias, on the other, to hold to a narrow and novel 'equivalence theory', the idea that Christ's sufferings were in exact equivalence to the punishment due to the elect. With the publication of the movement's Confession of Faith in 1823, a mature document which blends traditional covenant theology with a pronounced Christological emphasis and accent on the work of the Spirit in bringing about union with Christ, doctrinal balance was restored.

Different strains of Calvinistic orthodoxy characterized the thought of the Independents and the Baptists as well. George Lewis, minister at Llanuwchllyn and then principal of the Congregational Academy at Wrexham, issued his weighty systematic theology *Y Drych Ysgrythurol* ('The Scriptural Mirror') in 1796, which was complemented between 1802 and 1815 by his equally erudite five-volume exposition on the New Testament. If Lewis's Calvinism was of the 'high' variety, a more moderate version, much influenced by the thought of Dr Edward Williams of Rotherham, came to be espoused by John Roberts, minister at Llanbrynmair, Montgomeryshire, in which a balance was struck between the divine sovereignty and human responsibility. This so called 'New System' would characterize the doctrinal stance of the Independents into the middle of the century and beyond. Turning to the Baptists, in the *Gwelediad y Palas Arian* ('A Vision of the Silver Palace') written by John Jenkins, minister at Hengoed, Glamorgan, and published in 1811 with a second edition in 1820, the concept of election was foregrounded in a more blatant way than had been usual previously. This 'high' Calvinism, which was also perceptible in his three-volume *Esboniad ar y Bibl Sanctaidd* ('A Commentary on the Holy Bible') (1823–32), was challenged vigorously by J. P. Davies, minister at Tredegar, whose posthumous *Traethodau* ('Treatises') (1832) established 'Fullerism', or the moderate Calvinism of the English theologian Andrew Fuller, as the mainstream view of the Welsh Baptists until mid-century and beyond.

The most gifted theologian of that period was Lewis Edwards, a graduate of the University of Edinburgh and founding principal of the Calvinistic Methodists' college at Bala. His series of essays entitled 'Cysondeb y Ffydd' ('The Consistency of Faith') published in the quarterly review *Y Traethodydd* between 1845 and 1853 and latterly in his composite volume *Traethodau Duwinyddol* ('Theological Essays') in 1872, attempted to move beyond the older polarities by positing a new way of doing theology entirely. If, by insisting that God's elective will was absolute, the high Calvinists had made the mediating position of the moderate Calvinists inevitable, was there any way of stating, without contradiction, that God was *both* wholly sovereign *and* that the human will was fully free? In emphasizing human freedom, the Wesleyans, for their part, had limited God's sovereignty, something that Edwards was loath to do. On the other hand, in majoring on God's sovereignty even moderate Calvinists like Thomas Jones had not done justice fully to the freedom of the will. What this series of essays did was to attempt a way forward beyond these dualities. 'The correct opinion on all subjects', he claimed, 'includes two opposite truths and the contrast between them only appears to be irreconcilable.' This was not Aristotle's golden mean or Hegel's synthesis but a way of doing justice to the apparent logical inconsistencies of plain biblical truth. In the essays he worked the theory out in the context of specific themes: the freedom of the will; the nature of the atonement; the extent of the atonement; the concept of election; and the idea of sin. The series created a sensation. 'Nothing appeared in Welsh theological literature that created such a deep impression on the nation's most reflective readers of all denominations', one commentator wrote, 'than this series of articles . . . It created a *novum organum*, a new way, a new method for theology.'[65] By the second half of the century Welsh

Dissenters had learned to be more comfortable with the paradoxes of faith than they had been in the past.

Pulpit, hymnody, the 1859 Revival and beyond

Such was the power and popularity of the pulpit that by mid-century the Welsh came to think of themselves as being uniquely blessed. 'Taking everything into consideration', noted the Calvinistic Methodist Edward Matthews in a seminal essay on Welsh preaching published in 1863, 'Wales can take pride in the fact that although she is bereft of many things, she is the home to the best preaching in the world, and the strongest yearning among the people to listen to such preaching.'[66] Having inherited the tradition of Christmas Evans, Williams of Wern and John Elias, Matthews belonged to an equally gifted generation who not only perpetuated the practice with enduring success, but lionized its significance. By the latter part of the Victorian era the ideal of Wales as 'the land of the preacher' had been well established, with increasingly romanticized volumes such as David Davies's *Echoes from the Welsh Hills, or Reminiscences of the Preachers and People of Wales* (1883) and Owen Jones's *Some of the Great Preachers of Wales* (1886) maintaining the stereotype. Although gospel preaching remained an effective force in Nonconformist life between 1760 and 1890, by the end of the period the emphasis on oratorical performance and homiletic technique was in danger of threatening the spiritual integrity of the message.

By mid-century Wales was also coming to be known as 'the land of song'. Popular revivalism had been fuelled by vocal praise, and where Williams Pantycelyn led, others followed. Initially singing was raw and exuberant, but with the universal popularity of hymn-singing, Nonconformist leaders realized the need for a more disciplined approach. As early as first decade of the nineteenth century the Montgomeryshire Calvinistic Methodist Henry Mills had been appointed by his monthly meeting as a peripatetic music teacher, though it was with the work of John Mills, his grandson, that a level of professionalism was attained. Author of *Gramadeg Cerddoriaeth* ('A Musical Grammar') in 1838, he visited the burgeoning local music societies explaining technique, raising standards and initiating worshippers in the principles of sacred song. The singing unions of the 1820s and 1830s were interdenominational in nature, with worshippers coming together to share ideas, exchange best practice and enjoy the experience of united praise. Along with the works of Williams Pantycelyn, the Baptist Joseph Harris ('Gomer') and the Independent Samuel Roberts had issued collections of hymns by a range of different authors, though it was with the publication of the *Llyfr Tonau* ('Tune Book') by John Roberts, 'Ieuan Gwyllt', in 1859, with four-part harmonies in simple, unadorned style, that the fusion of words and music came together in an exceptional way. By its use of John Curwen's tonic sol-fa scheme rather than the older staff notation, Eleazer Roberts's *Llawlyfr Caniadaeth* ('Hymnodic Handbook') of 1861 revolutionized the practice. Soon every chapel had its modulator, and virtually all of their worshippers had been instructed in its use. The *cymanfa ganu* or communal singing festival dates from this period. It has been said that '[t]he development of the *cymanfa ganu* in the nineteenth century probably did more than anything to promote the proverbial Welsh love of congregational singing: it encouraged the learning of tunes in four parts and gave vent to powerful singing and powerful emotions.'[67]

As well as stimulating the influence of preaching and energizing popular hymnody, local awakenings culminating in the 1859 Revival remained key to the expansion of Welsh Nonconformity. Revivals, of course, were familiar, but by the late 1830s novel elements were emerging, inspired by the ideas of the American evangelist Charles G. Finney. The Arminian Finney had less interest in doctrinal minutiae than even the most non-dogmatic Welsh Wesleyan, but his *Darlithiau ar Adfywiadau Crefyddol* (1839), a Welsh translation of his practical handbook *Lectures on Revivals of Religion*, became an unexpected best-seller. For Finney, conversion could be induced by a specific technique while revivals could be more or less manufactured. They were, in fact, 'the natural result of the correct adherence to given means'.[68] These means included: concerted prayer; the pointed preaching of Christ's sacrificial death as God's way of salvation; the deliberate application of this message to individuals' conscience in the context of 'protracted meetings' in a single location over a period of days; and the use of the 'anxious bench' where prospective converts could be pressed to respond to the gospel call. 'The result', he claimed, 'is as inevitable under the one circumstance as it is under the other.'[69] Whereas the older theology believed revival to be a sovereign work of the Holy Spirit, the awakenings which occurred throughout the 1840s and 1850s were much indebted to these methods. In April 1850 the Independent minister Thomas Rees implored Finney to visit Wales, ensuring him that his lectures had 'been instrumental in the conversion of hundreds if not thousands of our countrymen'.[70] Henry Hughes, historian of the nineteenth-century revivals, calculated that between 1849 and 1851, 20,000 were added to the chapels throughout the land, many of whom had been drawn through use of the new measures and techniques, even apart from the general preaching which had characterized Nonconformist evangelism in the past.

With the advent of the 1859 Revival, the measures first championed by Finney had been absorbed into the culture of Welsh evangelicalism. During the months before the awakening became widespread, Thomas Aubrey, Wesleyan minister in the Bangor circuit, had led a particularly effective campaign along Finney's lines within his congregations, though it was through the work of his fellow Wesleyan, Humphrey Jones, that the renewal became best known. Jones, a native of Llancynfelyn, Cardiganshire, had been ordained into the ministry of the Episcopal Methodists, a revivalist-based frontier denomination, in Wisconsin in 1855 following his emigration there a year earlier, and soon gained a name in the American mid-west as a fiery evangelist. Returning to Wales intent on spreading the spirit of renewal at home, between July and September 1858, following a series of protracted meetings replete with altar calls and use of the anxious bench, hundreds had been added to churches in the north Cardiganshire Wesleyan circuit. By October he had been joined by David Morgan, a Calvinistic Methodist from Ysbyty Ystwyth, also in northern-Cardiganshire, and thereafter the revival spread further afield. Although initially it had been felt mostly among the Wesleyans; by 1859, when it was at its most potent, it had spread through all the Nonconformist denominations, even touching the Established Church. By the time it had subsided in the spring of 1860, it was seen as being the most powerful awakening since the time of Howell Harris and Daniel Rowland: 'The 1859 Revival left an indelible mark on Welsh society. Membership [in the Calvinistic Methodist Church] soared by an estimated 110,000, the vast majority of whom remained faithful for the rest of their lives.'[71]

By then there were signs that the cultural and intellectual climate was changing. Tensions between the Calvinistic Methodists and the Arminian Wesleyans had long abated, while even the moderate Calvinistic consensus shared by the Independents and Baptists was being superseded. At this juncture Lewis Edwards's *Athrawiaeth yr Iawn* ('The Doctrine of the Atonement') of 1860 proved to be a watershed work. Published a year after Charles Darwin's *Origin of Species*, when thousands of new converts were being added to the chapels in the wake of the revival, it encapsulated perfectly the intellectual challenge which late nineteenth- and twentieth-century Dissent would have to face. In itself it was deeply traditional, holding to the orthodox concept of penal substitution: sin is a transgression of the divine law; God as lawgiver demands reparation for that transgression, otherwise God would not be righteous, while Christ has put himself in man's place in order to pay his penalty according to the divine demand. Written as a Socratic dialogue between teacher and pupil and in a winsome and irenic style, it was obviously a sign that the younger generation was beginning to question the presuppositions of their fathers. Was it true that God *demanded* a sacrifice of his Son in order to be merciful? The dialogue partners were the English liberals F. D. Maurice, Benjamin Jowett and the Scot McLeod Campbell, showing that the author and his readers were well aware of doctrinal developments elsewhere. Although Edwards rejected their views firmly and courteously, he did not anathematize them. He was sufficiently open to the sincere questions of an upcoming generation to feel their force. The book is part of the *Zeitgeist* described by the historian Boyd Hilton:

> It is clear that moral revulsion did play an important role in the softening of evangelical Christianity . . . Along with hellfire, liberal theologians of the 1850s and 60s surrendered the idea that a loving God would inflict excruciating

suffering on his Son as a vicarious sacrifice for other men's sins. Such an action now seemed both unjust and . . . inefficacious. [72]

Lewis Edwards never did this because he was never a liberal theologian, but he was sufficiently open to realize the problematic nature of the older explanations and to respond sensitively to questions that were being asked. It would become clear that in order to endure, Nonconformist Wales would need to meet the challenge of the times.

Welsh religion by 1890

'Sir', wrote Canon William Evans, the vicar of Rhymney, to the secretary of the Church Pastoral Aid Society in 1887, 'you have the satisfaction of helping not a dying Church, not a decaying Church, but a living, a reviving, a rising Church.'[73] The malaise which had previously afflicted Welsh Anglicanism and had been partially redressed by mid-century, now belonged to the past. Pluralities had been abolished, absenteeism had ceased, church buildings everywhere had been refurbished and finances had been released to facilitate church extension. With the appointment of Joshua Hughes to St Asaph in 1870, the baleful policy of appointing Englishmen to Welsh sees came to an end. Thereafter the bishops would be native-born Welshmen, all able to officiate through both English and Welsh. Significant parochial renewal had come through the preaching ministry of the evangelicals, especially potent in the recently industrialized Valleys communities, while the older High Church sacramentarianism had been rejuvenated through the influence of the Oxford Movement. Newly aware of their status within the apostolic succession, Jesus College ordinands returned home intent on enacting Tractarian principles within their parishes. In all, by 1890 the Welsh Church was in good heart.

The Catholic church too, by that time, was in buoyant mood. In 1760 in all but two small pockets, the Holywell area of Flintshire and Abergavenny and Usk in Monmouthshire, indigenous Welsh Catholicism had all but died out. According to a report sent to

Rome in 1773, Wales possessed a mere 750 Catholics served by nine missionary priests.[74] With industrialization however, and especially with early nineteenth-century immigration from Ireland, Catholic numbers increased, and for the first time since the Reformation the Mass began to be celebrated in such places as Newport (1809), Merthyr Tydfil (1824), Cardiff (1825) and in the north, Bangor (1827), Wrexham (1828) and Caernarfon. By 1838, nine years after the passing of the Catholic Emancipation Act, there were approximately 6,250 Catholics in Wales, mostly in the dock areas of Swansea, Cardiff and Newport but also in the iron-producing capital of Merthyr Tydfil and in Wrexham. By mid-century the need for priests became pressing; they were supplied, increasingly, by the religious orders: the Benedictines, the Rosaminians or Fathers of Charity, the Capuchin Franciscans and later by the Jesuits and the Passionists.

Between 1688 and 1849 Wales was part of the so-called Western District, and from 1840 placed within the new vicariate of Wales and Hereford with its own vicar-apostolic, Thomas Joseph Brown, formerly prior of Downside Abbey. Following the restoration of the hierarchy in 1850, north Wales became part of the diocese of Shrewsbury, its first bishop being James Brown, while Thomas Joseph Brown (no relation) was appointed first bishop of the new diocese of Newport and Menevia encompassing the south Wales counties and Herefordshire: 'When T. J. Brown began his work in Wales in 1840 there were sixteen stations and eighteen priests in the whole country; by the time of his death in 1880 there were forty stations and the same number of priests in his diocese alone.'[75]

In 1895, following Pope Leo XIII's apostolic brief *De Antimarum Salute*, structures changed yet again. The six north Wales counties which had been annexed to the diocese of Shrewsbury, were now joined to those in the south (excluding populous Glamorgan and Monmouthshire) in order to create a new vicariate-apostolic headed by Welsh-born Francis Mostyn, son of an old-established recusant family, the Mostyns of Talacre, Flintshire. Within three years the vicariate had become an independent diocese designated by the title of Menevia, while the two south-eastern counties along with Hereford became the new diocese of Newport. Led by the scholarly John Cuthbert Headley, who had been bishop of the old see of

Newport and Menevia since 1881, and now the youthful Mostyn, Welsh Catholicism looked towards the future with confidence. There were by then some 45,000 Catholics, the vast preponderance of whom were Irish, served by sixty-eight priests, in Newport, and a much smaller complement of 6,000 or so in Menevia, served by some thirty priests. Although still somewhat peripheral to the nation's life, and often mistrusted and despised, 'the Old Faith' of the Church of Rome had re-established itself as an essential element of the Christian witness in Wales.

Nevertheless, Protestant Nonconformity remained in the ascendancy and was massively influential still. The pattern which was noted in the religious census of 1851 and would be reaffirmed in the statistics contained in the *Report of the Royal Commission appointed to inquire into the Church and other Religious Bodies in Wales and Monmouthshire* (1910), showed that 'the nation of Nonconformists' felt itself to be assured of the future. It would not be long, however, before clouds would be visible on the horizon and the 'the dawn of a bright future' so confidently predicted in 1890,[76] would turn to a darker hue.

Notes

1   Henry Richard, *Letters and Essays on Wales* (1866) (London: James Clarke, 1884), p. 2.

2   Arianism was the belief that Christ did not share full deity with the Father, but was the greatest of God's creatures.

3   Standard volumes on the history of Welsh Dissent between 1760 and 1890 are listed in the guide to further reading at the end of this volume.

4   K. Monica Davies, 'Teulu Trefeca', in *Hanes Methodistiaeth Galfinaidd Cymru*, vol. 1: *Y Deffroad Mawr*, edited by Gomer M. Roberts (Caernarfon: Llyfrfa'r Methodistiaid, 1974), pp. 356–77.

5   Quoted in R. T. Jenkins, 'Methodistiaeth ym Mhapurau Thomas Morgan, Henllan', in *Yng Nghysgod Trefeca: Ysgrifau ar Hanes Crefydd a Chymdeithas yng Nghymru'r Ddeunawfed Ganrif* (Caernarfon: Llyfrfa'r Methodistiaid, 1968), p. 48.

6   *Llythyr, Oddi wrth y Gymanfa at yr eglwysi* (Caerfyrddin: John Ross,

1779), p. 2.

7   Quoted in John T. Griffith, *Hanes Eglwys Pen-y-fai* (Tonypandy: Evans & Short, 1916), p. 26.

8   M. J. Rhys to John Rippon, 23 November 1791, British Library Add.MS 24388.

9   William Morgan, *Cofiant, neu Hanes Bywyd y Diweddar Barch. Christmas Evans* (Caerdydd: Llewelyn Jenkins, 1839), p. 17.

10 'Hanes Christmas Evans', *Greal y Bedyddwyr* (1829), 321.

11 Christmas Evans, 'Cyflwr crefydd yng Nghymru' (1837), in *Gweithiau y Parchedig Christmas Evans*, cyf. 2, edited by Owen Davies (Caernarfon: Gwenlyn Evans, 1898), p. 13.

12 His actual word is 'periwigs', namely the headgear worn by the staid and respectable preachers of eighteenth-century Dissent.

13 John Rowlands, *Cofiant y Parchg Daniel Davies* (Llanelli: James Davies, 1879), p. 180.

14 Evans, 'Cyflwr crefydd yng Nghymru', p. 13.

15 Evans, 'Cyflwr crefydd yng Nghymru', p. 14.

16 Williams, Jacob, Yates and Knight, *The Welsh Church*, p. 165.

17 Eryn M. White, 'A "Poor, Benighted Church"? Church and Society in Mid–Eighteenth–Century Wales', in *From Medieval to Modern Wales: Historical Essays in Honour of Kenneth O. Morgan and Ralph A. Griffiths*, edited by R. R. Davies and Geraint H. Jenkins (Cardiff: University of Wales Press, 2004), p. 123.

18 Peter B. Nockles, *The Oxford Movement in Context: Anglican High Churchmanship, 1760–1857* (Cambridge: Cambridge University Press, 1994), p. 10.

19 John Warren, *The Duties of Parochial Clergy Considered in a Charge delivered to the clergy of the Diocese of Bangor* (London: Lockyer Davis, 1784), pp. 10–11.

20 Warren, *The Duties of Parochial Clergy Considered*, p. 5.

21 Warren, *The Duties of Parochial Clergy Considered*, p. 5.

22 Warren, *The Duties of Parochial Clergy Considered*, p. 3.

23 Warren, *The Duties of Parochial Clergy Considered*, p. 4.

24 Samuel Horsley, *The Charge of Samuel, Lord Bishop of St David's, to the Clergy of his Diocese* (London: R. Robson, 1790), p. 28.

25 Horsley, *Charge ... to the Clergy of his Diocese*, p. 33.

26 Horsley, *Charge ... to the Clergy of his Diocese*, p. 32.

27 For the 'Anglo–bishops', see Morgan, *Theologia Cambrensis*, vol. 1, pp. 389–90.

28 John R. Guy, *The Diocese of Llandaff in 1763* (Cardiff: South Wales Record Society, 1991), p. 34.

29 Gomer M. Roberts, *Y Pêr Ganiedydd [Pantycelyn]*, cyf. 1: *Trem ar ei Fywyd* (Aberystwyth: Gwasg Aberystwyth, 1949), p. 168.

30 D. E. Jenkins, *The Life of Thomas Charles of Bala*, vol. 2 (Denbigh: Llewelyn Jenkins, 1910), p. 45.

31 A letter written in 1812, quoted in D. E. Jenkins, *Calvinistic Methodist Holy Orders* (Caernarfon: Calvinistic Methodist Book-Room, 1911), p. 224.

32 Jonathan Jones, *Cofiant y Parchg Thomas Jones o Ddinbych* (Dinbych: Thomas Gee, 1897), pp. 230–1.

33 Quoted in *Hanes Methodistiaeth Galfinaidd Cymru*, vol. 2: *Cynnydd y Corff*, edited by Gomer M. Roberts (Caernarfon: Llyfrfa'r Methodistiaid Calfinaidd, 1978), pp. 293–4.

34 *The Religious Census of 1851: A Calendar of the Returns relating to Wales*, vol. 1: *South Wales*, edited by Ieuan Gwynedd Jones and David Williams (Cardiff: University of Wales Press, 1976), appendix B; *The Religious Census of 1851: A Calendar of the Returns relating to Wales*; vol. 2: *North Wales*, edited by Ieuan Gwynedd Jones (Cardiff: University of Wales Press, 1981), appendix.

35 See Bruce Hindmarsh, *John Newton and the English Evangelical Tradition* (Oxford: Clarendon Press, 1996).

36 D. E. Jenkins, *The Life of the Rev. Thomas Charles of Bala*, vol. 3 (Denbigh: Llewelyn Jenkins, 1911), pp. 301–2; Roger L. Brown, *Evangelicals in the Church of Wales* (Welshpool: Tair Eglwys Press), p. 94.

37 Letter to Josiah Pratt, secretary of the Church Missionary Society, quoted in Jenkins, *The Life of the Rev. Thomas Charles of Bala*, vol. 3, p. 303.

38 Quoted in St George Armstrong Williams, 'Memoir', in *The English Works of the Late Revd Eliezer Williams MA* (London: Cradock and Co., 1840), p. lxv.

39 St George Armstrong Williams, 'Memoir', pp. lxviii–lxix.

40 St George Armstrong Williams, 'Memoir', p. lxxi. Eliezer Williams is listed in both *DWB* and *ODNB*.

41 Peter Williams, *Casgliad o Bregethau . . . y pedwerydd llyfr* (Dolgellau: R. Jones. 1815), p. 137

42 Williams, *Casgliad o Bregethau . . . y pedwerydd llyfr*, pp. 148, 149.

43 Williams, *Casgliad o Bregethau . . . y pedwerydd llyfr*, p. 21.

44 Williams, *Casgliad o Bregethau . . . y pedwerydd llyfr*, pp. 207–8.

45 Williams, Jacob, Yates and Knight, *The Welsh Church*, p. 292.

46 Jenkins, *The Life of Thomas Charles of Bala*, vol. 3, p. 413.

47 As listed by R. Tudur Jones, *Blas ar Gristnogaeth Cymru*, edited by Euros Wyn Jones (Chwilog: Cyhoeddiadau'r Gair, 2018), p. 75.

48 Huw J. Hughes, 'Thomas Charles, llythrennedd a'r Ysgol Sul', in *Thomas Charles o'r Bala*, edited by D. Densil Morgan (Caerdydd: Gwasg Prifysgol Cymru, 2013), p. 33.

49 E. Wyn James, 'Thomas Charles, Ann Griffiths a Mary Jones', in *Thomas Charles o'r Bala*, edited by Morgan, pp. 135–56.

50 See White, *The Welsh Bible*, pp. 102–12.

51 Quoted in James, 'Thomas Charles, Ann Griffiths a Mary Jones', p. 150.

52 See Huw Walters, 'The Periodical Press', in *The Welsh Language and Its Social Domains, 1801–1911*, edited by Geraint H. Jenkins (Cardiff: University of Wales Press, 2000), pp. 349–78.

53 Quoted in Walters, 'The Periodical Press', p. 361.

54 Thomas Rees, *Miscellaneous Papers on Subjects relating to Wales* (London: John Snow, 1867), p. 49.

55 See J. Idwal Jones, *J. R. Jones Ramoth a'i Amserau* (Llandysul: Gwasg Gomer, 1966).

56 It should be remembered that out of a total Welsh population of over a million, it seems that over half remained beyond the reach of organized religion altogether: 'The irreligious are a lost element in Welsh historiography'; John Davies, *A History of Wales* (London: Penguin Books, 1993), p. 427.

57 *A Wandering Scholar: The Life and Opinions of Robert Roberts*, edited by J. Burnett and H. G. Williams (Cardiff: University of Wales Press, 1991), p. 63.

58 *The Religious Census of 1851*, vol. 1: *South Wales*, edited by Jones and Williams, p. 465.

59 *The Religious Census of 1851*, vol. 2: *North Wales*, edited by Jones, p. 338.

60 *The Religious Census of 1851*, vol. 2, edited by Jones, p. 181.

61 *The Religious Census of 1851*, vol. 1, edited by Jones and Williams, pp. 464–5.

62 *The Religious Census of 1851*, vol. 1, edited by Jones and Williams, p. 352.

63 *The Religious Census of 1851*, vol. 2, edited by Jones, p. 319.

64 The curate of Carn–guwch, Bangor diocese, in *The Religious Census of 1851*, vol. 2, edited by Jones, p. 292

65 Griffith Parry, 'Y Diweddar Barchedig Dr Edwards, Y Bala', *Y Drysorfa*, 57 (1887), 326–7.

66 Edward Matthews, 'Pregethwyr a Phregethu Cymru', *Bywgraffiad y Parch. Thomas Richard* (Abertawe: Joseph Rosser, 1863), p. xvi.

67 Rhidian Griffiths, 'Songs of Praises', in *The History of Welsh Calvinistic*

Methodism, vol. III: *Growth and Consolidation (c. 1814–1914)*, edited by
J. Gwynfor Jones (Cardiff: Presbyterian Church of Wales, 2013), p. 141.

[68] Charles G. Finney, *Darlithiau ar Adfywiadau Crefyddol*, translated by Evan
Griffiths (Abertawe: E. Griffiths, 1839), p. 8.

[69] Finney, *Darlithiau ar Adfywiadau Crefyddol*, p. 9.

[70] Quoted in Richard Carwardine, 'The Welsh Evangelical Community
and "Finney's Revival"', *Journal of Ecclesiastical History*, 29 (1978), 478.

[71] Goronwy Prys Owen, 'Worship and spiritual life', in *The History of
Welsh Calvinistic Methodism*, vol. III, edited by Jones, p. 41; for the
statistics see Henry Hughes, *Hanes Diwygiadau Crefyddol Cymru*
(Caernarfon: Swyddfa'r Genedl, 1906), p. 395.

[72] Boyd Hilton, *The Age of Atonement: The Influence of Evangelicalism on
Social and Economic Thought, 1785–1865* (Oxford: Clarendon Press,
1986), pp. 273, 281.

[73] Brown, *Evangelicals in the Church of Wales*, p. 143.

[74] Donald Attwater, *The Catholic Church in Modern Wales* (London: Burns
and Oates, 1935), p. 25.

[75] R. Tudur Jones, *Faith and the Crisis of a Nation: Wales 1890–1914*,
edited by Robert Pope (Cardiff: University of Wales Press, 2004),
p. 18.

[76] Jones, *Faith and the Crisis of a Nation: Wales 1890–1914*, p. 1.

Chapter 11

Adapting to a Secular Wales, 1890–2020

D. DENSIL MORGAN AND DAVID CERI JONES

By the final quarter of the nineteenth century Nonconformist Wales was flourishing as never before. Chapel life was vibrant while denominational structures everywhere were being strengthened. The first general assembly of the Calvinistic Methodists, now regarding itself increasingly as the Presbyterian Church of Wales, was convened in 1864, the Baptist Union of Wales met for the first time in 1866, as did the Union of Welsh Independents in 1872. The University College at Aberystwyth, forerunner of the University of Wales, was founded in 1872, followed by colleges at Cardiff in 1883 and Bangor in 1884. The University would be 'secular', not in the sense of being non-religious but purposely outside the control of the Established Church. The 'nation of Nonconformists' described in the previous chapter had come of age, yet some were already sensing that all was not well. If, for Lewis Edwards the intellectual challenges were like a cloud the size of a man's hand, for Thomas Charles Edwards, his son, founding principal of the 'national college' at Aberystwyth and premier theologian of the late Victorian era, the future was increasingly ominous. 'In our fathers' days', he told his church's general assembly in 1888, 'it could be taken for granted that theology was the abiding concern of a huge swath of the Welsh lay folk, but can that be said of today? Now it is politics or scientific theory, and is it not a fact that our young men not only have no theology but have no appetite for it at all?'[1] 'In the present condition of things in Wales', he informed the Pan-Presbyterian Council in London in that same year, 'you have a people actually weary of contending systems, keenly alive at the same time to the fascination of new ideas, political and scientific, and, for this reason, in danger of drifting away from theological truth altogether.' It was not that the gospel was failing to be preached. The basic soundness of the evangelical pulpit could not be faulted. What was new was that the listeners, still active in their chapels, were becoming more and more sceptical as to the reality of divine truth: 'In our age agnosticism has come to the front as a conscious phase of the human intellect and teaches our young men not that this or that solution to the problem is fallacious . . . but that the problem itself need not be solved either way.'[2]

Theology itself was changing. The 'age of atonement' had yielded to 'the age of incarnation', centred less on the Christ who had died to save humankind from sin and damnation as on the one who had affirmed the divine image borne by all.[3] Though evangelical truth was still being espoused, among some ministers, Congregationalists especially, the emphasis was being transferred from the sinfulness of humankind and its need for an objective redemption, to evolution, moral progression and the divine immanence. Christ the crucified Saviour was in danger of being eclipsed by the man Jesus, the prophet of human perfectibility. Thomas Charles Edwards's *God-Man* (1895), a brave attempt at preserving the substance of the faith while responding to the challenge of Idealist philosophy, was only partly successful. A more liberal creed, sceptical of such older staples as hell, the wrath of God and the divine judgement, and optimistic on the question of man's innate goodness, was gaining adherents steadily, especially among the young.

This being the case, the astounding religious revival of 1904–5 remains something of an enigma. Beginning in south Cardiganshire in the spring of 1904, rapidly spreading throughout the whole of Wales and beyond, and only abating around Christmas 1905, it brought myriads of people either back into the churches having received a fresh vision of the glory of the gospel, or else brought them to a saving knowledge of Christ for the first time. Prepared for assiduously by a band of committed younger ministers, its most high-profile leader would be Evan Roberts, a former coal miner and ministerial candidate with the Calvinistic Methodists. Unlike the revivals of the past, its doctrinal content was muted. Its emphasis – under Evan Roberts, at least – was upon the divine love sometimes at the expense of the divine justice, while its most obvious characteristic was not powerful preaching but high emotional intensity. Roberts, though patently sincere, was theologically untrained and given to intense subjectivism, a cause of much controversy at the time. As a result of the revival, church membership in the Nonconformist denominations increased by some 80,000, a rise of 18.6 per cent, though much backsliding and disenchantment was recorded during the subsequent years. An objective assessment, even at this juncture, is difficult to make. For some it was 'the swansong of the old religious tradition of Wales . . . the consumptive's flush of death'.[4] For others it was, and remained, a turning point in their lives and the basis of a lifetime's commitment and faithfulness. Although stubbornly difficult to evaluate, it remains 'one of the most remarkable events in twentieth-century Welsh history'.[5]

The Disestablishment campaign

The revival occurred in a Wales that was, in parts, heavily industrialized and increasingly Anglicized in speech, in the valleys of Monmouthshire and Glamorgan, the border counties and the larger towns especially. Socialism and a class-based labour politics were superseding Liberal and laissez-faire individualism while the Anglican church, previously shunned as being an alien and oppressive institution, had regained strength and popularity. Yet for Nonconformity, outwardly at least, things continued to flourish. 'We think that from the evidence advanced before us', wrote the authors of the *Report of the Royal Commission of the Church of England and other Religious Bodies in Wales and Monmouthshire* (1910), 'that the people of Wales show a marked tendency to avail themselves of the provision made by the churches of all denominations for their spiritual welfare.'[6] Whatever the truth of this assertion, more and more people were, in fact, becoming disenchanted with organized religion per se. This became nowhere more obvious than with the painful and protracted campaign to disestablish and disendow the Church of England in Wales. 'In its effect on the spiritual life of the nation', wrote R. Tudur Jones, 'this long battle was a major disaster.'[7] What had been in the 1870s a principled disagreement about a valid concern – whether religion should, or should not, maintain its historic link with the state – had become by the 1900s a vicious and mean-spirited squabble about privilege, status and money: 'It gave rise to hatred and cruelty which left deep scars on the spiritual life of the nation.'[8]

By the 1870s the resentment stoked by the 'Blue Books' controversy a quarter-century earlier found a fresh focus in the call to disestablish the Anglican Church in Wales. The English Congregationalist and radical MP Edward Miall's Society for the Liberation of Religion from State Control and Patronage, 'The Liberation Society', gained ground in Wales especially after 1865, and following the election of 1868 signalling the end of Tory supremacy in the principality, pressure for radical change increased. In May 1870 Watkin Williams, the Liberal member for Denbigh, forwarded a Commons measure calling for endowment capital from the four Welsh dioceses to be used for general educational purposes, and although heavily rejected by parliament, the move illustrated what was yet to come. The 1880 election saw Liberal candidates being returned for as many as twenty-nine of Wales's thirty-three seats, and four years later, following the Third Reform Act (1884) which widened the franchise even further, Liberal representation rose to thirty. In March 1886 Lewis Llewelyn Dillwyn, the veteran Liberal member for Swansea (and an Anglican), sponsored a motion calling for Welsh disestablishment, and although it failed to move beyond a first reading, it was supported by as many as 229 votes to 241. Popular support for the cause was escalating everywhere:

> I object to all civil establishments of religion [stated the Cardiff coal-owner, philanthropist and erstwhile Anglican, John Cory], believing it to be no part of the business of governments to interfere in matters of conscience, and having

a deep conviction that in doing so they violate the rights of conscience and injure the cause of religion.[9]

With pressure from a younger generation of fiery and nationalistic MPs such as D. A. Thomas, Samuel T. Evans, T. E. Ellis and David Lloyd George, disestablishment became a means of redressing much more widespread ills, the Church question being merely a symptom of age-old landed Tory oppression of the Welsh people. Although nominally Nonconformist, this generation partook fully of the religious scepticism which Thomas Charles Edwards had described, and as a consequence spiritual concerns became secondary. Unionist Nonconformists in England were now faced with the claim for disestablishment in Wales alone, with the Liberal Party, representing a minority of English seats, needing to be seen to respond to popular Welsh demand. With W. E. Gladstone's decision to support the cause in 1891, Welsh disestablishment became central to Liberal policy.

As the new generation of radical politicians came to the fore representing Nonconformists. 'Church Defence' or the campaign to preserve the link with the state found its champion in the recently appointed bishop of St Asaph, Alfred George Edwards. More pugnacious than his predecessors and although native-born and Welsh-speaking, deeply ambivalent about the claims of Welsh nationhood, he chose to defend the church wholly on Erastian and ultra-unionist lines. Aided with immense skill by his colleague, John Owen, dean of St Asaph and later bishop of St David's, a wrangle ensued between what was perceived as a privileged, Anglicized elite, and the voluntary and democratic Welsh-speaking culture which characterized popular Nonconformity. The financial matter of disendowment was particularly rancorous, and compromise proved impossible. Before long the situation was more akin to out-and-out war between chapel and church.

Following two unsuccessful attempts at passing a Welsh disestablishment bill, the first in April 1894 and the second a year later, with extensive Liberal losses following the general election of 1895, any further progress in parliament proved impossible. Agitation came to a virtual stop until 1906, and with the landslide victory of the Liberals, which saw the Tories forfeiting every single

Welsh seat – the Scot Keir Hardie retained Merthyr Tydfil for the new Independent Labour Party – there was nothing to prevent the disestablishment of the Church of England in Wales from going ahead. The times, alas, had changed. Interest in religious matters was abating everywhere, and the gripping concerns had become social and economic. Lloyd George, now a senior member of cabinet, was wholly absorbed with infinitely more pressing matters: the Pensions Act of 1908, the 'People's Budget' of 1909 and the equally revolutionary National Assurance Act of 1911, along with that year's Parliament Act curtailing the House of Lords' power of veto. The Royal Commission on Religion in Wales, established in 1906 in order to prepare for disestablishment and disendowment, was seen widely as a delaying tactic, with the more zealous among the Nonconformists being deeply dismayed at the government's prevarication. After the publication of its exhaustive (and for the historian, invaluable) report in 1910, action could no longer be postponed.

The 'Act to Terminate the Establishment of the Church of England in Wales and Monmouthshire and to make Provision for the Temporalities thereof', or what became 'The Welsh Church Act', was introduced to parliament on 23 April 1912, moving through its different stages until it was passed by the Commons in January 1913, only to be rejected by the Lords. A second iteration began its journey in July which met with the same fate, and it was only in September 1914 that success was finally and wearily conceded. By then war against Germany had been declared and, like the Government of Ireland Act of the same month, the proviso was that they be enacted within a year of the cessation of hostilities. According to the Act, all pre-1662 properties would be secularized and a number of Welsh Church Commissioners would be appointed to oversee the transferral of assets – namely cathedrals, deaneries and bishops' residences, churches, vicarages, rectories and all glebe lands – to a Representative Body of the new Welsh Church. Income from the Queen Anne's Bounty and parliamentary grants since 1800 would be discontinued while all parochial endowments would be transferred to the county councils. St David's College Lampeter, established by Bishop Burgess in 1822 for the training of clergy, and St Michael's College Llandaf, founded in

1892 for their postgraduate pastoral instruction, would be exempt from this process. The financial clauses of the measure were much less drastic than many churchmen had feared, though in terms of status and prestige, the changes still stung. Severed from the province of Canterbury, the monarch would no longer be the Church's titular head, the bishops would lose their seats in the House of Lords, and there would no longer be clerical representation in Convocation. Although the Welsh members sang *Hen Wlad fy Nhadau* in the Commons lobby to celebrate the occasion, the victory, nevertheless, felt hollow. By now interest was elsewhere, not least in events in Belgium and France.

The First World War

The First World War broke upon the nation unexpectedly. If the Church of England (to which all Welsh Anglicans still belonged), reflecting the values of the establishment, threw itself into the war effort wholesale, a quasi-pacifist Nonconformity surprised itself by supporting the conflict so enthusiastically. Edwardian Wales partook of the imperialist spirit as much as any other part of the United Kingdom, while the presence of the Baptist David Lloyd George at the centre of government swayed the judgement of many. 'As the Lord liveth, we had entered into no conspiracy against Germany', he assured a vast congregation at the City Temple, Westminster, in November 1914. 'We are in the war from motives of purest chivalry to defend the weak.' Belgium was, like Wales, a small nation, 'a poor little neighbour whose home was broken into by a hulking bully'. Were it not for the Christian resolve of her allies, she would surely perish. However regrettable, the war was just. 'We are all looking forward to the time when swords shall be beaten into ploughshares', but in the meantime there was no alternative but to fight.[10] Such rhetoric was replicated again and again, not only by those who sought to justify the war but by others who would persuade young men to volunteer for military service. This was nowhere more so than in the Welsh-speaking heartlands of Caernarfonshire and Anglesey, where Calvinistic Methodism's two most charismatic preachers, John Williams Brynsiencyn and Thomas Charles Williams, urged Christian youth to take up arms. Such uncritical zeal would prove their undoing. When the populace realized that the war would not be 'over by Christmas' and that the level of slaughter would be unprecedented, the reputation of such slick trumpeters of righteousness sank immeasurably. So too did that of all who had tried to vindicate the war as a religious crusade. Whatever was true of Christianity more widely, the integrity of the Nonconformist cause would suffer considerably.

The counterpoint to the rhetoric of the jingoistic ministers and clergy was the stand taken by those who raised questions as to the unambiguous purity of the state's cause in waging total war. Thomas Rees, principal of the Congregational college at Bala-Bangor, and John Puleston Jones, a supremely gifted Calvinistic Methodist minister from Pwllheli, suffered immense opprobrium for reminding the public of the moral ambiguities of war. 'I note that you have been expressing *Christian* views on this terrible European conflict', wrote one of Rees's correspondents in October 1914.

> To find anyone with sufficient courage at the present time to stand boldly for such obsolete opinions is to me at any rate wholesome and invigorating. The 'neutrality of Belgium argument', as it has been presented on its altruistic side, is of course irresistible. At the same time, it takes a rather 'strong man' possessing any knowledge of the tortuous ways of diplomats, to believe that anything so disinterested is possible on the part of any European chancellery.[11]

Any blanket support for the government's cause belied the need for a measured view of national policy, the correspondent stated, while the present atmosphere of fevered patriotism made a mockery of the claim that the only absolutes within Christendom were Christ and the Kingdom of God.

Although not initially out-and-out pacifists, Rees and Puleston Jones became mainstays of the Fellowship of Reconciliation, the Christian (and overwhelmingly non-Anglican) society founded in 1914 to counter the claims of war. It received an undoubted boost in January 1916 with the government's decision to impose conscription, thus calling into question Nonconformity's core conviction concerning the rights of individual conscience. Those who refused to bear arms found themselves having to defend their stand before local tribunals and were often imprisoned. The one figure who came to personify pacifist absolutism was George M. Ll. Davies, the grandson of John Jones Tal-sarn, one of Calvinistic Methodism's mid-nineteenth-century prince preachers. Davies, whose Tolstoyesque conversion from bourgeois religiosity to a highly idealist (if dogma-free) form of Christianity inspired many, while the pacifists' willingness to suffer for their convictions often elicited sympathy and respect even among those who remained unconvinced by their views. Always a radical minority, the pacifists' most substantial contribution was in helping create a post-war consensus, among Nonconformists at least, which put peace near the top of the political agenda. This fact was illustrated by George Davies's election, on a pacifist ticket, as MP for the University of Wales seat in 1923.

What, therefore, was the impact of the Great War on the future of Welsh Christianity? It is often said that the war destroyed people's faith in the reality of God and the goodness of humankind. Such an assessment is too stark and simplistic. Secularization would have happened anyway. What the war provided was a convenient divide between a religious and a post-religious phase in modern Welsh history. There is no doubt that on returning from the front, disenchanted with the ideals with which they had grown up, many did abandon a belief in God, divine providence and the comforts of the gospel. There were others, however – and the evidence points to the fact that they were many – who actually *found* their faith in the trenches. Whereas the question of how to justify God's existence in the face of human adversity has always been a conundrum, the biblical revelation contains unique resources to deal with (though never fully to understand) the fact of pain and suffering. This is especially true of a religion whose Saviour died on a cross. During the war, the work of the military chaplains, both Anglican and Nonconformist, was mostly revered. The words 'This is my body broken for you' took on a new reality for many who partook of the eucharist or Lord's Supper in the front line, having witnessed affliction, agony and extreme torment with their own eyes. One thoughtful Calvinistic Methodist ministerial student, soon to be killed, wrote to his college principal: 'The problems of war have always challenged faith, but a world organized for slaughter is something new.' Despite the horrors which the concept of total war had introduced, the religious questions being faced were more in scale than in kind: 'It would be truer as a general statement to say that the old difficulties have been intensified rather than new ones have arisen.'[12]

What was incontrovertible was that post-war Wales would be a different world and that the religious bodies would need to respond to its changes or face the consequences. 'The question that men will ask of the church when they return', wrote Alfred Jenkins, that same ministerial student, was:

Are you prepared to lead in the social movement that has declared war on a system based on monopolism, which keeps the land locked up in the interests of a few and which condemns millions of our population to live in rack-rented, overcrowded dwellings? The church must not count on the devotion and loyalty that were merely a family tradition and heritage, for these have been shrivelled up in the experiences of war ... [Moreover] if the basis of church membership will still invoke the pale ghosts of ancient creeds and musty dogmas rather than the challenge of the moral heroism of men, the church will not attract those who have learned to suffer and endure.[13]

What was needed was a radical social message, genuine personal conviction and a realistic and pertinent theology. By 1920 there were many in the Welsh churches, both Anglican and Nonconformist, who agreed that this was the case.

Welsh Anglicanism and Roman Catholicism between the wars

On 1 April 1920 the newly disestablished and autonomous Welsh Anglican church, soon to be called 'The Church in Wales', became a fact. Having been cushioned from the worst effects of disendowment by the government's financial guarantee, Welsh Anglicans began to accustom themselves to their new situation.

Realizing now that it could make its own rules, the Church established two new dioceses, Monmouth, carved from the overwhelmingly populous Llandaf, and Swansea and Brecon, formerly part of the huge diocese of St Davids. Though disestablished, the new body remained hierarchical in nature, in many places gentrified and still very hesitant about its status. In some quarters the old hostility towards the Welsh language persisted; many of its senior clergy and middle-class laity despised the vernacular as an uncouth throwback to the past, 'the last refuge of the uneducated' according to A. G. Edwards,[14] its first archbishop. Yet confidence was growing and churchmen began to appreciate, if not to relish, their new-found independence.

If some of the senior clergy remained Anglophile and still establishment-minded high Tories, there were many among the parish ministers for whom a commitment to the Church was no bar to being wholly Welsh. For them this was the opportunity for the new body to align itself with national sentiment. 'I hope', wrote one north Wales clergyman before the advent of disestablishment,

> that . . . [many] will make an effort at this juncture in its history to popularize, democratize and nationalize the old Church of our Fathers so that it may become once more the old spiritual home of the Welsh people. A fervent (Nonconformist) Welsh Nationalist . . . told a friend of mine the other day, 'I hear you are forming a scheme of government for the Church after Disestablishment. For God's sake, be wise. These – meaning Nonconformists – are tumbling to pieces. The people will come back to you if you proceed wisely'. This is the spirit that is abroad.[15]

Despite much social ambiguity, John Owen, bishop of St Davids and the most able champion of 'Church Defence', was indisputably Welsh in language and culture, as was Dr Maurice Jones, appointed in 1923 to a key position of influence, namely principal of St David's College, Lampeter. Owen, a former Calvinistic Methodist from Caernarfonshire's Llŷn peninsula, was the son of a tenant farmer, while Jones, from rural Trawsfynydd, was the son of a blacksmith.

Even more significant for the Church's profile was the unexpected election, in 1931, of Fr Timothy Rees, a monk of the Community of the Resurrection at Mirfield, Yorkshire, and son of a Cardiganshire sea captain, as bishop of Llandaf. As a Mirfield missionary based outside Wales since 1907, he had avoided the harsh polemics of the disestablishment campaign, while his social commitment, solidarity with the disadvantaged and warm-hearted Welsh patriotism were felt to be something new. 'We think it is fair to say', wrote London's *Church Times*, 'that it is quite certain that Fr Rees would not be the bishop-elect of Llandaff if the Welsh Church were not disestablished.'[16] The tenor of his ministry was made clear during his enthronement speech:

> My heart goes out in sympathy to the broken lives and the broken hearts that are the result of this depression. Would God that I could do something to help. Would God that I could make some contribution to the solution of this crushing problem . . .
>
> Let us remember that Almighty God is just as interested in the doings of the Borough Council as in the doings of the Diocesan Conference; that He is just as interested in the problem of providing decent houses for people to live in as in the problem of providing decent churches for people to worship in . . . There is nothing secular but sin.[17]

Not only were Welsh Anglicans energized and impressed by this new move, but so were Nonconformists. Present at the enthronement in Llandaf cathedral, the Revd J. Penry Thomas, secretary of the Cardiff Free Church Council, wrote: 'The event marked a new epoch in the history of the Church in Wales'.[18]

The potential of this new situation, however, was impeded by continued problems: the economic depression of the 1930s, an innate ecclesiastical conservatism and a deepening spiritual paralysis. Rees's radicalism was untypical. His fellow prelates, led by the patrician Charles Green, bishop of Monmouth from 1921, translated to Bangor in 1928 and archbishop between 1934 and his death in 1944, remained wedded to the older norms. But whoever led the church, what sapped its energy most was 'the dead weight of sheer indifference'.[19] 'This indifference to spiritual things which prevails in our parishes'[20] was a blight at the time and so it would remain. Rees's deteriorating health mirrored what he saw as the main challenge to the church's mission. His death, aged sixty-five, in 1939 after a protracted illness was a blow not only to the disestablished Church but to the nation as a whole.

The Roman Catholic Church in Wales was also gaining strength and confidence at this time. Benedict XV's apostolic letter *Cambria Celtica* of 1916 had freed the dioceses of Menevia and Newport from the province of Birmingham and created a separate Welsh province with its own archbishop. Newport was to be renamed the archdiocese of Cardiff with its church of St Davids becoming the metropolitan cathedral, while Menevia, the suffragan see, would have its cathedral at Wrexham. The province's first archbishop had been the Benedictine monk James Bilsborrow, a Lancastrian, who had been forced to resign in 1920 through ill health, to be replaced by the Welshman Francis Mostyn, bishop of Menevia. Apologizing for his absence at the enthronement in the metropolitan cathedral in April 1921, the prime minister David Lloyd George extolled Mostyn's 'famed Welsh lineage' and 'loyalty to Welsh traditions', and stated that 'Welshmen without distinction of creed will rejoice in today's ceremony'.[21] There is no doubt that the occasion signified that the Welsh Catholic church had finally arrived. As well as serving as bishop of Cardiff and the province's archbishop, Mostyn would continue as Menevia's apostolic administrator until 1926, when Pius XI appointed another Welshman, Francis Vaughan, nephew of Herbert Vaughan, cardinal archbishop of Westminster, to the see of Menevia. Like Mostyn, he too was the son of an old Welsh recusant family, the Vaughans of Courtfield in Monmouthshire, and equally zealous in his commitment to Wales.

Between 1921 and 1945, the Welsh Catholic church would expand impressively. By the end of the Second World War, the archdiocese of Cardiff's nearly 60,000 Catholics would become 85,000, its 95 priests would increase to 150 and its churches from 80 to 120. In geographically extensive Menevia, the Catholic total would more than double, from less than 10,000 to 22,000, its 90 priests growing to 150 and its fifty-two churches to ninety. This expansion was due to fecundity within Catholic families (which tended to be much larger than Protestant families), by those who embraced their partner's faith at marriage, and by conversion through religious conviction. 'There have been some notable conversions in the last few years', wrote the author T. P. Ellis in 1936, 'of men and women, most of them young, wholeheartedly devoted to Wales, and the leaven of their example will spread.'[22] The dramatist, nationalist and political activist Saunders Lewis, who had forsaken Calvinistic Methodism for the Catholic faith in 1932, would become perhaps the best known among them. Vaughan's premature death, aged fifty-seven, in 1935 led to the institution of the scholarly Michael McGrath, a Welsh-speaking Irishman, as leader of the see who, in 1940, would succeed Mostyn to the archiepiscopate of Cardiff.

Although beset by problems, mostly 'leakage' or the tendency of birth-Catholics to fall away from Mass attendance as well as an inordinate and obsessional 'No Popery' attitude within the wider community, the Welsh Catholic community would continue in good heart.

> In His time and in His season [lyricized one commentator] Wales will return to the Faith and to Catholic unity which were hers for a thousand years. Wales will be a holy land, her wind-vext Tegid a Sea of Galilee, her headlong Dee a Jordan, her Snowdon a Mount of Transfiguration.[23]

Nonconformity: the social challenge

The context in which the Church in Wales, the Catholic church and the Nonconformist denominations would have to function, in the industrial south at least, was one of strife and depression, while in Wales generally a fundamental switch of allegiance occurred from the Liberal Party to Labour. Whereas before the war its active support in Wales had been desultory, by 1935 Labour controlled every single seat in the industrial south, polling 400,000 votes or over 45 per cent of the Welsh total. By the 1930s most of Wales had rejected the individualism of its Liberal past in favour of a collectivist and more class-based Labour future.

Long before the deep dislocation of the 1930s, Christianity and the Labour movement had striven to accommodate one another. Early socialists such as Keir Hardie, founder of the Independent Labour Party, had used biblical language and a religiously inspired idealism in order to convince Welsh chapelgoers of socialism's compatibility with their faith. For Hardie socialism was Christianity at work, the practical application of the Sermon on the Mount in order to usher in God's Kingdom on earth. It was above all else a moral code rather than an economic dogma, and was commended as such not least by T. E. Nicholas of Glais in the Swansea valley, the ILP's most effective propagandist among the workers of south Wales before the Great War. If Nicholas, a neo-Marxist poet-preacher in the romantic style, was a skilled populist, there were other young Nonconformists like the Baptist Herbert Morgan and the Methodist Silyn Roberts whose apologia for the socialist creed was much more intellectually astute. James Griffiths, leader of the west Wales anthracite miners, later MP for Llanelli and a minister in successive Labour governments, recalled Silyn's immense influence on the youth of his generation:

> He preached God and evolution. He was a minister and a socialist . . . he became our inspirer and our justification. We could tell our parents, who feared this new gospel we talked of, 'but Silyn Roberts believes as we do'. How many devout but dubious fathers became reconciled to socialist sons by that assurance? He linked the South Wales of Evan Roberts to the South Wales of Keir Hardie.[24]

For these, there was no incompatibility between Labour and the chapels. 'There are thousands of Welshmen today', wrote one observer in 1923, 'who can find no inconsistency in singing *Diolch iddo* and *Ar ei ben bo'r goron*, with the Welsh *hwyl* at one meeting, and then proceeding to another meeting to sing *The Red Flag* with the same enthusiasm.'[25]

The problem, however, was that those who were keenest to forge the combination tended to see Christianity in terms of socialist ideology or a humanitarian faith. Nicholas had claimed that 'true Christianity recognizes the divinity of man ... not as a fallen being but one who is continually advancing to higher levels and who is endowed with unlimited possibilities'.[26] Even less radical chapel-going socialists sat very loosely to orthodox formulations of the creed. Whereas the outward trappings of Nonconformist culture were being preserved in the guise of attendance at worship, hymn singing and often an appreciation of a well-delivered sermon, specifically religious convictions were weakening daily. Basic theological truths concerning the holiness of God, the reality of human sinfulness and the deity of Christ were being refashioned according to the canons of a humanitarian creed. Rather than devising a doctrinally robust Christian socialism which was faithful to the gospel, the tendency in Wales was to spiritualize a basically materialist ideology according to Nonconformist values. In every compromise it was traditional Christianity and not the Labour movement which lost out.[27]

Nonconformity: the fundamentalist impulse and Pentecostalism

There were other young men (and women), however, for whom socialist politics or a dilution of Christian basics would have no allure. The 1904–5 Revival had been particularly intense among the working class, some of whose members found its primal spirituality and egalitarian nature to be vehemently potent. There is little doubt that the 'rootlessness' which characterized the vast influx from rural Wales and elsewhere to the Valleys, during these and preceding decades, made the young uniquely receptive to such powerful experiential religiosity:

> The young and women were drawn to the revival in particularly large numbers at a time of profound social dislocation . . . It was amongst many of these socially, economically and politically disenfranchised individuals that the exciting pieties of the revival seemed to be most attractive.[28]

As well as rejuvenating the mainline denominations, there were two specific emphases which sprang from the revival: fundamentalism and the newly minted Pentecostal faith. Both were separatist, world-denying and pietistic, eschewing politics and social engagement as being worldly and unspiritual, but both contributing in their different ways to the Welsh Nonconformist mix.

Fundamentalism, stemmed from the United States where a series of booklets called *The Fundamentals* (1910–15) had served to rally conservative-minded Protestants who believed that liberal theology was threatening the vitality of the cause. The movement soon became equated with a belligerent attitude to all aspects of secular culture, and by the early 1920s its militant temper and polemical defence of biblical inerrancy was being replicated in south Wales. Its main exemplar was R. B. Jones, Baptist minister at the Tabernacle church, Porth, in the Rhondda, whose reputation as a stern prophet of the divine wrath had been consolidated during the revival. By the inter-war period, the mores of fundamentalism: a literalist biblical hermeneutic (a six-day creation, a literal Adam, Eve and serpent, the historicity of the book of Jonah), premillennial eschatology and the call to separate from the world and a worldly church, had become deeply entrenched among a section of Welsh evangelicals, and its principles were upheld through such institutions as the annual Llandrindod convention, 'the Keswick of Wales', which espoused a 'second blessing' holiness doctrine, the Bible College of Wales at Derwen Fawr, Swansea, founded in 1924 by Rees Howells, another highly idiosyncratic Welsh evangelical, Jones's own South Wales Bible Training Institute at Porth, and the bi-monthly periodical *Yr Efengylydd*. The truculent nature of their witness often made withdrawal inevitable, either from their parent denominations or from what they believed were 'worldly' local churches, and by the 1930s a plethora of independent 'mission halls' had sprung up throughout the south Wales Valleys, though not further afield. Although never a major aspect of Welsh Nonconformity, classic fundamentalism did, however, have its part to play in the story.

The same is true of Pentecostalism. Although it became a major twentieth-century religious phenomenon, Pentecostalism never impacted Wales to the extent that it did elsewhere. Nevertheless the movement's historians always affirm that the 1904–5 Revival was one of its contributing factors.[29] Beginning with the revival at Azuza Street, Los Angeles, in 1906, its special characteristics, along with exuberant and emotion-fuelled gospel preaching, would be the 'baptism of the Spirit' replete with ecstatic phenomena such as prophecy, bodily healing and speaking with tongues. Daniel P. Williams, a Congregational convert of the Welsh revival, had separated from his local church in order to worship in the 'mission hall' in his native Pen-y-groes, Carmarthenshire, when, in 1909, he received 'the baptism in the Spirit'. One of the earliest British Pentecostalist preachers, W. O. Hutchinson, had already planted a church in Swansea which Williams began to attend. By then he and others had left the mission hall to establish their own fellowship, where the full range of spiritual gifts could be practised. In 1910 Williams was ordained by Hutchinson as pastor of the Pen-y-groes fellowship, later being appointed Apostle in Hutchinson's denomination. Predictably perhaps, tensions became manifest, and in 1916 'Pastor Dan' broke with Hutchinson and established the Apostolic Church. By 1922 it had merged with other Pentecostalist groups in Hereford, Glasgow and Bradford, though retaining its headquarters in Pen-y-groes, which from 1917 onwards attracted vast crowds to its annual August convention. It also developed a wide international profile, commissioning its first missionary, to Argentina, in 1922. Despite localized growth during the 1920s and early 1930s, mostly among the colliers and tinplate workers of east Carmarthenshire and west Glamorgan, real expansion occurred only outside Wales, though even then the highly centralized nature of the Apostolic Church was said to militate against it ever becoming a significant contributor to the wider Pentecostal witness.

Two other skilled charismatic evangelists, Stephen and George Jeffreys, initially Congregationalists from Maesteg, Glamorgan, had begun itinerating after being converted during the revival, and having experienced 'baptism in the Spirit', introduced healing, prophecy and speaking in tongues in their campaigns. Whereas after 1913 Stephen concentrated his ministry at Cwm-twrch in the Swansea valley, George, by then itinerating ever more widely, established the Elim Evangelistic Band, planting its first church in Belfast in 1916. Following further success throughout the British

Isles, the movement was renamed the Elim Foursquare Gospel Alliance in 1926. Although an important element of British Pentecostalism and despite there being a sprinkling of Elim churches, again in south Wales, by the 1930s, the Alliance never developed a specifically Welsh-based structure, though by the 1960s and 1970s Swansea's City Church and Cardiff's City Temple had become important centres of Pentecostal presence.

A third Pentecostal offshoot, the Assemblies of God, enjoying a much looser structure than either the Apostolic Church or Elim, was established in Birmingham in 1924, drawing together disparate fellowships, thirty-eight of them situated in Wales, mostly in the eastern Valleys of Monmouthshire. The Welsh fellowships comprised the largest segment of this new denomination, and although growth was steady during the inter-war years, by the 1950s it had tended to stagnate. The same pattern was seen throughout the Pentecostal bodies in Wales, and it was only with the advent of Charismatic renewal in the 1970s that the characteristic emphases of Pentecostal faith, especially informal worship and a renewed appreciation for the gifts of the Holy Spirit, came to be accepted beyond the Pentecostal bodies. It has been said, however, that

> What is deeply ironic about the story of Pentecostalism in Wales is that, despite the Welsh origin of so many of its leaders and organisations, the country has largely missed out on the tremendous growth of Pentecostal ... activity which has occurred in many parts of the world.[30]

Nonconformity: liberalism and a renewed orthodoxy

Whatever was true of the religious periphery, by the immediate post-war years the trend towards liberal theology, among the Congregationalists primarily, had established itself as something of a norm. Its watchwords, despite the tragedy of war, were progress, evolution and the immanence of God. More alarming was the fact that outside of fundamentalism and Pentecostalism, the miraculous was disappearing as a doctrinal concept across the board. Naturalism and the non-miraculous were becoming the *sina qua non* of mainline religious faith. Initiated by David Adams, minister at Grove Street Welsh Church in Liverpool until his death in 1923, the axioms of modernism were built into the thought of Congregationalism's most gifted post-war leaders: Thomas Rees principal of the Bala-Bangor College; his professorial colleague John Morgan Jones; and D. Miall Edwards, professor of Christian Doctrine at the Memorial College in Brecon. Blatant liberalism was not nearly as prevalent among the Baptists and Wesleyans, while, despite incipient tensions, the 1823 Confession of Faith preserved the Calvinistic Methodists from succumbing wholly to the liberal lure. The two most influential Calvinistic Methodist theologians were of the older generation, D. Cynddylan Jones and Puleston Jones, the one more conservative and the other tending towards the liberal, both affirmed a centrist and supernatural trinitarian orthodoxy.

Some of the younger ministers, however, were less enamoured of such views. 'Modern theology', according to one of their number, 'can be most satisfactoraly gauged by taking as the point of our departure the movement commonly known as philosophical Idealism of the absolute type.'[31] In surveying the history of Welsh theology since the mid-nineteenth century, Philip J. Jones, a Calvinistic Methodist from Cardiff, delighted in the fact that traditional formulations of the faith were fast disappearing and that a radical Nonconformity was taking its place. 'Fall from innocence into sin is a fall upwards and onwards', he claimed, 'and every stage of sin contributes to the ultimate realization of perfect goodness.' Christ was not so much the divine saviour but the archetype of human perfectibility. 'Atonement is, according to this teaching, a cosmic process', whereas the resurrection of the body could only be rationally interpreted in terms of the immortality of the soul, 'the loss of self by death implies the finding of self in the larger life of union in God.' 'Whatever may be the actual implications of this challenging and attractive teaching', he continued, 'there can be but no doubt that it gives rise to questions of great importance for theology', which indeed was the case. It seemed that, for some young preachers, philosophical Idealism had all but swallowed Christian faith whole. 'Hegelianism', he stated, with neither irony nor incongruity, 'is the most potent vindication of Christianity and

Christian doctrines which has as yet been offered to human intelligence.'[32] The time was ripe for a counter-movement, and it was provided not by the fundamentalists but by the more substantial and innovative thought of the Swiss theologian Karl Barth.

Barth had first come into the public purview in 1919 with his exposition of Paul's letter to the Romans, described by the Catholic Karl Adam as 'the bomb that fell on the playground of the theologians'.[33] The smooth naturalist theology of bourgeois European Protestantism, which happily synthesized spirituality and morality with a comfortable knowledge of God, was now disrupted by a radical discontinuity, making such a knowledge impossible. God was not an appendage of human religiosity but radically transcendent. He could only be known if he allowed himself to be known through a revelation which was not the result of human striving. The liberal ideal of a synthesis between the human and the divine would be challenged fundamentally. In Wales, scholarly liberalism had found its most lucid expression in Miall Edwards's *Bannau'r Ffydd* ('The Pinnacles of Faith') of 1929, a volume whose integrating theme was humankind's innate capacity for God. Christianity, claimed Edwards, begins with salvation interpreted as the believer's experience of the divine; it advances through Christology interpreted as Jesus of Nazareth's sense of sonship in relation to the Father; and concludes with a doctrine of God as the ground of all existence. 'It is apparent', he wrote, 'that we are working on the assumption that experience is the key to doctrine.'[34] So subjective was this principle that few truths remained inviolate: 'If in the future "evolution" produces one whose authority in the realm of the spiritual is higher than Jesus Christ, I would be obliged to pledge my most absolute loyalty to him.'[35] It was not the Christ of apostolic testimony that was absolute any longer, but an individual's 'authority in the realm of the spiritual' (even other than that of Jesus of Nazareth).

Just as Barth had challenged these views on the Continent, J. E. Daniel, the twenty-eight-year-old professor of Christian Doctrine at the Congregational College at Bala-Bangor, did likewise in response to Edwards's thesis. Daniel had been appointed to his post in 1926, and was one of the first in Wales to make Barth's spirited anti-modernism his own. He would spearhead a new phase in

Nonconformist theology in Wales. In an extended review in the students' journal *Yr Efrydydd*, he took Edwards to task on every single point: the axiomatic status of 'the modern mind', the use of experience as the sole criterion for truth, and the attempt to do theology on the basis of human perception rather than on God's objective revelation of himself as attested in Scripture. In an understandable though wholly misguided attempt to be relevant, what Edwards had done was to shear God of his radical otherness and make him nothing but a projection of the religious spirit of humankind. Such errors, he claimed, had already 'led to the theological and spiritual bankruptcy of Protestantism'.[36]

Daniel continued by challenging Edwards's adoptionist Christology and his truncated theory of atonement. If Jesus of Nazareth was a man whose particular attribute lay in his exquisite experience of the divine, anything resembling an objective salvation would be rendered impossible: 'The modernists' Christ could not perform an objective redemption even if they believed such a thing existed', he exclaimed. Yet man, as sinner, needed to be redeemed. What he required was not an example – Edwards's 'expert . . . in the realm of the spiritual' – but a saviour who was actually divine: 'For me atonement is something which is wrought for us, independently, a fountain opened *before* we drink from its waters.' Despite its pious talk of Jesus' fellowship with the Father and his experience of the divine, what liberal theology did was to posit an unbridgeable ontological divide between the Father and the Son which rendered true salvation impossible. On the basis of Edwards's theology, the church could no longer claim that *God* in Christ had reconciled the world to himself. Despite its elegance and undoubted appeal, this was in fact a theology of despair. For the sake of its present doctrinal integrity and its future spiritual health, Welsh Nonconformity should, 'with the undivided tradition of the Church, reject the concept of experience and return once more to the concept of revelation'.[37] What was needed, exhorted J. E. Daniel, was a restatement of classic orthodoxy according to a rejuvenated theology of the Word of God.

By the 1930s and into the war years and beyond, there occurred a partial return to a more balanced, biblical and orthodox faith by the Nonconformist pulpit, while an older conservative evangelicalism was revitalized, not least through the remarkable ministry of Martyn Lloyd-Jones, a London-Welsh doctor who had relinquished his prestigious role as chief assistant to the King's Physician in 1927 for the life of a lowly pastor-evangelist at Bethlehem Forward Movement Hall in Aberavon, Port Talbot. Even after returning to London as minister of Westminster Chapel in 1939, Lloyd-Jones would become a hugely revered figure in Welsh evangelicalism, and wield enormous influence during the post-war years.

Among the congregations, the faithful responded to the approaching war with quiet fortitude. The biblical categories of sin, redemption and the divine transcendence were infinitely more effective in interpreting the present crisis than those of a discredited liberalism. The striking difference between the quiet confidence of the mid-1940s and the facile optimism which had greeted the previous conflict, was its note of realism. Optimism may have vanished, but there was little despair. Although Nazism was perceived to be an unmitigated evil, neither hatred nor jingoism marred the national response. The unspeakable horrors of Belsen and Buchenwald revealed the depths of human depravity which no ready-made theology could comprehend; nevertheless the proven realities of biblical faith did serve to offer consolation and a chastened hope.

The post-war era and the challenge of the 1960s

Following the war, the signs were that Welsh Anglicanism was coming into its own. More confident than ever in its specific identity, it was facing the future with assertiveness. 'It may be fairly said', stated one of a younger generation of very able clergymen, 'there is among Welsh Churchmen at the present a widespread mood of expectancy.'[38] With Nonconformity in decline and Romanism alien, in the main, to the modern Welsh experience, Anglicanism, with its rounded orthodoxy and world-affirming sacramentalism, was poised to fill the nation's religious void. The church was busy with reconstruction: financial reorganization, religious education, a commission on the role of cathedrals, liturgical renewal and the Nation and Prayer Book Commission, which reported to the Governing Body in 1949, while a new and dynamic cohort of bishops was coming to the fore: the former missionary John Charles Jones, called to the Bangor diocese in 1949 and, following his untimely death aged fifty-two in 1956; Gwilym O. Williams; and Glyn Simon, appointed bishop of Swansea and Brecon in 1953 before his transferral to Llandaf in 1957. It all reflected a conviction that significant renewal was afoot:

> Wales today is a nation losing its vision of God [it was claimed] . . . Nor can that nation be brought back to the vision of God till the Church in Wales, the only agent among us capable of the task, sets herself in grim earnest to recall it to belief in the full Catholic faith. [39]

By the early 1950s, the signs were that the task was already in hand.

Throughout the late 1940s and most of the 1950s, church attendance not only kept steady but the trend was even upwards. Whereas Nonconformist congregations were becoming thinner, on Easter day 1945, 155,911 communicants partook of the eucharist at the church's altars, 170,338 did so on the same occasion in 1959 and as many as 182,864 in 1960. [40] Such success was due, it was said, to the fact that the Church in Wales alone possessed the fullness of the catholic faith. Such a claim bred conceit which was nowhere more manifest than in the comments of Edwin Morris, bishop of Monmouth, when consecrating Daniel Bartlett to the see of St Asaph in 1951. 'The Roman clergy and Nonconformist ministers are, strictly speaking, intruders', he claimed. 'There may be historical reasons for them being here, but we cannot recognize their right to be here.'[41] Both Nonconformists and Catholics were incensed, while the single word 'intruders' put paid to any serious attempt at rapprochement between the Church in Wales and the other Protestant denominations for a generation or more. This was not the only time that Morris's imprudence – he was appointed archbishop in 1957 – caused controversy, while his clash with Glyn Simon over the appointment of the non-Welsh-speaking John J. A. Thomas as bishop of Swansea and Brecon later the same year[42] revealed starkly some underlying, though previously well-hidden, tensions within the Welsh Anglican communion, especially as the

1960s drew near. Nevertheless, for most of this period, the Church in Wales was in a healthy state.

The same was true of the Catholic church in Wales. 'Wales is not Catholic', stated Archbishop McGrath at the consecration of John Pettit as bishop of Menevia in 1947, 'but it is fast becoming Catholicized . . . It is more than a dream of life that the future is with the Church of Rome in this country.'[43] A year later the ancient shrine of Our Lady of Pen-rhys in the Rhondda was rededicated, an act of witness which showed the boldness and vigour of Welsh Catholicism at the time: 'Today hundreds of pilgrims are demonstrating the return of the Faith; this is revival.'[44] Baptisms were on the increase, conversions were up, church building and school extension were progressing steadily, and despite residual Protestant hostility in many quarters still, confidence was sustained throughout the 1950s: 'It may well be tiresome and disquieting for some folks', wrote a correspondent in the *Western Mail* in 1960, 'but there is little doubt that the "Faith of our Fathers" is rapidly returning to the "Land of our Fathers".'[45]

No such optimism was apparent among Welsh Nonconformists. Although the statistics had shown a steady decline since their peak in 1926, by the mid-1950s the chief Nonconformist denominations could still boast a joint membership of 370,000 baptized communicants representing as many as one in seven of the total Welsh population, yet there was a feeling abroad that chapel life was stagnating and that Nonconformity itself was facing an enormous crisis. In a perceptive if gloomy analysis published in 1962, the tercentenary of the birth of English and Welsh Dissent, R. Ifor Parry, a senior Congregational minister in Aberdare, showed how Nonconformity was suffering through its cultural captivity to 'the Welsh way of life' which was currently in decline; that it was wedded to 'the Nonconformist Conscience', the puritanism of which was everywhere regarded as being antiquated and hypocritical; that the plainness of its worship had bred a negativity towards beauty and the senses; and that growing economic affluence had led to a materialism which dissolved the moral seriousness on which Dissenting conviction was built: 'This is the atmosphere in which Nonconformity is having to exist and today it is fighting for its very life.'[46]

There were, nonetheless, attempts to stem the decline. The Evangelical Movement of Wales, established in 1955 in the wake of a spiritual awakening among Bangor University students some six years earlier, had become the focus of considerable religious verve. Through its magazines, *Y Cylchgrawn Efengylaidd* and *The Evangelical Magazine of Wales*, its annual conferences, well-attended preaching meetings and local evangelistic campaigns, its youth activities and ministerial fraternals, the movement provided a network through which evangelical believers could share fellowship and nurture a vision for the nation's Christian renewal. Its tendency from the beginning however, was to mark itself off from those who did not fully endorse its aims, and by espousing a restrictive concept of biblical infallibility and increasingly a separatist ecclesiology, its effectiveness as a means of cross-denominational renewal was seriously curtailed. This was especially true after 1966–7 and the secession of some of its affiliated churches from their parent denominations following Martyn Lloyd-Jones's call for evangelical believers to secede from what he had come to believe were apostate religious bodies. Thereafter evangelical witness within the denominations tended to occur outside the ambit of the Evangelical Movement of Wales.

A second focus for renewal was ecumenism. Ever since the great Edinburgh Missionary Conference of 1910, the conviction had increased that for mission and evangelism to be effective, they must stem from a single and united Christian church. The British Council of Churches had been established in 1942, the World Council of Churches had been inaugurated in 1948 while the Council of Churches for Wales was formed in 1956. Just as the evangelical awakening among the Bangor students had led to the birth of the Evangelical Movement of Wales, lively evangelistic activity of a less restrictive kind had been happening there under the auspices of the Student Christian Movement (SCM), its focus being *Yr Ymgyrch Newydd yng Nghymru* ('The New Campaign in Wales'). As well as emphasizing the necessity for personal commitment, it was socially involved and held to the ecumenical vision of fashioning a single and unified Welsh church. The path to create such a body was tortuous and complex, and though it led, by 1975, to the ratification of a covenant for union between the Methodists, the United

Reformed Church, the Presbyterian Church in Wales, the Congregationalists and the Anglican Church in Wales, it amounted to little in the end. Organic union, or the abolition of denominational Christianity in favour of a single ecclesiastical body, would never happen, while the main contribution of the Ecumenical Movement would be to foster mutual respect among Welsh Christians whatever their church background, and to share a knowledge of the riches of the various traditions.

The theological ferment which affected Western Christianity generally during the 1960s did not bypass the Welsh churches. The Second Vatican Council, Bishop John Robinson's radical and unexpectedly popular paperback *Honest to God* (1963), the 'Death of God' movement and various secular theologies had their devotees within the land. A particularly vigorous theological discussion took place in the Welsh-language monthly *Barn* in 1963–4 between J. R. Jones, a Calvinistic Methodist layman and professor of philosophy at the University of Wales, Swansea, and H. D. Lewis, also a Calvinistic Methodist and professor of the philosophy of religion at King's College, London. Heavily influenced by the radical theologian Paul Tillich's 'Protestant Principle' and some of the most enigmatic sections of Dietrich Bonhoeffer's *Letters and Papers from Prison* (1951), Jones championed a highly idiosyncratic existential humanism which was openly antagonistic to Christian orthodoxy.[47] As well as reflecting faithfully each of the religious predilections of the 'secular sixties', this altercation was intensified by being linked to the concurrent crises of nationhood and that within Welsh Dissent. Despite its apparent malaise, Nonconformity was sufficiently healthy to fuel such an intellectually distinguished discussion and to provide work for renewal movements of both evangelical and ecumenical hues.

Nevertheless, by the late 1970s Welsh Nonconformity was in a parlous state. Membership in the Presbyterian Church in Wales was down to 55,500, the Baptists down to 47,000, Methodist membership (i.e. the Wesleyan tradition) was down to 27,000, the Welsh Independents down to 34,000 and other Nonconformist denominations to 46,000.[48] Thereafter the fall-off would be even more precipitous. Although their rate of decline was not so steep, the same pattern was visible across all the historic Christian churches in Wales. The 'nation of Nonconformists' which had been so creative, energetic and suffused with optimism a century earlier had long been lost to secularism, irreligion and a predominantly materialistic way of life. Neither did Anglican Wales nor Catholic Wales emerge to take its place. By 1979, the year of the first, and unsuccessful, devolution referendum and the year when Margaret Thatcher's Conservative government was swept to power, there was a feeling abroad that the old dispensation, replete with its religious presuppositions, was coming to an end: 'The old Wales was rapidly being transformed into something else and it was far from clear whether Christianity would have any significant part to play in its further development at all.'[49]

Into a new millennium

In the last two decades of the twentieth century, much that had been familiar was swept away. The heavy industries of steel making and coal mining that had formed Wales's industrial backbone for so long had been in terminal decline for much of the second half of the twentieth century. The mass closure of uneconomic pits in the mid-1980s following the bitter miners' strike of 1984–5, led for a time to higher unemployment and the weakening of many of the communities which had owed their growth to these industries. Considerable efforts were made to provide alternative employment and diversify the Welsh economy, but change came about only gradually, though by the turn of the millennium Cardiff had grown to become a vibrant and modern metropolitan centre, and the economic powerhouse of the country. There has also been far-reaching political change. A second devolution referendum was held following the coming to power of Tony Blair's Labour Party in 1997; the Welsh supported the establishment of the proposed National Assembly by the slimmest of democratic margins, and in the two decades since its opening the Assembly has gradually evolved, incrementally gaining additional powers, including in 2017 the ability to raise taxes. By 2020 the Assembly had gained enough confidence to rename itself Senedd Cymru/Welsh Parliament, an indication of the extent of the political change that had taken place.

When looking at the fortunes of the Christian churches during this period it can be difficult to see beyond the apparently inexorable decline of the traditional Welsh denominations and the marginalization of religion in contemporary Wales. The statistics make for stark reading. Although the 2011 census revealed that a surprisingly high 59 per cent of Welsh people still identified as Christian,[50] that figure has not been reflected in Sunday church attendance. The number of Easter communicants in the Church in Wales fell from 168,200 in 1980 to just 32,000 in 2020. A similar pattern can be observed in the main Nonconformist denominations: membership figures in the Baptist Union of Wales dropped from 47,900 in 1980 to a mere 9,800 in 2020, while the Presbyterian Church of Wales witnessed a similar haemorrhaging of members from 55,600 to 10,900 over the same period. Those who attend church on a regular basis, or hold membership in a religious denomination, represented just 4.3% of the population of Wales in 2020.[51] The country, it would seem, has 'journeyed rapidly towards secularism',[52] and many who apparently profess to believe often do so without necessarily belonging to an identifiable Christian community.[53]

Religious groups in Wales have responded to this situation in different ways, and there have been some surprising results. The story of decline and marginalization outlined above must be balanced by evidence that some religious communities have been able to resist decline a little more effectively than others. The Roman Catholic Church in Wales, as elsewhere in Britain, has been boosted by the presence of large numbers of Polish immigrants since the expansion of the European Union in 2004,[54] though scandals surrounding historic sexual abuse within the church have brought with them enormous challenges for contemporary Catholic witness.

In the evangelical community also, there have been churches that have experienced sustained growth over a long period. The advent of charismatic renewal in Wales in the 1970s[55] led to the revitalization of some churches in the mainstream denominations, and the establishment of a number of new church networks of an evangelical and Pentecostal flavour. Within the Church in Wales, St Michael's, Aberystwyth, experienced charismatic renewal and grew

significantly from the mid-1980s under the ministries of first Bertie
Lewis and then Stuart Bell, sustaining a large congregation in the
university town for almost thirty years.[56] Some of this growth has
been fuelled by the advent of innovative evangelistic strategies like
Alpha, a basic course introducing the Christian faith that, since its
nationwide launch in 1993, has been remarkably successful in
building bridges between churches and those who have traditionally
had little contact with religious belief. Other evangelicals have
abandoned traditional church structures altogether, preferring to
follow the apostolic pattern of meeting in homes.[57] In many
instances these house churches have evolved to look like more
traditional churches, some linking up with national and even
international charismatic church networks such as New Frontiers,
the Ichthus Christian Fellowship or Vineyard. Increased ethnic
diversity in early twenty-first-century Wales has also witnessed the
establishment of new congregations,[58] among which the Nigerian
Redeemed Christian Church of God appears to have been
especially successful, establishing seven churches in Wales following
the opening of their first congregation in Cardiff in 2013.

The churches represented by the Evangelical Movement of
Wales have also managed to hold their ground. For much of the
1970s the itinerant preaching of Martyn Lloyd-Jones provided an
important rallying point, and barely a month seemed to pass
without his preaching to very large congregations somewhere in
Wales. His message on these occasions invariably focused on the
pressing need for revival, but his death in 1981 seemed to mark the
end of an era. In many ways his power in the pulpit harked back to
the glory days of Welsh Nonconformity; no one has stepped
forward to fill the void. However, without Lloyd-Jones's galvanizing
ministry, the churches represented by the Evangelical Movement of
Wales seemed to lack direction.[59] Some like the Heath Evangelical
Church in Cardiff sustained a very large congregation well into the
new millennium, but the origins of many churches in secession
made them prone to further division, as churches continued to split,
whether in response to experimentation with the new worship
styles associated with the charismatic movement, the adoption of a
modern Bible translation, or the awkward succession from one
dominant minister to a new one who might be just learning the

ropes. The establishment of the Associating Evangelical Churches of Wales in 1988 was an attempt to bind these churches into a relationship of greater interdependence, though the distinction between the EMW and the AECW has not always been entirely clear.

However, by the early twenty-first century evangelicalism was itself becoming a more diverse movement. The majority of Welsh evangelicals tended not to belong to separatist bodies, but from 1986 came under the umbrella of Evangelical Alliance Wales. Representing churches from around thirty denominations, EA Wales brought together evangelicals from the older denominations (including the Church in Wales), Pentecostal bodies, and some of the newer house churches and charismatic networks as well. While the separatist churches have tended to have low expectations about transforming society, some suggesting that God might even have given up on contemporary Wales,[60] churches aligned with the Evangelical Alliance have often prioritized social action. The EA itself has sought to represent the evangelical voice to the Welsh government and the media, affording Welsh evangelicals a greater presence in Welsh civic life.

There has also been a further breaking down of some of the barriers that once existed between Wales's many Christian denominations. Ecumenical realignment took place in 1990 with the founding of Cytûn: Churches Together in Wales. It grew out of the 'Not Strangers but Pilgrims' initiative of 1986 when a large number of Christians from across the denominational spectrum came together during Lent for prayer, Bible study and mutual enrichment, culminating in the 20,000-strong 'Teulu Duw' festival on the Royal Welsh showground at which Archbishop Desmond Tutu thanked Welsh Christians for their support of the anti-apartheid movement in South Africa. The Roman Catholic church was fully engaged, seemingly reinvigorated after Pope John Paul II's visit to Cardiff in June 1982, and committed itself to Cytûn, a major step forward in terms of inter-church relations. For those who had long felt that the splintering of Christian witness among a plethora of competing denominations was a major barrier to the church's mission in Wales, this development has been 'nothing short of miraculous'.[61] Yet the founding of Cytûn has not brought about the anticipated renewal of the traditional denominations, and has not arrested the downward spiral of decline.

In the twenty-first century many of these denominations have been involved in a constant battle to stave off some of the worst consequences of the loss of numbers. This has sometimes involved a diversification in their ministries, with largely redundant church buildings being turned into community spaces, and churches hosting and running food banks and other agencies to support the marginalized. The shrinking of the Nonconformist denominations has also paradoxically brought the Church in Wales to greater national prominence. For a time, the profile of the Church in Wales was even raised internationally when the bishop of Monmouth and archbishop of Wales, Rowan Williams, was translated to Canterbury as the 104th archbishop in 2002. In Wales, as elsewhere in the Anglican world, much hope was pinned on the ordination of women to the priesthood in 1996, and the full inclusion of women into the leadership of the church following its decision to elect women as bishops in 2013.[62] Yet despite having the highest proportion of women bishops within the whole Anglican communion, endemic problems remain. This was reflected in the commissioning of an external review which, when it finally reported in 2012, recommended a fundamental overhaul of the structure of the Church in Wales. 'The parish system', it stated, 'as originally set up with a single priest serving a small community is no longer viable.'[63] It called on the church to draw its lay members into more prominent leadership roles as the only response to dwindling clergy numbers, and the replacement of parishes with Local Ministry Areas. The national coverage of the Church in Wales, one if its distinguishing features, has become impossible to maintain. Yet such institutional restructuring could not disguise some of the deep-seated divisions in the church, especially over the issue of same-sex relationships. The inauguration of Anglican Essentials Wales in 2019 drew together 'orthodox Anglicans' determined to resist the liberal direction of the Church in Wales. Whether these different traditions can be held together in the years to come remains deeply uncertain. Among the Nonconformist churches there have been occasional attempts to infuse them with a fresh enthusiasm for mission, and bodies like Waleswide have sought to engage in pioneer mission work to plant churches in communities where older churches and chapels have closed.[64] The future for Wales's old religious denominations, Anglican and Nonconformist, remains precarious, with most facing all but extinction if present rates of decline are not arrested.

The 2020–1 Coronavirus pandemic has witnessed churches, chapels and other places of worship shut their doors and move almost entirely online. For those concerned about the marginalization of the Christian church in Wales, while these circumstances have often been challenging, they have also presented churches with new opportunities, and through technologies like Zoom enabled them to reach people otherwise isolated by the regime of social distancing. Perhaps the pandemic will give churches throughout Wales an unexpected opportunity to recalibrate their approach to mission and to present the gospel of Christ afresh? This book has explored many of the ways in which Welsh Christians have over the course of almost two thousand years continually discovered new ways of praising their Lord. The future of Christian witness in Wales remains exceedingly challenging on many levels, but Christians down the ages have taken solace from Christ's promise that he will always 'build his church' (Matt. 16:18). As they do so they stand on the shoulders of the saints, monks, scholars, Reformers, evangelists, revivalists and theologians who have figured so prominently in Wales's Christian story, and live in hope, even expectation, that the fortunes of the Church in Wales can sometimes change, and do so in the twinkling of an eye.

Notes

[1] Thomas Charles Edwards, 'Prif nodwedd yr adeg bresennol ar grefydd yn y Cyfundeb', *Y Drysorfa*, 58 (1888), 288.

[2] 'Religious Thought in Wales', in *Thomas Charles Edwards*, edited by D. D. Williams (Liverpool: National Eisteddfod Transactions, 1921), pp. 110–11.

[3] This change is thoroughly described in Hilton, *The Age of Atonement*, pp. 253–378.

4   D. R. Davies, *In Search of Myself: An Autobiography* (London: Geoffrey Bles, 1961), p. 37.

5   Jones, *Faith and the Crisis of a Nation*, p. 283.

6   *Report of the Royal Commission of the Church of England and other Religious Bodies in Wales and Monmouthshire*, vol. 1 (London: HMSO, 1910), p. 19.

7   Jones, *Congregationalism in Wales*, edited by Pope, p. 208.

8   Jones, *Faith and the Crisis of a Nation*, p. 373.

9   John Cory, in *Why I Would Disestablish: A Representative Book by Representative Man*, edited by Andrew Reid (London: Longmans, Green and Co, 1886), p. 151.

10   *The Times* (11 November 1914), 3.

11   D. R. Daniel to Thomas Rees, 16 October 1914, Bala-Bangor MSS 65, Bangor University Archives.

12   Alfred Jenkins to Owen Prys, sometime in 1917, Owen Prys Papers 22283, Calvinistic Methodist Archives, National Library of Wales.

13   Owen Prys Papers 22283.

14   Quoted in Owain W. Jones, *Glyn Simon, his Life and Opinions* (Llandysul: Gomer Press, 1981), p. 55.

15   William Morgan, vicar of Glanogwen, Bethesda, to Rural Dean, July 1917, National Library of Wales MS 10938C.

16   *Church Times* (2 April 1931), 8.

17   *Sermons and Hymns by Timothy Rees, Bishop of Llandaff*, edited by J. Lambert Rees (London: Mowbrays, 1946), pp. 8, 12.

18   J. Lambert Rees, *Timothy Rees of Mirfield and Llandaff: A Biography* (London: Mowbrays, 1945), p. 107.

19   *Sermons and Hymns by Timothy Rees*, p. 99.

20   *Sermons and Hymns by Timothy Rees*, p. 107.

21   Menevia Diocese Archive; quoted by Tystan Owain Hughes in an unpublished paper, 'Francis Mostyn, Bishop of Menevia and Archbishop of Wales'.

22   *Western Mail* (18 May 1936), 7.

23   *The Tablet* (15 August 1925), 206.

24   Quoted in David Thomas, *Silyn (Cofiant Silyn Roberts)* (Liverpool: Gwasg y Brython, 1957), p. 77.

25   *The Labour Voice* (14 April 1923), 5.

26   Quoted in David Howell, *Nicholas of Glais; the People's Champion* (Clydach: Clydach Historical Society, 1991), p. 29.

[27] For an analysis of this theme, see Robert Pope, *Building Jerusalem: Nonconformity, Labour and the Social Question in Wales, 1906–1939*, second edition (Cardiff: University of Wales Press, 2014), and *Seeking God's Kingdom: The Nonconformist Social Gospel in Wales, 1906–39*, second edition (Cardiff: University of Wales Press, 2015).

[28] David Ceri Jones, 'Pentecostalism', in *The Religious History of Wales*, edited by Allen and Jones with Hughes, p. 133.

[29] See, for example, Allan Anderson, *An Introduction to Pentecostalism* (Cambridge: Cambridge University Press, 2014), pp. 37–8.

[30] Jones, 'Pentecostalism', p. 142.

[31] Philip J. Jones, 'Theology in Wales during the last eighty years', *The Treasury*, 15 (1927), 8.

[32] Jones, 'Theology in Wales during the last eighty years', 8, 9, 10, 9, 43.

[33] Quoted in John McConnachie, 'The teaching of Karl Barth: a new positive movement in German theology', *The Hibbert Journal*, 25 (1926–7), 385.

[34] D. Miall Edwards, *Bannau'r Ffydd* (Wrecsam: Hughes a'i Fab, 1929), p. xiii.

[35] Edwards, *Bannau'r Ffydd* , p. 374.

[36] J. E. Daniel, 'Diwinyddiaeth Cymru', *Yr Efrydydd*, 5 (1929), 174.

[37] Daniel, 'Diwinyddiaeth Cymru', 197, 198, 121.

[38] Ewart Lewis, *The Church in Wales, the Catholic Faith and the Future* (Llandybïe: Silurian Books, 1945), p. 5.

[39] Lewis, *The Church in Wales, the Catholic Faith and the Future*, p. 10.

[40] For the statistical breakdown across the dioceses, see D. Densil Morgan, *The Span of the Cross: Christian Religion and Society in Wales, 1914–2000*, second edition (Cardiff: University of Wales Press, 2011), p. 189.

[41] Quoted in John S. Peart-Binns, *Edwin Morris: Archbishop of Wales* (Llandysul: Gomer Press, 1990), p. 81.

[42] The controversy is discussed fully by both biographers: Jones, *Glyn Simon, his Life and Opinions*, pp. 62–73 and Peart-Binns, *Edwin Morris: Archbishop of Wales*, pp. 106–37.

[43] *Western Mail* (26 March 1947), 3.

[44] *Catholic Herald* (17 March 1948), 1.

[45] *Western Mail* (15 March 1960), 4

[46] R. Ifor Parry, *Ymneilltuaeth* (Llandysul: Gwasg Gomer, 1962), p. 175.

47 See Robert Pope, 'Dolur Dwfn Diffyg Ystyr: J. R. Jones a Chrefydd', in E. Gwynn Matthews, *Astudiaethau Athronyddol*, 6 (Talybont:Y Lolfa, 2017), pp. 31–59.

48 The statistical evidence in R. Tudur Jones, *Blas ar Gristnogaeth Cymru*, edited by Euros Wyn Jones (Chwilog: Cyhoeddiadau'r Gair, 2018), p. 101.

49 Morgan, *Span of the Cross*, p. 260.

50 Robert Pigott, '2011 Census: Is Christianity shrinking of just changing?', BBC News report (11 December 2012), *https://www.bbc.co.uk/news/uk–20683744* (accessed 5 January 2021).

51 *UK Church Statistics, No. 4: 2021 Edition*, edited by Peter Brierley (Tonbridge: ADBC Publishing, 2020), table 13.6.2.

52 John I. Morgans and Peter C. Noble, *Our Holy Ground: The Welsh Christian Experience* (Talybont:Y Lolfa, 2016), p. 176.

53 Grace Davie, *Religion in Britain since 1945: Believing without Belonging* (London: Wiley, 1994).

54 Hughes, 'Roman Catholicism', in *The Religious History of Wales*, edited by Allen and Jones with Hughes, pp. 76–7.

55 David Ceri Jones, '"On the edge of spiritual revival": Charismatic Renewal in Wales', in *Transatlantic Charismatic Renewal, c.1950–2000*, edited by Andrew Atherstone, Mark Hutchinson and John Maiden (Leiden: Brill, 2021), pp. 101–22.

56 Noel Butler, *You are My Witnesses: St Michael's, Aberystwyth, 1890–1990* (Aberystwyth: Aber Art, 1990), pp. 41–7 and 49–54.

57 Paul Chambers, '"On or Off the Bus": Identity, Belonging and Schism. A Case Study of a Neo–Pentecostal House Church', in *Charismatic Christianity: Sociological Perspectives*, edited by Stephen Hunt, Malcolm Hamilton and Tony Walter (Houndmills: Macmillan, 1997), pp. 140–59.

58 Paul Chambers, 'Religious Diversity in Wales', in *A Tolerant Nation? Revisiting Ethnic Diversity in a Devolved Wales*, edited by Charlotte Williams, Neil Evans and Paul O'Leary (Cardiff: University of Wales Press, 2015), pp. 147–58.

59 David Ceri Jones, 'Lloyd-Jones and Wales', in *Engaging with Lloyd-Jones: The Life and Legacy of 'the Doctor'*, edited by Andrew Atherstone and David Ceri Jones (Nottingham: Apollos, 2011), pp. 87–90.

60 *Contemporary Welsh Preachers*, vol 1: *Where is Faith?*, edited by Llewellyn Jenkins (Harleston: Leaping Cat Press, 2004), p. 164.

61 Morgans and Noble, *Our Holy Ground*, p. 189.

[62] William Price, 'The Church in Wales across the Century', in *A New History of the Church in Wales: Governance and Ministry, Theology and Society*, edited by Norman Doe (Cambridge: Cambridge University Press, 2020), pp. 75–8.

[63] *Church in Wales Review* (July 2012), 6.

[64] David Ollerton, *A New Mission to Wales: Seeing Churches Prosper across Wales in the Twenty–first Century* (Pwllheli: Cyhoeddiadau'r Gair, 2016).

A GUIDE TO FURTHER READING

This final section is not designed to be an exhaustive bibliography listing every work referred to throughout this volume. It is, rather, an annotated guide to the main scholarly works on each of the themes and periods covered, providing interested readers with a roadmap through much of the extensive specialist literature on the history and development of Christian witness in Wales.

Chapter 1: Roman Beginnings, c.AD 1–c.AD 400

Roman Wales is almost entirely a matter for archaeology, which makes the study of religion particularly difficult. There is not a large bibliography for this period. Britain as a whole is better served, but the same problems apply, and only slightly less severely. In contrast, for the wider Roman empire and religion and the growth of early Christianity, the difficulty is in finding something particular to recommend among the numberless books and articles published on these subjects.

For Roman Britain, a recent survey is David Mattingly, *An Imperial Possession: Britain in the Roman Empire, 54 BC–AD 409* (London: Allen Lane, 2006), which takes a post-colonial, critical view of Roman imperialism. A briefer, but still thorough introduction is *The Roman Era*, edited by Peter Salway (Oxford: Oxford University Press, 2002), part of the Short Oxford History of the British Isles series. For Wales, the standard book is Christopher J. Arnold and Jeffrey L. Davies, *Roman and Early Medieval Wales* (Stroud: Tempus, 2000), very much an archaeological survey. For Roman military sites in Wales – which make up the great majority of the Roman archaeology – this is updated by the splendidly illustrated Barry C. Burnham and Jeffrey L. Davies, *Roman Frontiers in Wales and the Marches* (Aberystwyth: Royal Commission on Ancient and Historical Monuments in Wales, 2010). On Caerwent, the Cadw guide by Richard J. Brewer, *Caerwent Roman Town* (Cardiff: Cadw, 2006), is excellent.

As an introduction to Roman religion, I recommend Mary Beard, John North and Simon Price, *Religions of Rome*, vol. 1: *A History* (Cambridge: Cambridge University Press, 1998). It is excellent, and though focused on the city, it covers the rest of the empire too. For Britain, M. Henig, *Religion in Roman Britain* (London: Batsford, 1984) is the main guide, though now quite old. On Celtic religion, various works by Miranda [Aldhouse-]Green, such as *The Gods of the Celts* (Gloucester: Alan Sutton, 1986), illustrate an approach that tries to extract as much as possible from Roman and medieval literary evidence. For contrasting recent approaches see Jane Webster, '*Interpretatio*: Roman Word Power and the Celtic Gods', *Britannia*, 26 (1995), 153–61, insisting on the colonial, imperialist nature of Roman approaches to local religion, and Ralph Häussler, 'How to identify Celtic religion(s) in Roman Britain and Gaul', in *Divinidades indígenas em análise: Divinités pré-romaines – bilan et perspectives d'une recherche*, edited by José d'Encarnação (Coimbra and Porto: CEAUCP, 2008), pp. 13–63, and Anthony King, 'The emergence of Romano-Celtic religion', in *The Early Roman Empire in the West*, edited by Thomas Blagg and Martin Millett (Oxford: Oxbow, 1990), pp. 221–41, who give more scope to local and native initiative. On Celtic gods in literature, see Ronald Hutton, 'Medieval Welsh Literature and Pre-Christian Deities', *Cambrian Medieval Celtic Studies*, 61 (Summer 2011), 57–85.

Turning to Christianity: Charles Thomas, *Christianity in Roman Britain to AD 500* (London: Batsford, 1981) is monumental and fundamental. It is brought up to date by David Petts, *Christianity in Roman Britain* (Stroud: Tempus, 2003), which is also shorter and more digestible. Petts takes, however, a very positive view of the evidence. Contrast, on Wales, the more negative view expressed in A. P. Seaman, 'Tempora Christiana? Conversion and Christianization in Western Britain AD 300–700', *Church Archaeology*, 16 (2014), 1–22.

On the transition to Christianity in the wider Roman world, I recommend Robin Lane Fox, *Pagans and Christians in the Mediterranean World from the Second Century to the Conversion of Constantine* (London:Viking, 1986). It is a marvellous portrait of the depth of religious feeling on both sides. Anything by Peter Brown is worth reading: most relevant is his *The Rise of Western Christendom: Triumph and Diversity, A.D. 200–1000* (Chichester: Wiley-Blackwell, 2013).

Chapter 2: The Age of Conversion, c. 400–c. 600

In contrast to Roman Wales, there is a vast amount written on these centuries, even though the original sources are still quite poor. The classic introduction to early medieval Wales is Wendy Davies, *Wales in the Early Middle Ages* (Leicester: Leicester University Press, 1982). For archaeology the basic guide is the second half of Arnold and Davies, *Roman and Early Medieval Wales*. For the church, David Petts, *The Early Medieval Church in Wales* (Stroud: The History Press, 2009) is useful. All three of these works cover the whole period down to *c.*1100. For a wider context, T. M. Charles-Edwards, *After Rome*, Short Oxford History of the British Isles (Oxford: Oxford University Press, 2003), is concise and full of insights. But now by far the most imposing and essential work is T. M. Charles-Edwards, *Wales and the Britons 350–1063* (Oxford: Oxford University Press, 2012).

The conversion period is the subject of several recent analyses. For the literary sources, see Richard Sharpe, 'Martyrs and local saints in late antique Britain', in *Local Saints and Local Churches in the Early Medieval West*, edited by Alan Thacker and Richard Sharpe (Oxford: Oxford University Press, 2002), pp. 75–154. This study is now an absolutely indispensable starting point, and it is a pity that the volume it was published in is so expensive and hard to come-by, especially as it contains several other outstanding pieces that will feature below in later bibliographies. For the archaeological debates, see three articles by Nancy Edwards: 'Perspectives on conversion in Wales', in *The Introduction of Christianity into the Early Medieval Insular World: Converting the Isles I*, edited by Roy Flechner and Máire Ní

Mhaonaigh (Turnhout: Brepols, 2016), pp. 93–107; 'Chi-Rhos, crosses, and Pictish symbols: inscribed stones and stone sculpture in early medieval Wales and Scotland', in *Transforming Landscapes of Belief in the Early Medieval Insular World: Converting the Isles II*, edited by Nancy Edwards, Máire Ní Mhaonaigh and Roy Flechner (Turnhout: Brepols, 2017), pp. 381–407; and 'Christianising the landscape in early medieval Wales: the island of Anglesey', in *Making Christian Landscapes in Atlantic Europe: Conversion and Consolidation in the Early Middle Ages*, edited by Tomás Ó Carragáin and Sam Turner (Cork: Cork University Press, 2016), pp. 177–203. See also Seaman, 'Tempora Christiana'.

The inscriptions have been fully reanalysed in the huge three-volume work, *A Corpus of Early Medieval Inscribed Stones and Stone Sculpture in Wales* (Cardiff: University of Wales Press). Volume 1 covers *South-east Wales and the English Border* (Mark Redknap and John M. Lewis, 2007). Volumes 2 and 3 cover *South-West Wales* and *North Wales* (Nancy Edwards, 2007, 2013). They include full illustrations, and important linguistic discussions by Patrick Sims-Williams, and the introductions are also significant.

Burial in early medieval Wales is surveyed by David Longley, 'Early medieval burial in Wales', in *The Archaeology of the Early Medieval Celtic Churches*, edited by Nancy Edwards (Abingdon: Routledge, 2009), pp. 105–32. David Petts, 'Cemeteries and boundaries in western Britain', in *Burial in Early Medieval England and Wales*, edited by Sam Lucy and Andrew Reynolds (London: The Society for Medieval Archaeology, 2002), pp. 24–46, is an important contribution, though its treatment of the place-name evidence now needs revision (see Chapter 3 above). Also important are Nancy Edwards's various articles, listed above.

There is an excellent survey of Welsh Christian terminology, most of it from Latin, by Morfydd E. Owen, 'Some Welsh words: language and religion in early Wales', in *Language of Religion – Language of the People: Medieval Judaism, Christianity and Islam*, edited by Ernst Bremer, Jörg Jarnut, Michael Richter and Daniel J. Wasserstein (Munich: Wilhelm Fink Verlag, 2006), pp. 251–73.

Constantius' *Life of St Germanus* is included in *Constance de Lyon: Vie de Saint Germain d'Auxerre*, edited by R. Borius (Paris, 1965). There is an English translation of the *Life* in Thomas F. X. Noble

---

and Thomas Head, *Soldiers of Christ: Saints and Saints' Lives from Late Antiquity and the Early Middle Ages* (University Park: Pennsylvania State University Press, 1993), pp. 75–104. On the Palladian mission, T. M. Charles-Edwards, 'Palladius, Prosper and Leo the Great: mission and primatial authority', in *Saint Patrick A.D. 493–1993*, edited by David N. Dumville (Woodbridge: Boydell Press, 1993), pp. 1–12, is fundamental. St Patrick, obviously, has an impossibly large bibliography. To cut through the morass, readers should go back to his own words. See the excellent website *https://www.confessio.ie/#* for texts and translations. For his spirituality, any of the publications of Thomas O'Loughlin will be rewarding, for example *Discovering Saint Patrick* (London: Darton, Longman and Todd, 2005). On historical aspects, the collection edited by Dumville (above) is very valuable. Thomas Charles-Edwards, *Early Christian Ireland* (Cambridge: Cambridge University Press, 2000) is essential too.

Gildas is edited and translated in Michael Winterbottom, *Gildas: The Ruin of Britain and Other Documents* (Chichester: Phillimore, 1978). The essential discussion is *Gildas: New Approaches*, edited by Michael Lapidge and David N. Dumville (Woodbridge: Boydell, 1984), which contains a number of fundamental studies.

The *Life of St Samson* is edited and translated into French in *La vie ancienne de Saint Samson de Dol*, edited by P. Flobert (Paris: Institut de Recherche et d'Histoire des Textes, 1997). There is an elderly English translation in T. Taylor (trans.), *The Life of St Samson of Dol* (London: SPCK, 1925). An important recent study is Richard Sowerby, 'The Lives of St Samson: Rewriting the Ambitions of an Early Medieval Cult', *Francia*, 38 (2011), 1–31, especially for the date. A recent volume of essays, *St Samson of Dol and the Earliest History of Brittany, Cornwall and Wales*, edited by Lynette Olson (Woodbridge: Boydell Press, 2017), is valuable too.

The modern idea of an 'age of saints' in Wales owes a great deal to Rice Rees, *An Essay on the Welsh Saints* (London: Longman, etc., 1836). J. E. Lloyd was much more cautious, see his *A History of Wales from the Earliest Times to the Edwardian Conquest*, 2 vols (London: Longmans, Green and Co., 1911), vol. 1, pp. 143–59 on 'Monastic founders of the Welsh church'. The topic needs a complete historiographical study. John Reuben Davies deals with the construction of the idea in 'The saints of south Wales and the Welsh church', in *Local Saints and Local Churches in the Early Medieval West*, edited by Thacker and Sharpe, pp. 361–95. See further Jonathan Wooding, 'The representation of early British monasticism and *peregrinatio* in *Vita Prima S. Samsonis*', in *St Samson of Dol*, edited by Olson, pp. 137–61.

For the wider context in this period, the works of Peter Brown should be read. His *The Rise of Western Christendom* was recommended in the bibliography for Chapter 1. A very insightful and readable account of conversion is Richard Fletcher, *The Conversion of Europe: From Paganism to Christianity 371–1386 AD* (Hammersmith: Fontana, 1997).

Chapter 3: The Definition of Christian Wales, c. 600–c. 800

All the general works listed for Chapter 2 continue to be relevant. The most important synthesis remains Sharpe, 'Local saints and local churches'. An important collection of essays is *The Early Church in Wales and the West*, edited by Nancy Edwards and Alan Lane (Oxford: Oxbow, 1992).

The growth of local churches is an important and complex topic. Archaeologists long followed Charles Thomas's model, according to which early cemeteries developed into churchyards. His exposition will be found in his *The Early Christian Archaeology of North Britain* (London: Oxford University Press, 1971), especially Chapter 3. The whole book, though now dated in many regards, remains a valuable and very readable survey. More recent work on burial casts doubt on whether early cemeteries were enclosed: see David Petts, 'Cemeteries and boundaries in western Britain', in *Burial in Early Medieval England and Wales*, edited by Sam Lucy and Andrew Reynolds (London: Society for Medieval Archaeology, 2002), pp. 24–46. The works by Longley and Edwards in the bibliography for Chapter 2 present and develop this new understanding of the complexity of early medieval burial.

Since church sites are so hard to excavate, other forms of evidence are called on to establish that churches are early, notably dedications to 'Celtic' saints and certain types of place-name. This evidence, and its limitations, is now very much better understood. Three essays, all in the same volume, are indispensable: they are Sharpe, 'Martyrs and local saints', as above, and O. J. Padel, 'Local saints and place-names in Cornwall', in *Local Saints and Local Churches in the Early Medieval West*, edited by Thacker and Sharpe, pp. 303–60, and John Reuben Davies, 'The saints of south Wales and the Welsh church', in the same volume, pp. 361–95. Though Padel works on Cornwall, much of what he says transfers smoothly to Wales. He updates his work in O. J. Padel, 'Christianity in medieval Cornwall: Celtic aspects', in Nicholas Orme, *A History of the County of Cornwall*, II: *Religious History to 1560* (Woodbridge: Victoria County History, 2010), pp. 110–25. Note that Padel and Davies diverge on the dating of *lann/llan* place-names, a debate that looks set to continue. Still in Cornwall, Sam Turner, 'Making a Christian landscape: early medieval Cornwall', in *The Cross Goes North: Processes of Conversion in Northern Europe, AD 300–1300*, edited by M. Carver (Woodbridge: York Medieval Press, 2003), pp. 171–94, and his monograph, *Making a Christian Landscape: The Countryside in Early-Medieval Cornwall, Devon and Wessex* (Exeter: University of Exeter Press, 2006), are well worth reading for comparative purposes.

More specific studies on place-names are Tomos Roberts, 'Welsh ecclesiastical place-names and archaeology', in *The Early Church in Wales and the West*, edited by Nancy Edwards and Alan Lane (Oxford: Oxbow Press, 1992), pp. 41–4, and David N. Parsons, *Martyrs and Memorials: Merthyr Place-Names and the Church in Early Wales* (Aberystwyth: Centre for Advanced Welsh and Celtic Studies, 2013). The latter is an exemplary full study of one element. Parsons proposes in future to deal with *llan* in the same way, a study that is eagerly anticipated.

It had long been accepted that churches dedicated to 'Celtic' saints were founded by these individuals, many of whom must therefore have been great travellers. This was already the belief in the Middle Ages, as saints' *Lives* reveal. It was revived for modern scholarship by Rees in his *Essay* (see bibliography for Chapter 2), and in the twentieth century E. G. Bowen married it with historical geography in several very well-known works, especially his *The Settlements of the Celtic Saints in Wales* (Cardiff: University of Wales

Press, 1954) and *Saints, Seaways and Settlement in the Celtic Lands* (Cardiff: University of Wales Press, 1969). I have noted J. E. Lloyd's cautious discussion in the bibliography to Chapter 2. A warning about the reliability of dedications was given by Owen Chadwick, 'The evidence of dedications in the early history of the Welsh church', in *Studies in Early British History*, edited by Nora Kershaw Chadwick (Cambridge: Cambridge University Press, 1954), pp. 173–88, but not enough attention was paid to it. For a much more complex explanation of the evidence, see Davies, 'Saints of south Wales', as above, and compare Padel's approach to the Cornish material, also as above.

Turning to events, by far the most worthwhile text to read is Bede's *Historia Ecclesiastica*. It is edited and translated in *Bede's Ecclesiastical History of the English People*, edited and translated by B. Colgrave and R. A. B. Mynors (Oxford: Clarendon Press, 1969). The same translation is readily and cheaply available in the Oxford World's Classics volume, *Bede: The Ecclesiastical History of the English People, The Greater Chronicle, Bede's Letter to Egbert*, edited by Judith McClure and Roger Collins (Oxford: Oxford University Press, 1994). For Bede and the Britons, two important studies are T. M. Charles-Edwards, 'Bede, the Irish and the Britons', *Celtica*, 15 (1983), 42–52, and Clare Stancliffe, 'The British church and the mission of Augustine', in *St Augustine and the Conversion of England*, edited by Richard Gameson (Stroud: Sutton, 1999), pp. 107–51.

On the Easter question there is a vast bibliography, but as the evidence for the Insular Easter almost all comes from an Irish context, the specifically Welsh dimension is hard to access. The best survey is T. M. Charles-Edwards, *Early Christian Ireland* (Cambridge: Cambridge University Press), Chapter 9: 'The paschal controversy', which does a good job of explaining why people cared so much. Edward James, 'Bede and the Tonsure Question', *Peritia*, 3 (1984), 83–98, is also useful. Aldhelm's letter to Gerent of Dumnonia is available in English translation in *Aldhelm: The Prose Works*, translated by M. Lapidge and M. Herren (Cambridge: D. S. Brewer, 1979), pp. 155–60; see also their discussion of its date, pp. 140–3. For Columbanus, see the edition of his letters, *Sancti Columbani Opera*, edited by G. S. M. Walker (Dublin: Dublin Institute for Advanced

Studies, 1957), and Caitlin Corning, 'Columbanus and the Easter controversy: theological, social and political contexts', in *The Irish in Early Medieval Europe*, edited by Roy Flechner and Sven Meeder (London: Palgrave, 2016), pp. 101–15.

For the 'Celtic church' debate, the key works are Kathleen Hughes, 'The Celtic Church: Is This a Valid Concept?', *Cambridge Medieval Celtic Studies*, 1 (Summer 1981), 1–20, and Wendy Davies, 'The myth of the Celtic Church', in *The Early Church in Wales and the West*, edited by Edwards and Lane, pp. 12–21. On the broader ideological issues, see Donald Meek, *The Quest for Celtic Christianity* (Edinburgh: Handsel Press, 2000). On the other side, for an interesting attempt to define a Welsh spiritual tradition within 'Celtic Christianity', see Oliver Davies, *Celtic Christianity in Early Medieval Wales: The Origins of the Welsh Spiritual Tradition* (Cardiff: University of Wales Press, 1996), but note that virtually everything discussed there is of twelfth-century date or later.

4: Vikings to Normans, c. 800–c. 1070

Once again, refer to the bibliography for Chapters 2 and 3 for general works on early medieval Welsh history. Petts, *The Early Church in Wales*, is an up-to-date survey of the church. For the secular history of these centuries, add also Wendy Davies, *Patterns of Power in Early Wales* (Oxford: Oxford University Press, 1990) and also her edited volume, *From the Vikings to the Normans* (Oxford: Oxford University Press, 2003), part of the Short Oxford History of the British Isles.

Written sources become more abundant in this period, especially towards the end. We now have annals, historical writing (the *Historia Brittonum*), the legal documents in the Lichfield gospels, and many charters in the Book of Llandaf and elsewhere. Our oldest surviving manuscripts also belong to these centuries, all in Latin, though some include Welsh material too. At the end of the eleventh century we have the very valuable *Lives* of St David by Rhygyfarch of Llanbadarn Fawr and of St Cadog by Lifris of Llancarfan. From the twelfth century on the sources multiply profusely: many more *Lives*, religious poetry in Welsh, especially three long praise poems to Saints Cadfan, Tysilio and David, and the rich writings of Gerald of Wales. These texts contain much that is relevant to earlier centuries. The annals and *Historia Brittonum* are usefully available in *Nennius: British History and the Welsh Annals*, edited by John Morris (London and Chichester: Phillimore, 1980). The *Lives* of the saints are in A. W. Wade-Evans, *Vitae Sanctorum Britanniae et Genealogiae* (Cardiff: University of Wales Press, 1944), with English translations. However, a more up-to-date edition and translation of the *Life of St David* is Richard Sharpe and John Reuben Davies (edited and translated), 'Rhygyfarch's *Life* of St David', in *St David of Wales: Cult, Church and Nation*, edited by J. Wyn Evans and Jonathan Wooding (Woodbridge: Boydell, 2007), pp. 107–55. The rest of that volume is also full of interesting material. The Book of Llandaf has not been translated into English. The Latin text is in *The Text of the Book of Llan Dâv*, edited by J. G. Evans and J. Rhys (Oxford: privately published, 1893). An important study of the book is John Reuben Davies, *The Book of Llandaf and the Norman Church in Wales* (Woodbridge: The Boydell Press, 2003). For Welsh poems to the saints, see *www.seintiaucymru.ac.uk*. Gerald of Wales is translated by Lewis Thorpe in the Penguin Classics series, but for those who read Welsh, Thomas Jones, *Gerallt Gymro* (Caerdydd: Gwasg Prifysgol Cymru, 1938), is better.

On raiding and conflict between the church and secular rulers, see W. E. Davies, 'Property rights and property claims in Welsh *Uitae* of the eleventh Century', in *Hagiographie, culture et sociétés, IVe–XIIe siècles*, edited by Évelyne Patlagean and Pierre Riché (Paris, 1981), pp. 515–33, and John R. Davies, 'Church, Property, and Conflict in Wales, AD 600–1100', *Welsh History Review*, 18 (1996–7), 387–406.

Bishops are discussed in Charles-Edwards, *Wales and the Britons*, pp. 583–98, and Colmán Etchingham, 'Bishoprics in Ireland and Wales in the early Middle Ages: some comparisons', in *Contrasts and Comparisons: Studies in Irish and Welsh Church History*, edited by John R. Guy and W. G. Neely (Llandysul: Gomer, 1999), pp. 7–25. There is a large literature on the *clas* churches. Start with J. Wyn Evans, 'The survival of the *clas* as an institution in medieval Wales: some observations', in *The Early Church in Wales and the West*, edited by Nancy Edwards and Alan Lane (Oxford: Oxbow, 1992), pp. 33–40. Charles-Edwards, *Wales and the Britons*, pp. 602–14, is an up-to-date survey making good use of the Llancarfan documents. For the identification of major churches using archaeological criteria, see the four regional surveys, covering all of Wales, in *The Archaeology of the Early Medieval Celtic Churches*, edited by Nancy Edwards (Leeds: Maney, 2009), Chapters 2–5. On layouts, see Huw Pryce, *Native Law and the Church in Medieval Wales* (Oxford: Clarendon Press, 1993), Chapter 7: 'Ecclesiastical Sanctuary', and David Petts and Sam Turner, 'Early medieval church groups in Wales and western England', in *The Archaeology of the Early Medieval Celtic Churches*, edited by Edwards, pp. 281–99. Tomás Ó Carragáin's work on Ireland is a very fruitful source of comparisons; see his *Churches in Early Medieval Ireland: Architecture, Ritual and Memory* (New Haven: Yale University Press). On personnel, see again Charles-Edwards, *Wales and the Britons*, from pp. 602ff.

The huge debate about early medieval churches, monasticism and pastoral care can be approached through *Pastoral Care Before the Parish*, edited by John Blair and Richard Sharpe (Leicester: Leicester University Press, 1992). The most relevant essay in that collection is by Huw Pryce on Wales, but the other papers should be read as well, as the debate has largely concerned Ireland and England where the evidence is far richer. Sharpe's earlier paper, 'Some Problems Concerning the Organization of the Church in Early Medieval Ireland', *Peritia*, 3 (1984), 230–70, is required reading too. There is an important book-length study by Colmán Etchingham, *Church Organisation in Ireland AD 650 to 1000* (Maynooth: Laigin Publications, 1999), which is demanding and does not deal much with Wales. Unfortunately, the Welsh evidence is not really sufficient to allow us to write a treatment of this length. On the English side, John Blair's paper in *Pastoral Care Before the Parish* should be compared with Eric Cambridge and David Rollason, 'The Pastoral Organization of the Anglo-Saxon Church: A Review of the "Minster Hypothesis"', *Early Medieval Europe*, 4 (1995), 87–104.

On island hermitages, see Jonathan Wooding, 'Island and coastal churches in medieval Ireland and Wales', in *Ireland and Wales in the Middle Ages*, edited by Karen Jankulak and Jonathan M. Wooding (Dublin: Four Courts Press, 2007), pp. 201–28. The *Life* of St Ælfgar is in Karen Jankulak and Jonathan M. Wooding, 'The Life of St Elgar of Ynys Enlli', *Trivium*, 39 (2010), 15–47.

On the cult of saints in this period, an important survey of the written evidence is J. R. Davies, 'The saints of south Wales and the Welsh church', in *Local Saints and Local Churches in the Early Medieval West*, edited by Thacker and Sharpe, pp. 361–95. Nancy Edwards, 'Celtic saints and early medieval archaeology', in the same volume, pp. 224–65, covers the material culture of the cult of saints.

On writing, see Huw Pryce, 'The origins and the medieval period', in *A Nation and its Books: A History of the Book in Wales*, edited by Philip H. Jones and Eiluned Rees (Aberystwyth, National Library of Wales: 1998), pp. 1–16; Patrick Sims-Williams, 'The uses of literacy in early medieval Wales', in *Literacy in Medieval Celtic Societies*, edited by Huw Pryce (Cambridge: Cambridge University Press, 1998), pp. 15–38; *The Cambridge History of the Book in Britain*, vol. 1: *c. 400–1100*, edited by R. Gameson (Cambridge: Cambridge University Press, 2011), with chapters by Helen McKee on script and the circulation of books, and T. M. Charles-Edwards on books in Wales. The latter topic is covered very similarly but in slightly more detail in Chapter 19 of Charles-Edwards, *Wales and the Britons*, on 'Latin learning in Wales, *c.*400–1100'. Individual manuscripts are viewable online, see *https://digital.bodleian.ox.ac.uk/*, and *https://cudl.lib.cam.ac.uk/view/MS-FF-00004-00042/1 (Juvencus)*, and *https://www.llyfrgell.cymru/index.php?id=1667* (Book of Llandaf). The Juvencus *englynion* are edited in Ifor Williams, *The Beginnings of Welsh Poetry*, edited by Rachel Bromwich (Cardiff: University of Wales Press, 1980), pp. 101–2. There is a later edition in Marged Haycock, *Blodeugerdd Barddas o Ganu Crefyddol Cynnar* (Llandybïe: Cyhoeddiadau Barddas, 1994), no. 1.

For the *Historia Brittonum*, see various articles by David N. Dumville, especially 'The historical value of the *Historia Brittonum*', *Arthurian Literature*, 6 (1986), 1–26. On myth-making around the figure of St Germanus in particular, see Barry J. Lewis, 'The saints in narratives of conversion from the Brittonic-speaking regions', in *The Introduction of Christianity into the Early Medieval Insular World: Converting the Isles I*, edited by Roy Flechner and Máire Ní Mhaonaigh (Turnhout: Brepols, 2016), pp. 431–56, and the much fuller survey in Howard Huws, *Buchedd Garmon Sant* (Llanrwst: Gwasg Carreg Gwalch, 2008). On the family of Sulien, see Michael Lapidge, 'The Welsh-Latin Poetry of Sulien's Family', *Studia Celtica*,

8/9 (1973–4), 68–109. *Bonedd y Saint* is in Peter Bartrum, *Early Welsh Genealogical Tracts* (Cardiff: University of Wales Press, 1966), pp. 51–67; a new edition and study by Barry J. Lewis is in preparation.

Chapter 5: The Age of Definition and Hierarchy, c. 1066–c. 1200

Glanmor Williams, *The Welsh Church from Conquest to Reformation* (Cardiff: University of Wales Press, revised edition 1976) is still a very valuable guide to the later part of the period covered by this chapter. The more recent county histories also have useful studies: see, for example, Jeremy Knight, 'The Parish Churches', and David H. Williams, 'The Religious Orders', in *The Gwent County History*, vol. 2: *The Age of the Marcher Lords, c. 1070–1536*, edited by Ralph A. Griffiths, Tony Hopkins and Ray Howell (Cardiff: University of Wales Press, 2008), pp. 167–82 and 183–216; 'The Church', in A. D. Carr, *Medieval Anglesey* (Llangefni: Anglesey Antiquarian Society, revised edition, 2011), pp. 211-36; John Reuben Davies, 'The Medieval Church' and David Williams, 'The Cistercian Houses', in *Cardiganshire County History*, vol. 2: *Medieval and Early Modern Cardiganshire*, edited by Geraint Jenkins, Richard Suggett and Eryn White (Cardiff: University of Wales Press, 2019), pp. 179–96 and 197–240.

On the general background to the period, see R. R. Davies, *Conquest, Co-existence and Change: Wales, 1063–1415* (Oxford: Clarendon Press, 1987); David Stephenson, *Medieval Wales c. 1050–1332: Centuries of Ambiguity* (Cardiff: University of Wales Press, 2019); earlier chapters in Glanmor Williams, *Recovery, Reorientation and Reformation: Wales, 1415–1642* (Oxford: Clarendon Press, 1987); Melissa Julian-Jones, 'Reading the March: interpretations and constructions of the Welsh marcher lordships and the Church in Wales, c. 1100–1284', *History Compass*, 15/7 (2017). Relevant chapters in the various county histories are also useful.

For religious life at the coming of the Normans, see Thomas O'Loughlin, 'Rhigyfarch's *Vita Davidi*: An *Apparatus Biblicus*', *Studia Celtica*, 32 (1998), 179–88. On Rhigyfarch's extensive scriptural knowledge and the high intellectual standards and organization of the late eleventh-century church, see J. Wyn Evans, 'St David and

St David's and the Coming of the Normans', *Transactions of the Honourable Society of Cymmrodorion*, 11 (2005), 5–18.

The debate over the Book of Llandaf and the organization of the early church in Wales has produced an extensive literature. Patrick Sims-Williams, *The Book of Llandaf as a Historical Source*, Studies in Celtic History, 38 (Woodbridge: Boydell Press, 2019), reviews work on the subject since Wendy Davies's seminal *An Early Welsh Microcosm: Studies in the Llandaff Charters* (London: Royal Historical Society, 1978) and *The Llandaff Charters* (Aberystwyth: National Library of Wales, 1979). See also 'The Book of Llandaff' and 'The Significance of the Doublets', in T. M. Charles-Edwards, *Wales and the Britons, 350–1064* (Oxford: Oxford University Press, 2013), pp. 245–66.

John Reuben Davies, *The Book of Llandaf and the Norman Church in Wales*, Studies in Celtic History, 21 (Woodbridge: Boydell Press, 2003), is good on the general background of the period as well as the Book of Llandaf itself. C. N. L. Brooke has taken a different perspective on the Book of Llandaf, regarding it as a complete forgery; his *The Church and the Welsh Border in the Central Middle Ages* (Woodbridge: Boydell Press, 1986) revisits his earlier arguments and is also a good source for developments in the early Norman period. See also David Walker, 'Cultural Survival in an Age of Conquest', in *Welsh Society and Nationhood: Historical Essays Presented to Glanmor Williams*, edited by R. R. Davies, Ralph A. Griffiths, Ieuan Gwynedd Jones and Kenneth O. Morgan (Cardiff: University of Wales Press, 1984), pp. 35–50.

The introductions to *Llandaff Episcopal Acta 1140–1287*, edited by David Crouch (Cardiff: South Wales Record Society, 1988) and *St David's Episcopal Acta 1085–1280*, are a useful background to ecclesiastical reorganization. Huw Pryce, *Native Law and the Church in Medieval Wales* (Oxford: Clarendon Press, 1993), provides much of the legal background to these developments. Several of the essays in *Welsh Society and Nationhood*, edited by Davies, Griffiths, Jones and Morgan, cover this period. See the following essays: David Walker, 'Cultural Survival in an Age of Conquest', R. R. Davies, 'Law and National Identity in Thirteenth-Century Wales' and Ralph A. Griffiths, 'Medieval Severnside: The Welsh Connection', pp. 35–50, 51–69 and 70–89.

On church building, the volumes of the 'Buildings of Wales' series are a useful introduction. For the earlier period, see also Malcolm Thurlby, *Romanesque Architecture and Sculpture in Wales* (Almeley: Logaston Press, 2006). David Longley, 'Penmon Revisited', *Transactions of the Anglesey Antiquarian Society* (2012), 75–86, is wider in scope than the title suggests. Unfortunately the British Academy's Corpus of Romanesque Sculpture in Britain and Ireland has not to date made much headway into Wales.

Chapter 6: Conquest and Apocalypse, c. 1200–c. 1420

The *Lives* of the Welsh saints claim to relate to the fifth and sixth centuries, but they are arguably at least as informative for the beliefs and priorities of the time they were written down. For recent analysis, as well as the further reading for Chapter 4 and the series currently being edited by the Centre for Advanced Welsh and Celtic Studies and published online at *http://www.welshsaints.ac.uk/theedition/*, see *Buchedd Beuno: The Middle Welsh* Life *of St Beuno*, edited by Patrick Sims-Williams (Dublin: Dublin Institute for Advanced Studies, 2018); *St David of Wales: Cult, Church and Nation*, edited by J. Wyn Evans and Jonathan Wooding (Woodbridge: Boydell Press, 2007); *Celtic Hagiography and Saints' Cults*, edited by Jane Cartwright (Cardiff: University of Wales Press, 2003); Barry Lewis, *Medieval Welsh Poems to Saints and Shrines*, Medieval and Modern Welsh Series, 14 (Dublin: Institute for Advanced Studies, 2015). Elissa Henken's approach is more that of a folklorist: see her *The Welsh Saints: A Study in Patterned Lives* (Cambridge: Brewer, 1991), and *Traditions of the Welsh Saints* (Cambridge: Brewer, 1987).

Specifically on female saints, see Jane Cartwright, *Feminine Sanctity and Spirituality in Medieval Wales* (Cardiff: University of Wales Press, 2008). This is an updated version of her earlier *Y Forwyn Fair, Santesau a Lleianod* (Cardiff: University of Wales Press, 1999); Madeleine Gray *Rewriting Holiness: Reconfiguring Vitae, Re-signifying Cults* (London: Centre for Late Antique and Medieval Studies, 2017), pp. 89–108.

———

On the religious houses, the Monastic Wales web site at *http://www.monasticwales.org/* is backed up by *Abbeys and Priories of Medieval Wales*, edited by Janet Burton and Karen Stöber (Cardiff: University of Wales Press, 2015), and *Monastic Wales: New Approaches*, edited by Janet Burton and Karen Stöber (Cardiff: University of Wales Press, 2015). On specific orders, see also David Williams's work on the Cistercians, summed up in *The Welsh Cistercians* (Leominster: Gracewing, 2001). There are a number of studies of individual houses: see Alan Bott and Margaret Dunn, *The Priory and Parish Church of St Mary, Beddgelert* (Coastline Publications, 2005); *Anatomy of a Priory Church: The Archaeology, History and Conservation of St Mary's Priory Church, Abergavenny*, edited by George Nash (Oxford: Archaeopress, 2015). On the educational activities of religious foundations, including the later chantries, see Nicholas Orme, 'Education in Medieval Wales', *Welsh History Review*, 27/4 (December 2015), 607–44.

On crusades and pilgrimage, Kathryn Hurlock, *Wales and the Crusades c.1095–1291* (Cardiff: University of Wales Press, 2011), and *Medieval Welsh Pilgrimage c.1100–1500* (London: Palgrave Macmillan, 2018), summarize recent research. For the later period, see G. Williams, 'Poets and pilgrims in fifteenth- and sixteenth-century Wales', *Transactions of the Honourable Society of Cymmrodorion* (1991), 69–98. Specifically on miracle stories, see Madeleine Gray, '"Gwyrth yn y Coed Gynt": a rediscovered miracle collection from the shrine of the Virgin Mary at Penrhys?', *Studia Celtica*, 45 (2011), 105–9. On the Welsh miracles of Thomas of Cantilupe, see Ian L. Bass, 'St Thomas de Cantilupe's Welsh miracles', *Studia Celtica,,* 53/1 (December 2019), 83–102, and 'Rebellion and Miracles on the Welsh March: Accounts in the Miracle Collection of St Thomas de Cantilupe', *Welsh History Review*, 29/4 (December 2019), 503–31.

On the church and the struggle for Welsh independence, as well as the general histories listed above, there is useful background in David Stephenson, *The Governance of Gwynedd* (Cardiff: University of Wales Press, 1984), republished as *Political Power in Medieval Gwynedd: Governance and the Welsh Princes* (Cardiff: University of Wales Press, 2014).

Our evidence for the development of lay spirituality in this period comes mainly from the poetry of the *Gogynfeirdd*. General works on the poetry of the period include Dafydd Johnston, *Llên yr Uchelwyr: Hanes Beirniadol Llenyddiaeth Gymraeg, 1300–1525* (Cardiff: University of Wales Press, 2005). The best English-language guide to the *Gogynfeirdd* is still *A Guide to Welsh Literature*, vol. 1, edited by A. O. H. Jarman and Gwilym Rees Hughes (Cardiff: University of Wales Press, 1992), and for the later period *A Guide to Welsh Literature*, vol. 2: *1282–c.1550*, edited by A. O. H. Jarman, Gwilym Rees Hughes and Dafydd Johnston (Cardiff: University of Wales Press, 1997). The Wiley-Blackwell *Encyclopaedia of Medieval Literature in Britain* (2017) has a number of articles on Welsh topics across its four volumes. Introductions and translations of key texts can be found in *The Medieval Welsh Religious Lyric: Poems of the Gogynfeirdd, 1137–1282*, edited by Catherine A. McKenna (Belmont, MA: Ford & Baillie, 1991), and N. G. Costigan, *Defining the Divinity: Medieval Perceptions in Welsh Court Poetry* (Aberystwyth: University of Wales Centre for Advanced Welsh and Celtic Studies, 2002). Further texts (with an introduction in English but not translations) are in *Welsh Court Poems*, edited by Rhian M. Andrews (Cardiff: University of Wales Press, 2007). On specific themes, see Catherine McKenna, 'Performing Penance and Poetic Performance in the Medieval Welsh Court', *Speculum*, 82/1 (January 2007), 70–96.

On the background to the crisis of the fourteenth century, as well as the general histories mentioned above, see the relevant chapters in Matthew Frank Stevens, *The Economy of Medieval Wales 1067–1536* (Cardiff: University of Wales Press, 2019) and references therein. Specifically on the famine, Phillipp R. Schofield, 'Wales and the Great Famine of the Early Fourteenth Century', *Welsh History Review*, 29/2 (December 2018), 143–67. The Glyndŵr uprising has an extensive literature: for an introduction, see R. R. Davies, *The Revolt of Owain Glyn Dŵr* (Oxford: Oxford University Press, 1997). Specifically on the church, Ralph Griffiths, 'Owain Glyn Dŵr's Invasion of the Central March of Wales in 1402: The Evidence of Clerical Taxation', *Studia Celtica*, 46 (2012), 111–22, discusses the scale of destruction of church property. Paul Frame, 'Glyndŵr's Rebellion, the Bishop of Bangor and the Councils of Pisa and Constance', *Welsh History Review*, 28/2 (December 2016), 209–32, puts Glyn Dŵr in the context of the Papal schism.

Chapter 7:Y Ganrif Fawr: Christianity in Late Medieval Wales,
c.1420–c.1530

Katherine Olson, *Popular Religion, Culture, and Reformation in Wales and the Marches, c.1400–1603* (Oxford: Oxford University Press, forthcoming), will deal in detail with the period from the Glyn Dŵr uprising. For church rebuilding and redecoration in the fifteenth and early sixteenth centuries, see Madeleine Gray, *Images of Piety: The Iconography of Traditional Religion* (Oxford: Archaeopress, 2000) and the relevant sections of Peter Lord and John Morgan-Guy, *The Visual Culture of Wales: Medieval Vision* (Cardiff: University of Wales Press, 2003).

Specifically on stained glass, Mostyn Lewis, *Stained Glass in North Wales up to 1850* (Altrincham: John Sherratt and Son, 1970) is still a valuable survey, though it needs to be corrected in detail by the first chapter of Martin Crampin, *Stained Glass from Welsh Churches* (Talybont:Y Lolfa, 2014). On rood screens, both C. James, '"Y Grog Ddoluriog Loywrym": Golwg ar y Canu i Grog Llangynwyd', *Llên Cymru*, 29/1 (2006), 64–109, and Barry Lewis, *Welsh Poetry and English Pilgrimage: Gruffudd ap Maredud and the Rood at Chester* (Aberystwyth: University of Wales Centre for Advanced Welsh and Celtic Studies, 2005), are wider in scope than their titles suggest. Part 2 of Sally Harper's *Music in Welsh Culture before 1650* (Farnham: Ashgate, 2007) looks in detail at the evidence for liturgical music in monastic and secular churches.

On the art of the macabre, Madeleine Gray, 'The "Dawns o Bowls" and the macabre in late medieval Welsh art and poetry', *Studia Celtica*, 47 (2013), 41–57; Madeleine Gray and David Hale, 'Dancing and Dicing with Death: literary evidence for some lost wall paintings in Wales', *Transactions of the Ancient Monuments Society*, 65 (2021), 7–19. Recent studies of burial and commemoration include Rhianydd Biebrach, *Church Monuments in South Wales, c. 1200–1547* (Woodbridge: Boydell, 2017); David Hale, 'Death and commemoration in late medieval Wales' (unpublished Ph.D. thesis, University of South Wales, 2017). Madeleine Gray, 'Reforming Memory: commemoration of the dead in sixteenth-century Wales', *Welsh History Review*, 26/2 (December 2012), 186–214.

On the church in the early sixteenth century see Madeleine Gray, "'The Curious Incident of the Dog in the Night-time": The Pre-Reformation Church in Wales', in *Christianities in the Early Modern Celtic World*, edited by Robert Armstrong and T. Ó hAnnracháin (Basingstoke: Palgrave Macmillan, 2014), pp. 42–54. The Llandeilo Talybont wall paintings are discussed in *Saving St Teilo's: Bringing a Medieval Church to Life*, edited by Gerallt Nash (Cardiff: National Museum of Wales, 2009). For recent research on the well and chapel at Holywell, see Rick Turner, 'The architecture, patronage and date of St Winefride's Well, Holywell', *Archaeologia Cambrensis*, 168 (2019), 245–75.

Chapter 8: Reformation Wales, 1530–1603

Historical writing on the Reformation is Wales remains dominated by the work of Glanmor Williams. Among his voluminous writings over many years, his *Wales and the Reformation* (Cardiff: University of Wales Press, 1999) distils that work into a single accessible volume. For shorter accounts, chapters 12 and 13 of his *Renewal and Reformation: Wales, c. 1415–1642* (Oxford: Oxford University Press, 1987) are excellent, as are the relevant sections in the first chapter of his *The Welsh and their Religion: Historical Essays* (Cardiff: University of Wales Press, 1991). For Wales in the sixteenth century more generally, J. Gwynfor Jones, *Wales and the Tudor State: Government, Religious Change and the Social Order, 1534–1603* (Cardiff: University of Wales Press, 1989), explores the development of Wales in the wake of the 'Acts of Union', and Hugh Thomas, *A History of Wales, 1485–1660* (Cardiff: University of Wales, 1972), provides a useful overview of some of the main developments in the period more generally.

In recent years there has been some excellent new work on the resilience of traditional religion in sixteenth-century Wales. Katherine Olson's *Popular Religion, Culture, and Reformation in Wales and the Marches, c. 1400–1603* (Oxford: Oxford University Press, forthcoming) remains eagerly anticipated. Her "'Slow and Cold in the True Service of God": Popular Beliefs and Practices, Conformity and Reformation in Wales, c.1530–c.1600', in

Christianities in the Early Modern Celtic World, edited by Armstrong and Ó hAnnracháin, pp. 92–110, whets the appetite for the larger study. Madeleine Gray's, *Images of Piety: The Iconography of Traditional Religion* (Oxford: Archaeopress, 2002) is excellent on the survival of many aspects of the visual culture of late medieval Catholicism. For the changing perspectives of the Welsh poets, Chapter 3 in J. Gwynfor Jones, *Aspects of Religious Life in Wales, c. 1536–1660: Leadership, Opinion and the Local Community* (Aberystwyth: Centre for Educational Studies, 2003), provides a good overview as well as English translations of some of the key evidence.

Often work on the Welsh Reformation has focused on individual dioceses and bishops. John Morgan-Guy's two essays on the progress of the Reformation in south-west Wales down to 1660 in *Religion and Society in the Diocese of St Davids, 1485–2011*, edited by William Gibson and John Morgan-Guy (Farnham: Ashgate, 2015), reflects much of the latest scholarship, though somewhat contentiously suggests that the attractions of Protestantism have often been overplayed. For the Reformation bishops, two good examples are Nia M. W. Powell, 'Arthur Bulkeley: Reformation Bishop of Bangor, 1541–1552/3', *Journal of Welsh Religious History*, new series 3 (2003), 23–52, and Madeleine Gray, 'The Cloister and the Hearth: Anthony Kitchin and Hugh Jones, two Reformation bishops of Llandaff', *Journal of Welsh Religious History*, 3 (1995), 15–34.

For the introduction of more radical Protestantism into Wales, Glanmor Williams's 'The Protestant Experiment in the Diocese of St David's, 1534–1555', in his *Welsh Reformation Essays* (Cardiff: University of Wales Press, 1967), pp. 111–40, remains unsurpassed. Many historians have focused on the provision of Welsh-language Protestant literature in the later sixteenth century. Eryn M. White's *The Welsh Bible: A History* (Stroud: Tempus, 2007) is an excellent introduction. Various chapters in *A Guide to Welsh Literature, c. 1530–1700*, edited by Geraint Gruffydd (Cardiff: University of Wales Press, 1997) focus on the Welsh Renaissance, while James Pierce, *A Rare Scholar: William Salesbury* (Aberystwyth: Y Lolfa, 2016) is a substantial biography of Wales's greatest Renaissance scholar. For Richard Davies, Lloyd Bowen, 'The Battle of Britain: History and Reformation in Early Modern Wales', in *Christianities in the Early*

Modern Celtic World, edited by Armstrong and Ó hAnnracháin, pp. 135–50, contains some up-to-date reflections on his work and significance. For William Morgan and his magisterial 1588 translation of the Bible into Welsh, Glanmor Williams's 'Bishop William Morgan and the first Welsh Bible', in his *The Welsh and their Religion*, pp. 173–229, is excellent, as is Isaac Thomas, *William Morgan and his Bible* (Cardiff: University of Wales Press, 1988).

For residual Catholicism in Wales, D. Aneurin Thomas, *The Welsh Elizabethan Catholic Martyrs* (Cardiff: University of Press, 1971), is a good place to start. Geraint Bowen's *Welsh Recusant Writings* (Cardiff: University of Wales Press, 1999) remains an excellent short overview, while Alexandra Walsham's, 'The Holy Maid of Wales: Vision, Imposture and Catholicism in Elizabethan Britain', *English Historical Review*, 132/555 (2017), 250–85, examines the persistence of Catholic spirituality. Early Welsh Puritanism is perhaps best approached through John Penry, for example in J. Gwynfor Jones, 'John Penry: Government, Order and the "Perishing Souls" of Wales', *Transactions of the Honourable Society of Cymmrodorion* (1993), 47–81, while Penry's main writings are contextualized and reprinted in *Three Treatises Concerning Wales*, edited by David Williams (Cardiff: University of Wales Press, 1960). The beginnings of a distinctly Welsh theological tradition at the end of the sixteenth century are explored in D. Densil Morgan, *Theologia Cambrensis: Protestant Religion and Theology in Wales*, vol. 1: *From Reformation to Revival, 1588–1760* (Cardiff: University of Wales Press, 2018), pp. 11–34.

Chapter 9: Creating a Protestant Wales, 1603–1760

For an overview of Wales in the seventeenth century W. S. K. Thomas's *Stuart Wales* (Llandysul: Gomer Press, 1988), although short, remains the best single-volume introduction to some of the main themes and events. Lloyd Bowen's, *The Politics of the Principality: Wales, c. 1603–42* (Cardiff: University of Wales Press, 2007) is a detailed study of Welsh political life up to the outbreak of the civil war, containing much on religious developments. Chapters 1 and 2 in Geraint H. Jenkins, *The Foundations of Modern*

Wales, 1642–1780 (Oxford: University of Wales Press, 1987), provide an excellent overview of the English civil war and its impact in Wales, together with the experiment in republican government in the 1650s. Much, if not the vast majority, of historical writing on Wales in the early seventeenth century has focused on the origins and growth of Dissent and Nonconformity. Geraint H. Jenkins, *Protestant Dissenters in Wales, 1639–1689* (Cardiff: University Press, 1992), says a remarkable amount in a short compass. Lloyd Bowen's 'Wales, 1587–1689', in *The Oxford History of Protestant Dissenting Traditions*, vol. 1: *The Post-Reformation Era, 1559–1689*, edited by John Coffey (Oxford: Oxford University Press, 2020), pp. 224–43, is an excellent more recent treatment.

For more specialized literature on religious developments in the period, the first two chapters in Glanmor Williams, William Jacob, Nigel Yates and Frances Knight, *The Welsh Church: From Reformation to Disestablishment, 1630–1920* (Cardiff: University of Wales Press, 2007), provides a useful overview of the Church of England in Wales during this period. On the early Welsh Puritans themselves, Thomas Richards's work remains indispensable. *The Puritan Movement in Wales, 1639 to 1653* (London: National Eisteddfod Association, 1920) covers the early period. Geoffrey F. Nuttall's *The Welsh Saints, 1640–1660: Walter Cradock, Vavasor Powell and Morgan Llwyd* (Cardiff: University of Wales Press, 1957), while a little dated, remains stimulating. R. Geraint Gruffydd's *'In that Gentile Country': The Beginnings of Protestant Nonconformity in Wales* (Bridgend: Evangelical Library of Wales, 1976) is also worth seeking out as a short introduction. For individual figures, see John I. Morgans, *The Honest Heretique: The Life and Work of William Erbery* (1604–1654) (Talybont: Y Lolfa, 2012), and R. Tudur Jones, 'The healing herb and the rose of love: the piety of two Welsh Puritans', in *Reformation, Conformity and Dissent: Essays in Honour of Geoffrey F. Nuttall*, edited by R. Buick Knox (London: Epworth Press, 1978), pp. 154–9. Entries in the *Oxford Dictionary of National Biography* (2004) provide excellent studies of the key figures also. For theological trends and developments before the Restoration, see Morgan, *Theologia Cambrensis*, vol. 1, pp. 34–84 and Chapter 2.

The religious changes and opportunities brought about by the civil war and ensuing revolution can be approached through

Christopher Hill, 'Puritans and the "dark corners of the land"', *Transactions of the Royal Historical Society*, 13 (December 1963), 77–102; Stephen K. Roberts, 'Propagating the gospel in Wales: the making of the 1650 act', *Transactions of the Honourable Society of Cymmrodorion*, new series 9 (2004), 57–75; Lloyd Bowen. 'Oliver Cromwell (alias Williams) and Wales', in *Oliver Cromwell: New Perspectives*, edited by Patrick Little (Houndmills: Palgrave Macmillan, 2009), pp. 168–84; and Lloyd Bowen, "This murmuring and unthankful Peevish Land": Wales and the Protectorate', in *The Cromwellian Protectorate*, edited by Patrick Little (Woodbridge: Boydell and Brewer, 2007), pp. 144–64.

For the impact of the Great Ejection, and the emergence of Nonconformity after 1662 Eryn M. White, 'From Ejectment to Toleration in Wales, 1662–89', in *The Great Ejectment of 1662: Its Antecedents, Aftermath, and Ecumenical Significance*, edited by Alan F. P. Sell (Eugene, OR: Pickwick Publications, 2012), pp. 125–82 is an excellent distillation of the major scholarship. The early chapters in R. Tudur Jones, *Congregationalism in Wales*, edited by Robert Pope (Cardiff: University of Wales Press, 2004) are invaluable. One of the most important figures in these decades was Stephen Hughes, and Glanmor Williams's 'Stephen Hughes (1622–1688): "Apostol Sir Gâr", the Apostle of Wales', *Carmarthenshire Antiquary*, 37 (2001), 21–30, remains the best account. For the proliferation of religious literature in post-Restoration Wales, see Geraint H. Jenkins, *Literature, Religion and Society in Wales, 1660–1730* (Cardiff: University of Wales Press, 1978); on education and the charity schools, Eryn M. White, 'Popular Schooling and the Welsh Language', in *The Welsh Language before the Industrial Revolution*, edited by Geraint H. Jenkins (Cardiff: University of Wales Press, 1997), pp. 318–41, and Mary Clement, *The SPCK and Wales* (London: SPCK, 1954), are the best studies. For Griffith Jones and the circulating schools, see Geraint H Jenkins, '"An old and much honoured Soldier": Griffith Jones, Llanddowror', *Welsh History Review*, 11/4 (1983), 449–68, and for a major reassessment of Jones's importance as a theological thinker of some substance, see Morgan, *Theologia Cambrensis*, vol. 1, pp. 278–316.

Methodism and the evangelical revival remains one of the most thoroughly studied areas of Welsh religious history, and the literature is consequently voluminous. For a brief overview, Chapter 9 in Jenkins, *The Foundations of Modern Wales, 1642–1780*, is good. David Ceri Jones, Boyd Stanley Schlenther and Eryn Mant White, *The Elect Methodists: Calvinistic Methodism in England and Wales* (Cardiff: University of Wales Press, 2012), is a comprehensive introduction and overview. For Howell Harris, Geraint Tudur's, *Howell Harris: From Conversion to Separation, 1735–50* (Cardiff: University of Wales Press, 2000) is a major study based on Harris's incredibly detailed diaries. Daniel Rowland remains something of an enigma; Eifion Evans's *Daniel Rowland and the Great Evangelical Awakening in Wales* (Edinburgh: Banner of Truth, 1985) is the fullest biography, while the same author's *Bread of Heaven: The Life and Work of William Williams, Pantycelyn* (Bridgend: Bryntirion Press, 2010) provides excellent summaries of Williams's main writings – a real boon to non-Welsh-speakers. However, it should ideally be read alongside Derec Llwyd Morgan's *The Great Awakening in Wales* (London: Epworth Press, 1988) for a more scholarly examination of Williams. For the Welsh Methodist societies, Eryn M. White's, *The Welsh Methodist Society: The Early Societies in South-West Wales, 1737–1750* (Cardiff: University of Wales Press, 2020) is a detailed examination of their social composition. For the Welsh revival's place within the wider evangelical movement, David Ceri Jones's *The Fire Divine: Introducing the Evangelical Revival* (Nottingham: Inter-Varsity Press, 2015) provides the necessary contextualization in short compass.

Chapter 10: Building a Nonconformist Nation, 1760–1890

For the history of Protestant Dissent, the following texts are standard: R. Tudur Jones, *Congregationalism in Wales*, edited by Robert Pope (Cardiff: University of Wales Press, 2004); the Welsh-language original is entitled *Hanes Annibynwyr Cymru* (Abertawe: Gwasg John Penry, 1966) and has long been regarded as a classic; for the Baptists T. M. Bassett, *The Welsh Baptists* (Swansea: Ilston Press, 1977), can be complemented by the essays of D. Hugh Matthews, John Rice Rowlands and Gareth O. Watts in *Y Fywiol Ffrwd: Bywyd a Thystiolaeth Bedyddwyr Cymru, 1649–1999*, edited by D. Densil Morgan (Abertawe: Gwasg Ilston, 1999); Unitarianism is treated in D. Elwyn Davies, *'They Thought for Themselves': A Brief look at the Story of Unitarianism and the Liberal Tradition in Wales* (Llandysul: Gomer Press, 1982), and in Welsh *Y Smotiau Duon: Braslun o Hanes y Traddodiad Rhyddfrydol ac Undodiaeth* (Llandysul: Gwasg Gomer, 1981), while the most succinct account of Welsh Quakerism during the period is Richard C. Allen, 'The Religious Society of Friends (Quakers)', in *The Religious History of Wales*, edited by Richard C. Allen and David Ceri Jones with Trystan Owain Hughes (Cardiff: Welsh Academic Press, 2014), pp. 55–68. A detailed study of later nineteenth-century developments is to be found in Owain Gethin Evans, '"Benign Neglect": the activities and relationship of the London Yearly Meeting of the Religious Society of Friends to Wales, c.1860–1918' (unpublished Ph.D. thesis, University of Birmingham, 2009). For composite assessments, see D. Densil Morgan, 'Nonconformity in Wales', in *The T&T Clark Companion to Nonconformity*, edited by Robert Pope (London: T&T Clark, 2013), pp. 27–46, and Eryn M. White, 'Protestant Dissent in Wales', in *The Oxford History of Protestant Dissenting Traditions,* vol. II: *The Long Eighteenth Century c. 1689–c. 1828*, edited by Andrew Thompson (Oxford: Oxford University Press, 2018), pp. 160–82.

Calvinistic Methodism has long been excellently served by historians. The period leading to the 1811 secession is covered fully by Jones, Schlenther and White in *The Elect Methodists*, while volumes 2 and 3 of the official denominational history, *Hanes Methodistiaeth Galfinaidd Cymru*, cyf. 2: *Cynnydd y Corff*, edited by Gomer M. Roberts (Caernarfon: Llyfrfa'r Methodistiaid Calfinaidd 1978), and *Hanes Methodistiaeth Galfinaidd Cymru*, cyf. 3: *Y Twf a'r Cadarnhau (c.1814–1914)*, edited by J. Gwynfor Jones (Caernarfon: Gwasg Pantycelyn, 2011), include a wealth of detail. To date only volume 3 is available in English, namely *The History of Welsh Calvinistic Methodism III: Growth and Consolidation, c. 1814–1914*, edited by J. Gwynfor Jones (Cardiff: Presbyterian Church of Wales, 2013). For the principal first-generation revivalists see Evans, *Daniel Rowland and the Great Evangelical Awakening in Wales*, and *Bread of Heaven: The Life and Work of Williams Pantycelyn*. Williams, especially, has been subject to extensive study, texts of the long poems 'Theomemphus' and 'Golwg ar Deyrnas Crist' being available in

Gweithiau William Williams Pantycelyn, cyf. 1, edited by Gomer M. Roberts (Caerdydd: Gwasg Prifysgol Cymru, 1964), and the main prose works edited by Garfield H. Hughes in *Gweithiau William Williams Pantycelyn*, cyf. 2 (Caerdydd: Gwasg Prifysgol Cymru, 1967). Both the literary and theological aspects of their work are treated exquisitely by Derec Llwyd Morgan in *Y Diwygiad Mawr* (Llandysul: Gwasg Gomer, 1981) translated as *The Great Awakening in Wales* (London: Epworth Press, 1988); Glyn Tegai Hughes provides an accomplished English-language evaluation in *Williams Pantycelyn* (Cardiff: University of Wales Press, 1983).

In comparison with the Calvinistic tradition, Wesleyan Methodism suffers from a dearth of recent historical analysis. A brief résumé is to be found in *Methodism in Wales: A Short History of the Wesley Tradition*, edited by Lionel Madden (Llandudno: Welsh Methodist Conference 2003), along with David Ceri Jones, 'Wesleyan Methodism', in *The Religious History of Wales*, edited by Allen and Jones with Hughes, pp. 94–105.

For the impact of the evangelical revival on Nonconformity, see D. Densil Morgan's, '"Smoke, fire and light": Baptists and the revitalization of Welsh Dissent', *The Baptist Quarterly*, 32 (1988), 224–32; *Christmas Evans a'r Ymneilltuaeth Newydd* (Llandysul: Gwasg Gomer, 1991) and 'Christmas Evans and the birth of Nonconformist Wales', in *Wales and the Word: Historical Perspectives on Welsh Identity and Religion* (Cardiff: University of Wales Press, 2008), pp. 17–30. Eryn M. White provides an excellent historical overview and critical appraisal of revivalism generally (centring on south Wales): 'Religious Revivals in the Eighteenth, Nineteenth and Twentieth Centuries', in *Religion and Society in the Diocese of St Davids*, edited by William Gibson and John Morgan-Guy (Farnham: Ashgate, 2015), pp. 129–56. The change in preaching styles is mapped by D. Densil Morgan in 'Preaching in the vernacular: the Welsh sermon, 1689–1901', in *The Oxford Handbook of the British Sermon, 1689–1901*, edited by Keith A. Francis and William Gibson (Oxford: Oxford University Press, 2012), pp. 199–214.

For Welsh Anglicanism during this period, see the chapters by Jacob, Yates and Knight in Glanmor Williams, William Jacob, Nigel Yates and Frances Knight, *The Welsh Church from Reformation to Disestablishment, 1603–1920* (Cardiff: University of Wales Press,

2007), along with Chapters 3 and 5, 'The Established Church 1800–50' and 'The Revival of the Established Church, 1850–1920', in E. T. Davies, *A New History of Wales: Religion and Society in the Nineteenth Century* (Llandybïe: Christopher Davies, 1981). D. T. W. Price, *A History of Saint David's University College, Lampeter*, vol. 1: *To 1898* (Cardiff: University of Wales Press, 1977), also contains pertinent material on many aspects of the subject.

The 'High Church' theology of the Church of England in Wales at the beginning of this period is charted in Morgan, *Theologia Cambrensis*, vol. 1, pp. 274–8. The tensions between churchmen and revivalists is treated by John Morgan-Guy, '"Tinkers and other vermin": Methodists and the Established Church in Wales, 1735–1800', in *Revival, Renewal and the Holy Spirit*, edited by Dyfed Wyn Roberts (Milton Keynes: Paternoster Press, 2009), pp. 27–35, while Mark Smith provides an assessment of Thomas Burgess, bishop of St Davids: 'Burgess, Churchman and Reformer', in *Bishop Burgess and his World: Culture, Religion and Society in Britain, Europe and North America in the Eighteenth and Nineteenth Centuries*, edited by Nigel Yates (Cardiff: University of Wales Press, 2007), pp. 5–40.

Post-1811 evangelicalism is dealt with in detail by Roger L. Brown, *Evangelicals in the Church in Wales* (Welshpool: Tair Eglwys Press, 2007), while Tractarianism has been assessed by A. Tudno Williams, *Cymru a Mudiad Rhydychen* (Dinbych: Gwasg Gee, 1983), D. P. Freeman, 'The influence of the Oxford Movement on Welsh Anglicanism . . . in the 1840s and 1850s' (unpublished Ph.D. thesis: University of Wales, Swansea, 1999), and John Boneham, 'Isaac Williams and Welsh Tractarian theology', in *The Oxford Movement: Europe and the Wider World, 1830–1930*, edited by Stewart J. Brown and Peter B. Nockles (Cambridge: Cambridge University Press, 2012), pp. 37–55. For the Anglican contribution to the nineteenth-century cultural renaissance, see Bedwyr Lewis Jones, *Yr Hen Bersoniaid Llengar* (n.p.: Gwasg yr Eglwys Yng Nghymru, 1963), along with the composite article in *The Oxford Dictionary of National Biography* (2004) entitled 'Yr Hen Bersoniaid Llengar: Old literary Clerics'.

As well as being a biography, D. E. Jenkins's three-volume *The Life of Thomas Charles of Bala* (Denbigh: Llewelyn Jenkins, 1908–11) provides indispensable detail concerning immediate pre- and post-secession Welsh Calvinistic Methodism. For different aspects of his contribution, see the essays in *Thomas Charles o'r Bala*, edited by D. Densil Morgan (Caerdydd: Gwasg Prifysgol Cymru, 2013), while the ordination movement has been treated in D. Densil Morgan, 'Thomas Jones of Denbigh (1756–1820) and the ordination of 1811', *Welsh Journal of Religious History*, 6 (2011), 9–30. Along with his chapter in Morgan, *Thomas Charles o'r Bala*, Andras Llŷr Iago has provided the definitive study of Thomas Jones in his 'Bywyd a Gwaith Thomas Jones o Ddinbych, 1755–1820' (unpublished Ph.D. thesis: University of Wales Trinity St David, 2014).

For the Sunday School Movement, see Huw J. Hughes, *Coleg y Werin: Hanes yr Ysgol Sul yng Nghymru rhwng 1780 ac 1851* (Chwilog: Cyhoeddiadau'r Gair, 2014), the fruits of detailed research for a Bangor Ph.D., while the missionary movement has been assessed by D. Andrew Jones, '"O Dywyllwch i Oleuni": Y Genhadaeth Gartref a Thramor', in *Hanes Methodistiaeth Galfinaidd Cymru*, cyf. 3, edited by Jones, pp. 422–93, and more briefly in '"From Darkness into Light": The Home and Foreign Mission', in *The History of Welsh Calvinistic Methodism*, vol. III, edited by Jones, pp. 193–217. An exhaustive catalogue of Welsh periodical literature, almost exclusively religious in nature, is to be found in Huw Walters's two-volume *Bibliography of Welsh Periodicals*, 1735–1850 and 1851–1900 (Aberystwyth: National Library of Wales, 1993 and 2003), along with the author's estimation of their importance: 'The Periodical Press', in *The Welsh Language and Its Social Domains, 1801–1911*, edited by Geraint H. Jenkins (Cardiff: University of Wales Press, 2000), pp. 349–78.

Turning to the 1851 census, a transcript of the Welsh material is available in *The Religious Census of 1851: A Calendar of the Returns relating to Wales*, vol. 1: *South Wales*, edited by Ieuan Gwynedd Jones and David Williams (Cardiff: University of Wales Press, 1976), and *The Religious Census of 1851: A Calendar of the Returns relating to Wales*, vol. 2: *North Wales*, edited by Ieuan Gwynedd Jones (Cardiff: University of Wales Press, 1981), along with a magisterial evaluation of their significance by Glanmor Williams in 'Crefydda mewn Llan a Chapel: Cyflwr Cymru yn y flwyddyn 1851', *Grym Tafodau Tân: Ysgrifau Hanesyddol ar Grefydd a Diwylliant* (Llandysul: Gwasg Gomer, 1984), pp. 282–308.

———

For the Blue Books controversy, see *Brad y Llyfrau Gleision: Ysgrifau ar Hanes Cymru*, edited by Prys Morgan (Llandysul: Gwasg Gomer, 1991), and Gwyneth Tyson Roberts, *The Language of the Blue Books:Wales and Colonial Prejudice* (Cardiff: University of Wales Press, 2011).The social composition of Nonconformity from mid-century on, along with its politics, has been treated with superb erudition by Ieuan Gwynedd Jones in *Explorations and Explanations: Essays in the Social History of Victorian Wales* (Llandysul: Gomer Press, 1981); *Communities: Essays in the Social History of Victorian Wales* (Llandysul: Gomer Press, 1987) and *Mid-Victorian Wales: The Observers and the Observed* (Cardiff: University of Wales Press, 1992). The essays 'Merioneth Politics in Mid-Nineteenth Century' and 'The Liberation Society and Welsh Politics', in *Explorations and Explanations,* pp. 83–164, 236–68, are especially relevant. See also Matthew Cragoe, *Culture, Politics and National Identity in Wales, 1832–86* (Oxford: Oxford University Press, 2004).

For the significance of the pulpit see Morgan, 'Preaching in the vernacular: the Welsh sermon, 1689–1901', in *The Oxford Handbook of the British Sermon,* edited by Francis and Gibson, pp. 199–214, and W. P. Griffith, '"Preaching second to no other under the sun": Edward Matthews, the Nonconformist pulpit and Welsh identity during the mid-nineteenth century', in *Religion and National Identity: Wales and Scotland, c. 1700–2000,* edited by Robert Pope (Cardiff: University of Wales Press, 2001), pp. 61–83. Hymnody is assessed by Alan Luff in *Welsh Hymns and their Tunes, their Background and Place in Welsh History and Culture* (London: Stainer & Bell, 2003), E. Wyn James, 'The evolution of the Welsh hymn', in *Dissenting Praise: Religious Dissent and the Hymn in England and Wales,* edited by Isabel Rivers and David L.Wykes (Oxford: Oxford University Press, 2011), pp. 229–68, and Rhidian Griffiths, 'Songs of Praises', in *The History of Welsh Calvinistic Methodism,* vol. III, edited by Jones, pp. 139–49.

For Charles Finney and the 1859 Revival, see Dyfed Wyn Roberts, 'Dylanwad diwygiadaeth Charles Finney ar ddiwygiad 1858–60 yng Nghymru' (unpublished Ph.D. thesis: Bangor University, 2005), along with his essay, 'The effect of Charles Finney's revivalism on the 1858–60 revival in Wales', in *Revival, Renewal and the Holy Spirit,* edited by Dyfed Wyn Roberts (Milton

Keynes: Paternoster, 2009), pp. 36–44. Also J. J. Morgan, *Hanes Dafydd Morgan Ysbyty a Diwygiad '59* (Yr Wyddgrug: dros yr awdur, 1906); Evan Isaac, *Humphrey Jones a Diwygiad 1859* (Y Bala: Gwasg y Bala, 1930), and Eifion Evans, *Two Welsh Revivalists: Humphrey Jones, Dafydd Morgan and the 1859 Revival in Wales* (Bridgend: Bryntirion Press, 1985).

For the most recent and comprehensive analysis of the development of theology and doctrine in the nineteenth century, see D. Densil Morgan, *Theologia Cambrensis*, vol. 2: *The Long Nineteenth Century, 1760–1900* (Cardiff: University of Wales Press, 2021). The standard Victorian assessment was contained in two exhaustive chapters of Owen Thomas *Cofiant y Parchedig John Jones, Talsarn* (Wrexham: Hughes a'i Fab, 1874), some of which has been translated by John Aaron as *The Atonement Controversy in Welsh Theological Literature and Debate, 1707–1841* (Edinburgh: Banner of Truth, 2002). A critical analysis and summary of the Calvinistic Methodist material has been attempted by D. Densil Morgan, in 'Credo ac Athrawiaeth', *Hanes Methodistiaeth Galfinaidd Cymru*, cyf. 3, edited by Jones, pp.112–86, and more succinctly in 'Theology among the Welsh Calvinistic Methodists, *c.*1811–1914', in *The History of Welsh Calvinistic Methodism*, vol. III, edited by Jones, pp. 70–89. Two early to mid-twentieth-century studies are still valuable: T. Ellis Jones's essay on moderate Calvinism, 'Ffwleriaeth yng Nghymru', *Trafodion Cymdeithas Hanes Bedyddwyr Cymru* (1936), 1–49, and Glyn Richard's 'A study of the theological developments among Nonconformists in Wales during the nineteenth century' (unpublished B.Litt., University of Oxford, 1957). For mid- to late nineteenth-century Calvinism, see D. Densil Morgan, *Lewis Edwards* (Caerdydd: Gwasg Prifysgol Cymru, 2009) (in Welsh) along with a précis in 'Lewis Edwards (1809–87) and Theology in Wales', *The Welsh Journal of Religious History*, 3 (2008), 15–28.

By far the best recent assessment of nineteenth-century Welsh Catholicism is Daniel J. Mullins, 'The Catholic Church in Wales', in *From Without the Flaminian Gate: 150 Years of Roman Catholicism in England and Wales, 1850–2000*, edited by V. Alan McClelland and Michael Hodgetts (Darton, Longman and Todd, 1999), pp. 272–94, though Donald Attwater, *The Catholic Church in Modern Wales* (London: Burns and Oates, 1935), remains useful.

Chapter 11: Adapting to a Secular Wales, 1890–2020

The key text on religion in late Victorian and Edwardian Wales, is R. Tudur Jones, *Faith and the Crisis of a Nation: Wales 1890–1914*, edited by Robert Pope (Cardiff: University of Wales Press, 2004), which includes a full analysis of the social context, doctrinal content and development of Welsh religion during these years. The original two-volume work was written in Welsh: R. Tudur Jones, *Ffydd ac Argyfwng Cenedl: Hanes Crefydd yng Nghymru, 1890–1914*, cyf. 1: *Prysurdeb a Phryder* (Abertawe: Gwasg John Penry, 1981), and cyf. 2: *Dryswch a Diwygiad* (Abertawe: Gwasg John Penry, 1982). For theological trends, see D. Densil Morgan, 'Et Incarnatus Est: the Christology of Thomas Charles Edwards (1837–1900)', *Transactions of the Honourable Society of Cymmrodorion*, 18 (2012), 56–66; '"Y Prins"': agweddau ar fywyd a gwaith Thomas Charles Edwards (1837–1900)', *Y Traethodydd*, 704 (2013), 30–9.

The best assessment of the 1904–5 Revival remains Chapters 12–14 in Tudur Jones, *Faith and the Crisis of a Nation*. The centenary engendered considerable new research and analysis, including Noel Gibbard, *On the Wings of a Dove: The International Effects of the 1904–05 Revival* (Bridgend: Bryntirion Press, 2004); *Fire on the Altar: A History and Evaluation of the 1904–05 Revival in Wales* (Bridgend: Bryntirion Press, 2005); John Gwynfor Jones, '"Ebychiad mawr olaf Anghydffurfiaeth Cymru"': Diwygiad 1904–5', *Transactions of the Honourable Society of Cymmrodorion*, 11 (2005), 105–43; 'Reflections on the Religious Revival in Wales, 1904–5', *Journal of the United Reformed Church History Society*, 7/7 (2005), 427–45; Robert Pope, 'Evan Roberts in Theological Context', *Transactions of the Honourable Society of Cymmrodorion*, 11 (2005), 144–69, and 'Demythologising the Evan Roberts Revival, 1904–1905', *The Journal of Ecclesiastical History*, 57 (2006), 515–34. Some of the essays in *Revival, Renewal and the Holy Spirit*, edited by Roberts deal with the Welsh Revival. For an uncritical biography of the best-known of the revivalists, see Brynmor Pierce Jones, *An Instrument of Revival: The Complete Life of Evan Roberts, 1878–1951* (Newbury, FL: Bridge Logos, 1995).

Most modern assessments of the disestablishment campaign begin with Kenneth O. Morgan, *Freedom or Sacrilege: A History of the Campaign for Welsh Disestablishment* (Penarth: Church in Wales Publications, 1966), reprinted in *Modern Wales: Politics, Places and People* (Cardiff: University of Wales Press, 1995), pp. 142–76; Roger L. Brown describes the negative aspect of the campaign as exemplified by A. G. Edwards in 'Traitors and Compromisers: The Shadow Side of the Church's Fight against Disestablishment', *Journal of Welsh Religious History*, 3 (1995) 35–53; also Paul O'Leary, 'Religion, Nationality and Politics: Disestablishment in Ireland and Wales 1868–1914', in *Contrasts and Comparisons: Studies in Irish and Welsh Church History*, edited by J. R. Guy and W. G. Neely (Welshpool: Welsh Religious History Society, 1999), pp. 89–113, and Simon J. Taylor 'Disestablished Establishment: High and Earthed Establishment in the Church in Wales', *Journal of Contemporary Religion*, 18 (2003), 227–40. John Owen's contribution to 'Church Defence' is assessed by Harri Williams in 'St Davids and Disestablishment: Reassessing the role of Bishop John Owen', in *Religion and Society in the Diocese of St Davids 1485–2011*, edited by John Morgan-Guy and William Gibson (Farnham: Ashgate, 2015), pp. 179–202, and more extensively in his 'The life and work of Bishop John Owen (1854–1926), with particular reference to the disestablishment of the Anglican Church in Wales' (unpublished Ph.D. thesis, University of Wales Trinity Saint David, 2018). The most recent short study is Jeffrey Gainer, 'The Road to Disestablishment', in *A New History of the Church in Wales*, edited by Norman Doe (Cambridge: Cambridge University Press, 2020), pp. 27–44, while David William Jones' 'The campaign for the disestablishment of the Welsh Anglican church: a study in political intrigue and popular frustration' (unpublished Ph.D. thesis, Swansea University, 2019), though revisionist, is very insightful.

For the First World War, see D. Densil Morgan, *The Span of the Cross: Christian Religion and Society in Wales, 1914–2000* (Cardiff: University of Wales Press, 2011), pp. 41–77; Robert Pope discusses Nonconformist attitudes to the conflict in 'Christ and Caesar? Welsh Nonconformists and the State, 1914–1918', in *Wales and War: Society, Politics and Religion in the Nineteenth and Twentieth Centuries*, edited by Matthew Cragoe and Chris Williams (Cardiff: University of Wales Press, 2007), pp. 165–83; '"Duw ar Drai ar Orwel Pell": Capeli Cymru a'r Rhyfel Mawr', *Y Traethodydd*, 169 (2014), 213–

30; and 'Conscription, Conscience and Building God's Kingdom: Welsh Nonconformists and the Great War', *The Journal of the United Reformed Church History Society*, 9/10 (2017), 575–97. Harri Parri discusses the tragic ambiguity of the recruiting campaign in *Gwn Glân a Beibl Budr: John Williams Brynsiencyn a'r Rhyfel Mawr* (Caernarfon: Gwasg y Bwthyn, 2014).

For the chaplains see D. Densil Morgan, 'Ffydd yn y ffosydd: bywyd a gwaith y Caplan D. Cynddelw Williams', *National Library of Wales Journal*, 29 (1995), 77–100, reprinted in *Cedyrn Canrif: Crefydd a Chymdeithas yng Nghymru'r Ugeinfed Ganrif* (Caerdydd: Gwasg Prifysgol Cymru, 2001), pp. 1–27, and Ieuan Elfryn Jones, 'Welsh army Chaplains in the First World War: an historical appraisal' (unpublished M.Phil. dissertation, Bangor University, 2014).

Pacifism is treated in Aled Eirug, *The Opposition to the Great War in Wales* (Cardiff: University of Wales Press, 2018), building upon an earlier work by Dewi Eirug Davies, *Byddin y Brenin: Cymru a'i Chrefydd yn y Rhyfel Mawr* (Abertawe: Gwasg John Penry, 1988) which is more specifically religious in scope. For biographical studies of individual Christian pacifists, see Jen Llywelyn, *Pilgrim of Peace: A Life of George M. Ll. Davies, Pacifist, Conscientious Objector and Peace-Maker* (Tal-y-bont: Y Lolfa, 2016) and Harri Parri, *Cannwyll yn Olau: Stori John Puleston Jones* (Caernarfon: Gwasg y Bwthyn, 2018).

For a general account of Welsh Anglicanism during the period, see David Walker, 'Disestablishment and Independence', in *A History of the Church in Wales*, edited by David Walker (Penarth: Church in Wales Publications, 1976), pp. 164–87; D. T. W Price, *A History of the Church in Wales in the Twentieth Century* (Penarth: Church in Wales Publications, 1991), and his 'The Church across the Century', in *A New History of the Church in Wales* edited by Doe, pp. 63–80, while the contribution of the bishops is analysed in Chapter 6 of the same work, Arthur Edwards, 'The Bishops and Archbishops', pp. 102–21; see also his *Archbishop Green, his Life and Opinions* (Llandysul: Gomer Press, 1986). For Timothy Rees, see Dafydd Jenkins, 'Timothy Rees CR, Esgob Llandaf, 1931–9', *Ceredigion*, 11 (1992), 405–24, and D. Densil Morgan, 'Lampeter, Mirfield and the world: the life and work of Bishop Timothy Rees (1874–1939)', *Welsh Journal of Religious History*, 7– 8 (2012–13), 100–17.

———

Essential reading for twentieth-century Roman Catholicism is Daniel J. Mullins, 'The Catholic Church in Wales', in *From Without the Flaminian Gate*, edited by McClelland and Hodgetts, pp. 272–94, and Trystan Owain Hughes, *Winds of Change: Roman Catholic Church and Society in Wales 1916–62* (Cardiff: University of Wales Press, 2015). See also his 'Roman Catholicism', in *The Religious History of Wales*, edited by Allen and Jones with Hughes, pp. 69–78, and his essays, '"No longer will we call ourselves Catholics in Wales but Welsh Catholics": Roman Catholicism, the Welsh language and Welsh national identity in the twentieth century', *Welsh History Review*, 20 (2000), 336–50, and 'Anti-Catholicism in Wales', *Journal of Ecclesiastical History*, 53 (2002), 312–25.

For the Congregationalists, see R. Tudur Jones, *Congregationalism in Wales*, edited by Robert Pope (Cardiff: University of Wales Press, 2004); the Welsh-language original is entitled *Hanes Annibynwyr Cymru* (Abertawe: Gwasg John Penry, 1966), but see also his *Yr Undeb: Hanes Undeb yr Annibynwyr Cymraeg, 1872–1972* (Abertawe: Gwasg John Penry, 1975), both of which are superb. The story of twentieth-century Welsh Presbyterianism is now available in *Hanes Methodistiaeth Galfinaidd Cymru, cyf. 4: Yr Ugenfed Ganrif (c. 1914–2014)*, edited by J. Gwynfor Jones and Marian Beech Hughes (Caernarfon: Gwasg Pantycelyn, 2017), along with R. Buick Knox's earlier study of the English-language churches, *Voices from the Past: History of the English Conference of the Presbyterian Church of Wales, 1889–1938* (Llandysul: J. D. Lewis, 1969). For the Welsh-speaking Baptists, see Gareth O. Watts, 'Yr Adran Gymraeg, 1866–1999', in *Y Fywiol Ffrwd: Bywyd a Thystiolaeth Bedyddwyr Cymru, 1649–1999*, edited by D. Densil Morgan (Abertawe: Gwasg Ilston, 1999), pp. 30–70. Unfortunately, there is no corresponding study of the English-language Baptists in Wales for this period though Brynmor Pierce Jones's *Sowing Beside all Waters: The Baptist Heritage of Gwent* (Blaenavon: Gwent Baptist Association, 1985) is useful.

For religion, the labour movement and the social gospel, see Robert Pope, *Building Jerusalem: Nonconformity, Labour and the Social Question in Wales, 1906–1939* (Cardiff: University of Wales Press, 2014); *Seeking God's Kingdom: The Nonconformist Social Gospel in Wales, 1906–39* (Cardiff: University of Wales Press, 2015); and his collection of essays, *Codi Muriau Dinas Duw: Anghydffurfiaeth ac*

Anghyddfurfwyr Cymru'r Ugeinfed Ganrif (Bangor: Canolfan Uwchefrydiau Crefydd yng Nghymru, 2005). There is also a colourful biography of the Marxist poet-preacher T. E. Nicholas in Hefin Wyn, *Ar Drywydd Niclas y Glais: Comiwnydd Rhonc a Christion Gloyw* (Tal-y-bont: Y Lolfa, 2017).

For inter-war fundamentalism, see Brynmor Pierce Jones, *The King's Champions: Revival and Reaction, 1905–35* (Cwmbran: Christian Literature Press, 1986); *The Spiritual History of Keswick in Wales, 1903–83* (Cwmbran: Christian Literature Press, 1989); and his history of the 'Mission Halls', *How Lovely are Thy Dwellings* (Newport: Wellspring, 1999), all of which are informative but lack academic rigour. Norman Grubb's *Rees Howells, Intercessor*, originally published in 1952 by Lutterworth Press but reissued numerous times subsequently, is similarly hagiographic. See also Noel Gibbard, *Taught to Serve: History of Barry and Bryntirion Colleges* (Bridgend: Evangelical Press of Wales, 1986); *R. B. Jones: Gospel Ministry in Turbulent Times* (Bridgend: Bryntirion Press, 2009).

Pentecostalism is treated by David Ceri Jones, in *The Religious History of Wales*, edited by Allen and Jones with Hughes, pp. 131–46; also, Thomas Napier Turnbull, *What God hath Wrought: A Short History of the Apostolic Church* (n.p.: Puritan Press, 1959), and H. B. Llewellyn, 'A study of the history of thought of the Apostolic Church in Wales in the context of Pentecostalism' (unpublished M.Phil. thesis, University of Wales, 1997). For Elim, see Desmond Cartwright, *The Great Evangelists: The Remarkable Lives of George and Stephen Jeffreys* (Basingstoke: Marshall Pickering, 1986); William K. Kay, *George Jeffreys: Pentecostal Apostle and Revivalist* (Cleveland, TN: CPT Press, 2017), and for the Assemblies of God, Christopher Palmer, *The Emergence of Pentecostalism in Wales: An Evaluation of the Early Development of the Assemblies of God Denomination in South Wales* (London: Apostolos, 2016).

Doctrinal issues within Nonconformity, including liberal theology and the Barthian response, have been discussed by Morgan in 'Confessing the Faith', Chapter 4 of *Span of the Cross*, pp. 107–47; *Barth Reception in Britain* (London: T&T Clark, 2010), pp. 56–62, and 'A Chapter in the History of Welsh Theology', in *The Bible in Church, Academy and Culture: Essays in Honour of the Revd Dr John Tudno Williams*, edited by Alan Sell (Eugene, OR: Pickwick

Publications, 2011), pp. 227–53. For theological developments within the Presbyterian Church in Wales, see Elwyn Richards, 'Credo a Diwinyddiaeth', in *Hanes Methodistiaeth Galfinaidd Cymru*, cyf. 4, edited by Jones and Hughes, pp. 181–214. The conservative evangelical renewal during the inter-war period has been analysed by David Ceri Jones, 'Lloyd-Jones and Wales', in *Engaging with Martyn Lloyd-Jones: The Life and Legacy of 'the Doctor'*, edited by Andrew Atherstone and David Ceri Jones (Nottingham: Apollos, 2011), pp. 59–90.

As well as the works listed above, much can gleaned on the Church in Wales after the war from the episcopal biographies: Edward Lewis, *John Bangor: The People's Bishop* (London: SPCK, 1962), Owain W. Jones, *Glyn Simon: His Life and Opinions* (Llandysul: Gomer Press, 1981), John S. Peart Binns, *Edwin Morris: Archbishop of Wales* (Llandysul: Gomer Press, 1990), and D. T. W. Price, *Archbishop Gwilym Owen Williams, 'G. O.': His Life and Opinions* (Cardiff: Church in Wales Publications, 2017). There is also an insightful essay by D. P. Davies, 'Welsh Anglicanism: a renewed Church for a reviving nation', in *Anglicanism: Essays in History, Belief and Practice*, edited by Nigel Yates (Lampeter: Trivium Publications, 2008), pp. 105–23. See also Chapters 7 and 8 in Roger L. Brown, *Evangelicals in the Church in Wales* (Welshpool: Tair Eglwys Press, 2007).

For Welsh Nonconformist Evangelicalism, see Noel Gibbard, *The First Fifty Years: The History of the Evangelical Movement of Wales, 1948–98* (Bridgend: Evangelical Press of Wales, 1998) and David Ceri Jones, 'Evangelicalism and Fundamentalism in Post-War Wales, 1947–81', in *Fundamentalism and Evangelicalism in the United Kingdom during the Twentieth Century*, edited by David W. Bebbington and David Ceri Jones (Oxford: Oxford University Press, 2013), pp. 289–308.

The essential text for Welsh Ecumenism is Noel A. Davies, *A History of Ecumenism in Wales, 1956–90* (Cardiff: University of Wales Press, 2008), though equally enlightening, especially on the Student Christian Movement (SCM), 'The New Campaign in Wales' and ministry following the Aberfan disaster, is Erastus Jones, *Croesi Ffiniau: Gyda'r Eglwys yn y Byd* (Abertawe: Gwasg John Penry, 2000).

Historical writing on Christianity in Wales in the very recent past is in its early stages. Paul Chambers, 'Religious Diversity in

Wales', in *A Tolerant Nation? Revisiting Ethnic Diversity in a Devolved Wales*, edited by Charlotte Williams, Neil Evans and Paul O'Leary (Cardiff: University of Wales Press, 2015), pp. 147–58, looks at the diversification of Christian groups, as well as the contribution of other faith communities to Welsh civic life. His *Religion, Secularization and Social Change in Wales: Congregational Studies in Post-Christian Wales* (Cardiff: University of Wales Press, 2005) is a sociological study which focuses on how different Christian congregations have adapted to life in contemporary Wales. There is some reflection on the recent history and future direction of the Church in Wales in a number of the chapters in *A New History of the Church in Wales*, edited by Doe, while David Ceri Jones has explored the advent of charismatic evangelicalism in Wales in '"On the edge of spiritual revival"? Charismatic Renewal in Wales', in *Transatlantic Charismatic Renewal c.1950–2000*, edited by Andrew Atherstone, John Maiden and Mark P. Hutchinson (Leiden: Brill, 2021), pp. 101–22. For the place of religion in British society more widely, Grace Davie's *Religion in Britain since 1945: Believing without Belonging* (London: Wiley, 1994) remains an important and highly influential work.

Index

౨

Jones, John Charles (1904–56)
302
Jones, John Morgan (1873–1946)
298
Jones, John Puleston (1862–1925)
286, 298
Jones, J. R. (philosopher)
(1911–70) 305
Jones, J. R. (Ramoth)
(1765–1822) 262
Jones, Mary (1784–1864) 260
Jones, Maurice (1863–1937) 289
Jones, Michael D. (1822–98) 268
Jones, Owen
Some of the Great Preachers of Wales (1886) 268
Jones, Philip J. 298–9
Jones, R. B. (1870–1933) 295
Jones, R. Tudur (1921–98) 282
Jones, Thomas (Creaton)
(1752–1845) 251
Jones, Thomas (Denbigh)
(1756–1820) 251–2, 253, 266
Y Drych Athrawiaethol (1806)
266
Ymddiddanion . . . ar Brynedigaeth (1816 and 1819)
266
Ymddiddanion Crefyddol (1807)
266
Jones, William (d.1700) 222
Joseph, bishop of Llandaf
(d.c.1045) 74, 102
Joseph of Arimathea 196
Jowett, Benjamin (1817–93) 271
Julius Caesar (100–44 BC) 4, 6, 7,
42
Julius, martyr 14, 30
Juvencus (*fl. c.*330), manuscript of
his work in Cambridge 89

K

Katherine, St *see* Catherine
Kent, early English kingdom 49,
57, 59
Kentigern, St 80
Kerry 78
'Keswick in Wales' 295
Kitchen, Anthony, bishop of
Llandaf (1471–1563) 193
Knights Hospitaller 116
Knights Templar 116
Kyffin, Maurice (1555–98) 202

L

Labour Party 292–3
'Lament of the Pilgrim' 120
Landkey, Devon 54
Langford, John
Holl Ddledswydd Dyn (1672)
Lanfranc, archbishop of
Canterbury (*c.*1010–89) 102
Lantokay, church site in Somerset
54
Last Judgement 136, 138–9,
159–60, 162–3
Latercus 60, 61, 62, 68
Latin language in Roman Britain
and early medieval Wales 25,
27, 31–2, 37–8, 89–91
Latin names and words in Welsh 5,
31–2, 36, 53
Laud, William (1573–1645)
213–14
law, medieval Welsh 76, 79
Lawrence, archbishop of
Canterbury (in office
604 × 609–619) 61
lay brothers, Cistercian 115
lay control of church 97
lay impropriators 194